MEDIEVAL
AND
RENAISSANCE
FLORENCE

VOLUME II

VIEW OF FLORENCE FROM THE CONVENT OF SAN FRANCESCO ABOVE FIESOLE

MEDIEVAL
AND
RENAISSANCE
FLORENCE

VOLUME II: THE AGE OF THE MEDICI
AND THE COMING OF HUMANISM

by Ferdinand Schevill

HARPER TORCHBOOKS ❧ The Academy Library

Harper & Row, Publishers New York, Evanston, and London

To Clara

FOR WHOM THIS BOOK WAS BEGUN

AND TO WHOSE BRIGHT AND GALLANT SPIRIT

IT IS DEDICATED

CONTENTS TO VOLUME II

LIST OF ILLUSTRATIONS TO VOLUME II
All photographs from Alinari through Art Reference Bureau, Inc.

LIST OF ILLUSTRATIONS

LIST OF MAPS

MEDIEVAL
AND
RENAISSANCE
FLORENCE

XVI. Democracy versus Oligarchy: The Final Struggle (1343–82)

WHATEVER the system of gild rule seemed to promise at its inception, from the time of the defeat and exile in 1295 of the popular champion, Giano della Bella, it had worked out in effect as an oligarchy which recruited its members from the greater gilds. By their intelligence, their energy, and, let us not forget to add, their entire lack of scruple, the oligarchs had in the course of the first half of the fourteenth century succeeded in making their city the leading financial and industrial center of the contemporary world. When we reflect that Florence was an inland town on a small river, that it boasted neither an exceptionably favorable location nor an easy access to abundant and cheap supplies of raw material, we cannot deny these bold adventurers and enterprisers our frank admiration. However, in measure as their fortunes rose higher and higher, their activities became more and more speculative until they found themselves inextricably tied up with numerous governments to which they had advanced the funds required to conduct unprofitable wars of conquest. When, beginning with Edward III of England, one of these governments after another defaulted on its loans there followed the great crash and crisis of the forties. It is chiefly connected in the minds of men with the names of the Bardi and Peruzzi, but, in point of fact, it brought down every trading firm of any consequence, robbed hundreds of large and small investors of their savings, and plunged the town into the trough of a prolonged depression.

It need hardly be expressly said that the crisis of the forties struck a terrific blow at the prestige of the ruling oligarchy. Since the rapid expansion of Florentine business and political power following the establishment of the priorate had not improperly been attributed by the ruling merchants to their own energy and sagacity, it was inevitable that the common people, who were the chief sufferers from the collapse, should with equal propriety ascribe the unexampled crash to this same group. In a supreme effort to avoid bankruptcy the bankers had promoted the rule of the duke of Athens; and when, disappointed with his lack of subserviency to their interests, they drove him from the town, the last remaining chance to escape destruction lay in their own bold seizure of the state. But this intrigue was promptly defeated by the now fully aroused democratic masses; and when the series of revolutions inaugurated by the rising against the French adventurer was over, the old government of the priors had been reconstituted, but on so different a basis as to present a greatly altered appearance to the world.

We have agreed that ever since the overthrow of Giano della Bella the power in the state had rested with the seven greater gilds. This was a clear departure from the Ordinances of Justice which attributed the new executive, the priorate, to the twenty-one gilds, great, medium, and small, recognized by that famous constitutional document. But so great, owing to their wealth, was the authority of the seven greater gilds that their usurpation, modified by the occasional magnanimous admission of a lesser gildsman to office, was not challenged so long as the prosperity and, let us add, the territorial expansion of Florence moved forward in an unbroken line. Men are not given to worrying about constitutional orthodoxy so long as success smiles on the efforts of their rulers. So it was with the Florentines, until with alarming suddenness and with the cumulative effect of successive deadly blows came the disastrous Lucchese war, the crumbling of the town's financial foundations, the industrial stagnation with its attendant unemployment, the disappointing and disgraceful episode of the duke of Athens. When, as a sequel to all these calamities, the constitution of the priors was rehabilitated, no one should be surprised to hear that the common people were resolved to assert themselves. They took the stand that the undue authority so long exercised by the seven upper gilds must terminate in order to be replaced by the government of the whole body of the twenty-one gilds, exactly as the law prescribed. It was therefore decreed that of the eight priors two were henceforth to represent the seven greater gilds, three the five middle gilds, and three the nine lesser gilds. The ninth prior, the gonfalonier of Justice, was to be chosen from each of the three groups in turn. Although this arrangement did not punish the merchant gilds for the recent catastrophes by excluding them from office, it secured a definite preponderance to the small bourgeoisie and the organized craftsmen. As, on the other hand, the reorganization made no concession whatever to the great mass of the textile proletariat, it cannot possibly be said to have had a distinctly radical or revolutionary character.[1]

Nevertheless it remains a fact that the government inaugurated in the autumn of 1343 assumed a popular cast entirely unfamiliar to its oligarchic predecessor. We may even assert with regard to it that more or less consciously and consistently it indicated an attempt to move forward along democratic lines. Modest as was this tendency, it represented so wide a departure from past

---

[1] Even though our knowledge of Florentine history, which, originally derived exclusively from the chroniclers, has in recent years been greatly broadened by the use of documents, extensive periods remain in contention, and none has aroused livelier disputes than the period (1343-82) treated in this chapter. The disputes are in part due to the loose use by the men of the trecento of class terms such as magnates, popolo grasso, mezzana gente, popolo minuto, plebe, etc. Until present-day students agree upon these terms they will always be writing at cross-purposes. A valiant attempt not only to avoid weasel words but also accurately to define the classes making up Florentine society in the trecento has been made by G. Scaramella, *Firenze allo Scoppio del Tumulto dei Ciompi*. Pisa, 1914. According to Scaramella it is a mistake to interpret the chroniclers as conceding a preponderance to the arti minori after 1343; they did not win control till 1378 and only the next three years (1378-81) constitute a genuine democratic interlude. If this is true, the present chapter ascribes to the government between 1343 and 1378 more of a democratic character than it actually had. While this is not unimportant, it belongs to the always disputable realm of interpretation and does not impugn the correctness of the events themselves as here set forth.

practice that it elicited frequent and usually alarmed contemporary comment. To Giovanni Villani, for instance, identified through a long life with the fallen oligarchs, the new government was the occasion of ever-renewed carping. And when, after Giovanni's death during the great pestilence of 1348, Matteo Villani undertook to continue his brother's chronicle, Matteo, too, never ceased to ring the changes on the stock lament that "every vile craftsman of the city aspires to reach the priorate and the great offices of the commune." [2] As Matteo died in 1363, his work has not the importance for the period treated in this chapter as that of his younger contemporary, Stefani, which covers the whole democratic interval. Granting that Stefani is much better disposed toward the popolo minuto than the two Villanis, he is hardly less emphatic in his criticism of the doubtless often arrogant demeanor of the little folk, whose sudden rise to power went to their head with the explosive energy of new wine.[3] Boccaccio, too, he of the hundred spicy tales composed to tickle the palate of a jaded bourgeoisie, repeatedly flung out against the new democracy in the most cutting manner. In short, the writers of the age and spokesmen of the new culture were without exception, though with varying emphasis, on the conservative side. Since the well-to-do and the educated have always been outraged by the assumption of the honors of government by their social and intellectual inferiors, we need not feel any surprise at the discontent manifested by these groups at Florence when the middle and minor arts appropriated the lion's share of the offices. Our sole concern at this juncture is that, beginning with the autumn of 1343, shopkeepers and artisans actually sat in the seats of power and with varying fortune clung to them till 1382. This period of almost forty years therefore constitutes a democratic interlude inviting the closest scrutiny. When, owing to the mistakes of the small people and, far more than to measurable human shortcomings, to the operation of blind social forces beyond the control of feeble men, the democracy lost the battle, the oligarchs again resumed the reins, thenceforth to retain them in one guise or another as long as the republic lasted.

We may therefore very properly begin our story of the democratic episode with a general survey of the impersonal factors which explain why it was bound to end in failure. And here, first and foremost, belongs the circumstance revealed by all the preceding chapters of this book that from the earliest days the destiny of Florence had been shaped by its merchants prompt to take advantage of the economic opportunities springing from the revival of trade and industrial enterprise. By their matchless energy spread over many generations these undaunted adventurers had committed the Arno city to a policy of economic imperialism, the earliest object of which was the mastery of Tuscany. The most immediate and palpable evidence of the immense success of these endeavors was Florence itself in its purely physical aspect. Just before the devastation wrought by the Black Death (1348) the town had swollen to a population of approximately 120,000, if to the dwellers within the third cir-

---

[2] M. Villani, II, 2.

[3] ". . . They are arrogant without judgment, and because the offices had come into their hands each one thought he was a king [*parea loro essere ciascuno un re*]." Marchionne di Coppo Stefani, *Cronica Fiorentina*. Ed. by N. Rodolico. Muratori (new ed.), Vol. XXX, r. 616.

cumvallation we add the crowded suburbs.[4] The fivefold increase in the course
of a single century was largely represented by the proletarian workers of the
two wool gilds; and these former peasants, who had migrated to the city to
serve as carders, spinners, dyers, and weavers, made a living by manufacturing
or refining the cloth which the merchants undertook to distribute to all parts
of the known world. Once assembled, the industrial population could not be
maintained save by the perpetuation of the system which had brought it into
being. Every society is the beneficiary or victim, as the case may be, of its own
past and cannot, unless it wishes to make an entirely new start, abandon its
foundations. Nor may the psychological implications of a body of inherited
customs and activities be overlooked. To keep pace with the imperialist program of the merchants and government the whole Florentine population had
developed a corresponding imperialist mentality. From the lowly beggars and
day laborers up to the great merchant princes, the Arno dwellers were passionate patriots, committed to a man to a forward policy in Tuscany holding
out the hope of an ever larger participation in peninsular and world-decisions.

This was the situation, these were the problems which faced the petty bourgeoisie when it took over the power in 1343. If, as a rule, the actions of men were
determined by purely logical considerations, the renunciation of the far-ranging
imperialism of the great merchants in favor of a narrow stay-at-home policy
would now have been a not unreasonable expectation. But there, in their
crowded, dingy quarters were the working masses, which could under no circumstances be ignored. For one thing, they had to be fed, a problem which
had been one of the most troublesome concerns of the old government and
which offered no prospect of becoming less pressing in the years to come.
Furthermore, with the bread question was tied up the wages question, and,
as matters stood, the wages necessary to buy the bread could be furnished from
no other source than the capitalists in touch with the world-markets. But even
assuming that the wheel of Time could have been turned back and the wool
workers redistributed among the farms they had abandoned—which is of course
absurd—the new rulers would have refused to carry out the measure since they,
too, took pride in the recently won glories and were patriotically averse to a
policy calculated to reduce Florence to its original parochial dimensions.

The net result was that the new government did not reverse the course but
continued in the main along the path blazed by its predecessors. This is particularly true of the foreign field. In fact it is difficult, if not impossible, to
detect any departure whatever from the territorial aims which had become
traditional. For several generations Florence had been engaged in creating a
state as nearly commensurate with Tuscany as possible; and if this purpose
had never been quite attained, the Red Lily had at least become provincially
dominant and, as a clear indication of its program, had brought all its smaller
neighbors under its rule. However, during the despotism of the duke of Athens
the various subject towns had seized the opportunity to renounce their allegiance. Consequently we must agree that when, after the duke's expulsion,
Florence resumed its independence, it was in a singularly advantageous posi-

---

[4] On these incurably uncertain figures the reader is referred to Rodolico, *La Democrazia Fiorentina,* chap. I.

Top: THE MEDICI PALACE, WITH THE MEDICI COAT OF ARMS. MICHELOZZI.
Bottom: THE COURT OF THE MEDICI PALACE. MICHELOZZI

THE PITTI PALACE

THE STROZZI PALACE. BENEDETTO DA MAIANO AND IL CRONACA

Left: GIOVANNI DI BICCI DE' MEDICI. MEDICI PALACE. *Right:* COSIMO DE' MEDICI. MEDICI PALACE

DEATH MASK IN PLASTER OF LORENZO THE MAG-
NIFICENT. MEDICI PALACE

tion to break with the policy of expansion once and for all. It flatly refused to do anything of the sort. To be sure, the priors exercised a wise restraint toward the rebellious subject communities; but never for a moment did they entertain the least doubt regarding the necessity of territorially reconstituting the Florentine state. And already after a few years their watchful waiting brought them a considerable success, for by a little past the middle of the century Colle di Val d'Elsa, San Gimignano, Prato, and Pistoia, either voluntarily or as the result of a tactfully applied pressure, again submitted to Florentine control. If it might be argued that the new government differed from its predecessor in being somewhat less prompt to appeal to arms, it was far from submitting humbly to the aggression of an arrogant neighbor. Thus when the archbishop of Milan, Giovanni Visconti, in pursuit of his ambitious design to create a strong north-Italian state, in 1351 invaded Tuscany, the government met the attack with energy, nor did it come off second best in the encounter.

That Archbishop Giovanni, who operated with hired mercenaries, had to be confronted with precisely the same kind of gentry was unfortunate but cannot be blamed on the artisan regime. The national army of the early days of the republic had gone to pieces during the rule of the greater gilds and, as we have seen, beginning with the early decades of the fourteenth century, Florence, yielding to a general Italian precedent, had wholeheartedly committed itself to the system of professional soldiers. When these professionals, organized in so-called companies of adventure, became aware that they were less the servants than the masters of the rich cities of Italy alike estranged from the use of arms, they flaunted their power through the length and breadth of the peninsula, levying ransom on every community in their path and, in case money was denied, stripping the country like a plague of locusts. We shall have frequent occasion to treat of these soldier or, more properly, robber bands, which constituted one of the major disasters of the peninsula during the second half of the fourteenth century. At this point we are content to note that the Florentines, too, were exposed to their insolence and repeatedly saved themselves from a threatened harrying of their territory by a lavish payment of blood money. Disgusting as this submission to blackmail was, it constituted no specialty of the Florentine democracy and, if contemptible, may be declared to have been unavoidable under the military conditions which had come to prevail in the Italy of that age.

Having touched on events in the foreign field, we may note that throughout the period here considered this field is of subordinate interest, and that no event following the Visconti aggression of 1351 arrests our attention till we come to 1362, when the ancient feud with Pisa flared up in a new war. It was precipitated by Florence and furnished the clearest possible evidence that the inland town was as attached as ever to its imperialist dream. In a sudden access of fury against Pisa, which, contrary to treaty, undertook to lay a small tax on Florentine goods in transit through its port, the injured city revived the project of a former generation to develop the hopelessly embogged Talamone on the Maremma coast as a Florentine harbor. Of course Pisa resisted this move, war followed, a cruel war of rival mercenary hosts, and the struggle continued for over two years till both sides were financially and economically exhausted. In the end Florence gave up the Talamone delusion and Pisa accepted the long-established Florentine immunity from transit dues. The episode bears an exasperating character of futility and was not very different in this respect from the innumerable earlier conflicts between the two towns. But it has historical significance nonetheless, inasmuch as it proves that under the little tradesmen, precisely as under the great merchants, the leading territorial aim of Florence continued to be the control of the Tuscan coast, and that attachment to this purpose meant a struggle with Pisa which would not terminate till Pisa had been conquered. In fine, we can but repeat that the Florentine foreign policy underwent no change of principle during the democratic interlude, and that the priorate dominated by the minor gilds was not perceptibly less expansionist than the priorate of the merchant period.

But it is by its domestic policy that the democratic character of a government is best gauged. And as the local happenings are peculiarly interesting, and as at the same time they are better documented than at any earlier period, they hold out the promise of a most profitable investigation. Indeed so revealing regarding the structure of Florentine society and the various pressures to which it was subject are the internal events of the four decades under consideration that the historian may under no circumstances overlook them. As our point of departure let us take the three main social-economic groups of which the population was at this time composed: the merchants of the seven greater gilds, the shopkeepers and artisans of the fourteen lesser gilds, and the proletarian masses which constituted the unorganized popolo minuto. The most important single feature of a very complex situation may without hesitation be declared to have been the desire and resolution of the last-named group, the industrial workers, to improve their lot through imitating the two superior classes by acquiring the advantages of organization. This was an entirely novel tendency, since during the long-continued advance of Florentine industry the workers had in the main been so thoroughly quiescent that they had come to be looked on by their employers as no better than dumb animals.

It was the misery inflicted by repeatedly experienced major and minor depressions that gradually convinced the lowly wage-earners of the need of action. Notwithstanding, it was not till 1342, when the duke of Athens had become master of the city, that they made their first appeal to the government for relief from conditions that threatened to crush them. In view of the fact that their complaint was directed against the popolo grasso, whom the tyrant, too, regarded as his special enemies, he was pleased not only to lend the petitioners a gracious ear but actually to authorize them to form a gild of their own. This was a first success; but it promptly went by the boards on the duke's expulsion. While the fourteen lesser gilds, which on the tyrant's disappearance secured a preponderant authority, were also in more or less declared opposition to the greater gilds, they had unfortunately no sympathy for the industrial proletariat, from which they felt themselves separated as by a wide chasm. They were concerned with keeping the workers fed, thereby forestalling hunger riots and social revolution, but they had no inclination whatever to raise the despised mass of carders, spinners, and dyers to their own level. This selfish interest of the lesser gilds in their own predominance defines the character of their democracy. In respect of their superiors, the merchant oligarchs, they present themselves to view as the democracy of the gild system, but in respect of their inferiors, the workingmen, they constituted a privileged class as averse to relinquishing their privileges as the privileged have ever been. The democratic or popular issue of the period under review has therefore a twofold aspect: there is first the struggle of the lesser gilds to hold fast to the concessions recently wrested from the burgher oligarchs; and second, there is the effort of the proletarians to win the right to organize in order to overcome the worst evils of their lot. Owing to the class tension between the petty bourgeoisie and the workers, the two democratic movements unfolded side by side in all but complete isolation until, after some thirty years, they were drawn into a single comprehensive action in the great revolution of 1378.

Taking up the second and more radical democratic movement first, we are obliged to begin by defining the legal status of the former peasants who had drifted into Florence and become the industrial workers of the merchant gilds of the Lana and the Calimala. The gilds in question, and the other greater gilds as well, were associations of masters, and the workers employed by them were their subordinates or *sottoposti*. The masters alone determined the wages of the workers and, in order to keep them at a minimum level and the workers themselves in secure subjection, declared every attempt of their subordinates to form a gild of their own a punishable crime. If we turn for confirmation of this statement to the statutes of the wool gild bearing the date 1338, we learn not only that they prohibited every organization of the sottoposti but that, in order to close every possible avenue to proletarian action, they went the length of declaring unlawful any meeting of more than ten workers for any purpose whatever.[5] Every least breach of these injunctions was subject to action by the court of the gild enjoying a sweeping jurisdiction over masters and sottoposti alike, and was punished by the *divieto,* that is, the exclusion of the transgressor from the list of approved workers for one or more years. Tantamount to a sentence of death by starvation, the mere threat of the divieto was like a sword perpetually suspended over the worker's head. We cannot get away from the conclusion that in the view of the masters of the Lana as revealed in their own statutes, the wool workers were no better than human chattels required to subsist on a submarginal wage and forbidden under the severest penalties to attempt to increase their pittance of a salary by collective bargaining. As all the labor-employing gilds boasted similarly repressive legislation, and as the government of Florence lay entirely in gild hands, we should feel no surprise to learn that the gild enactments against every sort of association or collegium of workers had been incorporated in the public law of the land. Both the constitution of the podestà and that of the captain contained articles which obliged these political officials to defend the economic privileges of the masters by alertly detecting and promptly punishing every attempt at association on the part of the sottoposti.[6]

[5] Rodolico, *La Democrazia Fiorentina*, p. 114. The author cites the relevant restrictions as given in the Statuti dell'Arte della Lana of 1338 preserved in the Archivio di Stato.

[6] Rodolico, *La Democrazia*, etc., p. 116. The author reproduces the relevant rubrics of both the statute of the podestà and that of the captain.

Here, if ever, was regulative legislation with teeth in it. However, stronger than any law is necessity. Immediately after the overthrow of the duke of Athens it gripped the workers in the form of the crisis precipitated by the bank failures of 1343–46 and the attendant unemployment and starvation. The indefinitely prolonged agony could not fail to produce repercussions among a group, which by its recent brief enjoyment under the duke of Athens of gild autonomy had seen a faint ray of light flash across its somber sky. To illustrate the kind of outbreak which following the economic crisis became common among the proletarians, a single instance will suffice. In the year 1345 a certain Ciuto Brandini, a wool-carder, tried to reconstitute the shattered gild of his fellow-workers. Seized one night in his bed, he was haled before the capitano del popolo and promptly sentenced to be hanged.[7] The arrest and condemnation carried out by a public official strikingly bring home to us the extent to which the state was the obedient tool of the masters of the gilds. In spite of Ciuto's cruel fate, irregular outbreaks against the ruling system continued until the Black Death of 1348 swung its giant scythe among both masters and men and temporarily weighted the scales in favor of the latter. The catastrophic mortality, especially in the crowded quarters of the poor, produced a deficiency of hands and a consequent increase of wages. But immediately on the cessation of the pestilence the peasants, tempted by the higher pay, poured into the town in such numbers that before long the proletarian ranks were again filled, inviting a return to the old wage scale. Whatever economic achievements the Black Death may be credited with in other respects, it brought only a very ephemeral advantage to the harassed wage slaves of Florence.

In the legislation of the fifties there is noticeable an occasional attempt to attract immigrants to Florence by the relaxation of some of the laws dealing with citizenship; but all enactments of this nature were sporadic and sprang solely from the desire to strengthen the lesser gilds. These were the people in power, and except insofar as a measure planned to advance their own cause may incidentally have helped the workers, they did not so much as lift a finger in behalf of their oppressed fellow-citizens. During the whole period here considered the scarcity of food continued to be felt throughout Tuscany and large sections of Italy; and again and again, in the wake of a famine, came the inevitable pestilence. Whipped by this double scourge, the tormented workers might have burst through every restraint, if the situation had not carried with it its own ironical alleviation. When there were more workers than there was food to go round and hunger lashed the starved masses till they were ready to rebel, a pestilence would providentially appear out of nowhere, kill enough workers to ease the pressure on the bread supply, and enable the quaking government to congratulate itself on having escaped a violent overturn. That even, under this appalling system, movements of protest were not unusual may be

---

[7] Rodolico, *Il Popolo Minuto (1343-78)*. Bologna, 1899. The official record of Ciuto's trial is printed as Document 14. This particular book of Rodolico represents the first attempt ever made to investigate the movements among the exploited workers of the greater arts. On the class struggle as well as on the numerous other problems of the democratic interlude the histories of Capponi, Perrens, and Caggese make suggestive contributions. Capponi offers a valuable Appendix of Documents. The contemporary diaries and chronicles are numerous. The most important after Stefani is the *Diario d'Anonimo Fiorentino dall'Anno 1358 al 1389* (Documenti di Storia Italiana, Tomo VI).

confirmed by recounting certain events of the year 1368.[8] On an August day of that year a famished and ragged crowd invaded the grain market to the cry of "Viva il Popolo" and seized and carried off twenty sacks of wheat. The action was no more than a riot induced by the not unusual scarcity, and the demonstrators were quickly dispersed. But immediately after, and due to the same incurable deficiency of bread, there occurred something so novel and ominous that it may be set up as a landmark: a strike on the part of the very important group of the sottoposti, the dyers. Although the dyers did not on this occasion quite go the length of forming a gild, they did by calling a strike indicate that they were engaged in what the law called a collegium or conspiracy and automatically drew on themselves the dreaded divieto or lockout. Under the application of this penalty the dyers' strike was quickly broken up. However, a new method of threatening the employers had been discovered and was not likely to be again forgotten. While the material which has come down to us bearing on the labor situation during this period is casual and incomplete, it yet suffices to attest so continuous a restlessness among the proletarians that the view of the older historians, who held that the revolution of 1378 fell like a bolt from the blue, must be abandoned. It is a fact, however, that the upheaval of that year, famous under the name of the rebellion of the Ciompi, was not originally instigated by the working masses but that it developed from an intensification of the struggle for power between the greater and the lesser gilds. This, a conflict among legally constituted groups, supplies the master-thread of the domestic history of the period. We shall now follow this conflict from its inception in the year 1343 to the outbreak of 1378, when it was reenforced and for a time completely overshadowed by an irresistible general rising of the proletariat.

The increased political power of the lesser gilds after the overthrow of the duke of Athens was an intolerable offense to the great merchants, which to remove as soon as possible they were prepared to leave no stone unturned. Nor was it long before they discovered an instrument admirably suited to their purpose. This was the parte Guelfa, which had risen to power in the days of Charles I of Anjou and which in the name of Charles had actually governed the city till the reorganization of 1280 dictated by Cardinal Latino. But, though forced thenceforward somewhat into the background, the party had by no means lost its grip. Owing to its having acquired title to immense Ghibelline properties, it had vast revenues at its disposal requiring a permanent administration. The party was accordingly housed in an imposing palazzo[9] not far from the Mercato Nuovo; and since the Guelphs were an organization with governors and councils and with many kinds of political and economic interests, there were larger and smaller rooms adapted to these several purposes. Although the party had originally been a society of magnates, from the first it had not hesitated to open its doors also to rich popolani. When Florence in the first half of the trecento became a world-center, the merchant element, which had raised it to that eminence, did not fail to win increased recognition.

[8] Caggese, Vol. II, pp. 224-26. The pertinent documents in Rodolico, *Il Popolo Minuto* (Nos. 11, 26).

[9] The great Gothic palace, recently restored, is admirably suited to convey an impression of the power of the party.

It thus came about that while, according to the original constitution of the party, the governors, called captains, had been six in number and had all to be of the noble class, in 1323 it was ordained that three of the captains were thenceforward to be popolani. By that time the distinction between nobles and wealthy commoners had become so artificial as to have all but lost its meaning and, for all practical purposes, the party membership may be regarded as a singularly coherent group of individuals of established means who, swayed by strictly conservative sentiments, regarded the state as the indispensable tool for the protection of their interests. Throughout the period of oligarchic control ending with the usurpation of the duke of Athens we may think of the government of the arti maggiori as effectively identified with the parte Guelfa.

When, on the expulsion of the duke, the merchants and bankers had been obliged to concede a preponderant political power to shopkeepers and artisans, the vanquished groups did not have to despair chiefly for the reason that their natural ally, the parte Guelfa, was still intact. The merchants and bankers, or at least their leading representatives, were members of the party in good standing and, as such, could freely air their grievances in its sessions. In point of fact there was no need whatever of impressing the desirability of action on the captains of the party since the vigorous tradition behind these powerful officials prompted them to an impassioned opposition to any government even faintly redolent of democracy. True, as a private association, the party could not, at least at once, step into the open and carry on the political struggle in behalf of the greater gilds. The proprieties had to be respected. But it could and did without delay make itself the secret rallying-point of the conservative influences in the city until such a time as it would feel strong enough to cast off the mask and in its own name to inaugurate the movement to drive the usurping little folk back to their shops and alleys.

As it took some years for the party's action to get under way it was not till 1346 that the first success was achieved. In that year the priors and councils were persuaded to pass a bill which declared that no citizen could hold office unless he and his father before him had been born in Florence. The act was a blow aimed at the small gildsmen, whose ranks were being uninterruptedly swollen by immigration from the country. As the malice of the measure was a trifle too apparent, it was almost immediately resolved to substitute a more subtle procedure, and by a supplementary act passed a few months later (1347), not recent immigration but Ghibellinism was defined as the blot punishable by exclusion from office. By this time Ghibellinism per se was undoubtedly a dead issue. Neither in Florence nor in its contado did any Ghibelline any longer venture to raise his head, so complete had been the house-cleaning effected by the Guelphs in the course of three and more generations. But during the prolonged Guelph-Ghibelline feud, originally purely a concern of the upper class, the whole Florentine population had become so imbued with guelfismo that even after the city had no further reason to fear the empire—and dread of the empire was the meat and kernel of Guelph sentiment—the Ghibelline bogey, as ancient bogies have the habit of doing, lived on in the hearts of the citizens. Consequently no more serious charge could be presented against a fellow-townsman than to allege that he was openly or secretly an imperial partisan; and so spontaneous was the heat engendered by the mere imputation of Ghibellinism that guilt was at once assumed without the tedious formality of legal proofs. Without this emotional background the role played by the parte Guelfa, which before long carried it to an all but complete domination of the state, cannot possibly be understood. The party was the dragon which for almost a century had guarded the treasure of guelfismo, the spiritual food of the Florentine population. Surely no one knew better than the lords of the party what constituted a genuine Guelph; and therefore should the captains render a decision, averring that this or that other citizen did not measure up to proper Guelph standards, it was as if judgment had fallen on him from on high. It was this immense moral prestige enjoyed by the party that it now resolved to exploit in the interest of big business, which was also its own interest. There were no indubitable, hall-marked Ghibellines left, or as good as none; the existing enemies of the party were the gildsmen of the lesser arts who by no reasonable procedure could be classified as either Guelph or Ghibelline. But if a small inn-keeper or waggoner recently arrived from the countryside should on the strength of the law of 1347 have the Ghibelline label clapped on him, he would not be permitted to take public office, even if his name should be regularly drawn from the borse. By claiming and exercising the right to detect Ghibellines and by their detection to exclude them from office the parte Guelfa completely dominated the elections and filled the ruling artisans with a vague fear.

Then something happened which nullified the victory. After a law was passed its execution rested with the authorities, and if the authorities declined to apply the law, the new statute, being still-born, was quietly buried. It was the peculiarity of the Florentine republic, and of all the other Italian republics as well, that they passed laws in such profusion and precipitation that it was a physical impossibility to have them all enforced, especially if it happened that they encountered opposition within the government.[10] Besides, before the parte Guelfa could take its next step in pursuit of its plans of indirect control, the Black Death intervened (1348) and for a time forced the issue between the greater and the lesser gilds into the background. But no sooner had recovery from the pestilence begun than the conflict again reared its head, and in the year 1354 the party renewed its offensive by sponsoring the revival, in a far more rigorous form than before, of the law forbidding Ghibellines to hold public office. But again the difficulty of applying the law put in an appearance, for the arti minori, more acutely aware by now of what was concealed under the Ghibelline legislation, utilized every political trick in their repertory to block the execution of the act. The issue was tossed to and fro until in high dudgeon the party put an end to continued subterfuge by proposing and carrying (1358) under loud threats and violent intimidation of the government a law which gave the determining of who was and who was not a Ghibelline exclusively into the hands of the party executive. Thus become a supplementary government outside the frame of the constitution, the party adopted a procedure which was simplicity itself. Whenever there was drawn

---

[10] Stefani, r. 728, joins the long list of witnesses who complain of the abundant and often contradictory enactments which were not enforced.

for office the name of an artisan who had invited the enmity of the party, or whenever there was drawn the name of a member of a greater gild even remotely tainted with democratic sympathies, he was handed a warning (*ammonizione*) by the captains of the party to the effect that he was a Ghibelline and could not serve. In case he should pay no attention to the remonstrance, the captains were prepared to summon him before the podestà on the charge of treason, for which offense the penalty was death or exile. As no one was willing to run this risk, the curious device of the ammonizione sufficed to give to the party the control to which it aspired. In connection with each successive election to the magistracies a number of citizens, whose names were regularly drawn from the borse but who were distasteful to the all-powerful captains, were served warning to keep off the premises with the result that in the course of a few years the "warned" or *ammoniti* were a body, and a very angry body as can be readily imagined, of several hundred persons. Turn and twist as the government would, it found no way of casting off the Guelph incubus. For eight unbroken years it suffered an intolerable infringement of its normal powers and might have suffered it longer, had it not been for a conflict which developed in the ranks of the arrogant Guelphs themselves.

The parte Guelfa was an oligarchy and it is the nature of an oligarchy, while united by a common interest, to be divided by personal ambitions. Oligarchies have regularly split upon this rock, as the case of Florence itself convincingly demonstrated by such earlier conflicts as those between the Uberti and the Buondelmonti and between the Cerchi and the Donati. And now history repeated itself, for hardly had the parte Guelfe acquired the mastery of Florence,[11] when the conflict within the party began over the question who was to be the party's master. The two leading claimants to the honor were a Ricci and an Albizzi, behind whom gathered their large and powerful respective clans. When Piero degli Albizzi, although rated a popolano, sought the support of the conservatives of the strictest observation, who were papalists and magnates, Uguccione de' Ricci inevitably was driven to establish contact with the moderates. Indeed in the manner of men who play for the stakes of power he did not hesitate to go for help to the enemy himself, to the arti minori. In the year 1366, when serving as one of the priors, he seized the occasion to trip his rival Piero by having a law passed which put certain obstacles in the way of finding a citizen guilty of Ghibellinism, chiefly by a reorganization of the executive of the parte Guelfa. On the strength of this law representatives of the lesser gilds were given seats among the all-powerful captains, who by this unwelcome association found themselves greatly hampered in the pleasant game of knocking down their enemies like so many tenpins. For a few years the practice of ammonizione signally declined until the two rival oligarchs, patching up their quarrel, arranged for a new law which invalidated its predecessor, and by re-establishing harmony within the parte Guelfa enabled it to resume its reign of terror. It is unnecessary and would be extremely tedious to trace the new moves by which the harassed government tried to

---

[11] Stefani's phrase, r. 778, is memorable in this connection. He says: "Chi era signore della parte era signore di Firenze."

escape the reknotted Guelph noose. Suffice it to say, and it goes without saying, that larger and ever larger groups of citizens lost patience with a situation that made mock of constitutional forms and hung a pall of fear over the whole city. The resentment against the overbearing tyrants who dared set up a subsidiary government in their private palace grew till, bursting all bounds, it led to an act as spontaneous as it was irrational: a war against the pope.

It is true that there were other causes besides the inflammatory domestic issue which contributed to this conflict. To understand them we must lift ourselves above the Tuscan scene to a height affording a survey of the contemporary situation of the papacy. Although planted since the first decade of the fourteenth century at Avignon, the papacy had never ceased to affirm that its appointed seat was Rome, whither it planned to return as soon as the time was ripe. But either conditions matured slowly or Avignon proved a too seductive garden, for it was not till past the middle of the century that a pope, the unusually enterprising Innocent VI, took the first step necessary to clear the way for a return. He intrusted a Spanish cardinal, Albornoz, who had been bred a soldier, with the task of bringing back to papal obedience the State of the Church, commonly designated by clerics as the *patrimonium Petri*. This undertaking Albornoz carried out with such a judicious mixture of military might and conciliatory diplomacy that by 1357 he could publish a constitution for the central Italian territories which for the first time since their acquisition by the papacy gave them something like a coherent political organization. With that achievement the papacy was at last prepared to assume the character of an Italian state capable on the strength of its own resources of entering the game of Italian politics. Moreover, with the patrimonium pacified the last excuse for clinging to the haven of Avignon was removed, and hesitantly and regretfully a new pope, Urban V, made ready to resume the abandoned Roman seat. In 1367 he came to Italy and, urged onward by most of the European sovereigns, including the emperor, triumphantly entered the Eternal City.

The reigning emperor, Charles IV, was of so different a stripe from all his predecessors that we are obliged at this point to bring him into historical focus. If we have long ago agreed that the empire, as a power capable of struggling with the church for world-supremacy, perished with Emperor Frederick II in 1250, we have not failed to note that its theoretical claims lived on and that they were not unworthily represented by such Hohenstaufen princes as Manfred and Conradin and by such a blameless knight as Henry VII. Even Ludwig the Bavarian, although suffering personal shipwreck in Italy, had clung tenaciously to the traditional luster of his office. But when Charles IV was elevated to the German kingship (and to remember that he was the grandson of Dante's *alto Arrigo* gives the measure of the immense reversal), he made a clean break with the past. From a purely common-sense angle the course which he adopted might well be called judicious and prudent, for it was based on recognition of the fact that he lived in a changed world, that the universal empire could not be revived, and that even to acquire the bare title of emperor, he would have to seek and retain the favor of the pope. In line with this political realism Charles openly avowed himself a Guelph and was rewarded by being formally invited by his triumphant rival to cross the Alps to have himself crowned emperor. The event occurred in 1355, and it characterizes the submissiveness of this strange Caesar that he left the Tiber city on the evening of the very day of his coronation. His purpose was scrupulously to avoid giving the impression that he any longer regarded Rome as his or the empire's capital.

When, twelve years after Charles's coronation, Pope Urban V plucked up courage for the long-delayed return to Italy, in expectation of difficulties with which he might be confronted, he called on Charles for support, and the humble papalist actually crossed the Alps a second time to add his mite toward making the pope secure in the regained dominion. On this occasion, exactly as during his former visit, Charles lingered for some months in northern and central Italy, where the Saxon and Hohenstaufen emperors had chiefly unfolded their might. Even here, where the empire still enjoyed a considerable following, he was content to adopt a purely practical attitude toward a society which had visibly slipped its medieval moorings. The usurping tyrants in person and the city-republics through representatives visited his court in crowds in order to have their new political status confirmed by an imperial charter. In this situation the calculating merchant-monarch detected remarkable opportunities for profit, offered documents of the most liberal scope to all comers, and in 1368, as he had already done in 1355, returned to Germany laden with Italian gold but totally shorn of respect for himself and for his diadem.[12] When, following his second journey, he disappeared behind the Alps, the empire may be said to have vanished with him: *exit imperium*. We shall encounter an occasional emperor after Charles coming almost stealthily to Italy lured by the bauble of the imperial crown; but as even the theory of the empire now began to evaporate from the minds of men, that institution lost its last shred of meaning and all but ceased to figure in the busy interplay of peninsular political forces.

However, the other universal power, the papacy, vigorously lived on, although not without a certain loss of prestige, owing to its abandonment of Rome and to its concomitant subjection to French national interests. When Albornoz for the first time fused the papal provinces in Italy into a political unit, he may well be said to have inaugurated a new phase of papal history. The long, world-shaking struggle between the popes and the emperors had been conducted, on the part of the popes, with their vast spiritual and financial resources and with as good as no help from the dominions immediately subject to their rule. Of course, in the future as in the past, the pope would continue to owe his authority, in the main, to his lordship over the church; but in consequence of the statesmanlike services of Cardinal Albornoz, he would, from the second half of the fourteenth century on, have also a not inconsiderable civil state on which to lean. To be sure, even after the labors of Albornoz the papal state long continued to rest on insecure foundations and

<hr>

12 "Colla borsa piena di danari, ma con assai vergogna in abbassamento dell'imperiale maestà." Thus Matteo Villani, V, 54, had already commented in 1355. On the occasion of this same earlier visit Charles sold a charter to Florence for one hundred thousand gold florins. The tranaction has received detailed treatment from F. Baldasseroni, "Relazioni tra Firenze, la Chiesa, e Carlo IV (1353-55)," in *Arch. Stor. It.,* Serie 5, Vol. XXXVII, pp. 2 ff.

was beset by many difficulties. One of them of particular weight at this time was the French nationality of the Avignon popes. While Urban V had again established his seat at Rome, he never felt happy in Italy, and after a two years' residence on the Tiber, succumbed to an overmastering nostalgia and returned to his seat on the Rhone. His successor, another Frenchman, who took the title Gregory XI, pledged himself on his elevation to office in 1370 to realize the plan that Urban had abandoned, but such was the pressure brought to bear on him by his French college of cardinals that years passed before he could summon the energy to redeem his pledge.

Meanwhile the State of the Church, as we shall henceforth call Albornoz' creation, had to be governed and, as might be expected, a French pope intrusted the task to French agents. To win the obedience of the local powers accustomed for generations to an anarchic independence was no light matter, and the foreign rectors, high prelates to a man, were frequently obliged to resort to harsh measures to enforce their rule. It is the essentially upstart papal state governed or, as its subjects claimed, misgoverned by French ecclesiastics in the name of an absentee pope, which is the first fact to hold in mind as we now return to the apparently so irrational war that Guelph Florence declared against the church.

To the republic of Florence, accustomed to regard itself as the leading central Italian state, the creation of a State of the Church was a disturbing phenomenon. Enveloping Florence on the north, east, and south, it threatened the republic's freedom of movement and might under certain conditions even endanger its independence. Without any doubt the Florentines preferred the former anarchy, for it had enabled them to deal individually with such cities as Perugia and Bologna and with the innumerable little Romagnese tyrants, such as the Ordelaffi of Forlì, the Montefeltri of Urbino, and the Malatesti of Rimini. Consequently, when with the enforcement of the new system the local powers raised their voices in clamorous complaint against the French ecclesiastics, the Arno republicans were lavish with their sympathy. A number of other incidents contributed to irritate the Florentines. When in the winter of 1374-75 they were overtaken by a food scarcity of famine proportions and turned, as their habit was, to the Romagna for relief, they learned with indignation that the papal legate at Bologna had put an embargo on the exportation of grain. Apparently there was a scarcity in the Romagna, too, and the legate felt that his first duty was toward his own subjects. While the Florentines were still fretting over what was to them an unfriendly act, behold in June, 1375, an invasion of their territory by John Hawkwood and his band of foreign devils. Hawkwood, who had been in the service of the legate, was dismissed when no longer needed and turned his steps toward Florence in the hope either of plunder or of ransom money. That was the familiar alternative with which the companies of adventure confronted their victims, and we do not need to believe that the ruffian Englishman required any prompting from the Bolognese governor to undertake his incursion. But the Florentines would not have it other than that the soldiers had burst into Tuscany at the instance of the legate. They bought off the unwelcome guests with a painfully high tribute and then proceeded to revenge themselves by making war upon the church.

The daughter against the mother, the consistent champion of the Guelph idea against the institution which embodied that idea! It seemed incredible. Without any doubt Florence had frequently in the past resisted demands made on it by the popes to the point of inviting excommunication and interdict. But it had never drawn the sword against the representative of Christ, and the orthodox Guelph doctrine as expounded on the Arno by the hierophants of the parte Guelfa regarded the mere suggestion as utterly wicked and blasphemous. If we now recall that with its "warnings" and its indirect control of the government, the parte Guelfa had by 1375 made itself the object of a livid hatred on the part of the vast majority of the citizens, we shall put ourselves in possession of the master-key to the astonishing event. So closely allied with the party as to be identified with it, the church together with the party had insensibly become the target of Florentine animosity. However, the resentment against the church had developed by such gradual stages that it remained hidden under the threshold of consciousness until the incidents just reported, no one of which was particularly significant in itself, brought it to the surface with an irresistible momentum. On an overmastering wave of anti-clerical sentiment the Florentines plunged into war with the pope, partly no doubt to express their ill-will toward the papal state in process of formation, but chiefly in the hope of shaking off the intolerable yoke of the papalist parte Guelfa.[13]

Considered as war, the conflict between Florence and the pope is completely uninteresting. It was fought on both sides by hireling companies of adventure, which saw no reason for the spilling of blood, considering that, if they discreetly survived the campaign, they could count on an easy existence at the expense of their unarmed employers. Aside from the occasional brutal excesses of a soldiery that could not always be kept under control, there are really no military events for the historian to chronicle. Moreover, in view of the unreliable character of their troops, the Florentines were prudent enough to count on winning the war not so much by fighting as by diplomacy. Their plan was to incite the innumerable local powers of the State of the Church, cities and tyrants, to rebellion, to aid the rebels against the pope with money and men, and by the eloquence at the command of their diplomatic secretary, the celebrated humanist, Coluccio Salutati, to present the struggle to the world as the insurrection of oppressed subjects against an overbearing master. In hundreds of communications to the states of Europe, great and small, Salutati affirmed that the single issue involved was Liberty, for which his fellow-citizens were represented as unselfishly sacrificing themselves to the sole end that the brave little communities of central Italy might not perish under the heel of an inhuman tyrant. So successful was the Florentine agitation among the subjects of the pope that by the spring of 1376 the whole papal state was in convulsions and the pope's hold on it reduced to a few scattered strong-

[13] The most thorough study of the war is by A. Gherardi, "La Guerra dei Fiorentini con Papa Gregorio XI," in *Arch. Stor. It.,* Serie 3, Vol. V, Parte II, pp. 35-131. The supporting documents in *Arch. Stor. It.,* Serie 3, Vols. VI, VII, VIII.

THE CLOISTER OF SAN MARCO. MICHELOZZI

THE LOGGIA DELGI INNOCENTI. BRUNELLESCHI

Bottom: THE CHURCH OF SAN LORENZO. BRUNELLESCHI. *Top:* THE SACRISTY OF
SAN LORENZO. BRUNELLESCHI AND DONATELLO

THE CATHEDRAL OF SANTA MARIA DEL FIORE AFTER THE COMPLETION OF BRUNEL-
LESCHI'S CUPOLA

holds. But that the hard-pressed pontiff still commanded the spiritual weapons with which he had once brought great emperors to their knees, the sons of the Red Lily were now regretfully to learn. Not only did Gregory XI place the city under interdict, but he invited all and sundry peoples of the earth at their pleasure to appropriate the goods and seize the persons of Florentines when and wherever they might lay hands on them.

It might be supposed that the papal reprisals would have quickly dampened the ardor of the self-appointed champions of Liberty. This was so far from being the case that the enthusiasm which the war elicited on the Arno is its most amazing feature. Its conduct was from the first assigned to a special committee of Eight, *I Otto della Guerra,* and when this committee became the object of the deadly hatred of the papal partisans within the gates, it gained from a war-crazed population the extravagant designation of the Eight Saints, *I Otto Santi.* Supported by the suffrages and prayers of the vast majority of the population, the government was able to go to incredible lengths in answering the violence of the pope with appropriate counterviolence. Hard pressed for cash in the long-drawn-out struggle, it ordered the seizure and progressive sale of ecclesiastical property; and, as a crowning measure of resistance to ecclesiastical authority, it made mock of the papal interdict by ordering the local clergy under heavy penalties to unveil the altars and celebrate the divine offices. That such extraordinary measures of religious revolt could be proposed and carried through is the best possible evidence of the popularity of the war and of the continuing support by the people of the Eight Saints and the rest of the government. In the autumn of 1376 Pope Gregory XI at last left Avignon and in January of the following year entered Rome amidst the acclamations of the inhabitants. It is well known that the fiery exhortations of the saintly Catherine of Siena were a factor in the papal decision to restore Rome to its ancient primacy in the Christian world. But it is more than probable that, as much as by St. Catherine's magnetic appeal, Gregory XI was brought to the sticking-point by purely political considerations. Among these figured prominently his desire to end the rebellion of the dominion and bring the dangerous war with Florence to a close.

That for its part the Arno town could not go on indefinitely with the struggle was becoming apparent to even its most intransigent supporters. Not only had the expenses reached a fantastic figure but the merchants, who were each day returning from abroad with stories of the brutal confiscation of their goods under the blanket order of the pope, filled the town with their laments. Naturally the parte Guelfa made all the capital possible out of the accumulated public and private calamities. Although opposed to the war from the start, it had been silenced by the spontaneous nature of the outbreak; but no sooner had the inevitable revulsion set in than the party made itself the rallying-point of the various groups of critics. When it at length felt encouraged experimentally to resume the ammonizioni, which the war had obliged it to abandon, the government became sufficiently alarmed to open negotiations with the pope. They might have quickly led to peace, had not the death of Gregory in March, 1378, caused them to be broken off. Nonetheless fighting was not resumed, although the formal treaty ending the conflict had to wait on the pleasure of a new pope and was not signed till July.

Throughout the last and dying phase of the passionately waged war with the pope the domestic situation had been becoming more and more tense. Encouraged by the failing popularity of the conflict and the manifest strengthening of the ranks in favor of peace, the leaders of the parte Guelfa concluded that their hour had struck and resolved to overthrow their enemies by violence. Since their indirect control of the government was no longer effective, they fastened on direct control as alone calculated to assure their ascendancy and set June 24 for the bold stroke. That was St. John's day, the Florentine national holiday. But the secret, shared by too many initiates, leaked out and prompted the enemies of the party to strike first. We are aware that from the earliest showing of the party's hand the opposition to its tactics centered in the lesser gilds. To them there had gravitated by slow degrees a not unimpressive percentage of the members of the greater gilds. It was the capricious am- monizioni of the parte Guelfa that had given offense to these elements of the popolo grasso till in their alarm they made ready to stand shoulder to shoul- der with the lesser gilds to defeat the projected *coup d'état*. But how to pro- ceed? Fortunately, a merchant of proved hostility to the party held the crucial office of gonfalonier of Justice. He was Salvestro de' Medici, and at the mere mention of his name something somber and ominous seems to inject itself into the plot about to unfold. That is because the historians, aware of the subse- quent role of the family to which Salvestro belonged, have ascribed to this fourteenth-century figure the subtle intelligence and sly intrigue displayed by later Medici representatives in bringing Florence under their yoke. For this reading of Salvestro's character there is entirely insufficient justification in the few facts which have come down to us. He belonged to a family which, be- ginning with the thirteenth century, had been steadily coming to the front by the usual avenue of trade and which by the fourteenth century had gained a se- cure position among the popolo grasso by its merchant enterprise coupled with its strict adherence to Guelph principles. While there were many Florentine families both richer and more prominent, the Medici by Salvestro's time were already an "old" clan in the sense that for several generations their repre- sentatives had been admitted to all the offices of the republic. It was therefore a man of established reputation that served as gonfalonier of Justice in the May-June period of 1378. While in the main it was the accident of the parte Guelfa resolving to seize the power during his official headship of the state that brought him to the front, we cannot but agree that to have profited from this circumstance as he did testifies that he was a man of swift intel- ligence and virile resolution.

Salvestro delayed launching his counterstroke until the close approach of the critical St. John's day had filled the city with waxing apprehension over the coming events. Then on June 18 with the support of some merchant leaders of the same stripe he made an appeal which brought the people into the piazza. To the cry, "Viva il Popolo," they rallied around the government until a few days later, their fury bursting every bound, they took the offensive and plundered and set fire to the houses of all the plotting leaders of the parte

Guelfa. Only by precipitate flight did the leaders themselves escape destruction. Under pressure from the exultant mob the defeated plotters were exiled from the city, the laws which had enabled them to play their sinister part were canceled, and their victims, the ammoniti, were formally absolved of their public taint. The parte Guelfa had succumbed to the might of the lesser gilds under the leadership of an allied faction of the great merchants. So far as Salvestro and his political associates were concerned the revolution had done its work and was over.

But it was not over, by reason of the feature so common to revolutions through the ages: it got out of hand. The June commotions leading to the discomfiture of the conservative parte Guelfa turned out to be only a first revolutionary stage, followed a month later, in July, by the second stage, in which the June victors had little or no share, since the leading part was taken by the hitherto disfranchised popolo minuto. Made up of the workers and sottoposti of the greater gilds, the starved and oppressed multitude had during the preceding decades given so many evidences of restless discontent that its seizure of an opportunity so favorable for a rising as the disturbed state of the city in the summer of 1378 should cause no surprise. It will be recalled that the sottoposti had owed a first, though very ephemeral, recognition as an independent gild to the favor of the duke of Athens. The memory of that triumph still lingered, spurring the successors of the earlier leaders to renewed action. Another memory of the famous French episode was preserved in the curious name of *ciompi,* which dated from 1343 and was loosely used to designate the popolo minuto. We hear that the French soldiers of the duke had in the manner of their country addressed the man encountered in the street and wineshop as *compère.* Of this the Florentine tongue by some strange philological alchemy had made ciompo; and owing to some quality of humor in the hybrid term, it had quickly acquired universal currency.[14] While the word seems to have covered the whole mass of the common people, this mass consisted so largely of the workers of the woolen industry that they have been sometimes singled out as the only genuine and indubitable ciompi. That is an unimportant subtlety. Our excuse for this etymological digression is that it explains how it came about that the famous workers' rising of 1378 figures in Florentine history as the revolt of the ciompi.

In accordance with usage, on July 1 Salvestro de' Medici had been replaced as banner-bearer of Justice by Luigi Guicciardini, and together with the latter a fresh body of priors had taken office. But the new government did not enjoy a single day of peace, for the public agitation begun on June 18, instead of abating, grew more intense, especially when it became known that conferences were taking place among the workers which pointed to their early descent upon the Palazzo Pubblico. At length on July 21 the ciompi in an irresistible wave swept into the piazza carrying a petition boldly demanding the right of association and of consequent participation in the government as an acknowledged gild. While the frightened signori tried to gain time, the mob got out of hand and, scattering through the town, engaged in plunder and arson. On

[14] This is the explanation given by Stefani, r. 575, which most modern historians have not hesitated to accept.

the following day the wild demonstration was repeated, and this time its leaders resolved to make a clean sweep by driving the government from the palace. One after another the overawed officials beat a retreat at the demand of the roaring mob until at last the building had been vacated and the shouting, sweating, and triumphant ciompi took possession. At the head of the dense column which, ascending the stone stairway, burst into the deserted council chamber was a young wool-comber, Michele di Lando by name. Dressed in a ragged shirt and bare-legged except for a pair of sandals, he carried the abandoned banner of the gonfalonier of Justice and dramatically came to a halt under it in the captured hall. Immediately his followers proclaimed him gonfalonier, thus making him, in view of the collapse of the legal government, the master of the city. The next day a parliament was called and gave to Michele and the sindics of the gilds authority (*balìa*) to exercise rule till the end of August with the special prerogative to reform the government.

As the old government before dissolving had accepted the petition of July 21, the interim government with the humble wool-carder, Michele di Lando, at its head, at once set about realizing the main demands of the victors. It was a single gild of all the workers which had been asked for and conceded during the most recent convulsion. On the balìa's canvassing the situation, it resolved, probably because of the vast number of the workers, to organize them not in one but in three gilds, the *Tintori* or dyers, the *Farsettai* or shirt-makers, and a gild of the *Popolo Minuto,* which was by far the largest of the three and which, because it embraced most of the wool workers, was commonly called the gild of the ciompi. As the three new gilds, which swelled the total of the constitutionally recognized gilds to twenty-four, were at the same time conceded an appropriate share of the offices, it looked as if the workers had at last reached port and might rest comfortably on their oars.

But the hubbub and excitement had become so great that the revolution could not be arrested. For the greater gilds the July developments, permitting the legally dependent workingmen to escape the control of their masters, signified a defeat certain to bring financial ruin in its train. Though ousted for the moment from the seats of power, they still had at their disposal an economic weapon of the highest efficacy. They closed their shops and, as the keys creaked in the locks, hollow-eyed starvation entered the dwelling of every workingman, lashing him to renewed fury at the sight of the suffering of his wife and children. Instantly the disenchanted proletarians resolved on a fresh revolt, the third in the agitated series of this topsyturvy summer. Like simple people of our own and every period, they had an unshakable faith in the magic power of politics and never doubted that their employers could be brought to terms by resolute pressure on the government. Once more therefore, toward the end of August, they made a succession of maddened demonstrations before the Palazzo Pubblico. Finally, an ultra-radical group took a decisive step and, setting up a rival government in the broad piazza before the church of Santa Maria Novella, on August 31 sent two messengers to the interim rulers at the palace insolently demanding that the rebels be admitted to a share in the state. It was too much for the former wool-carder, Michele di Lando, temporarily the leading official of the city and intoxicated with a naïve pride of place. Seizing a sword, he drove the two emissaries of the insurgents from the chamber and down the stone stairway. Then mounting a horse, he bade all those who loved their city to join him in routing the enemy. The larger portion of the bystanders enthusiastically followed his lead and, throwing themselves on the radical rebels encamped on the Piazza Santa Maria Novella, pursued them through the streets and out of the gates until they lost track of them among the vineyards and olive orchards of the rolling countryside. By the resolute action of a single individual clothed with visible authority the radicals had been overwhelmed. When with the day's work done Banner-bearer Michele returned to the Palazzo Pubblico, he was hailed on all hands as the man who had saved his country.[15]

On the next day (September 1) the balìa presided over by Michele came to an end and a new group of priors, taking office, undertook such a house-cleaning as the sweeping character of the victory over the rebels seemed to authorize. The insurgents had been largely made up of the ciompi of the woolen industry aggregated in the newly created gild of the Popolo Minuto. The other two workers' gilds, the Tintori and Farsettai, had at the critical moment detached themselves from the ciompi and thrown in their lot with the government. In consequence a distinction was made; and while the insurrectionary gild of the Popolo Minuto was abolished, the gilds of the Tintori and Farsettai received renewed approval as arti minori in good standing. There were therefore now sixteen lesser gilds against the unchanged number of seven greater gilds. The eternally contested issue of power between the two groups was met by decreeing a substantial equality of representatives in the various magistracies with, however, a slight preponderance of the lesser gilds in most of them. The salient feature of the settlement was that, although the defeat of the radicals without doubt benefited the major arts, these did not at once achieve an ascendancy. On the contrary, the minor arts resumed the place in the state which they had held ever since the great overturn of 1343. Indeed it might be contended that, as the net result of the revolutionary summer just passed, they had even somewhat improved their position, since two new arts, representing certain groups of formerly disfranchised workers, had been added to their number. Unquestionably class jealousy continued as before to dig a chasm between the petty bourgeoisie of the original body of the lesser gilds and the wage-workers of the two recent additions. This was admittedly a difficulty and a weakness. Nonetheless the common people and

---

[15] It need hardly be said that the most diverse opinions have been voiced on the disturbances of 1378, on the roles and characters of Salvestro de' Medici and Michele di Lando, and on the causes and objectives of the third and most radical revolt. I have preferred not to pronounce on the motives of Salvestro and Michele since, owing to the slightness of the contemporary material dealing with them, every statement is no better than conjecture. It is amusing to note that when in the course of his history that incurable romantic, Machiavelli, got to the ambiguous Michele di Lando, he had him play a role that wins him a niche in the author's pantheon of heroes not much below those occupied by Castruccio Castracane and Caesar Borgia. To the authorities already cited the following, particularly concerned with the events of 1378, should be added: C. Falletti-Fossati, *Il Tumulto dei Ciompi*. Rome, 1882. G. Corazzini, *I Ciompi: Cronache e Documenti con Notizie intorno alla Vita di Michele di Lando*. Florence, 1888. *Il Tumulto dei Ciompi: Cronache e Memorie*. Muratori (New Ed.), Tomo XVIII, Parte 3.

not the great merchants were in the saddle, and the democratic experiment, inaugurated in 1343 and subjected to terrific strain in the summer of 1378, was found to have been salvaged when the storm was over. It continued to stamp its peculiar imprint on Florentine history for the next three years.

In some respects this last phase of the Florentine democracy is its most interesting period, largely because the strengthened people were somewhat more free to give effect to their peculiar purposes. No longer as before the revolution of 1378 was the parte Guelfa able to nullify the democratic policy of the rulers, for the party had had its teeth drawn and was at least temporarily innocuous. The elimination of this ultra-conservative club was perhaps the outstanding achievement of the disturbances through which the city had just passed. For the present resistance to the new government was centered in the great gilds, which, although they were still strong enough in law and tenacious enough in character to make the passage of democratic legislation extremely difficult, had to concede something to their opponents in order to have something conceded to themselves in return. With this constitutional balance in mind we can profitably pass in review the events of the next few years to the moment when a combination of circumstances drove the minor gilds from the helm, thereby once more giving over the ship of state to the exclusive control of the merchants of the arti maggiori.

The first concern of the government that issued from the third and final revolution and that began its rule on September 1 was to defend itself against its many enemies. At the head of the list were the exiled magnates of the parte Guelfa. Without exception men of consequence, they were so passionately bent on effecting their return that they never ceased stirring up the enemies of Florence against their native city. The same animosity characterized the beaten and fugitive ciompi. Regardless of whether he was of high or low degree, no Florentine ever meekly accepted the verdict that made him an outcast from his place of birth. Dangerous as were these two groups of enemies outside the city, the enemies within the walls constituted an even graver problem. They consisted of all those who for one reason or another held a political grudge against the government or nursed a personal ambition. While such ciompi as, driven by hunger, had returned to Florence in search of employment were the most numerous internal enemy group, the magnates and merchants of an uncompromising conservative outlook constituted a more immediate danger. No doubt, however, the greatest of all the perils to which the democratic regime was exposed, sprang from its false friends, ambitious ex-magnates, like Giorgio Scali, and ambitious popolani, like Tommaso Strozzi, who assumed the role of demagogue and flattered the people in the selfish hope of being carried by some lucky turn to the lordship of the city. The sheer endless succession of plots and crises that followed from the activities of both the inner and the outer enemies of the regime fills many a wearisome page in such contemporary records as that of Stefani. Ever on its guard, the republic usually seized and ruthlessly executed its opponents before their plot was ready to be touched off; sooner or later, however, somewhere, somehow a cog would be sure to slip and a combination of accidents bring down the precariously established democratic government.

In no single political field did the government succeed in giving more unambiguous evidence of its democratic character than in that of finance. In an earlier chapter [16] we took occasion to look into the revenue policy imposed on Florence by the triumphant merchant oligarchy. In last analysis we found it reduced itself to a simple scheme of endlessly multiplied consumption taxes (gabelle), supplemented by forced loans (prestanze) bearing a high rate of interest. When at length in 1343 the lesser gilds gained a greater weight in affairs, they attempted, with very little success it must be conceded, to break with a system so favorable to the rich and so injurious to the already heavily burdened masses. The only really important reform they carried through was a consolidation of the prestanze into a unified national debt (Il Monte), carrying a modest interest rate of 5 per cent, which it was decreed was never again to be exceeded. The Monte was an achievement of the first years (1343-47) of the new regime and with this one act the whole financial reform movement had come to a halt. In point of fact, owing to budgetary difficulties that reared their head on the occasion of the war with Pisa in 1362, even this single reform had suffered impairment. With the government sorely needing a loan and the well-to-do unwilling to furnish it for the niggardly 5 per cent fixed by law, a cunning notary, ser Piero di ser Grifo, found a way out. He suggested that every lender be entered in the books of a new Monte for three times the amount of his actual subscription; he would then receive a handsome 15 per cent without the government appearing to pay more than the 5 per cent fixed by the law. The Monte thus created became known as *dell'uno tre* (three for one), and the fraud was so generally acceptable that on the occasion of a later war there was created a more modest Monte—one wonders why more modest—yielding but 10 per cent and commonly called *dell'uno due* (two for one). Should we ask how under a popular regime it was possible to introduce financial practices so unfavorable to the lesser gilds in power, the answer is supplied by the persistent vigor of the conservatives amply attested for the years when these new Monti came into existence by the directive activities of the parte Guelfa.

But the parte Guelfa fell in 1378, the lesser gilds were strengthened by being increased from fourteen to sixteen in number, and with a refreshed spirit the critics of oligarchic finance attacked the problem of reform. It is gratifying to note that in and out of season these critics brought the question of how to relieve the poor of the burdens under which they groaned before the various councils. Granted that the measures which became law did not go very far and that, besides, they were usually but partially enforced, nonetheless a spirit manifested itself presenting such a lively contrast to the notions hitherto in vogue that it claims our respectful attention. Of course the recent fraudulent circumvention of the original Monte was the financial crime that aroused the most furious discussion. Indignant artisans did not mince words in denouncing the scandalous subterfuge connected with the name of ser Piero; and at length in December, 1380, a law was passed which suppressed the falsely inflated existing Monti and substituted for them a single Monte yielding an inalterable 5 per cent on the actual, not on the supposititious, sums loaned to the government.[17] As a result of this adjustment of a monstrous wrong the state saved annually an item of sixty thousand gold florins, of itself an emphatic justification of the measure. It was inevitable that the lesser gilds should attempt to pass on from this success to a correction of the unjust and greatly overworked system of indirect taxation. The memory of the direct tax, the estimo, current in the early years of the century, had not perished and an effort was made again to re-establish it in order to oblige the well-to-do to contribute to the support of the state in some adequate proportion to their wealth. And actually an estimo was voted and put in force; but it encountered so much secret and open opposition that it failed of its purpose and, in the face of insurmountable difficulties, had to be abandoned. Perhaps the most important deduction to be drawn from these rather timid and certainly sketchy achievements in the realm of financial reform is that, while the minor arts may have enjoyed a small preponderance of votes in the colleges and councils, the major arts through their unbroken economic power commanded the hidden resources enabling them substantially to nullify the reform measures of their opponents.

In the perpetually disturbed domestic situation of the Florentine republic the three years constituting the last phase of the rule of the lesser gilds represent an apex. Plots, denunciations, executions, sentences of exile, repatriations followed each other in unbroken, frenzied succession. With these agitations drawing the attention of the citizens the members of the sixteen lesser gilds often forgot or at least were not steadily mindful of the fact that the great merchants were sleeplessly on the watch to restore their political power and to bring the two remaining gilds of workers, the Tintori and Farsettai, back into the dependence to which the gild of the ciompi had already been obliged to return. In January, 1382, a violent uprising against the capitano del popolo headed by Giorgio Scali, the magnate demagogue who had imposed himself on the people as their leader, was the occasion of a new domestic crisis. The determined co-operation of all the authorities with the threatened capitano led to the quick seizure and execution of the unlamented Giorgio. The event filled the leaders of the greater gilds with rejoicing. As in their eyes the popular leader had fallen and the people were moved by divided counsels, the long-awaited hour for merchant action had come. Making the most of the favorable moment, the employers of labor, above all the employers of the great woolen gild, organized an armed assault on the shops and dwellings of the Tintori and Farsettai. They followed this by the measure which had become conventional whenever a change was to be effected in the government: they induced the priors to summon a parliament which gave the power (balìa) to reform the government to a handpicked committee.

As the balìa was voted on January 21, 1382, we may accept this date as marking the formal demise of the Florentine democracy. Of course the commission impeccably did its duty as defined by the victors. It canceled the charters of the two workers' gilds, thereby once more reducing the minor arts to

---

[17] For detailed information on this and all the other financial reforms see Rodolico, *La Democrazia Fiorentina*, chap. VI (Parte Seconda). Our authority for the trick of ser Piero is Stefani, r. 883.

fourteen in number. In the hope of amicably persuading the fourteen minor gilds to detach their fortunes from the proletarians, once more degraded to the level of sottoposti of the greater gilds, these latter, though victors, exercised a certain measure of restraint. They accepted an arrangement of the governing commission whereby, although the preponderance of power recently exercised by the lesser gilds was shifted to the greater gilds, the former were still conceded a relatively liberal participation in the government. There was no denying, however, that the oligarchy had triumphed. In the next few years it steadily added to its strength until its victory became sweeping and complete. Without doing violence to the truth a funeral orator of the defunct Florentine democracy might point out that it had made a firmer and more prolonged stand than that of any other Italian town. While it went down to defeat because of its lack of intelligence, leadership, and organization, much more, after all, than to its own defects, its overthrow must be attributed to the numerous economic and political forces which co-operated to favor the oligarchs and which in their sum were irresistible.

We end as we began by calling the episode of 1343 to 1382 a democratic interlude. It owed its origin to a temporary setback of the triumphant oligarchy which had reared its might on the gild system as formulated by the Ordinances of Justice. As soon as the setback was overcome the underlying forces, once more surging to the top, re-established the oligarchic system. Under these circumstances we are justified in accepting that system as a reasonably accurate expression of the distribution of power among the social classes making up the Florentine state.

XVII. Aspects and Problems of the New Urban Economy

THUS far in this book we have been concerned in the main with Florence as a political organism and, beginning with its origin, we have traced the stages of its development till the final victory in 1382 of the oligarchic principle. We have been at pains to point out that, like every other commune, Florence owed its existence to the revival of commerce around the year 1000, and that it grew to strength and achieved a virile dignity by adopting an urban way of life which brought it into violent conflict with the dominant agrarian forms identified with the feudal age. The unfolding of this epochal struggle obliged us to take account of trade routes, goods exchanged, money, merchant companies, and a score of similar economic items entering into the situation; we have dealt with the Florentine woolen industry as the leading source of the national prosperity; and, above all, we have taken account of those primal economic cells, the gilds, which so completely dictated the pattern of the city's material activity that they were enabled to take over the government. Should anyone ever be tempted to forget that Florence owed its greatness in the first place to the vigorous economic forces of which it was the focus, let him remember that throughout the two leading centuries of its history it was, at least in form, nothing other than a democracy of twenty-one constitutive gild units. Nonetheless we have thus far regularly subordinated the economic factors to our main problem, which was the consolidation of the Florentine state and the part it succeeded in playing between the two world-powers of the church and the empire. The time has now come to examine the economic activities systematically and for their own sake in order that we may arrive at as clear a picture as possible of the forces and institutions which contributed, each in its degree, to raise the city to its commercial and industrial eminence.

The communal movement which ended the long stagnation of the early Middle Ages was chiefly prompted by the renewal of the broken ties between the backward European west and the more advanced countries strung along the coast of the eastern Mediterranean. The Arab conquest, inaugurated by the Prophet Mohammed in the seventh century, had driven the already feeble Christian commerce from the Mediterranean and converted that sea into a Moslem lake; and, although the Arab empire had in the course of the eighth and ninth centuries lost some of its energy by falling into many separate emirates, these Arab succession states were alike interested in keeping Christian shipping from a sea which they regarded as the special preserve of the children of Allah. Some of the Moslem political units, especially in the western region of the Mediterranean, in Africa and Spain, were no better than pirate federations and, in addition to preying on such commerce as the Christians still ventured to conduct, they periodically descended on the Christian coasts to kill and plunder the inhabitants. We have learned in an early chapter [1] how Pisa on the Tuscan and Genoa on the Ligurian littoral about the year 1000 A.D. summoned the courage not only to resist the invaders but also to pay them home with raids so successfully conducted that after a few generations the Christians were permitted to regard the western Mediterranean as again at least in part their own.

At the same time Amalfi and Naples, cities of the southern coast, and, more energetically still, Venice, at the head of the Adriatic, took advantage of their never wholly interrupted association with the Byzantine empire to intensify their commerce with Constantinople. It was the Byzantine connection which enabled them to act as the distributors of the luxury articles of the orient among the rude peoples of the west. These articles consisted, besides the much-prized spices for the flavoring of the extremely simple and monotonous diet of the occident, of products indicative of a highly developed civilization, such as jewelry, silks, ivory, and ornaments of gold and silver. It was these precious articles which gave birth among the western barbarians to the idea of the fabulous wealth of the orient and which were, though certainly not the main cause, a contributory element in those stirring and perplexing invasions of the near east called the Crusades. Taken purely at their face value, the Crusades were an attempt to free by force of arms the Holy Land of Palestine from its Mohammedan masters and give it back to Christendom. We are aware that, apart from occasional successes of relatively short duration, the movement conspicuously failed, and that the vast crusading effort, many times renewed in a period of something less than two hundred years, would have to be enumerated among the major fiascos of history, had not consequences in other than the military field made the successive penetrations of the Levant something like a turning-point in western civilization. For one thing, to the western half of the Mediterranean, which the Genoese and Pisans had by their unaided effort reclaimed as a field of enterprise for Christendom, the eastern half was now added. This is not to say that the Crusades made the great middle sea a Christian instead of a Mohammedan lake, but merely that thenceforward the Mohammedans were sufficiently held in check no longer to be able to hinder the Christians from sailing the Mediterranean from one end to the other. From this extension of the physical range of the Christian mariners it gradually followed that the backward and self-repressed west, confronted with what its imagination pictured as the "gorgeous east," surrendered many of its narrow provincial customs and achieved a new mental and moral perspective. And since cause and effect in the realm of both mind and nature constitute an endless chain of energy, the communal movement, which was in its first infancy when the Crusades began, received a stimulus from them enabling it

[1] Chap. V.

steadily to wax in vigor till it was at last strong enough to overthrow the reigning feudal order.

The invaluable unity of occidental civilization attributable to a common faith and church, far from being disrupted by the commercial movement, was actually confirmed and fortified by it. This would not have been the case had not the awakening reached all the western lands without distinction. Since, however, the movement originated in the Mediterranean, the southern countries responded to it somewhat earlier than those bordering on the North and Baltic Seas; and among the Mediterranean areas the peninsula of Italy, owing to its central location, became the predestined clearing-house for an east-west exchange of goods. On this advantage, conferred by an accident of geography, the alert Italian towns seized without delay, thereby converting the very profitable trade in eastern spices and luxury articles into an Italian monopoly. Adriatic Venice, as first in the field, led the way but, even before the launching of the First Crusade (1096), it had already to reckon with the competition of such energetic upstarts from the west-Italian coast as Genoa and Pisa. Engaged chiefly in the importation of the much-esteemed eastern goods, the three leading seaports were spurred to develop appropriate organizations for their distribution through France, Germany, and England; and in measure as these western, as yet preponderantly agrarian countries in their turn acquired a taste for luxury and display, the Italian merchants increased the volume of both their business and their profits. It was accordingly the seaports which first waxed powerful in Italy as well as, for that matter, in the rest of Europe. But inasmuch as the commercial movement spread until it became general, inland towns favorably located on navigable rivers or on important cross-roads began before long to prosper in their turn.

We learned in an earlier section of this book that Tuscany, the province inviting our particular regard, experienced the gradual vitalization of a considerable group of inland towns intent each one on making the most of the novel opportunities. An identical situation developed in Lombardy, Liguria, Umbria, and the Romagna. The amazingly large number of communes between Verona at the foot of the Alps and Perugia in the heart of the Apennines that sprang to life and made a bid for power and wealth is a tribute to the magnificent animation of the period. They recognized, subconsciously probably rather than consciously, that if they wished to advance their fortunes by trade they would have to have something to trade with, and this perception led to the stimulation of the local crafts. Presently it came about that the towns which were most energetic in developing a manufacturing specialty, or which had an advantage in the matter of certain desirable raw products, or which enjoyed a supply of water sufficient to turn a mill wheel, or which commanded a system of convenient roads, forged ahead of their neighbors and ended by dominating them. In this way Bologna became the commercial metropolis of the Romagna, Genoa of Liguria, Milan of Lombardy; and rather surprisingly, in view of Pisa's earlier start and more favorable position on the coast, Florence slowly forged ahead and became the metropolis of Tuscany.[2]

---

[2] For the economic history of the whole of Italy there is now available an excellent survey by A. Doren, *Italienische Wirtschaftsgeschichte*. Jena, 1934.

That Florence for some generations after the communal movement had begun was economically inferior to Pisa and even to Pisa's near neighbor, Lucca,
is undeniable. Indeed it cannot be asserted that in that early time it counted
for more than any of its fellows of the Tuscan inland such as Pistoia, Siena,
and Arezzo. Lucca, as the capital of Tuscany during the Lombard period,
enjoyed a prestige within the province which continued well into the new
period of urban self-assertion. Among other ways, this primacy expressed
itself in the prerogative to mint the silver penny (*denarius*), the common
medium of exchange for all Tuscany. Moreover, the presence within its walls
during several centuries of a powerful duke or margrave attended by a
numerous court had stimulated the crafts, which got well under way in
Lucca some generations before they came to the front in the other Tuscan
towns. True, as soon as Pisa roused itself to cast off the incubus of Moslem
piracy, its development, though more along commercial than industrial lines,
carried it well beyond Lucca in economic power. As commanding the sea
route to Rome and southern Italy, it acquired a very special significance for
the emperors of the Franconian and Hohenstaufen lines and was able to sell
its assistance to its imperial masters in return for extensive privileges of an
economic-political nature. Among these was the right conceded by Barbarossa
in 1155 to issue a silver penny of its own and by this means to terminate the
monopoly hitherto enjoyed by the Lucchese mint.[3] Naturally this thrust at
the already shaken Lucchese supremacy only added fresh fuel to the fierce
rivalry of the two close neighbors dating from their birth as self-conscious
political organisms.

For lagging Florence the unquenchable feud between the two leading Tuscan communities constituted a brilliant opportunity. Coolly examining the
situation with an eye to the main chance, the as yet inconsiderable commune
dedicated to St. John and Santa Reparata resolved to align itself with Pisa.
The reader will recall that when Pisa, fighting for its life against the Moslem
corsairs, issued a general appeal for help, Florence made wholehearted response
and shared in the famous expedition, which in 1115 captured the island of
Majorca. The two porphyry columns, still guarding the main portal of the
baptistery, serve as a perpetual reminder of the early sworn brotherhood of
the two Arno towns.

Felicitous as the twelfth-century association of Florence and Pisa was, let
us not close our eyes to the fact that it rested on a solid basis of interest.
Pisa was naturally willing to accept aid against its pirate enemies from any
quarter that offered, while land-locked Florence had a clear perception of the
advantage for her trade of an outlet to the sea. In the years following the
Majorcan campaign of 1115 the inland town with few exceptions clung fast to
its Pisan friend and doubtless to a considerable extent owed its steady advance
to this association. The reward for its continued devotion reached a peak in
a famous treaty signed in 1171. This is so important as an economic mile-
stone that the privileges Pisa therein conceded to Florence must be enumerated
with some detail. The first of them touches the silver penny coined by Pisa
under the imperial concession obtained sixteen years before. In order to

[3] Davidsohn, Vol. I, p. 467.

persuade Florence to put and keep its influence behind that coin the Pisans conceded to the Florentines one half the profits of their mint. Next, in order to remove every obstacle in the way of the maritime trade of Florence, Pisa promised to carry Florentine citizens and their goods across the water on the same terms as those offered to Pisans. Finally, to make the measure of Pisan good-will full and overflowing the Florentines were in the matter of the shore tolls in Pisa to be treated even better than the Pisans themselves, since the guests were to be charged only half the dues levied on natives.[4]

Of this treaty with its amazing favors the unescapable interpretation is that, while the Pisans were as yet too far in front to reckon with the Florentines as rivals, the inland town was already formidable enough to be courted and won with favors. In view of the fact that Florence enjoyed the concessions embodied in the treaty for half a century without a break, the opinion may be ventured that the alliance of 1171 was a significant factor in the steady rise of its fortunes. During those fifty years constantly increasing numbers of Florentines with their goods made their way to Pisa and from Pisa to the Pisan settlements across the sea in Africa and the Levant. Even more important for Florence, however, was the continuous movement of rough woolen cloth from France which, after subjecting to certain refining processes, the enterprising merchants of the Calimala with expert salesmanship distributed over half of Europe. This cloth trade was the earliest source of Florentine prosperity. It swelled to such proportions that the traders, waxing proud, after a while no longer willingly accepted the traditional Pisan supremacy. To their rising resentment the Pisans responded in kind, and a brief reign of these dangerous emotions sufficed to undermine the ancient friendship between the two towns. In the year 1220 occurred the first overt act indicative of the new state of feeling. The Florentine and Pisan delegations dispatched by their respective communes to Rome to attend the coronation ceremonies of Emperor Frederick II indulged in an exchange of taunts while encamped before the Eternal City which culminated in blows and bloodshed. Two years later (1222) war broke out; and although this first serious quarrel was after some years patched up, the old partners had come to the parting of the ways and were henceforth irreconcilable enemies. This dramatic revulsion in their relations admits of but one interpretation: having grown in strength till it was able to challenge the ascendancy which Pisa had exercised in Tuscany for two hundred years, Florence resolved not to rest until it had forced the maritime town into a dependence which would oblige it to become the serviceable instrument of Florentine commercial expansion.

The political history of Florence as traced in this book has revealed a sum of moral qualities on the part of the merchant leaders which the economic history, constituting our present concern, will be found to confirm at every point. More clearly than any other Italian commune the Florentine burghers recognized that they were bringing a new social order into the world and that, as a consequence of their revolutionary activity, the emperor, who stood at the head of the traditional feudal system, was their inalterable enemy. In this enlightened perception much more than in any sentimental devotion to the

---

[4] Davidsohn, Vol. I, pp. 518-19. For exact details see Santini, *Documenti*, etc., No. IV.

pope lies the explanation of their consistent Guelph partisanship. They became the obstinate and aggressive opponents of the imperial power, not, however, without resorting to a flexibility of judgment and action which, especially in the early days, was absolutely necessary in the face of the possession by the emperor of an irresistible army. With the death in 1250 of Frederick II, the last emperor to command respect by reason of his military might, the Florentine opposition to the wielder of the imperial scepter became fixed and immutable. On the passing of the great Hohenstaufen the commune felt encouraged to treat the empire as though it had itself expired and at once seized all the prerogatives it needed to round out its sovereignty. This was less a novel than a culminating act since, as our exposition has made clear, having begun its usurpations of authority at its birth, the Arno town had never failed to appropriate a new imperial right whenever the favorable moment beckoned. It is therefore certain that if Florence may be said to have achieved its independence in the year 1250, it had been steadily moving toward that goal for almost two hundred years before that time.

All this is recalled at this point because the daring, the elasticity, and the vigorous grasp of the actualities which Florence exhibited in the political field characterized the citizens also in the realm of business. Not that the two departments can be strictly kept apart. It is rare indeed that a political action does not imply economic considerations or that economic considerations do not inspire political action. But as in the present chapter we are putting economic matters to the fore, it will be permissible and proper to emphasize the economic aspect of events which, viewed from another angle, may be considered as possessing also a political, a juridicial, or a social import. In the light of this opinion we desire to draw attention to two usurpations of sovereign rights on the part of Florence which befell, one a little before, the other a little after, the demise of the second Frederick, and which, though highly political, greatly affected the business world and therefore call for an evaluation on their economic side.

In discussing the coinage situation we observed that the silver penny of Lucca, an inheritance from the long-vanished ducal regime, ruled the realm of Tuscan business till Pisa in 1155 obtained from Frederick I the right to issue a silver penny of its own. Presently a number of other towns, such as Siena, Arezzo, and Volterra, gained by imperial diploma the same privilege as Pisa and the Tuscan monetary situation fell into confusion. This was owing not so much to the great number of legal pennies in circulation as to the circumstance that each town, as soon as it found itself in financial straits, took the immediately convenient course of relieving its treasury by debasing the currency. With a variable silver content in the competitive municipal pennies expert money-changers had to come to the rescue to determine their intrinsic worth and this intervention of a third party hampered traffic, besides afflicting it with a burdensome service charge. The Florentines bore the situation for a time with great patience. They minted no penny of their own for the simple reason that they had never been willing to kneel at the throne of the emperor as humble petitioners. In their characteristically cautious way they waited for a favorable opportunity and in the period 1234-1237 (the exact moment has thus far escaped detection) resolutely took action. The reigning emperor at the time was that Frederick II who figured so prominently in Italian and Tuscan affairs in his day. In the year 1235 he was obliged to hurry to Germany in order to crush a dangerous rebellion led by his own son. The imperial overlord entangled in perilous civil strife far from the Italian scene—that was a situation than which Florence could not imagine anything more auspicious. In the light of what has already been said touching Tuscan coinage we are aware that the mint was un unchallenged imperial prerogative: only the emperor issued money or those lords and towns to whom he had conceded the right by formal patent. The Florentines knew this as well as everybody else but, fiercely opposed to the emperor, they preferred to filch his rights from him rather than to get them by meek submission and money paid in hand. In this frame of mind they watched his disappearance behind the Alps with quiet glee and in the spirit of reckless bravado issued their first coin, the silver solidus.[5]

Not only was the silver solidus, politically considered, a revolutionary act but economically it was a startling innovation. From the early Middle Ages the common circulating medium not only in Italy but throughout Europe had been the thin silver penny (denarius), of which twelve made a solidus (called soldo in Italian). Twenty solidi or two hundred and forty denarii made a libra (called lira in Italian). As both solidus and libra were merely reckoning units and were not minted, it must be understood that only the penny was in actual circulation. The penny met every need so long as the commercial movement, which set in around the year 1000, was in its infancy and trade was conducted on a relatively small scale. However, by the thirteenth century trade had assumed considerable proportions and a larger unit than the silver penny, which, small of value in itself, had been still further reduced by admixture with baser metals, had become imperative. The Florentine solution of the difficulty was the silver solidus, a creative act! Confronted with the new coin, worth twelve of the old pennies, the Lucchese, Pisans, and Sienese must have wondered why they had not thought of it themselves, for they immediately paid it the flattery of imitation. The sudden plethora of solidi did not alter the impression that the Florentines had proved themselves to be the most original thinkers along financial lines in Tuscany.

Not much more than a decade later, in 1252, they took a step which carried their name far beyond the limits of Tuscany and, in connection with the whole capitalist movement to be presently discussed, made them the financial leaders of the western world. They issued a gold coin, the florin, which showed their patron saint, St. John the Baptist, on one side and their coat of arms, the lily, on the other.[6] It must be granted that they had been preceded in the issuance of a gold coin by Emperor Frederick II with his famous augustales. His were the first gold coins put out by any western sovereign

---

[5] Although Villani, VI, 53, casually mentions the issue of this coin, it remained for Davidsohn to clear up the details (Vol. II[1], p. 213; *Forschungen*, Vol. IV, pp. 316-22).

[6] Villani, VI, 53; Davidsohn, Vol. II[1], pp. 411-12.

since the passing of the Roman empire. But Frederick's mint was closed at his death, and again we receive confirmation of the mental alertness of the Arno merchants in that they at once filled the gap with their own gold coin, the *fiorino d'oro*. It was issued as the equivalent of twenty solidi or of one libra.[7] Thenceforward the commune regarded it a matter of pride as well as of sound business to maintain the full gold value of the new coin to the intent of thus creating a stable unit of exchange. Its success in this respect is attested by the rapidity and completeness with which the florin conquered the markets of Italy, the Mediterranean, and even the European north. It became and remained for several generations the most prized of the many scores of gold and silver coins put into circulation in competition with the florin. For in an attempt to keep abreast of the Florentines numerous towns and sovereigns put forth gold coins of their own and, in witness of the success of the piece bearing the lily and the Baptist, many of the rival issues were nothing other than impudent counterfeits of the revolutionary florin. According to David-sohn no less than forty-eight European mints were guilty of this barefaced fraud.

By serving themselves in pertinent and intelligent fashion the Florentines had served the whole contemporary world, and their prestige rose enormously. The name of Florence was whispered and finally shouted through all the lands until fifty years after the issuance of the gold florin Pope Boniface VIII, on the occasion of the reception in 1300, the year of the Great Jubilee, of a number of special ambassadors, who, although representing different com-munities, were all Florentines by birth, was moved to greet them with the smiling compliment: "You Florentines are the fifth element." In Boniface's opinion, as in that of all his contemporaries, the world was made up of four substances called elements: water, fire, earth, and air. These had constituted the universe until the Florentines came along and manifestly enriched the mixture with the fifth element of their fine ingenuity. Of this the florin, invented half a century earlier, was for most Italians of Boniface's time the outstanding instance.

Since the new coin made its influence felt to the ends of the earth, it natu-rally became a factor also in the local Tuscan struggle for supremacy between Florence and Pisa which had begun around 1220. On this particular situation Villani throws light with such a sparkling tale that, although his *novelletta,* as he calls it, may not be strictly true, it cannot be passed over because it illustrates the waxing Florentine reputation more effectively than a volume of statistics.[8]

[7] "E contavasi l'uno soldi venti" (Villani, VI, 53). However, the fiorino d'oro steadily appre-ciated. By the early fourteenth century it was usually worth more than thirty solidi; and a hundred years after its appearance frequently rose to the value of sixty silver solidi or three librae of silver pennies. The appreciation was chiefly due to the continuation of the evil practices of the Tuscan and European mints in general of debasing the silver penny by increasing the ratio of cop-per. With the process continuing indefinitely the penny was bound in the long run to reach the state when, with its silver content gone, it would be wholly a copper coin. Undoubtedly a second factor in the gradual appreciation of the florin was the burden put upon gold in supporting the world's business. With the demand for gold constantly increasing the metal naturally rose in value.

[8] VI, 53.

When the said new florins had begun to travel through the world some of them reached Tunis in Barbary and, brought to the attention of the king of Tunis, a wise and valiant lord, they pleased him greatly. And he ordered that they be assayed and, on learning that they were of fine gold, praised them much and bade his interpreters explain the imprint, which showed John the Baptist on one side, and on the other, the lily with the word Fiorenza. Seeing that it was money of Christians, he sent for the Pisan merchants, who, as privileged traders, stood high in the king's esteem [even the Florentines in Tunis passed as Pisans] [9] and asked them what sort of a city among Christians this Fiorenza might be that made the said fiorini. Out of envy the Pisans answered contemptuously saying: "They are the Arabs of our hinterland," by which they meant to signify the equivalent of our own [Florentine] mountaineers. Thereupon the king responded wisely: "This does not look to me like the money of Arabs; and you Pisans, what gold coin do you issue?" On this they were confused and gave no answer, and he next asked if there was not someone from Florence in their midst. And such an one was found, a wide-awake fellow from Oltrarno by the name of Pera Balducci. Him the king asked concerning these Florentines, who, according to the Pisans, were their Arabs. And Pera answered wisely, exhibiting the power and magnificence of Florence and that Pisa in strength and population did not amount to half of Florence; and that Pisa had no gold coin; and that the florin was the result of the many victories won by Florence over Pisa. By which statements the Pisans were shamed and the king on account of the florin . . . issued a charter to the Florentines which gave them the same privileges as those enjoyed by Pisa. And by virtue of them the Florentines were to have at Tunis a warehouse [*fondaco*], dwellings, and a church.

Granting that the gold florin was a factor in the mounting commercial importance of Florence, an even greater factor was the merchant company; and as this institution, far from being a Florentine specialty, sprang from the complex phenomenon called the rise of capitalism, we shall have to give this larger issue our close consideration. Among the most prominent analysts and historians of capitalism is Sombart, who has made himself the champion of the view that the most common source of the earliest accumulations of capital in medieval times were the surplus ground rents of the great feudal landowners. Sombart argues that the magnates were obliged to put their excess returns to work, thereby instituting a new system. In his view capitalist production differs from manorial production, which preceded it, by being conducted with free funds to the sole end of profit. Conceding that he makes out a good case for his ground-rent theory for many parts of medieval Europe, we are obliged to insist that its application to Florentine conditions is much less convincing. The leading Florentine authority, Davidsohn, does not hesitate to declare that Sombart has so patently misinterpreted the Florentine evidence that what he alleges about capitalist beginnings on the Arno is completely erroneous. Davidsohn thereupon advances a theory of his own, which he buttresses with such a wealth of documents that it is difficult to see how it can be successfully attacked. Let us see how, according to him, it came about that Florence rose to be the foremost center of the new and

[9] This identification of Florentines as Pisans in Tunis and other ports, where the Pisans enjoyed special privileges, was a consequence of the treaty of 1171. For details of this fusion of Florentines and Pisans abroad see Davidsohn, Vol. IV[2], pp. 2, 256.

revolutionary system of production and exchange that passes under the name of capitalism.[10]

In the early Middle Ages wealth took the form of land and was concentrated in the hands of great prelates, such as bishops and abbots, and of secular lords. Our interest in what happened to this wealth on the coming of the communal revolution is limited to Tuscany, which constitutes no more than a particular instance within the general situation. Far from accumulating pecuniary reserves, from the time of the earliest records which have come down to us the landlords of this province are found to be in the most serious financial straits. While commanding ample returns from their vassals and serfs in the form of services and supplies, they received little or no ready money. Consequently when, by the intensified distribution of oriental goods, commerce and the crusades had raised the western standard of living, the feudal masters found it difficult to satisfy their newly acquired tastes.

While the new time called for expensive amusements in the form of feasts, hunts, and tournaments, there were, besides, campaigns to be conducted and periodic journeys to be undertaken to the court of pope or emperor. As these various activities signified for the ruling lords the need of providing costly apparel and elaborate armament for themselves and their train, it became incumbent on them to borrow money from the *mercatores,* the new class of traders born of the urban movement. We must remember that we are dealing with a small upper stratum of society as improvident as it was pleasure-loving. A great nobleman would ride into the nearest town, tap at the door of a trader with his spear, and putting his cross, in lieu of his name which he could not write, to a mysterious Latin document, would vanish as soon as a few pounds of pennies had been delivered into his hands. Likely enough he did not actually handle the cash, for the money-lender was also a merchant and cunningly supplied the goods the money was intended to buy from his own stock. When after a few months the debt had to be repaid, the improvident borrower, incapable of making restitution, grasped eagerly at an extension offered him at a higher rate of interest and registered no objection against throwing in an additional field or vineyard as security for his loan. The process, begun in the eleventh century, was accelerated in the twelfth and carried to a climax in the thirteenth century. The documents tell a clear and entirely unambiguous story.[11] They show, for instance, how the Florentine family of the Gianfigliazzi began its career by lending money in a small way to the bishop of Fiesole. Once begun, the movement continued until the Gianfigliazzi and other families associated with them had stripped his lordship of all of his possessions and left him a pauper. In the same way the Cerchi battened on the abbot of the Badia, the Cavalcanti on the nuns of Santa Felicità on the left bank of the Arno near the Ponte Vecchio. And the bloodsucking of the bish-

[10] In his work, *Der Moderne Kapitalismus,* in addition to accumulated ground rents, Sombart operates with two other sources of early capitalism, mining and colonial enterprises. Of these, however, he does not affirm that they apply to Florence. Davidsohn's position is most fully stated in his study, "Uber die Entstehung des Kapitalismus," *Forschungen,* Vol. IV, pp. 268-94. See also Vol. I, pp. 796 ff.; Vol. II², pp. 402 ff.

[11] Davidsohn, *Forschungen,* Vol. IV, pp. 281-94. For the detailed record of the impoverishment through continued borrowing of a great prelate, the bishop of Volterra, see F. Schneider, *Bistum und Geldwirtschaft.* Vols. VIII and IX of *Quellen und Forschungen aus Ital. Archiven.*

oprics and monasteries was strictly paralleled by what happened to the temporal lords. The Guidi, the Ubertini, and the other great barons of the Tuscan
countryside found that, once in the clutches of the money-lenders, they could
not again extricate themselves and had to suffer the gradual transfer of their
houses and lands to the Spini, the Mozzi, the Frescobaldi, the Peruzzi, and
other similar urban residents. By the thirteenth century each of the families
named, and many others besides, had risen from a level akin to that of small
pawnshop dealers to the status of great bankers and, forgetting their plebeian
origin, looked upon themselves in comparison with their poorer fellow-townsmen as born to the purple. Like the new-rich from the beginning of time, they
aped the old-rich whom they supplanted and ordered their existence as far as
possible according to the military standards of their victims. Within a span of
perhaps two centuries the whole landed wealth of the Florentine contado and
of a large part of Tuscany as well had passed from the original feudal owners
into the possession of townsmen who, regardless of their social pretensions,
were, or at least had begun their existence, as traders and bankers.

Traders and bankers, yes; but in unvarnished speech they were nothing but
usurers. Far from this being an unfair modern judgment, it was shared by
their contemporaries, as we can still learn from a document of the year 1294
which referred to the Gianfigliazzi as "mercatores, immo usurarii," merchants,
nay rather, usurers.[12] It is of course well known that usury, meaning interest
on a money loan, high or low, fair or unfair, interest of any sort, was forbidden by the church; and it is or should be equally well known that no one,
including the highest dignitaries of the church up to and including the popes
themselves, paid any attention to the prohibition in their daily affairs. Doc-
trinally, however, the church never budged from its traditional position. Whenever the issue of usury was brought before a church council or whenever the
pope pronounced on it *ex cathedra*, the declaration against the lending of
money at interest was solemnly renewed and usury was denounced as a deadly
sin. Accordingly, Dante was doing no more than giving expression to sound
Catholic doctrine when he reserved one of the least comfortable compartments
of hell for usurers, although we may agree that when he could not restrain
his satisfaction at finding so large a Florentine contingent there, he was voic-
ing a purely personal animosity.[13] The chasm yawning between profession and
practice has been a feature of every society since Priam was king in Troy, but
in no age was it wider and deeper than in medieval Europe. That a usurer on
his deathbed was often obliged by the priest, before he would administer extreme unction, to restore to his victims some of his ill-gotten gains or, as a
substitute measure, to leave a lump sum to the church to distribute in charity
as it saw fit, cannot alter our view of the shocking hypocrisy of the whole
business. High as interest would normally have been in the Middle Ages,
owing to the scarcity of money and to the general public insecurity, the official
sinfulness of usury, perpetually exposing the usurer to seizure and condemnation as a heretic, added to his risk and helped make money dear to the pur-
chaser. In any case the usual interest rate was appallingly high, 30 and 40 per

.12 Davidsohn, *Forschungen*, Vol. III, document 221.
18 *Inferno*, XVII, 34-75.

cent per annum being not unusual during the infancy of commerce.[14] In the course of the fourteenth century, by which time the volume of trade had greatly increased, the original opinion regarding usury underwent a modification and the Florentine merchant world developed the distinction between interest and usury familiar to our own business practice. Exactly as with us a reasonable charge came to be considered legitimate and the word usury experienced a restriction in scope, being limited to excessive percentages. However, as a rate up to 20 per cent lay within the fourteenth-century criterion of reasonableness, we may agree that the returns from money-lending of even the respectable sort enjoying the support of the municipal law courts remained very high; and from this continued height we may draw the further conclusion that the huge profits of the banking business were an expression of its heavy risks and of the undiminished scarcity of money.[15]

The dizzy rate of interest had to be injected into the argument at this point because it helps explain the ease and completeness with which many or most of the original feudal lords lost their property to the money-lenders graciously prepared to relieve their necessity with a loan. It was only after the money-lenders had in their turn become the proprietors of houses and farms and had utilized them to broaden their credit structure that they achieved the dignity of bankers. But their great reputation rests on their next step, which was to rise from the level of local bankers to world-bankers; and in order to make this advance they had to be helped by a world-event. This was the struggle between the church and the empire which in the last years of the reign of Frederick II developed into a fight to the finish. Pope Gregory IX took the view that in order to win the victory he might levy on the ecclesiastical property of all Christendom, while his successor, Innocent IV, went a step farther and by rating the struggle against Frederick as a crusade in behalf of the Cross claimed and exercised the right to collect the crusading tithe. There is no occasion to retell at this point the ferocious combat of Frederick's last years nor the dramatic crises associated with the Guelph-Ghibelline wars of the second half of the thirteenth century. It will suffice if we recall that the church in the end won the day; but particularly pertinent to the economic matter treated in this chapter is the fact that the Guelph victory resulted to a very large extent from the superior resources of the pope. Neither Gregory IX nor Innocent IV nor any of their successors failed to strain every nerve to assemble in their hands subsidies and tithes levied on abbots and bishops throughout the west with which to equip the armies required to stamp out the accursed seed of the Hohenstaufens. To collect these dues the popes used the Italian merchants and bankers, whose business enterprise had scattered them over the western world. While their profits merely as papal collectors

---

[14] These are the figures of Davidsohn (Vol. I, p. 795; *Forschungen*, Vol. I, p. 158) based on an examination of thirty Florentine loans covering the years 1016 to 1210.

[15] In an excellent article by A. Sapori, "L'Interesse del Denaro a Firenze nel Trecento," in *Arch. Stor. It.*, Serie 7, Vol. X, pp. 161-86, the distinction gradually made between legitimate and usurious interest is discussed as well as the height of each toward the end of the fourteenth century. The author also shows how the doctors of both the civil and the canon law were gradually moved to descend from their ivory towers and to exercise their ingenuity to accommodate the original stark theory regarding usury to current business practice. Divine law beat a strategic retreat before common utility.

must have been considerable, they enjoyed even greater rewards from advancing the papal assessment to the bishops and abbots at a variable but regularly stiff rate of interest. In other words, they performed a variety of offices which, ranking as war services, were urgent in character and yielded an inordinate return; and although the popes at first used Italian bankers indiscriminately and, if they showed a preference at all, may be said to have favored the Sienese, the battle of Montaperti (1260) produced a crisis which revolutionized the situation.

As Montaperti was a Ghibelline success, and as no more sweeping victory had ever been won in Tuscany, it followed that all the Tuscan towns, with or against their will, were brought under the Ghibelline banner. Therewith the only effective means left in the pope's hands for undermining the hated Ghibelline hegemony was his so-called spiritual power. Accordingly, he laid every Ghibelline commune under interdict and ordered the debtors of merchants of these communes in every country of Europe to refuse to pay their debts under pain of excommunication. At the same time he let it be known that he would individually readmit to the Christian communion all merchant-bankers prepared to desert the Ghibelline cause, and that he would favor the reconciled firms by intrusting the papal business to their care. Almost precipitately the Florentines, especially those who, as confirmed Guelphs, had fled from their native city after Montaperti, accepted the papal offer. Since Siena was too closely and officially tied up with the Ghibelline ascendancy, the Sienese could not to anything like the same extent come to terms with the pope, and as a result the men of Arno gradually replaced their rivals of the City of the Virgin at the papal court. When, a few years after Montaperti, the pope resolved to draw Charles of Anjou across the Alps in order to oust Manfred from southern Italy, he committed the financial preliminaries of the campaign chiefly, if not exclusively, to good Florentine Guelphs. And before another decade had passed so great an intimacy had been established between Florence, now become passionately and uncompromisingly Guelph, and the venerable and unchanging head of the Guelph cause that the Arno merchants crowded out all rivals and came into a virtual monopoly of the vast and lucrative papal business.[16]

The bankers, whom the world-struggle between pope and emperor had made an international power, were organized in partnerships or merchant companies, and the characteristic feature of the merchant company was that it engaged not only in banking but also in trade. Representatives of the Florentine firms appeared at all the great European fairs, particularly at the fairs of Champagne in eastern France, which were the largest trade gatherings of the thirteenth century, while with the expansion of international commerce in the following century agents of the Florentine houses settled permanently in France, England, Flanders, Sicily, Catalonia, Tunis, and every town and country affording commercial opportunities. It was the Italians and, among them of course our Florentines, who chiefly profited from the commercial movement because, as the earliest European people in the field, they possessed special information about goods, markets, and costs, besides commanding all the new technical

[16] Davidsohn, Vol. II, chap. 7, pp. 532, 546, 551-54.

devices, such as the bill of exchange. The way in which a Florentine company would utilize its position as financial agent of the papacy in order to extend its trade may be illustrated by reference to England. When the pope laid a tax on the English monasteries, a Florentine agent residing in England would present the bill. Since in all probability the abbots could not immediately pay, the ingratiating stranger, in his capacity of banker, advanced the assessment as a loan secured by the wool which the English monasteries produced in great quantities; or, in case a loan was not necessary, the Arno visitor, in his capacity of merchant, offered to buy the wool outright in order to ship it to the continent, where it was in demand for the manufacture of cloth. While the wool at first went generally to the cities of Flanders, toward the end of the thirteenth century the dealers widened their range and diverted the English wool in ever larger quantities to the banks of the Arno as an aid to the further development of the native woolen industry.

By this measure the merchant company added to banking and trade a third department, industrial promotion, and in the course of the fourteenth century fairly outstripped with this activity the other two. It has already been stated that when industry in Florence first transcended a purely local scale, it rested exclusively on the refining and dyeing of a very rough kind of cloth imported from the markets of Champagne in eastern France. These were the so-called *panni franceschi*. Merchant companies, the members of which belonged overwhelmingly to the gild of the Calimala, undertook both the import and re-export of the French cloths. However, at the side of this purely processing industry there existed from an early time a modest manufacture of cloth from native wool. Owing to the poor quality of the home-grown article this industry remained insignificant till the merchants bethought themselves to bring in better foreign wool, first from Spain and finally from England. The latter long-stapled product was considered to be the best wool grown; and when the Florentine merchants, having in their capacity of papal agents become acquainted with the English article, resolved to direct it to their native city, Florentine industrial development entered on a new phase. By taking advantage of the skill and taste which had been developed by the native workmen, above all, in the selection and use of dyes, the merchants calculated that they could produce from imported wool a cloth which would be without a rival. If only the necessary capital was supplied, manufacture might be started on a large scale and all accessible markets be captured with the prospect of very handsome profits. The enterprisers who went in for this particular venture gradually congregated in a second wool gild, the Lana; and as shortly after the turn of the century, in the early days of the victory of the Blacks, the volume of business done by the Lana began to outstrip that of the older Calimala gild, we have evidence of the quick success of the plan to intensify the city's industry. Before the middle of the trecento, the production of woolen cloth, according to Villani, furnished a livelihood for thirty thousand people and completely dominated the local economic situation. However, the industry continued to be ruled as from the first by traders, who, apart from financing by the putting-out method the various operations of spinning, dyeing, and weaving, were content to assemble the finished cloth in order to distribute it over Europe.

This will explain why, although Florence owed its rapid fourteenth-century expansion to manufacture, the leading men of the town always present themselves to view not as industrialists but as merchants. It follows that the organization through which they operated continued to be the merchant company. These associations were of all sizes, great and small, with much or little capital, with many or few partners, and the goods they most commonly bought and sold were raw wool and finished cloth together with the various materials necessary for textile manufacture, such as alum and dyestuffs. But they dealt also in leather, weapons, salt, spices, wheat, wine, linen, in fact in every article that sought a market and from the buying and selling of which there was likely to result a profit.[17] Since in the course of the fourteenth century banking became a more highly specialized occupation than had been the case in the preceding centuries and required more ample resources for its successful conduct, only the larger merchant companies, such as the Bardi, the Peruzzi, and the Acciaiuoli, continued to act as banks. The smaller trading firms felt more and more constrained to limit their scope to purely commercial transactions. However, so closely did their interests remain tied up with the great houses that, when a financial crisis befell they were sympathetically affected; and in case the big companies crashed to the ground, there was every likelihood that the smaller companies, inextricably entangled with the leading firms, would also go down.

The fourteenth century repeatedly supplies the proof of this statement and in no instance more convincingly than in the famous crisis of the forties. We heard in an earlier chapter how this was precipitated, at least in its first phase, by the circumstance that the two great companies of the Bardi and Peruzzi had overextended themselves by continued and excessive loans to Edward III of England in support of his madly ambitious project to conquer France. When the king defaulted on both interest and principal, not only the two firms directly involved but the whole business structure of Florence was shaken to its foundations. The threatened interests made a desperate effort to save the situation, but when the republic of Florence in its turn was obliged to cease payment on its huge war debt piled up in connection with the attempt to conquer Lucca there was no further staving off the avalanche of bankruptcies (1343–46).

It is a tribute to the undaunted energy of the Florentine merchants that they would not admit defeat in spite of this unparalleled disaster. They formed new companies which manifested no less zeal and resolution than their predecessors and which operated with such success that Florence was enabled to retain the same dominating place in the European business world during the second half of the fourteenth century as it had held in the first half. Among the great houses of the new period of prosperity were the Alberti, the Albizzi,

[17] The recent spurt of interest in economic history has produced many valuable studies dealing with the innumerable economic and juridical problems connected with the merchant, such as contracts of partnership, the draft, the fondaco, transportation, insurance, etc. Such are: E. Bensa, *Francesco di Marco da Prato. Notizie e Documenti sulla Mercatura Italiana del Secolo XIV.* Milan, 1928. A. Sapori, *Una Compagnia di Calimala ai Primi del Trecento.* Florence, 1932.

the Strozzi, and the Medici. Let the fresh set of upstarts remind us that there had been in Florence from the earliest days a constant rise and fall of merchant companies. It should serve to bring home to us that the opportunities which offered of inordinate gain were matched by the risks which were equally inordinate, and that only the happy concomitance of business acumen and good fortune would secure to a merchant company an even relative permanence of existence. In point of fact it was the exception and not the rule for a merchant company to continue in business for the length of more than a human generation.[18]

If we turn now to examine the field of operation of the merchant companies, let us begin with France where we have encountered them as active from an early date and from where they radiated toward Flanders, on the one hand, and toward England, on the other. All three of these northern areas continued throughout the fourteenth century to receive the attention of the Florentines; but it was France which, as from the first, exercised the greatest attraction and with which the business ties became most numerous and intimate. After the decline of the Fairs of Champagne, a movement already well advanced before the year 1300, the city of Paris became the great emporium of the kingdom, and at Paris and the nearby towns to the north and east innumerable young Florentines served their business apprenticeship in representation of the trading houses which had their seat on the Arno. Already by Villani's time it was a business commonplace that the exploitation of the French market was the main source of Florentine prosperity. It has been repeatedly pointed out in these pages that the obstinate guelphism of the City of the Baptist has one of its leading roots in this dependence of Florentine business on the protection and good-will of the kings of France. In a natural effort to sentimentalize the hard reality, the Florentines were at pains to represent themselves as standing shoulder to shoulder with the house of Capet, its Angevin offshoot in southern Italy, and the popes in an idealistic undertaking to advance the cause of Holy church. As final and conclusive proof of the spontaneous and preordained nature of the association between themselves and the French kingdom the Arno folk were wont to point to the circumstance that both states boasted the lily as their emblem. This was of course a mere accident, but it helped to strengthen the pro-French enthusiasm and contributed its share toward introducing into Florence French customs, fashions, and epics of chivalry, which in their turn operated as a by no means negligible factor in shaping the local social and literary developments. However, let us make no mistake. The decisive reason for the historical intimacy between the Kingdom of the White and the City of the Red Lily was the very substantial advantage Florence enjoyed during many generations in France through its domination of the French markets due to the commercial acumen and the superior organizing skill of its merchants.

While northern France was undoubtedly the chief magnet of the Florentine merchant-adventurers, they were to be encountered also in practically every

---

[18] O. Meltzing, *Das Bankhaus der Medici und seine Vorläufer*. Jena, 1906. This is still the most serviceable history of the leading Florentine trading companies, disclosing, as it does, their organization, their activities, their wealth, and their swift decline.

Christian land and in many Mohammedan realms besides. It goes therefore without saying that they were to be found in such leading contemporary emporia as ·Bruges, London, Barcelona, Avignon, Marseilles, Naples, Genoa, Venice, Constantinople, and Tunis; but even inconspicuous communities, provided they were strategically located along the great trade routes, were favored with their presence. Wherever they went, and whether in small or large numbers, they settled among their hosts in a tight little native group, which constituted a solid phalanx for the defense of common interests and which enjoyed considerable rights of self-government. We shall not find our merchants in great numbers in Germany because Germany belonged to the area of Venetian exploitation. However, in spite of the near east, too, having been from the earliest days of the commercial awakening the special preserve of Venice and such other seaports as Genoa and Pisa, so alluring were the prospects of profit in this opulent field that the Florentines refused to be excluded from it. The earliest Florentine merchants came to the Levant by taking advantage of the treaty with Pisa of 1171, which, as we have noted, secured to them all the rights enjoyed by the Pisans themselves. When war with Pisa closed this easy avenue and dried up the eastern profits, the Florentines, in revenge, nursed the resentful design of bringing Pisa under their rule. Since this was not effected till 1406, it was only after that time that Florence was enabled to send out merchant fleets under its own flag and to aspire to a much larger share than before in the Levantine trade. That in the fifteenth century the town succeeded in postponing the already threatening decline of its prosperity by finding a partial substitute for its shrinking western business in the east is a not unimportant economic detail; but that Florence, even after acquiring Pisa, ever became a great maritime power, able to take its place at the side of Genoa and Venice, must be emphatically denied.

Of all the countries invaded by Florentine enterprise none experienced a more thorough and heartless exploitation than the allied Angevin kingdom of Naples. Under the Norman kings and their Hohenstaufen successors this kingdom in its earlier and larger form of a kingdom of Sicily had been in many ways the most advanced region of the occident. A disastrous turning dates from the resolution of the popes to replace the hostile Hohenstaufens with the more subservient house of Anjou. In order to effect the overthrow of the older line the successors of St. Peter determined to mobilize every possible resource at their command and turned for help to their Italian financial agents, among whom the Florentines soon gained the lead. The Arno bankers and usurers may be said to have arrived at Naples and Palermo simultaneously with the victorious Charles and, like their parasitic kind before and since, never again left his side. Toward the end of Charles's reign the island of Sicily revolted (1282) and could not be again subdued, although the attempt was constantly renewed during a span of fifty years. The prolonged struggle signified an increasing dependence of the ·Neapolitan court on the Florentine money-lenders, who, as a reward for their advances, demanded trade concessions which in the end and in their sum became an all-inclusive and crushing monopoly.

The southern kingdom was then and still is the granary of Italy. Pisa and Venice, as sea cities, had been the first to become aware of the value of the

Neapolitan grain trade. They succeeded in dividing it between them, Pisa acting as distributor of the grain of the west coast, Venice of that of the east coast. Although they arrived late, the Florentines, when they came, labored so thoroughly and systematically that they gradually drove out both rivals and won the whole grain trade for themselves. As at the same time they secured their money loans to the sovereign by an assignment on the taxes, and as they brought into the kingdom all the manufactured goods which the inhabitants required, we may speak of an exploitation than which it is impossible to imagine anything more complete. The Bardi and Peruzzi, who played so large a financial role in England, were the leaders among the many Florentine companies which in the days of King Robert of Naples (1309–43) took possession of this lucrative field. When they failed and vanished from the scene, other Florentine houses succeeded them and squeezed fresh fortunes out of their hapless victim. It was the Acciaiuoli, who, although they had co-operated with the Bardi and Peruzzi and had failed with them, brought the game to an unexampled climax. A certain Niccolò Acciaiuoli rose to be the greatest man of the kingdom, virtually exercised the royal power under the title of grand seneschal, and became the possessor of one of the great fortunes of his age. Never, in spite of his lofty state and years of absence, forgetting that he was a Florentine, he founded the Certosa outside of Porta Romana, where he was buried when he died in 1365 and where a monument by a follower of the great sculptor Orcagna still recites his honors and merits.[19]

Nothing brings us humanly so close to these hard-headed traders and unscrupulous profiteers as the dangers to which they were exposed and the courage they exhibited and had to possess in inexhaustible abundance if their labors were to be crowned with success. The goods that went by land were loaded in bales or rolls on pack animals, which for better protection traveled over Europe in long, well-guarded caravans. The roads were in pitiful case, generally not surfaced roads at all but rutted paths churned into knee-deep mud in the rainy season and in hot summer weather heaped high with choking dust. The streams and rivers had usually to be forded, for bridges were few, and at these few some lord invariably exacted the payment of a toll. But not only at bridges but at scores of points along the road feudal noblemen, who dominated the local situation, collected dues allegedly to meet the cost of maintenance. Without even alleging a reason other than their good swords, other nobles, indistinguishable from common highwaymen, exacted a payment for safe conduct through their territory, and if refused, attacked and plundered the caravan. If romance is born of chances defying calculation, there has surely never been a time when it is more fitting to speak of business as romance than in the days of the merchant companies.

But we are only at the beginning of the long tale of merchant hazards. In the earliest phase of the commercial movement a visiting merchant was a foreigner without rights, who was admitted into an alien community purely on sufferance and at his own risk. If he defaulted on a payment and fled, the local judge allowed the creditor to indemnify himself by seizing the goods of any

---

[19] For the details of the ruthless Florentine exploitation of Il Regno see Davidsohn, Vol. IV², chap. VIII. See also L. Tanfani, *Nicola Acciaiuoli*. Florence, 1863.

of the defaulter's fellow-citizens who happened to be at hand. On or even before the delivery of the sentence the implicated innocent strangers gathered together what they could of their possessions and ran for their lives. On arriving breathless in their own commune they lodged a complaint with their government, which promptly avenged the insult to its subjects by ordering the wholesale confiscation of such goods in its midst as pertained to the citizens of the offending commonwealth. This frenzied exchange of injuries went by the name of reprisals and was a universal concomitant of commercial intercourse in its earliest and still barbarous phase. It was inevitable that, in measure as trade became more intensive, all traders alike should become interested in abolishing the monstrous system worthy of Bushmen and Mohawks. The reasonable solution was to concede a foreigner legal protection by the local court and to declare the contracting individual alone responsible for his debt according to the principle *a cui dato a colui richiesto* (payment is to be exacted solely from him who received the goods). By slow degrees this saner system won recognition, largely because it met the interest of all alike, but also because it accorded with the principles of Roman law, the revival and growing empire of which was a significant feature of the waxing communal movement. By the twelfth and, more commonly still, by the thirteenth century the Italian municipalities adopted the practice of negotiating commercial treaties with each other in which they took steps, first to mitigate, and finally to abolish reprisals altogether. In connection with this more humane and rational procedure the merchants themselves of a given town would set up a commercial court capable of receiving suits from both native and foreign traders and prepared to pronounce sentence according to generally accepted principles of justice and without regard to nationality. This type of trade court culminated in the case of Florence in the *mercanzia,* established in 1308. It was created by the united action of all the trade gilds, the arti maggiori, and acquired a great and merited reputation among the commercial classes of all Italy. Finally, in sweeping evidence of the advance made by rational procedure during the thirteenth century let it be said that by the time the Florentine mercanzia was established reprisals in their original raw, collective form had already become the exception and were no longer the rule of Italian commerce.[20]

However, in some countries not subject to Italian inter-communal regulations, reprisals long continued. France was such a land. From time to time the French government, yielding to the clamor of the debtors among its subjects unwilling or unable to pay the foreign merchants doing business under its aegis, liberated its subjects from their obligation to pay; and to make the measure of the punishment full and overflowing the government might go farther and authorize the seizure of both goods and persons of the foreign traders. If it seemed desirable to justify these violent procedures, this could be done by referring to the allegedly usurious practices of the visitors. Royal decrees illustrative of this exercise of retributive justice were issued by Louis

[20] On reprisals and the long fight to overcome them see Del Vecchio and Casanova, *Le Rappresaglie nei Comuni Medievali e specialmente in Firenze.* Bologna, 1894. G. Arias, *I Trattati Commerciali della Repubblica Fiorentina.* Florence, 1901. On the mercanzia see pp. 745-51 of A. Doren, *Das Florentiner Zunftwesen.* Stuttgart, 1908. G. Bonolis, *La Giurisdizione della Mercanzia in Firenze nel Secolo XIV.* Florence, 1901.

IX in 1269, by Philip III in 1274 and 1277, and by all their successors well through the fourteenth century. The frequency of the confiscations arouses the suspicion that they were not thoroughly carried out and that in launching their thunderbolt the sovereigns had their eye much more on their own advantage than on that of their subjects. Surviving documents make it perfectly clear that on satisfactory payment to the royal agents the Italians, among whom the Florentines easily preponderated, were considered to have compounded their felonies. While the original decree of the king's chancellery gave eloquent and moving utterance to the moral indignation of the monarch over the sinful usury practiced by the foreigners, the subsequent action of the royal officials induces us to believe that the whole upflare was nothing other than a financial maneuver to fill the royal treasury, since such traders as promptly paid tribute were not further molested.[21] Agreeing that the confiscations of the French and of occasional other sovereigns were not so disastrous to the Italian merchants as would appear on the surface, they nevertheless constituted a serious risk and should not be overlooked in an estimate of the extremely aleatory character of the activities of the great merchant companies.

Of all the continued reprisals uncured and incurable by treaty, the most generally injurious were those imposed by the pope. Let it be said at once that the two most deadly weapons of the supreme pontiff, excommunication and interdict, do not in and by themselves belong to an economic discussion. They were of a spiritual nature and visited spiritual penalties on the evil-doers at whom they were aimed. Over and over again since the first emergence of self-government, Florence had been put under interdict by the pope in connection with some ecclesiastical transgression, such, for example, as subjecting the clergy within its jurisdiction to a municipal tax. This, as threatening the independence of the clergy, was denounced at Rome as an infringement on the liberty of the church. Undoubtedly the pope was on sound canonical ground when he held it to be his right and duty to defend the supremacy of the institution of which he was the head and in that defense to employ as legitimate, if extreme, measures the interdict and excommunication. But become a leading political power, the pontiff had fallen into the habit of using his spiritual prerogatives to punish a purely political opposition; and on the on the whole rare occasions when Florence deserted the Guelph banner, interdict and excommunication were brought into play to smite the citizens exactly as if they had made themselves guilty of an ecclesiastical transgression. Thus in 1261 when, following the battle of Montaperti, Florence was compelled to become Ghibelline, Pope Urban IV not only punished the city with the interdict but added the invitation to the governments of the whole world to seize Florentine goods and imprison Florentine traders when and wherever encountered. It has already been told how quickly this threat induced the bankers at all costs to seek an accommodation with the pontiff. If the companies of the Arno town did not on this particular occasion suffer heavy losses, those of many other Ghibelline communities visited by the same anathema did; and in any case the power which the pope arrogated to himself in his interest and at his pleasure to level a destructive blow at trade deserves to be set down in every catalogue of the special disadvantages under which merchants labored in the communal age. While reaffirming that Florence, as the most devoted Guelph government of Italy, was not often in political opposition to the pope and that it was therefore relatively untouched by the pope's political wrath, let us not forget that its business had always to be conducted with an eye to reprisals which it lay within the pope's power to impose. As late as 1376, on occasion of the war between Florence and the State of the Church, the so-called War of the Eight Saints, Pope Gregory XI attempted to break Florentine resistance by coupling with his interdict the order to good Christians throughout the west to throw Florentine merchants into prison and to appropriate their goods.[22] Since the war lasted till 1378 the losses suffered by Florence under the papal enactments ran into the hundreds of thousands of gold florins. In short, the hazards under which Florentine and medieval commerce in general labored were extraordinary. They helped to account for such characteristic features of contemporary business as the high rate of interest, the sudden enrichment of a trading company by a bold, successful stroke, and the early collapse of every company practically without exception.

We have learned that, beginning with the awakening of commerce, the great feudal properties of Tuscany, whether belonging to bishops, abbots, or temporal lords, began to pass into the possession of the merchants of the towns. Not improbably these merchants were at the same time themselves landowners, though on a small scale. Become by their acquisitions landowners on a large scale, they not only achieved a more elevated social status but also gained a valuable credit basis for their expanding commercial transactions. There followed a notable agricultural expansion from this amassing of land by urban families. In the main the great manorial properties of the past had been cultivated by the labor of serfs, although surviving records prove that even in the deep feudal age land was frequently cultivated under a lease, by the terms of which the worker or peasant paid the owner an agreed portion of the crop. The ratio at which the harvest was shared varied greatly, but the trend from an early time was toward an equal division between the two contracting parties. This is substantially the *mezzeria* system, which afterward became and which remains to this day the characteristic form of land tenure throughout Tuscany. As the specialists assure us, the first faint beginnings of the mezzeria reach so far back that they may even antedate the Germanic invasions. With the downfall of feudalism and the taking over of the fields and orchards by burgher interests, the disappearance of serfdom, a system suited to resident landlords, was accelerated and the partnership of the mezzeria which, while raising the status of the peasant, freed the city owner from the necessity of immediate superintendence became more and more common. When in the year 1289 a decree of the new government of the priors abolished serfdom throughout the Florentine jurisdiction, this characteristic institution of feudalism had already declined to such an extent that there was but little of it left. We may therefore think of the often cited act of liberation of 1289 as crowning a development which had been inaugurated many generations before and which was an inseparable feature of the whole communal movement. Owing

[22] See chap. XVI, p. 275.

to the radical character of that movement even the Tuscan land, the stronghold of the feudal classes, passed into possession of the burghers, who favored the mezzeria and gradually made it all but universal in the province. Thus we see that it was a sum of historical conditions and not the hypothetical generosity of the ruling merchants which brought about the abolition of serfdom.

Nonetheless the merchant successors of the nobles, far from being just a passive landlord group, made an important contribution to the practice of agriculture. They poured capital into the farms they took over in order to increase the return, and as skilled business men they contributed to the enlarged venture a valuable element of management. In Florence, a rapidly expanding industrial town, they had close at hand a market capable of absorbing all the foodstuffs they could possibly grow. No wonder that Tuscan farmland became a much-prized form of investment, and if it did not yield as high a return on capital as trade, the latter, as much more speculative, suffered recurrent severe losses unknown to the former. On the whole, the advancing fourteenth century showed a distinct tendency on the part of merchants to give up trade as carrying too many risks and to be content with the smaller but safer return from farms worked by free peasants on the mezzeria plan.

The foregoing condensed history of the Florentine adventurers and their characteristic organization, the merchant company, will have served its purpose if it has made clear that the town of the Red Lily owed its rise and importance to this enterprising class. Fully conscious of their value, the merchants undertook from a very early time to safeguard their interests at home by joining forces in an association or gild. That there was a gild of merchants in Florence as early as the beginning of the twelfth century is as good as certain, although it is true that the oldest existing document referring to such a gild belongs to the year 1182. As the leading merchants of that period were the importers of foreign cloth, and as they were installed in shops (*botteghe*) along a narrow street near the Mercato Vecchio, they came to be known from this street as the merchants of the Calimala. Not long afterward we hear of other merchant associations. In 1202 there is reference to a gild of cambiatores or money-changers and ten years later we first hear of a wool gild (arte di Lana). The merchants of the Por Santa Maria gild are mentioned for the first time in 1218. With the spirit of association abroad in the land and with the gild offering itself to the individual as the most suitable means of self-protection, it was natural for the humble craftsmen to follow the example set by the wealthy traders. A document of the year 1193, according to which in a political crisis an unnamed number of craft gilds acted together in order to make their weight felt with the government, makes it clear that organization had by that time reached down into the artisan strata of society.[23] Again, as in the case of the merchant gild, let it be said that the craft gilds go far back of their earliest documentary mention, but the only authority for the statement is reasonable conjecture.

Although the thirteenth century constitutes a period of rapid economic de-

---

[23] A. Doren, *Entwicklung und Organisation der Florentiner Zünfte im 13. und 14. Jahrhundert* (Schmoller's *Forschungen*, Vol. XV). Two further works conclude Doren's invaluable studies of the Florentine gilds. They are: *Die Florentiner Wollentuchindustrie* (Stuttgart, 1901) and *Das Florentiner Zunftwesen* (Stuttgart, 1908).

velopment, very little information touching the gilds is available till we reach the political revolution of 1282. Aware as we are that the considerable expansion of Florence, which had occurred during the period prior to 1282, was primarily the work of the merchants, we have no occasion to register surprise at learning that it was they who made the above-mentioned revolution and, what is more, that they made it for the express purpose of taking over the government. By 1282 the merchants were organized in seven gilds representing a vast economic power. Quite possibly the seven could have appropriated the government by their own strength alone; but as their action was not without certain risks, they resolved to move cautiously and invited the five strongest craft gilds to join them in their undertaking. The result was the successful setting up of a government of twelve gilds, from the membership of which the new executive of the priors had to be chosen. When, ten years later, the twelve undertook to crown their revolution by that famous blow at the magnates familiar under the name of the Ordinances of Justice, they prudently resolved still further to strengthen their hand by drawing nine additional craft gilds to their side. There thus came into being the government of the twenty-one gilds, of which, seven qualified as arti maggiori, five as arti medie, and nine as arti minori.[24] However, the distinction between the middle and minor gilds is artificial and did not long survive. Compared with the seven merchant gilds, the middle and minor gilds alike were so plainly the organizations of artisans and shopkeepers, and furthermore, so wide an economic chasm yawned between the merchants on the one hand, and the artisans and shopkeepers on the other, that common parlance soon grouped all the craft associations together as the fourteen minor gilds. Nor did it take long for the distinction between what was major and minor economically to achieve political expression. While the theoretical participation in the government of the fourteen craft gilds was not disputed, the priors, especially after the fall of Giano della Bella (1295), were so generally chosen from the membership of the greater gilds that we may without fear of contradiction speak of the priorate as a merchant government. To be sure, owing to circumstances considered in the previous chapter, the merchant ascendancy was challenged during the period 1343-82; but when the popular movement failed, the merchant oligarchy resumed and thenceforward retained control until the development out of its midst of the principate of the Medici. Most of what has been said about Florentine democracy by historians, and especially by literary essayists, savors of exaggeration or sentimentality. In spite of Florence being an industrial city populated by shopkeepers and workers, it was dominated by its merchants who, distributed among seven major gilds, constituted a privileged political body.

The twenty-one gilds which gained political recognition by the constitution of 1293 were, generally speaking, not single but composite gilds. A constituent unit was called a *membrum,* and as new units continued to be added, especially during the early decades of the fourteenth century, the gilds tended to become compounded of more and more membra. To illustrate by reference to the gild of the *medici* and *speziali,* usually listed sixth in order among the

[24] See chap. XI where the gilds are listed under their historical names.

seven arti maggiori: to the medici (physicians) and speziali (apothecaries) there were gradually added the *merciai* (retail merchants), *sellai* (saddlers), *borsai* (purse-makers), and *dipintori* (painters). An examination of this rather artisan-like list of membra makes the claim of this gild to be a great merchant gild appear rather doubtful.[25] Skepticism also assails us in the case of the seventh of the greater gilds, the *pellicciai* or furriers, although this gild undoubtedly imported pelts from the Black Sea and elsewhere and made them up into garments for distribution. While the furriers indisputably had the character of a merchant gild, the volume of their business cannot have been very large. The fact is there were gradations of importance among the greater gilds just as there were gradations among the lesser gilds; and the deeper we penetrate into Florentine economic history the more we are persuaded that its ruling element was not the seven great gilds as such, but rather the two wool gilds (Calimala, Lana), the Cambio (bankers), and later, when the silk industry developed, the Por Santa Maria. It was substantially in these four gilds that were concentrated the wealth and influence of the merchants who guided the fortunes of the city.

But we have drifted away from the issue of the many occupations united in a single gild. On the whole the lesser gilds were more likely to be constituted of many members than the powerful gilds, whose very power derived in part from their more perfect unification. The *pizzicagnoli* had four membra, generally small retailers like the pizzicagnoli themselves. The *fabri* (smiths) had six membra, while the *albergatori* (inn-keepers), the *rigattieri* (second-hand dealers), and the other lesser gilds regularly embraced several constituent groups, although, owing to frequent changes, the exact number is not always easy to determine.[26] The conclusion to be drawn from these data is that, while there were only twenty-one gilds recognized by the law, three and four times this number of occupational groups were associated together within the gilds, thereby enabling these societies to embrace a larger membership and develop a richer existence than the conventional figure of twenty-one gilds would lead us to believe.

But while a considerable body of local craftsmen and small shopkeepers enjoyed organization and the political rights which organization alone conferred, the much larger mass of the workers of the two woolen gilds, and later of the silk gild (Por Santa Maria), could claim none of these benefits. Technically incorporated in one or another of the textile gilds, the workers were subjected to sharp regulations and prohibitions without any corresponding benefits. The textile gilds were gilds exclusively of masters, while the textile workers were industrial serfs or sottoposti required to subsist on starvation wages and forbidden under heavy penalties to form gilds of their own. In the previous chapter we have dealt with the attempt the sottoposti made in the period 1343–82 to improve their lot. Their main effort was directed to getting from under the heel of their masters by the formation of independent gilds. In the

[25] The character of this gild is treated in detail by R. Ciasca, *L'Arte dei Medici e Speziali nella Storia e nel Commercio dal Secolo XII al XV*. Florence, 1927.

[26] The frequent shifts in membership are treated in detail by Doren, *Entwickelung und Organisation*, etc., chap. III.

great rising of 1378 they realized their dream by the creation of three gilds of workers, thus raising the official list of gilds endowed with political rights to twenty-four. But what was medicine for the workers was poison for the masters, who neither slumbered nor slept till they had destroyed the three workers' gilds and again reduced their employees to mere sottoposti of their own organizations. The defeat of 1382 must have broken the spirit of the proletarians, for they gave up the fight and never again, as long as the republic lasted, challenged the control of their superiors. The struggle of the fourteenth century constitutes an early chapter in the very modern conflict between capital and labor, and in the relatively easy victory won by capital reveals the difficulties which then and ever since have confronted capital's opponent.

The inner organization of the gilds is disclosed by their statutes, innumerable manuscripts of which are still preserved in the Florentine Archives.[27] The oldest existing statutes are those of the rigattieri of the year 1295; immediately after them come the Calimala statutes of 1301. The vast majority of the manuscripts belong to the fourteenth century, the period when the gilds were most active and vigorous. They show that, though there was considerable difference in detail in the organization of the different gilds, they all had so much in common that a generalized description is not impossible. The gild was governed by a college of consuls, who held office for half a year and who were obliged in all important matters to seek the advice of a council. Since, to satisfy its self-respect, the gild owned a house (*casa*)—only the great woolen gild, the Lana, boasted a palazzo—collected dues and fines, paid out money for salaries, festivals, and benefactions, it had to have a treasurer and a budget. Moreover, as is indicated by the innumerable prescriptions and prohibitions imposed by the statutes touching production and distribution, the gild claimed police power over its members. This was exercised by bailiffs, who on receiving a denunciation haled the offender before the gild court for trial and punishment. While the statutes cannot be said to have aimed at destroying the initiative of the individual member, they so rigorously provided for a just price and a high standard of excellence in the article produced that the gildsman was never able to forget that he labored not only for himself but also for the community. In spite of the worldly temper induced by the general character of the urban movement, the medieval religious spirit was still strong and gave each gild something of the character of a fraternal organization. In daily practice the social and religious implications of the gild may not always have successfully imposed themselves, but they were subtly intermingled with the system and account for much of its strength.

It admits of no dispute that the economic, social, and political life of Florence during the two hundred years following the establishment of the government of the priors received its characteristic imprint from the gilds. Not only were most of the officials beginning with the highest executive, the priors, chosen from the gild membership, but the consuls of the gilds (*capitudines artium*) had a seat in the council of the captain and were, besides, called into consulta-

<hr/>

[27] The manuscripts are described by Doren, *Das Florentiner Zunftwesen*, Anhang I. Doren's work rests firmly on this original material. The first step toward a systematic publication of these manuscripts has been taken by the issuance of the *Statuti dell'Arte dei Medici e Speziali . . . per cura di R. Ciasca.* Florence, 1922.

tion by the priors in all issues affecting the welfare of the state. While there were gilds in all the Italian communes without exception, and while in many communes they acquired a measure of political importance, they did not anywhere else so completely take over the government as in Florence. And in spite of difficulties, risings, and disastrous lapses, the gild-controlled government of Florence developed a greater measure of effectiveness than that of any other commune with the single exception of Venice. Our analysis cannot fail to have made clear that at the core of the system was the compact oligarchy of the upper gilds. For better and for worse the gild system of Florence operated strictly as a class regime. And since the governing class were the merchants, who, beginning with the twelfth century, had been engaged in opening new paths to adventure and wealth, we may instance Florence as a community in which the political responsibilities very accurately reflected the distribution of economic power.

XVIII. Intellectual Change: The Coming of Humanism

IN THIS chapter it is proposed to show how in the fourteenth century Florence and Italy provided themselves if not with a new, at least with the beginnings of a new, mentality. Before making a start, however, it will be necessary to engage in a brief discussion of a general nature. In the Introduction, in which the author passed in review the movement through the centuries of Florentine historiography, he explained how the concept of history has so greatly broadened during recent generations that a work calling itself a history will no longer meet present-day requirements unless, in addition to politics, it gives attention to various other aspects of society so intimately interwoven with politics that politics remains incomprehensible without them. Inevitably therefore a modern history will have something of the character of a history of civilization. Although the author continues to uphold this contention, he has now arrived at a point in his own history when he feels urged to elaborate his position. Above all, he wishes to guard against possible misconceptions to which his statement in its bare, overgeneralized form is exposed.

If it is agreed that history, so long limited to affairs of state, has recently widened its outlook, it must not be understood that the new procedure imposed on the historian obliges him simply to enlarge his scope and that his revised task consists in adding to a history of the traditional political type an indefinite number of other histories dealing respectively with the economic, social, intellectual, artistic, and other similar developments. Apart from the circumstance that such a production, lacking the unity characteristic of a work of art, would be an encyclopedia rather than a history, the fact is that no single individual can in our day hope even remotely to master the various techniques and bodies of information which such an undertaking would require. Let us therefore agree at once that it will be wise to let the specialists in political economy, philosophy, literature, and art, in the future as in the past, write the histories for which they alone possess the indispensable preparation and training. The enlarged task of the traditional historian, who has burst the too narrow bounds of his subject, is neither to enter into competition with all the other kinds of existing historians nor to attempt the impossible enterprise of occupying the whole field of human knowledge. His concern is still with politics, the state must continue to be the core of the subject matter inviting his investigation. But having learned from the developments in his field since the middle of the nineteenth century that the state may no longer be regarded as an isolated, self-contained unit, and that without any doubt whatever the nature and undertakings of the state are determined by the activities unfolded in the economic, social, philosophic, and other related fields, he will have to take account of these other matters, not so much for their own sake as in the interest of his primary, his political preoccupations. Moreover, as he will not be expected to be an expert save in his immediate department, he will have to content himself with the results furnished by the experts in the departments that neighbor on his own, and he will have to present their findings in summary form and in due subordination to his main, his political theme.

It is this conception of the enlarged requirements of a present-day history which the author has attempted to apply in the work in hand. While making the formation and development of the Florentine state his main concern, he has been at pains to discard the political blinders, which were so integral a part of the authoritative classical tradition, and to see the Arno commune from its first appearance amidst the chaos of the feudal system as a social-economic entity. What, in contrast to or, more accurately, in supplementation of, the political emphasis, may be called the social-economic viewpoint has dominated his narrative throughout its course. But, beginning with the preceding chapter, the moment seemed to have come for a separate and more concentrated presentation of some of the special agencies that figured in the shaping of the state and society under review. That chapter therefore was devoted to a cursory sketch of the economic activities in which the Florentines succeeded in peculiarly distinguishing themselves. While it is hoped that it makes an appreciable contribution to the understanding of the general Florentine situation, not for a moment does it pretend to be a reasoned economic history of the Arno town during the period in question. For this the reader especially interested in economic matters is invited to consult the economic historians. The same statement applies to the intellectual and artistic material which will be offered respectively in the present and in the succeeding chapter. The two chapters together markedly contribute, in the author's view, to the understanding of Florentine social and political conditions and accordingly serve the central purpose of this book; but they present data for which the author has been obliged to go to the specialists in these particular fields, and which he hopes to succeed in fusing with his main matter into an intelligible and vital whole.

The intellectual background of the Middle Ages is relatively simple and incomparably unified. This is due to the fact that when the new or western civilization came into existence, it was dominated by Christianity in the organized form of the Roman Catholic church. The clergy inculcated the Christian doctrines of the Fall of Adam, the Atonement through Christ Jesus, and the Last Judgment, which were the central features of a magnificently elaborated system defining the relations between God and man; and far from encouraging, they deprecated any intellectual curiosity in excess of the official matter, which, as divinely revealed, possessed the character of final and incontrovertible truth. Faith exercised exclusive rule, and the intelligence, with which man is endowed by nature and which a deep-seated instinct urges him to employ in order to increase his knowledge, was for several centuries treated with suspicion and systematically restrained. But when after the year 1000 the urban development set in, producing a stimulating and greatly multiplied movement of men and goods, it occasioned also a spontaneous generation of ideas until the clergy found themselves unable to hold the Christian flock to the original static norm of thought. In fact the clergy, as the most cultivated members of society, were themselves the first to raise their voices in behalf of a more liberal use of the intellect; but as at the same time they remained convinced Christian believers, they finally, but only after lively and at times perilous disputes, agreed on the exercise of mind, or of *ratio* (reason) as they called mind in the terminology of the period, provided always that reason would keep within bounds and would modestly refrain from invading the hallowed ground of Christian dogma.

It was in the eleventh and twelfth centuries that the struggle in behalf of reason began, and so eager was the interest in the issue that it gave birth to a special institution, the university. In the course of still another century, the thirteenth, not only did the intellectual turmoil at the new university centers reach its height, but in the person of Thomas of Aquinas (1225-74) it brought forth its most eminent representative. In his famous work, the *Summa Theologica,* Thomas harmonized faith and reason in so just a manner that the church gave his exposition its formal indorsement. According to the position adopted by him there need be no quarrel between faith and reason, since each of them could lay claim to a special function and dominion. However, harnessed together though the two were henceforth to be, they were not to be considered equals, for, should a dispute arise between them, it was reason and not faith that must give way since the continued primacy of faith was undebatable and axiomatic. It follows that, while it is unexceptional to speak of the early Middle Ages up to about 1000 as an age of faith, the statement holds good of the later Middle Ages only with a certain reservation. For characteristic of the period coming after the year 1000 is the fact that it cultivated and even exalted reason, provided always that reason would agree to respect as inviolable the special dominion of faith. It will not escape the reader's attention that the true age of faith coincides in the main with the backward agrarian period dominated by feudalism, whereas the successful, if limited, assertion of reason is a concomitant and result of the disturbance introduced into the conservative agrarian mentality by the communal revolution.

Now our town of Florence had no part in shaping either the earlier or the later medieval mentality. Both outlooks derived from the only existing learned class, the clergy, with the interesting difference that the members of the order who effected the recognition of reason expounded their views not from ecclesiastical pulpits but from the lecture platforms of universities at which they served as professors. As such they were often denominated *doctores scholastici* or schoolmen, while the philosophy they propounded was commonly designated as scholasticism. By the thirteenth century scholasticism had become the possession of the whole body of European intellectuals, who in the expanding towns, especially of Italy, came gradually to include, besides priests, monks, and friars, considerable numbers of the laity. In that age of increasing intercourse among the nations of the west as well as between the opposed oriental and occidental worlds, many laymen by reading books and attending the universities had acquired the same learning as their clerical contemporaries. The time therefore came when a layman might feel as free as a clergyman to expound the newer Christian system in which faith had made a pact with reason and reason had become faith's ally. It was only when this particular development had been reached that Florence projected itself into the intellectual history of Europe. And the layman who by thus stepping forward indicated that the exclusive rule of the clergy in the realm of thought was passing was the city's greatest son, the greatest not only of his own but of every age, Dante Alighieri.

We have already dealt with Dante as a poet, who at the call of patriotism plunged into politics, found himself on the losing side, and was driven into exile. There is no need of entering again into his story, for at this point we are concerned exclusively with the intellectual significance of his great poem, the *Divine Comedy*. In that work Dante planned to set forth the Christian scheme of salvation, as he himself had learned it from the writings of the Fathers and, in greater detail still, from the recent great scholastics with the saintly Thomas at their head. Disinclined to elaborate his theme heavily and argumentatively like a theologian and impelled by his peculiar genius to body it forth in the pictorial fashion appropriate to the artist, he represented himself as taking a journey through the world-to-come beginning in the depths of hell and ending in high heaven in order by this device to inform his readers through the evidence of an eye-witness of the rewards and punishments meted out to souls for their conduct while inhabiting the house of flesh on earth. There is no question at this point of our evaluing the *Divine Comedy* as poetry. Let it suffice to refer to the chorus of approbation which, sounded by critics through the ages, places it among the masterpieces of world-literature. It is the intellectual significance of the poem that here alone concerns us; and on this score it is not too bold an affirmation to declare that Dante, a Florentine layman writing in the first quarter of the trecento, crowned the labors of the scholastic philosophers by setting forth the Christian order of the universe with such understanding, faith, and fullness that later generations have not hesitated to regard him, if not as the most authoritative, certainly as the most exalted, voice that made itself heard in the whole course of the Middle Ages.

Thus belatedly did Florence make a richly imaginative contribution to the intellectual development of medieval Europe. But instead of a starting-point it proved to be an ending: the *Divine Comedy* was the swan song of the Middle Ages. For even as Dante was writing his passionate verses, the communal revolution, entering a new phase, began to respond to forces other than those of medieval Christianity and to give shape to other purposes. For the communal revolution, uninterruptedly continuing, signified uninterrupted change, with the result that no sooner would a foreshadowed goal be approached than another more distant goal would be descried and the strenuous onward march resumed. Closely studied, the scholastic movement itself was no more than a manifestation in the realm of thought of the social-economic changes brought about in the twelfth and thirteenth centuries. While the scholastic doctors declared and honestly believed that they had projected a philosophy which would serve as a frame for human thinking to the end of time, after the manner of ephemeral men they deluded themselves by ascribing to a purely temporary system the quality of eternity. The very next university generation after that of the great Aquinas began to gnaw at his structure. At the same time something far more ominous than academic criticism put in an appearance by reason of the circumstance that increasing numbers of the intelligentsia frankly and definitely turned their backs on the issues that had been involved in the scholastic movement. Apparently these issues ceased to interest the new generation, which threw itself on a new set of problems more immediately relevant to the altered aspects of society. In the intellectual history of Europe scholasticism was succeeded by humanism, and humanism is so largely an Italian and even a distinctly Florentine product that we shall have to give it our close attention.

The early Middle Ages, the true age of faith, had a markedly transcendental character, for they inculcated the vanity of the brief and imperfect Here and exalted the eternity of the Hereafter as alone worthy of the regard of a true Christian. Even though the later Middle Ages made a concession to our mortal state by authorizing the pursuit of mundane knowledge through the exercise of reason, the transcendental emphasis was not greatly modified. While the thirteenth-century intellectuals, overwhelmingly members of the clergy confined within the barriers of their class, wrestled with the difficult abstractions of philosophy, the great body of the laity, composed of merchants, lawyers, physicians, and artisans, continued to occupy themselves with the pressing practical problems of living. They struggled to rise in the world by the successful exercise of their craft or profession; they traveled and became acquainted with other peoples, other countries, other customs; and, as citizens of an expanding town, they tried to contribute to its expansion and to win the right to participate in the conduct of its affairs. For these men constituting the urban laity, the transcendental message of the clergy imperceptibly began to lose its lure. Passionately concerned with the earth and with their human kind, they gradually, so gradually that it long escaped their own notice, set up for themselves a new scale of values. Inevitably the heaven of the teachers and preachers faded from view in measure as the urban laymen became increasingly absorbed with the engrossing concerns of everyday life. In brief, there took place a switch of attention, a mental re-orientation, which in the course of time received the name of humanism. Humanism is derived from the Latin *humanitas* (and ultimately from *homo,* that is, man), and its becoming a banner and a watch cry signified that the intellectual revolution produced by the urban movement had reached the stage when the Hereafter with its remote, presumptive glories would be gradually dethroned to be replaced by the Here with its pungent, ever-present, life-giving realities.

It was in the fourteenth century that humanism came clearly into view under its first great champion, Petrarch. But since it was, as we have been insisting, a consequence of the earth-directed communal movement, it had been in obscure gestation for several generations before, in the person of Petrarch, it presented itself to the eyes of men. From our own town of Florence we may learn by a particular instance how the movement was prepared in the womb of time. A leading lay intellectual of the generation before

Dante was Dante's teacher, Brunetto Latini (d. 1294?). As he was at the same time the first permanent chancellor of the Florentine republic, he was in his day one of the outstanding personages of the town. Latini became so absorbed in the fresh secular knowledge which was being slowly accumulated in consequence of the unwonted contemporary curiosity that he wrote a kind of encyclopedia under the name of *Il Tesoro* (the Treasure).[1] It contained very simple matter, indeed so incredibly simple that nothing short of a perusal of its offerings in the way of physiology, zoölogy, and astronomy will serve to convey an idea of what in Latini's time was able to pass for knowledge. Nonetheless the work denotes a mental tendency which was bound to gain strength with every fresh generation. In proof of this assertion we may adduce the case of Latini's great pupil, Dante. For Dante was moved to undertake a secular encyclopedia of his own, *Il Convivio,* though it is true that he never brought it to completion. Perhaps he tired of the effort because, absorbed as a visionary poet in the religious idealism of the Middle Ages, he found an imperfect satisfaction in a prolonged occupation with purely mundane matter. The fact remains, however, that he was extraordinarily responsive to the colorful and palpable sense-world about him, as every reader of his great poem will readily recall. There is certainly no occasion to entertain a doubt as to his strong attachment to the earth on which he stood and from which he drew the solid substance of his verse. Only because he was stirred to his depths by the inexhaustible moods of nature and the striking aspects of men in their characteristic activities did he succeed in incorporating them in his poem with a vivacity and power that have never been surpassed.

And so we come to Francesco Petrarca, the conscious herald of a new day. As his father, a notary and man of law, had been banished from Florence in 1302 along with Dante and the other leading Whites, it happened that when, two years later, Francesco was born, the event took place not in Florence but at Arezzo on the upper Arno. Eagerly seeking employment in order to win a living for himself and his family, the father settled finally at Avignon, which as the new papal capital had become the busiest legal center of Europe. When Francesco was approaching early manhood, he was sent to the University of Bologna to study law and make ready to follow in his father's footsteps. But the youth revolted against the intricate and tedious matter of the civil code and boldly decided to devote his life to literature.[2] Let the immense fame he acquired in his day with the sonnet sequence dedicated to Madonna Laura stand as proof that he persisted in his purpose.

---

[1] As Latini composed his encyclopedia while living as an exile in France during the brief period of Ghibelline ascendancy in Florence (1260-66), he actually wrote his book in the French tongue under the French equivalent of the Treasure, *Le Trésor*. It was later translated and circulated, not in Latin, let it be observed, but in Italian. The literary use of the vulgar tongue was a feature of the advancing secularization.

[2] In accordance with the procedure followed thus far no attempt will be made to list the immense literature dealing with Petrarch. Absolutely essential to an understanding of his historical service are his Italian poems and his Latin letters. The poems under the collective title of *Il Canzoniere* (The Book of Songs) are accessible in scores of editions. The most convenient edition of the Letters, sometimes with, sometimes without, an Italian translation, has been issued by Fracassetti. A handy selection from Petrarch's correspondence translated into English from the original Latin has been issued by J. H. Robinson and H. W. Rolfe under the title *Petrarch, The First Modern Scholar and Man of Letters*. New York, 1898.

In the opinion of some of his contemporaries he had with the plaintive music of his *Canzoniere* proved himself an even greater poet than his predecessor, Dante, but that is a view which no longer enjoys the support of discerning readers. In fact Petrarch is one of those poets who in the course of the most recent generations have experienced a notable deflation. For the historians as distinct from the critics of literature, however, he continues to be the second figure in the great Italian trinity of Dante, Petrarch, and Boccaccio, and properly enough from their viewpoint they make much of the enormous influence exercised by him upon the subsequent literature not only of Italy but also of all the other countries of Europe.[3]

Engaged in this chapter in tracing the development of Italian thought, we willingly abandon Petrarch, the poet, to give our attention to Petrarch, the humanist. While the secular tendencies, which had for many generations been gathering strength, came to a head in him, they took a form which requires a word of explanation. Contrary to an opinion which still stubbornly maintains its hold, the literature of classical antiquity never ceased to be admired during the Middle Ages, especially in Italy, which always felt itself to be the legitimate heir of Rome in both blood and institutions. Nor was the authority and expressiveness of the Latin language questioned, since it completely ruled the intellectual world by its position at the very center of the medieval curriculum. But there were countervailing influences which tended to nullify this great heritage of speech and letters. For one thing, the content of the pagan authors was so far removed from the ruling norms of medieval thought that it was seen as through a veil and was often grossly misinterpreted; and for another thing, the ascendancy of scholasticism had recently given an additional impulse to the barbarization to which the Latin language had been exposed for centuries by adapting it to the purposes and needs of the scholastic dialectic. If we once more instance Dante, his extraordinary eminence must serve as the excuse for our frequent use of him as a point of reference. Not only was the Florentine poet familiar with the Latin language as the indispensable medium of the dominant scholastic philosophy, but he also had a wide acquaintance with Latin literature. In thinking of the Divine Comedy we immediately recall his boundless admiration for Virgil; however, as the Dante specialists have been at pains to point out, he was familiar not only with the Mantuan bard but with the whole extant body of the Latin authors. And yet, diligently as he read the classics, he read them through Christian medieval glasses and gave them an interpretation far removed from their original meaning.

It was by casting aside the medieval glasses and facing the world with so direct a gaze that he has been called the First Modern Man that Petrarch was able to render both the language and literature of Rome a revolutionary service. A circumstance absolutely determinative of his outlook was that, although educated under the scholastic curriculum, he reacted violently against its dialectical exercises and the domination of the crabbed, abused Latin to which the needs of dialectics had reduced the once proud speech of the former rulers of the world. He wanted the original beauty of the language to be re-

[3] For the most recent exposition of Petrarch's wide literary empire see J. B. Fletcher, *Literature of the Italian Renaissance*. New York, 1934.

stored and the ancient authors to be studied for their value as literature. Not content to preach, he set an example by teaching himself to write Latin in at least an approach to the older manner and by probing the Latin authors to their stylistic core. An outstanding feature of the literature of Rome was that it represented an urban civilization which, having freed itself from religious tutelage, faced the world relying on no other support than our five frail senses and our imperfect reason. In the fourteenth century a new urban civilization was arising, and to it, still groping in the dark, the older civilization, as disclosed by its literary remains, became a light and an inspiration. In short, the time was ripe and Petrarch's message found an extraordinary response throughout the length and breadth of Italy. In measure as ever larger bodies of men discarded the old scholastic in favor of the new classical learning, there arose a demand for copies of the Latin writings, which Petrarch was extolling as the fountainhead of wisdom. While the existing works were rapidly multiplied by copyists, a feverish search began for missing works which ancient or recent neglect had permitted to drop from sight. In case the preserved or rediscovered texts of a given work showed different readings these had to be carefully compared in the hope of restoring as far as possible the exact words and turns of phrase the classical master had used. Such labor called for scholarly diligence and critical acumen and laid the foundations of classical philology, an entirely new field of study. Finally, in measure as the enthusiasm elicited by the reglimpsed world of antiquity continued to grow, the Latin literary monuments figured more and more prominently in the education of the young, thereby preparing the way for a revised curriculum which should no longer be dominated by the logical exercises and philosophic teachings of the schoolman.

From its practitioners beginning with Petrarch himself the new literary interests received the name of *studia humaniora,* for which the approximate English equivalent is humanism. Later generations, however, adopted a different emphasis and brought other terms into vogue, such as the revival of learning (or antiquity) and the Renaissance. As they still figure with humanism in all discussions of the period, we have three vaguely synonymous terms which have been subjected to a distressingly loose usage by many generations of writers. Under the circumstances every new writer should feel obliged to make clear the meaning he proposes to attach to each expression. To begin with humanism, after what has just gone before there should not be any doubt as to how it is here employed. We hold it to be a movement of the human mind which began when, following the rise of the towns, the urban intelligentsia slowly turned away from the transcendental values imposed by religion to the more immediately perceptible values of nature and of man. Inaugurated timidly in the twelfth and thirteenth centuries, humanism first arrived at consciousness of itself in the fourteenth century and, holding the scene ever since, has, apart from an occasional setback, steadily widened its empire. For reasons heretofore set forth it happened that, beginning with Petrarch, the mounting secular interests were deflected toward classical literature and led to an eager revival of antiquity. Consequently, since humanism did not become an active force till Petrarch's time, there has been a tendency to equate it with the revival of learning. But that is an ill-advised procedure as the part can never be equal to the whole. In other words, the revival of learning was the particular turn taken under Petrarch's direction by the great secularizing movement which had set in with the communal revolution and which in one form or another has gone on uninterruptedly to our own day. It is therefore the writer's contention that humanism is a force which has been a factor in the civilization of the occident ever since the communal revolution, while the revival of learning is no more than the first conscious phase of humanism dating from the fourteenth century and owing its special character to an inspired leader. It helps to maintain the distinction between the two terms to think of the revival of learning as a literary movement of limited duration and of humanism as a far more inclusive and continuous social and intellectual phenomenon. Accepting this relation to each other of humanism and the revival of learning (or antiquity), we should not find it difficult to differentiate them both from a term of much later origin, the Renaissance. When this gained a foothold in the sixteenth century, it signified exactly what it etymologically denotes, rebirth, and had reference to the rebirth of that antiquity in which everybody gloried. However, in recent generations the word has been assigned a somewhat different use and the practice has come into vogue, to which the present writer wholeheartedly subscribes, of applying the term Renaissance, without the aesthetic and moral connotation it originally carried, to the particular period or phase of western civilization which, beginning with the fourteenth century, marks the close of the Middle Ages and continues for some two or three hundred years. In this book the Renaissance signifies an European epoch with an indeterminate beginning and end.[4]

It might be argued that when humanism, which was developing normally and naturally through the steadily widening experiences of an adventurous society, submitted to the direction of the dead world of antiquity it did itself an injury rather than a service. On the other hand, it is undeniable that for the Italians, who held the lead over the rest of Europe, the submitting, on the widening of their mundane knowledge, to classical leadership had a perfectly logical character, for they had never ceased to consider themselves as the direct descendants of Rome. To them to revive antiquity appeared as nothing other than to re-establish connection with their past, from which they had been unhappily divorced by the Germanic conquest. And by enthusiastically entering under Petrarch's captaincy into the possession of a highly finished and substantially unified body of secular thought, they undoubtedly greatly accelerated their emancipation from the medieval way of life. We have only to throw a glance at the following, the fifteenth, century to discover that Frenchmen, Englishmen, and Germans are still substantially and contentedly medieval, whereas the Italians already possess a strikingly modern appearance. The

---

[4] By far the largest number of books dealing with humanism regard it as identical with the revival of learning and therefore as purely or at least overwhelmingly literary. Such are G. Voigt, *Die Wiederbelebung des Classischen Alterthums.* 3d ed. Berlin, 1893. P. Le Monnier, *Le Quattrocento.* 2 vols. Paris, 1901. J. A. Symonds, *The Revival of Learning* (Vol. II of his *The Renaissance in Italy*). The larger social point of view is taken by J. Burckhardt, *Die Kultur der Renaissance in Italien.* The original edition republished by Kroener, Leipzig, 1922. Two excellent Italian works are: G. Volpi, *Il Trecento.* Milan; V. Rossi, *Il Quattrocento.* Milan.

Italians were therefore greatly transformed by the revival of learning; but what may under no circumstances be overlooked, they also suffered a heavy loss in exchange for whatever it was they gained. To bring this out it will suffice to consider what happened in the single field of Italian letters. So persuaded were the humanists that the Latin language was the only worthy vehicle of literature and so withering was the scorn they entertained for the youthful Italian idiom that its employment for literary purposes was almost completely abandoned. The result was that the light which had risen over Italy in the work of Dante, and to the diffusion of which Petrarch and Boccaccio made each a significant contribution, practically went out with Boccaccio's death not to be rekindled for a hundred years. For this calamity, a calamity of national scope, the Latin literature produced by the humanists could by no stretch of the imagination be called a compensation. While they conscientiously tried their hand at every literary category known to the older tongue, at poetry, philosophy, oratory, and history, their productions proved so feeble a progeny that they but rarely outlived their begetters. By reducing themselves in both form and language to slavish imitators of their great exemplars they sacrificed the freshness and originality, without which no work of art is ever other than a tinkling cymbal.

While there is thus a humanistic debit account which may not be overlooked, we should have no difficulty in agreeing that it is the positive achievement of the humanists which is our real concern. We have already seen that with Petrarch pointing the way their labors took the form of discovering lost classical works, of collecting and editing texts, and of transfusing their minds with the wisdom of the ancients in order to free themselves from the bonds of medieval thought and to widen and enrich their lives. When Petrarch died in 1374, his cause had already made such headway that it was not at all likely that the conservative opposition of the clergy and the schoolmen, active and virulent though it was, would succeed in blocking its advance. The great poet and scholar had been a tireless traveler, and in every community of Italy he visited he left behind him a body of disciples. In our town of Florence his leading spokesman was Giovanni Boccaccio (1313–75). Only a little younger than Petrarch, Boccaccio did not till middle life experience the Petrarcan influence. In his early period he accordingly followed his native bent and became a poet and writer. In his poetry he followed the current romantic and chivalrous tradition not without developing in the shepherd idyll an important literary form of his own; but his great vogue came to him when, on abandoning poetry, he turned to prose and composed the collection of one hundred tales known as the *Decameron*. While some of the tales are indefensibly slippery and immoral, not only are they in their majority free from these taints but they underscore and pointedly commend the sentiments which hold and have ever held society together. Taken as a whole the *Decameron* is an amazingly colorful reproduction of the aspirations, plots, accidents, disasters, and triumphs which have made up human destiny from the beginning of time and well deserves its reputation as an animated, pictorial presentation of the eternal human comedy.

But Boccaccio, too, could not escape the impact of antiquity, especially when, after having already passed the summit of existence, he became personally acquainted with Petrarch and fell completely under his spell. From that moment his mind, which had never aimed at a higher goal than to provide entertainment for his contemporaries, turned away from literature and became absorbed with classical research. From insufficient training as well as from lack of natural aptitude Boccaccio did not succeed in achieving distinction as a humanist; but that he took his new interest seriously is indicated by his compiling two dictionaries dealing respectively with classical geography and classical mythology. To his credit in our eyes, he never, like Petrarch, developed an active hostility toward his native Italian tongue; and, again in honorable distinction from his revered leader, to the end of his days he worshiped the memory of Dante, regarding his famous fellow-townsman as quite the equal of the very best of the fabulous ancients.

By the time of the death of Boccaccio Florence was so well won over to the new learning that the movement continued to rise like a flood through the next three or four generations. And although, as already said, the movement embraced all Italy, it found particular favor and touched its highest mark in the Arno city. The most prominent humanist of the generation following Boccaccio was Coluccio Salutati. He was the type of the pure scholar destined to become more and more common in the years ahead, who regarded philological pursuits as sufficient by themselves and having no need to be justified by parallel literary production. As he had to make a living, he became a notary and in middle life was appointed as head of the Florentine chancellery. This was one of the few permanent positions in the service of the Florentine state, which, as we are aware, was headed by an executive of eight priors and a gonfalonier with a term of office lasting only two months. The chancellor's permanence in the midst of so much flux made him a leading political figure. Among other duties Salutati had charge of the foreign correspondence and made a point of conducting it with the rhetorical elegance of a proud and culture-conscious humanist. It is proof of the spread to the governing circles of all Italy of the new literary mode that the Milanese tyrant, Gian Galeazzo Visconti, once let drop the remark that a state paper composed by Salutati fell into the political scales with the weight of a thousand horsemen.

Salutati lived into the fifteenth century—he died in 1406—and had the pleasure before his end of contributing to an immense extension of the field of learning. Owing to the break during the Middle Ages of the Latin west with the Greek world, the Greek language and literature had completely dropped from view in the countries west of the Adriatic Sea. No less a person than Petrarch had sensed the gravity of this misfortune, but his efforts to remedy it were rendered vain by his inability to find more than a very bungling preceptor of the lost language. Petrarch was hardly dead when a world-event played into the hands of his successors. By their steady pressure on the Byzantine empire and their successful encroachment, beginning with the fourteenth century, on its European territory the Ottoman Turks induced an intermittent migration of scholarly Greeks to Italy, where they were eagerly welcomed. In the year 1396 the Florentines invited one of these refugees, Manuel Chrysoloras, to give public instruction in Greek in their city, and the example set was so generally imitated that before long the Greek language and literature were expounded from academic platforms throughout the land. With the opening of this door such a fresh wave of fervor passed over the whole brotherhood of the humanists that not only did they in a surprisingly short time master the new tongue but before fifty years had passed they had, either through importation by fugitive Greeks or by their own voyages of discovery to Constantinople, possessed themselves of the whole extant body of Greek literature.

Only when the conquest of Greek had been effected was the foundation laid for a really solid structure of classical learning. For Latin literature was, after all, no more than a limited supply of neatly dressed stones compared with the inexhaustible Greek quarry from which it derived. Many quattro-cento scholars, without deserting the Latin tradition to which they were patriotically attached, fell strongly under the spell of the older and richer literature. Two such scholars were Leonardo Bruni of Arezzo (1369–1444) and Poggio Bracciolini (1380–1459). Both of them served for a time as Floren-tine chancellors and both of them acquired an immense reputation through writing histories of Florence by which, because they employed the Latin tongue and slavishly imitated the ancient masters, they were supposed to have revived the glory of Rome. But that is an estimate which has long ago ceased to enlist support. Without the least hesitation we may assert sweepingly of the whole tribe of humanists that as creative artists they are, in spite of their fine passion for letters, a quite negligible quantity. We give them their full due when we declare first, that by rediscovering antiquity they disclosed new horizons for mankind; second, that by wrestling with the details of their discovery they gave birth to an important branch of learning, namely, classical philology; and third, that they discredited the medieval curriculum and gradually replaced it by one which had the classics as its core. The many other claims which enthusiasts have made in their behalf may be regarded as completely lacking in foundation.

Generally speaking, the humanists did not settle in a particular town but preferred to live their lives as wanderers seeking a precarious existence in the houses of sympathetic burghers or at the courts of princes. In spite of this characteristic unsteadiness there was always an assembly of greater and lesser members of the genus at Florence with the result that not merely a small upper class of the studious but a broad section of the well-to-do citizen element became thoroughly indoctrinated with the new learning. To its many other claims to greatness the city in the quattrocento added the distinction of serving as the leading center of the new scholarship.

If we now turn to examine the various factors that co-operated to bring about the primacy of Florence as an intellectual center we may begin with the university. A university, called *studio* by the Italians, was so simple an affair compared with our present-day institutions for advanced studies that a word of explanation is not out of place. All that was needed in the thirteenth and fourteenth centuries to call a university into being was for a government to appropriate an amount of money for a staff of teachers qualified to offer instruction in the recognized professional studies of theology, law, and medicine. For good measure it might also provide a chair of logic or philosophy; and by the fifteenth century it could hardly avoid endowing a professorship dedicated to the new studia humaniora. Till far into this same century libraries were non-existent and even a book, which was a hand-produced and costly object, was a considerable rarity. It is hardly an exaggeration to say that it was his fortunate possession of a few books pertaining to his professional field that raised a man above his fellows and enabled him to qualify as a professor. Under these circumstances the present-day problem of providing an expensive equipment of libraries and laboratories in connection with a university caused no concern. Nor did stately lecture halls have to be erected since the modest classroom facilities demanded by that simple society could be secured by hiring a private house and repartitioning its interior according to immediate needs.

It was not till 1321, by which time universities had become established in many towns throughout Italy, that the Florentine republic first voted to create a university of its own. But the execution was delayed, and when at length a few lecturers had been engaged, owing to heavy pressure on the public purse their appointments were before long permitted again to lapse. Consequently the studio remained a feeble plant for many decades, although it deserves to be remembered that it was during this drab period, in 1373 to be exact, that Giovanni Boccaccio was appointed to a lectureship and that his contract invited him to honor the city's greatest son by expounding the *Divine Comedy*. Not till 1387 did the government resolve to end its trifling with the university idea and make a consistent effort to call an institution into being which might presume to vie with such ancient and celebrated universities as those of Bologna, Padua, and Pavia. While, as might be expected, attention was chiefly directed to providing teachers of reputation for the students of the two practical professions, law and medicine, one or more chairs were reserved for the apostles of the new humanistic learning. By being the first university, which by engaging Manuel Chrysoloras (1396) introduced Greek into the curriculum, the Florentine studio revealed a leaning toward the literary innovators. Never at any time in the past had the Arno town been a stronghold of scholasticism. In the course of the first half of the fifteenth century such elements of learning as the medieval system may have deposited among its citizens were all but completely swept away before the advancing tide of humanistic enlightenment.[5]

It will not be supposed that the university, chiefly concerned with supplying the Florentine state with lawyers, administrators, and physicians, was more than one of many factors in the unusually busy intellectual life of Florence at the end of the fourteenth and the beginning of the fifteenth century. Unquestionably the fires of local thought were mainly fed by the private activities of leading citizens either directly as scholars or indirectly as patrons. If we take the case of Chancellor Salutati, we learn that it was his pleasure to gather about him an eager circle of old and young for the discussion of the educational and philological problems precipitated by the humanistic

---

[5] Whatever is worth knowing about the studio can be learned from the *Statuti della Università e Studio Fiorentino . . .* pubblicati da A. Gherardi. Vol. VII of *Documenti di Storia Italiana.*

Left: GHIBERTI. SACRIFICE OF ABRAHAM FOR THE COMPETITION OF 1401. *Right:* BRUNELLESCHI. SACRIFICE OF ABRAHAM FOR THE COMPETITION OF 1401.

Left: DONATELLO. ST. GEORGE. MARBLE. MUSEO NAZIONALE. FORMERLY IN AN OUTER NICHE OF OR SAN MICHELE. *Right:* DONATELLO. NICCOLÒ DA UZZANO. COLORED TERRA COTTA. MUSEO NAZIONALE

DONATELLO. ORGAN LOFT. MUSEO DELL' OPERA DEL DUOMO

LUCA DELLA ROBBIA. ORGAN LOFT. MUSEO DELL' OPERA DEL DUOMO

movement. By his resounding success in his office he created such a prejudice among the citizens in favor of the intellectual tendency represented by him that he was followed by a long row of chancellors imbued with the same humanistic doctrine and alike eager to give it currency. Effective propagandist centers as the successive chancellors proved themselves to be, they did not by any means stand alone. While Salutati was still alive and active a cultivated friar of an ancient Florentine family made the Augustinian monastery of Santo Spirito on the left bank of the Arno an unofficial academy of learning. His name was Luigi Marsigli, and although he opened his mind freely to the knowledge propagated by the humanists, he did not let himself be seduced from the Christian faith. In the pleasant cloisters of Santo Spirito Marsigli and a large body of friends and disciples met daily to discourse upon the delights of classical literature, while at the same time they attempted to reconcile the ancient secular wisdom with the inspired declarations of the Fathers. Marsigli died in 1394 but his academy continued to assemble far into the next century, spreading a stimulus that was widely felt and gratefully acknowledged.

By the early quattrocento Florence had become the seat of a veritable republic of letters and to its perpetuation and enlargement the merchants who acted as patrons contributed no less than the scholars. The greatest single service of the patrons was their activity as book-collectors. Books, let us again remind ourselves, still meant manuscripts, and the absence of great libraries of manuscripts had been bemoaned by Petrarch, the brilliant innovator, as the most damaging handicap of scholarship. Accordingly, he employed much of his time and all of his limited resources to assemble as large a library as possible. When he died he left this treasure to the city of Venice on the understanding that it should be made freely accessible to scholars, but the neglect of his heirs permitted the bequest to be dispersed. Boccaccio, too, acquired a modest library which on his death he gave to the monastery of Santo Spirito, but we do not hear that it became the nucleus of a serviceable public collection. Without doubt the most tireless and successful early collector of books was the Florentine merchant, Niccolò Niccoli (d. 1437). He was not a leading merchant, and when he retired from business in order to devote himself exclusively to his literary hobby, he commanded no more than a modest competence. Had he not been at pains to acquire a fine handwriting with which to produce his own books, he would never have been able to assemble the eight hundred volumes in his possession on his demise. Even so, he died a bankrupt, and his collection would have been scattered to pay his debts, had not a great merchant-prince come to the rescue. Niccoli belonged to the circle of the much younger Cosimo de' Medici, who already at Niccoli's death had become the secret ruler of Florence. Cosimo is deservedly celebrated as the greatest patron not only of letters but also of the Fine Arts of his age. By satisfying his friend Niccoli's debts he acquired title to his books and by depositing them in a beautiful building, incorporated in the monastery of San Marco and erected at his expense, he created what was probably the first broadly serviceable public library of modern times. Besides steadily increasing the San Marco collection by judicious purchases, the lordly Cosimo assembled another, a second, library which he lodged in the monastery under Fiesole known as La Badia.[6] When Pope Nicholas V (1447–55) who, although not a citizen of Florence, had spent many years of his life on the Arno, mounted the papal throne, he at once leapt to the front as a patron and collector. Not only did he employ the most eminent humanists to translate the Greek masters into Latin and pay them lavishly for their services but he also brought together what was easily the largest library of medieval and classical authors of the contemporary world. Although Nicholas did not live to carry out his plan of housing his collection in an appropriate structure, he did not labor in vain as his cherished manuscripts constitute the nucleus of the present great Vatican library.[7] Stimulated by the example of Cosimo and Nicholas many princes of Italy, both secular and ecclesiastical, collected libraries according to their means. In the story of the advance of scholarship the beginning made in the quattrocento toward the creation of great repositories of books holds a place of hardly to be exaggerated importance.

As the Florentine humanism of the second half of the fifteenth century will be treated in a later chapter, we shall close this brief sketch of early humanism by referring to a significant change very generally noticeable in humanist mentality by, let us say, the year 1450. It is characteristic of men's thoughts that they take their color from the element in which they are steeped. The enthusiasts of antiquity are no exception to the rule; and after they had for several generations saturated themselves in classical paganism it was inevitable that they should be shaken in their devotion to the Christian faith. When Petrarch launched the new learning he was not visited by any suspicion of this possibility. In spite of his classical enthusiasm, he was and remained an earnest Christian believer and an obedient son of Mother church. In fact there persisted in him a strong medieval vein and he was consequently often visited by compunctions touching the worldly implications of his beloved literary studies. The incident of his ascent of Mont Ventoux, related in one of his own letters,[8] is well known. He made the ascent for the very unmedieval reason of mere pleasure and, arrived at the top, he indulged himself in an ecstasy of classical memories by recalling Livy's description of Hannibal's crossing of the Alps. Then suddenly his exultation died, as he bethought himself of the vanity of his undertaking, and drawing St. Augustine's *Confessions* from his pocket, he gave not another glance to the vast and glorious prospect under his feet as he pored over the dark warnings of his ghostly companion. Boccaccio, too, in spite of the very worldly matter of his *Decameron* became not less, but actually more, devoted to the faith of his fathers with his advancing years. By the early fifteenth century, however, we encounter evidence of the spread of religious indifference which in the course of another genera-

[6] Counting the collection Cosimo made for his private residence, we may even think of him as the founder of three libraries.

[7] According to the book-dealer Vespasiano da Bisticci, the library of Pope Nicholas reached the extraordinary figure of five thousand volumes. This same well-informed and garrulous old gentleman has left us in his *Vite di Uomini Illustri del Secolo XV* a very precious record of the fun, envy, and excitement experienced by such men as Niccolò Niccoli, Cosimo de' Medici, and Nicholas V in connection with the game of book-collection at a time when a book was a hand-written treasure.

[8] Robinson and Rolfe, *Petrarch*, pp. 307 ff.

tion frequently took the form of an active skepticism. At its peak it manifested itself as a rejection of the truth of revelation in favor of a truth to be attained by our unaided natural endowment of sense and intellect. It would be an exaggeration to charge the whole body of humanists with turning skeptic in the course of the fifteenth century. Some people always managed to make Petrarch's compromise and to live in two worlds at once, in the world of revelation and the world of private judgment. But there is no denying that the tendency toward skepticism gained ground and that in a few extreme instances it ended in outright agnosticism.

In Petrarch's day the Inquisition would have had a word, and a loaded word, to say about so sharp a departure from the beaten path. However, in the course of the fifteenth century this grim institution lost both its vigor and its teeth. That, too, was an effect of the new learning, for classical antiquity had succeeded in enlisting the favor of a large section of the clergy, especially of the great prelates, including a generous number of cardinals and popes. We have heard of the activity of Pope Nicholas V which was so little of an exceptional order that a number of ecclesiastical princes competed with him as patrons of letters and collectors of classical manuscripts. It followed from these secular pursuits that Rome became a nursery of humanistic scholarship which after Nicholas's time yielded in no respect to Florence. Who under these circumstances will wonder that the Inquisition fell into general disuse and that the right of free opinion exercised by the neo-pagans remained unrebuked by the institution which during the previous two hundred years had regarded the defense of orthodoxy as its real reason for existence? To turn from the trecento to the quattrocento is to face an entirely different intellectual landscape. For, at least as far as the upper classes of the Italian peninsula are concerned, the Middle Ages have passed away and we are gazing at the modern world.

XIX. The Fine Arts: The First or Medieval Phase

A S THE purely ancillary character of the chapters of this book dealing with Florentine culture has already been set forth, it will not be necessary to preface the following story of the Fine Arts with another declaration of purpose. Since what by long-established usage passes under the name of the Fine Arts are the three sister-skills of architecture, sculpture, and painting, we would begin our presentation of the field of art with architecture, were it not that we had found it convenient to recount the building history of medieval Florence in the chapter in which we accepted the guidance of that most excellent of ciceroni, Giovanni Villani.[1] Villani was the kind of intelligent and patriotic burgher who in his capacity of chronicler and diarist would not fail to take proud note of every new fine structure that arose in his day. On the other hand, he would be much less attentive to the more concealed and intimate work of the sculptor and painter, and accordingly we find that he made very little mention of it in his book. It is therefore sculpture and painting that will be treated in this chapter, and we shall trace the development of each in turn through the Middle Ages to the threshold of the great change marked by the coming of humanism and the revival of antiquity.

Just as Florence, a backward inland town during the early generations of the communal movement, lagged behind maritime Pisa in political and economic development, so also it was outstripped by its neighbor on the lower Arno in the practice of the arts. True, the church of San Miniato, begun in 1018, points to an early artistic activity at Florence; but unfortunately San Miniato remained an isolated achievement and cannot in regard to the influence it exercised remotely vie with the great cathedral of which the Pisans laid the foundation stone in the year 1062. With this structure they created an ecclesiastical type which was admired and imitated over a large area of Tuscany. In the following century they raised the neighboring structure of the baptistery, and with these two handsome buildings completed or approaching completion, the desire made itself felt to enrich them with ornament and figure work. Thus was supplied the impulse which led to a local, a Pisan, school of sculpture. While the earliest work of the native artists, examples of which still adorn the cathedral façade, was very crude, a gradual improvement may be observed in the later work on the façade till suddenly, a little past the middle of the thirteenth century, a giant forward step was taken by

[1] Chap. XV.

a man of genius, Niccolò Pisano. It was in the year 1260 that Niccolò completed his famous pulpit for the Pisan baptistery. In the six scenes in relief which constitute the sides of the hexagonal structure he returned to the forms and costumes of antiquity, as he had become acquainted with them on certain late Roman sarcophagi which had outlived the storms of the migrations and which may still be seen at Pisa at the present day. With his pulpit Niccolò proclaimed the greatness of classical art, of a very inferior and decadent classical art it is true, because the inferior and decadent phase was the only one to which through the above-mentioned sarcophagi he had access. Nonetheless he turned his face resolutely to the past, and if his enthusiasm had taken general hold the rinascimento might have captured the Fine Arts a century and more before it did. But the time was not ripe and Niccolò's own son, Giovanni (1250?–1328), reacted violently against his father's tendencies. The period was, after all, the Middle Ages, when men were swayed by strong religious emotion and were not likely to be deeply impressed with a purely imitative classic calm. Giovanni Pisano therefore developed an animated subjective art, which derived its inspiration from contemporary French rather than from ancient Roman models, and which was essentially Gothic in spirit. So greatly did this Gothic art of Giovanni's appeal to his age that through him and his numerous followers it established its empire over a large part of Tuscany and Lombardy.

It was the vogue given to sculpture by the Pisan school that first called sculpture to life in Florence. Although the Florentines possessed in their baptistery of San Giovanni a noble monument of essentially classical design, even if it cannot be indisputably proved to have been erected in the classical period, and although as early as the eleventh century they had with San Miniato revived ecclesiastical construction of the Christian basilican type, they had gone no farther on the road of decoration than to supply the façade of these two buildings with a marble incrustation of interesting, if simple, pattern. Figure work, manifestly a higher form of sculptural invention than abstract ornament, remained for a long time outside the range of their ambition. Not till the first quarter of the thirteenth century do we come upon a considerable piece of figured sculpture of distinctly Florentine provenience. It is the pulpit which once adorned the vanished temple of San Piero Scheraggio and which is now set up in the small suburban church of San Leonardo in Arcetri outside Porta San Giorgio. The pulpit is inclosed by a number of panels in high relief, the human figures of which, though of extremely crude workmanship, are occasionally assembled into a naïvely effective composition. Granting that here was a promising beginning, the fact remains that the art continued to languish for another hundred years, when at last the Pisan torch lit a native fire and Florentine sculpture came not alone to life but arrived immediately at manhood with the magnificent bronze doors which between 1330 and 1336 Andrea Pisano fashioned for the baptistery.[2]

While the name of this artist serves to recall his Pisan origin, he developed

[2] On the beginnings of sculpture in Tuscany (and of architecture as well) see E. W. Anthony, *Early Florentine Architecture and Decoration.* Cambridge (Mass.), 1927.

a sculptural language which is so different from that of his master, Giovanni Pisano, that we may accept him as marking the advent of a genuine Florentine style. The most reasonable explanation of the very individual manner developed by Andrea Pisano is that, summoned to Florence to undertake a monumental work, he fell under the influence of Giotto, one of the greatest innovators of all time and predominantly, although by no means exclusively, active as a painter. By his noble types of men and women, his simple and dramatic compositions, and his unpaltering honesty of spirit, Giotto had acquired an authority in the art world of the first third of the trecento which established him as its unquestioned leader. By the best of all evidence, the evidence of his work, it is clear that Andrea passed under Giotto's spell. In addition to eight single figures, representative of the theological and moral virtues, the baptistery gate exhibits in relief twenty scenes from the life of St. John. The simplicity and directness of both figures and scenes point unerringly to Giotto, although the compositions would never have attained their high measure of expressiveness if Andrea had not been a master in his own right. In the free movement of the human body in much of this work the artist even scored an advance over the art of Giotto, who, pursuing an ideal of static dignity, only rarely strove to impress movement on his figures.

Andrea was also employed in Florence in connection with the sculptures that adorn the base of Giotto's campanile. He worked on them in such intimate collaboration with the great master that the exact share of each in the completed work will never be determined. From evidences of style it would seem probable that the seven panels on the west face of the campanile are mainly by the hand of Giotto. The series begins with the creation of Adam and continues with the creation of Eve and with the Fall; in this, the third panel, Adam and Eve are delving and spinning according to the curse they have drawn on their heads. On this strictly Christian and orthodox introduction to human history there succeeds in a continuous band inclosing the four sides of the tower a fascinating record of the inventions and occupations by which the descendants of our first parents forced the stubborn earth to yield them a satisfying living. However, as only three sides were finished in Giotto's and Andrea's time, the panels of the fourth, which is the northern, face remained blank until filled in a hundred years later by Luca della Robbia, an artist of an entirely different inspiration.

Together with the three introductory panels, but without those of Luca della Robbia, the reliefs are twenty-one in number and tell with extraordinary skill the heartening tale of how man, who for his disobedience had been cast forth from paradise into a hostile world, rose to a new and self-earned dignity by his restless energy and amazing ingenuity. What is here offered is in sum a picture-book of civilization, and not only is it the earliest work of its kind but as a statement of man's achievements in the language of a graphic art it has perhaps not been excelled down to our time. We can hardly go astray if we attribute this broad and eminently pictorial vision of man's upward journey to the master artist, Giotto. But if he was responsible for the plan, it is more than likely that he left the execution of the individual panels, with the possible exception of the first six or seven, to the younger craftsman who with his baptistery gate had proved himself a worthy associate.[3]

Following this first creative burst of energy there was a lull. Not that sculpture failed to receive due recognition from the church, the state, and occasional private patrons, or that there was a dearth of plastic workers desirous of winning honor by following the path blazed by the two great masterpieces, the bronze gate of the baptistery and the marble story-book strung about the base of Giotto's campanile. The cathedral, Santa Croce, Santa Maria Novella, and the smaller houses of worship which abounded in the town were at this time still far from that state of adornment in which they presented themselves to view at a later age. Consequently their façades and portals required statues commemorative of the saints, while the bare interiors needed to be furnished with carved stone altars, pulpits, and holy water fountains. In the decades following Andrea Pisano, work of this kind was produced in considerable quantity, to which should be added a funeral monument characteristic of the time, consisting of a marble sarcophagus adorned with figures of the saints and presenting, amidst a wealth of Gothic ornament, the image of the deceased asleep upon the tomb. Serving in most instances as the coffin of some great ecclesiastical dignitary, such a monument was usually. placed high above the ground along the wall of aisle or transept. Examples of all these kinds of work can still be seen in the Florentine churches and the names of their makers can in practically every case be identified. But almost without exception they suffer from a mortal flaw in that they are the uninspired handiwork of mere craftsmen. The decades immediately following Giotto and Andrea might be dismissed by us without another word, were it not that one sculptor, deserting the common herd, proved that he was a man and artist.

This exceptional individual was Andrea Orcagna (active 1344–68). Like the other artists of his time he by no means limited himself to sculpture, but it is as a sculptor that we involuntarily think of him by reason of his famous tabernacle of Or San Michele. Wrought as a shrine for an exquisite panel painting of the Madonna by Bernardo Daddi, it engrossed Orcagna's heart and soul to such an extent and for so many years that it became in his hands one of the most unusual combinations of jewel-like inlay and decoration with sculpture in the round and in relief within the whole range of Italian art. It could not be more unfortunately placed than it is at present, for, owing to the walling up of the windows of Or San Michele, it is now practically invisible except with the aid of artificial illumination. In its plan and proportions as well as in its details the tabernacle is a thoroughly Gothic monument and proves that Orcagna was in sympathy with the tradition of northern art as represented by Giovanni Pisano and his successors. But like all Florentines from the first moment that Gothic gained a foothold in their territory, he took of the importation only what he could use without injury to the genius

[3] The fundamental history of Italian art is still Vasari's *Lives,* accessible in many English translations. The standard Italian edition is by Gaetano Milanesi. The main facts of the medieval phase of Italian art, and of the subsequent phases as well, are obtainable in innumerable handbooks, which need not be listed here. We shall limit ourselves in the footnotes to the mention of an occasional special work of outstanding worth.

of his race. To this he remained inalterably attached, for his love of fine ornament patterned in many colors goes back to the baptistery and San Miniato,
while in his figure work he is the faithful follower of that most pungent and
solid of Florentines, Giotto. By their gravity and poise the prophets and
apostles, who either as full or half-figures adorn the shrine, proclaim their
relationship to that master; but as they have also a novel flavor of realism
and are more carefully individualized than is usually the case with Giotto's
more generalized men and women, they announce that Orcagna was an independent artist, who without denying his indebtedness to his forerunners
stood firmly on his own feet. The sculptor reached his highest level in some
of the scenes in relief from the life of the Virgin, and in the last and crowning
episode he fairly surpassed himself. This is in two related sections. Below we
have the death of Mary surrounded by the mourning apostles, while above
she is seen already floating in the sky, lifted upward by attending angels. By
reason of its movement, its unity, and fine reserve this composition takes rank
as one of the great achievements of the trecento.

The single figure of Orcagna cannot alter the impression that Florentine
sculpture was becoming enfeebled in the latter half of the fourteenth century
and that it was doomed unless it managed to tap a fresh source of inspiration.
And this is the very thing it succeeded in doing, thereby inaugurating its second
or quattrocento phase. The event is closely tied up with the contemporary
revolution which we have agreed to call humanism, and which actually and
simply was humanism until Petrarch and his followers gave it the narrower
significance of a revival of ancient learning. As, toward the close of the trecento, the outlook of the upper and learned classes was being rapidly transformed, it was inevitable that the artists should be caught by the prevailing
thought currents and be revolutionized in their turn. Thus it happened that,
beginning about 1400, the architects, sculptors, and painters shed their old
and acquired a new, or at least a partially new, mentality. The man who was
chiefly instrumental in mediating the change so far as sculpture is concerned
was Donatello (1386–1466). Than this nothing more fortunate could have
happened, for while Donatello became fascinated by the art of the ancients
and to develop his skill diligently copied the classical remains still relatively
rare in his day because buried in the ground, even more than to the ancients
he was drawn to nature itself. Seeking renewal for his art by every available
path, by some profound instinct which defies analysis he turned most avidly
to the earth and its inhabitants. In this way, instead of leading sculpture up
the blind alley of antiquity, he conducted it into fresh pastures and made its
quattrocento phase one of the glories of his town and country.

In turning, next, to painting we approach the art which the Florentines
found peculiarly suited to their genius and in which their contribution was
so significant that it has largely determined the whole subsequent course of
European expression in design and color. Their starting-point was the later
Greek or Byzantine practice of the art. In the eleventh and twelfth centuries
there had been a revival of painting at Constantinople, and the religious altar
pieces which issued from this movement had in many instances found their
way to Italy. Occasionally a Greek artist had even established direct touch

with his western patrons by setting up his shop at Rome or Venice or some other rising commune. In the course of time native-born Italians took up the Greek practice, thereby giving birth to a considerable number of local schools dominated in varying degree by the Byzantine manner. One such school arose in Florence and one of its earliest adepts was a certain Cimabue. A veritable man of flesh and blood in his time, he has for us dwindled to a rather ghostly figure since hardly a single work exists in which present-day experts agree in recognizing his hand. However, the Cimabue problem does not greatly concern the general student, since the real fountainhead of Florentine painting was Cimabue's pupil, Giotto. Of Giotto we luckily still possess a large body of authentic works enabling us to detect exactly what the elements were he introduced into the art and which his contemporaries hailed as novel and quickening beyond compare.[4]

In spite of there having come down to us much work by Giotto's hand, and in spite of the positively bewildering amount of painting by his trecento successors still extant in churches and museums, we are met with a difficulty in attempting to enjoy and understand the master and his followers which it is well to face at once. With very few exceptions the handiwork of all this group of artists has suffered and continues to suffer such grave impairment that we may speak of it as a body of remains slowly crumbling to complete ruin. While the accidents of time coupled with human neglect and maltreatment are largely responsible for this lamentable state of affairs, it has been brought about also by the technical processes under which the work was produced. These are materially and aesthetically so important that without a measure of acquaintance with them the fourteenth-century artists and their works will always remain outside our comprehension. Like everything else about early painting the technical processes go back to the Byzantines and fall under the two heads of wall (or fresco) and panel painting. In either case the colors were carried in a medium of yolk of egg mixed with water, that is, as the saying went, they were "tempered" by these ingredients to the desired consistency. Commonly called tempera, the indicated method of color preparation was usual for both techniques. In every other respect, however, wall painting and panel painting were very different, although the same artist would and usually did practice both methods.

On being assigned to the wall of a church or a convent the wall painter encountered as his immediate task the preparation of the surface with the best and smoothest kind of plaster available. At the same time he set about drawing his designs in bare outline on large sheets of paper and in charcoal, making careful measurements in order that they might fit exactly into the space at his disposal. When he had transferred his outlined designs to the wall by tracing, and then, as his first step in color, had underpainted all the figures in shaded monochrome, he was ready for the crucial operation which was to cover with a fresh coat of thin lime plaster just so much of his design

---

[4] Berenson, *The Florentine Painters of the Renaissance*. 3d ed. New York, 1909. C. Carra, *Giotto: 192 Riproduzioni in Fototipia*. Rome, 1924. F. J. Mather, *A History of Italian Painting*. New York, 1923.

Attention should be called to a monumental work on Florentine painting now in course of preparation. R. Offner, *A Corpus of Florentine Painting*. Planned in 30 volumes.

as he thought he could finish coloring in a single day. The fresh paint fusing with the wet lime dried before the next morning, when the artist would repeat the process with the adjoining section. It was this application of paint to a fresh coat of lime which gave the method its name of fresco or, more correctly, of *al fresco* painting. Fresco called for good drawing, clear color, and a resolute attack, and, whenever it was successfully employed, resulted in a strikingly monumental style of work. Michelangelo, who was among the last Florentine painters successfully to practice fresco and who, putting aside the oil method popular in his day, chose it as his medium for the famous ceiling of the Sistine Chapel, expressed his admiration for it by saying that it made possible the kind of painting alone worthy of men.

Panel painting was painting on a wooden board overlaid with an absorptive ground of plaster of Paris and was on a smaller scale than fresco and much more delicate. It was concerned largely with altar pieces, which were to be made as luminous as possible by presenting a saint or a group of saints with stamped gold aureoles and in raiments of various colors projected against a background of shining gold. The first step following the tracing of the design upon the panel consisted in underpainting the figures in a greenish monotone. Next, the draperies were brought to the desired color key and, last of all, the heads and hands were delicately enameled by means of a succession of thin coats of white and red. As it was the heads and hands that were intended particularly to draw the eyes of the spectators, all other features were treated as subordinate. The artist entertained no desire to be realistic in any sense whatever of that very elastic term. It sufficed him that the panel should exhibit one or more of the accredited inhabitants of heaven and that it should shine with the color and light of a jewel. So painstaking and delicate was panel painting that it had many of the qualities of miniature.[5]

Now while both these techniques yielded paintings of a high degree of durability, they were not proof against all the vicissitudes of nature and of chance. As for wall paintings, they will begin to flake when exposed to humidity, while the fine enamel finish, the glory of the altar pieces, will vanish under gradually accumulating dust and grime. As soon as in the past ages such physical deterioration manifested itself in either kind of work, the question arose as to how it was to be met. The issue presented itself to men, who, belonging to a later period, had little or no just appreciation of the work of the earlier generation. Whatever they might do under the altered standards of taste was therefore almost certain to be wrong. Let what happened to the Giotto frescos of the Bardi and Peruzzi chapels at Santa Croce, frescos probably as great as any in the world, serve for illustration. Having through persistent flaking lost much of what constituted pictorial beauty according to the canons of eighteenth-century art, they were in that century quietly and unceremoniously buried under an obliterating coat of whitewash. On being rediscovered toward the middle of the nineteenth century, an almost worse barbarism was committed, for they were "restored" by two daubers who

---

[5] For the technical processes the great authority is the painter Cennino Cennini, who lived at the end of the trecento and the beginning of the quattrocento. His work is available in English under the title: *The Book of the Art of Cennino Cennini*. Translated from the Italian with notes on Medieval Art Methods by Christiana J. Herringham. London, 1922.

wantonly repainted large sections, and especially the faces, according to their private pitiful standards of what constitutes good painting. As for the delicate panels, most of them now torn from the altars for which they were intended and herded in cold, uncongenial museums, they have so often had the dirt and soot scraped off them by insensitive hands that not only has the fine surface enamel very generally disappeared but in many instances hardly more is left than the original green underpainting turned black by time and human abuse.

With these vicissitudes in mind we are prepared to understand why it is that the novice taking up Giotto for the first time is likely to be disappointed. However, he will reveal himself as impervious to the message of painting or of any other art, should he not, by repeatedly returning to what, after all, still are radiant and inspiring remains, discover for himself the superb merits of this genius. Coming, as he did, at the beginning of the development of painting, Giotto (1270?–1337) lacked much of the purely technical ability that was afterward acquired by those who trod in his footsteps. He knew nothing of anatomy or perspective and very little of movement. Deprived of these valuable resources, he undertook to communicate what he had to say by the exclusive means of the draped human figure. It was by reason of this all-important decision of its founder that Florentine painting became essentially a figure art. Moreover, as the subject matter presented by Giotto was exclusively religious, he may at least in part be charged with having brought it about that Florentine painting became and for a long time to come remained a figure art with an essentially religious import. Giotto's world is a world of very humanly conceived saints, who possess an unmatched dignity and go with the greatest gravity about their saintly concerns. In depicting them in a particular attitude or engaged in a particular act he aimed to give the essence of the situation stripped of all useless side issues and accessories. This is the reason why we never cease to be impressed with his simplicity and sincerity, as it also explains the dramatic concentration of his compositions. With such unerring judgment did he seize upon the significant elements of the event to be depicted that we are convinced that precisely as he presented it and in no other conceivable manner must it have taken place.

Giotto's fame was so great that he had many patrons, at whose orders he worked in widely separated sections of Italy. His chief fresco series are to be found in certain churches at Padua, Assisi, and Florence. As any one work of his, carefully examined, will serve as a concrete instance of his qualities, we may turn for illumination touching his manner to the Peruzzi chapel at Santa Croce, where at the summit of his powers he painted on one wall scenes from the life of St. John the Baptist and on the opposite wall scenes from the life of the Baptist's namesake, the Evangelist. It is these frescos to which we referred as having experienced so miraculous a resurrection almost a century ago. In spite of the damage done by the unsympathetic restorer, the outlines of the figures are unimpaired and patches of the original color are still intact. If we turn to the wall at the right hand dedicated to St. John the Evangelist, we have two scenes, one above the other, showing respectively the raising by John of Drusiana and John's death and ascension to heaven. They are both magnificent compositions giving the essence of the event so

directly and succinctly that there is nothing to be added. Attempted explanation becomes prattle and impertinence. John and the other dramatis personae
are intensely human. But while they have unmistakably the quality of earth-
born folk, they at the same time breathe an earnestness and solemnity that
leaves no doubt in our mind that we have entered the realm of the religious
sanctities. If Giotto was an artist with a definite aesthetic endowment placing
him in the front rank of the artists of all ages, he never permits us to forget
that he lived by the light of faith and that he was not a secular but a religious
painter.

Giotto so overwhelmed his Florentine contemporaries that with few exceptions they all flocked to his banner and tried to work in his style; and when
his contemporaries had passed from the scene, a second and a third generation
of artists continued to copy his types and rethink his thoughts. Being so manifestly his followers, the painters of the later trecento have been grouped together under the name of Giotteschi; and if there is a touch of contempt in
the designation, it is not unmerited. On the other hand, it is a mistake to conceive of the Giotteschi as a completely unindividualized mass of lifeless imitators. There were men of talent among them, like Giotto's favorite pupil,
Taddeo Gaddi; and as one decade after another of the trecento slipped away,
certain novel features began to appear among the men who to the casual eye
seem to constitute just a docile following. To mention but a single matter:
the austere, idealistic human types of Giotto began to recede in favor of figures
closer to actual life. In itself such realism was neither good nor bad, but insofar as it indicated emancipation from blind authoritarianism, it may be regarded as the promise of a richer productivity. However, on the whole, the
Giotteschi cannot be thought of other than as copyists. Undoubtedly they
have all the weaknesses of copyists, of which by far the worst is that they do
not understand what they copy. His followers picked up the externals of
Giotto's art without comprehending its spirit with the result that their work
falls unescapably under the curse of mediocrity.

But, as already said, these were exceptions to the rule, and one at least of
the exceptional men must come in for a word, especially as we have already
had occasion to note his contribution to sculpture. As a matter of fact Andrea
Orcagna (d. 1368) was chiefly a painter, although, according to the custom of
his age, he practiced many of the sister-arts of painting whenever the occasion
arose to do so. We see him at his best as a painter in the Strozzi chapel at
Santa Maria Novella. All the work here is by his hand, not only the altar piece
in the middle exhibiting Christ with a number of saints, but also the two
frescos of hell and heaven on the right and left wall respectively. While,
owing to ruthless cleaning, the altar piece has lost much of its original luster,
it is still a beautiful panel nobly and religiously conceived. The hell we will
pass over as something which, however frequently attempted, has always de-
fied pictorial presentation. But turn to the heaven and you will encounter a
great, a breath-taking revelation! Its injury through restoration is immense,
especially by reason of the modern artist's attempt to sweeten the faces of the
women and to smooth out the wrinkles of the men. Notwithstanding this
corruption, in its energy, its rhythmic balance, and its monumental propor-

tions the composition is one of the exultant visions left us by the Middle Ages.

Lacking new impulses, Florentine painting would have perished of inanition if, a little past the year 1400, it had not responded to the new energy radiated by the humanistic movement. What happened to the art of painting constitutes a close parallel to the contemporary renovation of sculpture even to the point of the leadership furnished by a surpassing genius. Admitting that there was a blind groping on the part of many painters to find a new means of expression, not till Masaccio did his Carmine frescos around 1426 was the path to be taken indicated in clear and unambiguous terms. Masaccio turned for inspiration to the fresh life and knowledge of his time and thereby inaugurated the quattrocento phase of painting. As no classical painting had survived to be admired and imitated, he was influenced by antiquity even less than the sculptor Donatello. No lover of originality will doubt that this was a fortunate circumstance since it obliged the quattrocento painters to carry their art forward by the exercise of their own strength.

With a new day dawning for sculpture and painting it was impossible for architecture not to feel in its turn the call for renewal. Between 1255, when the palace of the people, now called the Bargello, was projected, and 1389, when the city celebrated the completion of the loggia of the priors, Florence had acquired those churches and public buildings which to a very large extent determine its physical character to this day. They possess stylistically so strong a kinship and reveal so great a unity of spirit that we are justified to speak of them as a distinctly native product. However, even a superficial analysis will at once show that their underlying principles, far from being indigenous to Florence, were widely distributed over Italy and all western Europe. The historic fact is that the earliest builders of the city drew upon the general body of architectural information that passed under the name of Romanesque, and that their successors from about the time of Arnolfo di Cambio (active around 1300) cautiously took over some of the features of the northern art, commonly called Gothic. Their attachment to Gothic or, we should perhaps say, their understanding of it was so incomplete that every structure they erected in what passes as the Gothic manner exhibits a substantial Romanesque core. In this often overlooked circumstance we have the explanation of how it came about that, whether they are early or late, the medieval structures of the town, fundamentally considered, carry an identical imprint.

As soon as the revival of antiquity became the passion of the Florentine learned and professional classes, the very feeble dominion that the foreign importation called Gothic had exercised in the town came to an abrupt end. The new generation reverted to the older, never quite forgotten Romanesque until, carried farther and farther back by its classical enthusiasm, it directed its attention to the remains of Roman architecture, of which Romanesque was, after all, no more than a barbarous corruption. By the early fifteenth century it was only necessary for a born leader to appear to establish architecture on a new and classical foundation. This leader was Filippo Brunelleschi (1379–1446), and from him dates the quattrocento phase of Florentine building. In Brunelleschi, Donatello, and Masaccio we have the three men under whose inspiration the Fine Arts were born again and came to a second and astonishing flowering.

XX. The Triumphant Oligarchy (1382–1434)

W E LEARNED in the chapter dealing with Florentine political developments in the decades leading up to 1382 how the democratic movement was defeated by uncompromising oligarchical hostility, by paralyzing cross-currents among its own supporters, and by the absence of anything even remotely resembling honest, courageous, and authoritative leadership. But even had the democracy which went down to defeat in 1382 been more compact and unified, it could not have survived for long in the Italy which was taking shape in the fourteenth century, for the anarchy of the innumerable small tyrants, which already in the last years of Dante's life had stood out as the leading aspect of the peninsula, was being gradually replaced by the absolutism of a few large states, which based their power on the successful absorption of their weaker neighbors. The outstanding development of this character was the Milan of the Visconti family. The mounting power of the Milanese state moved the sea city, Venice, to seek protection against a possible attack from the west by means of a line of outposts on the mainland. Become thus a contender for land power, the Venetian commonwealth, which under the name of a republic was organized into one of the tightest oligarchies recorded in history, had projected itself as an important and permanent factor into the Italian political system. The oldest large-scale polity of the peninsula was the kingdom of Naples. Following the death of King Robert I in 1343, it was frequently threatened with dissolution owing to fatal divisions among the members of the ruling dynasty. Grave difficulties notwithstanding, the southern kingdom never ceased to figure prominently in the Italian parallelogram of forces. Although the papal dominion had presented itself to view during the medieval period as a mere mass of *disjecta membra,* a little past the middle of the fourteenth century the political genius of Cardinal Albornoz had shown that the scattered elements could be fused into a unified structure; and while we must admit that almost as soon as that able churchman's hand had been removed from his creation it had again collapsed, the proof had been furnished that a great papal state in the heart of the peninsula was a political feasibility and would henceforth have to be reckoned with.

It was in the midst of a chaos from which the above-mentioned four states, Milan, Venice, Naples, and the State of the Church, were slowly disengaging themselves that Florence raised its head with the plan of reaching the approximate level of these neighbors by making Tuscany the basis of its power. It was a program every whit as expansionist as that of the rival states, two of which lay to the north of Florence and two to the south. But that to carry out a program requiring the application of an unwavering resolution was an enterprise particularly suited to the nature of a democracy was very doubtful. For a democracy, driven as it invariably is by opposing winds of opinion, generally follows an impulsive, zigzag course. Frequently canceling today what it enacted yesterday, it exhibits a capriciousness hopelessly incompatible with the steady pursuit of a policy of conquest. On conquest, however, all Florentine classes alike had set their hearts, although the merchant class with its far-flung commercial interests may be considered to have originated the program. The merchants were probably right in thinking that with their greater compactness they could carry the town to its goal much more surely than the ignorant, disputatious masses. This explains why it was that, as soon as by the victory of 1382 they had re-established their power, they prosecuted with a much greater energy than their democratic predecessors had shown the territorial policy, which with a somewhat different emphasis the whole population, regardless of economic status, eagerly indorsed.

In the military conditions of the age lay another reason for conceding a higher probability of successful conquest to an oligarchic than to a democratic system. War was conducted by mercenary troops which by the second half of the trecento had greatly improved their organization. The mercenaries, held permanently together under condottieri enjoying their confidence, were willing to serve any employer capable of meeting their wage bill. Nonetheless it was natural that they should put more trust in the spokesmen of a system possessed of a certain promise of permanence than in the representatives of an ever-shifting democratic ruling group. A recent experience through which Florence had gone will confirm the argument. During the War of the Eight Saints the most famous condottiere of his day, the Englishman John Hawkwood, had not hesitated to sell his services to the democratic government then in power; but that he had no sympathy for his employers' system is proved by the support he gave the oligarchic plotters in connection with their successful revolution. In the critical month of January of the year 1382 this Giovanni Acuto, as the Italians called him, was present in Florence in the pay of the government. However, when the rising occurred, instead of putting himself behind the democracy to which he was under contract, he backed the opposition and was a factor in its victory. From that day onward Hawkwood served the oligarchy with such unusual devotion that there was established a bond of peculiar intimacy between it and him.[1] In sign thereof he was accorded the rare favor of Florentine citizenship together with a pension for life and exemption from taxation; and when he died in 1394 the grateful government not only honored him with a splendid funeral at public expense, but also commemorated his services by having him painted on the wall of the inner façade of the cathedral mounted on horseback in full panoply of war. Half a century later the same honor was accorded to another condottiere, Niccolò da Tolentino. To this day these two hireling soldiers proudly sit their war steeds on the entrance wall of the great central temple of the city, recalling to the reflective visitor one of the

[1] J. Temple-Leader and G. Marcotti, *Sir John Hawkwood: Story of a Condottiere.* London, 1889.

most curious perversions of the sentiment of patriotism recorded in history.

A much-remarked feature of this period regarding the condottieri and their troops must not be overlooked, although we may agree that it possesses no intrinsic importance. Hawkwood concludes the long line of foreign condottieri who operated in Italy preponderantly with foreign men-at-arms. After him Italian condottieri, preferably employing troopers of their own nationality, took over the lucrative business of mercenary warfare. More especially in the following, the fifteenth, century these native adventurers rose to great fame, and some of them became so powerful that they were able to appropriate the government they were supposed to serve and to found a dynasty. The outstanding example of this sort is Francesco Sforza, who became duke of Milan. But other heads of military companies, such as Jacopo del Verme, Niccolò Fortebraccio, and Niccolò Piccinino hardly made less stir in their day. Our concern with them at this point goes no farther than to bring out that it was by them and their likes that Florence got its fighting done in the oligarchic, and in the subsequent Medicean, period as well. It need hardly be expressly said that on taking the field the mercenaries failed to show conspicuous zeal for their employer and that not infrequently their conduct during a campaign was dictated by directly treasonable considerations. On the whole, however, the oligarchy during this, its last lease of power, may be judged to have received a fair return for its money, for, although frequently involved in extremely perilous wars, it managed to conclude them with reasonably satisfactory terms of peace. Indeed in view of its having made so many territorial gains that by the time it was superseded by the rule of Cosimo de' Medici it had brought under its control all Tuscany with the exception of Lucca and Siena, we may credit it with having put forth more power—and that means essentially military power—than any government with which Florence had been thus far provided. We shall be obliged to examine the foreign policy of the oligarchy and the wars in which it engaged with some detail, but before doing so it will be well to turn to the domestic story and trace the line of internal development taken by the government in the half-century between its birth and its demise.

From the moment the oligarchy had regained the preponderant influence in the government its main concern was not again to lose control. It had been moderate in the hour of victory and had conceded to the lesser gilds a share in the offices just short of that attributed to itself. However, democratic rule was too recent an experience not to be the cause of constant alarm to the new rulers. The moment there were mutterings among the discomfited proletarians or vague movements of protest among the members of the lesser gilds, such inevitable discontent was promptly exaggerated into a conspiracy against the regime and made to serve as an excuse for severe repressive action. And since repression looks less draconic when disguised under a harmless name, it was designated euphemistically as a "reform." The first such reform occurred in 1387 and laid down the procedure for a number of others that followed in due course. It had long been customary to suspend the constitution from time to time by calling a general assembly or parlamentum and by having it vote special power (balìa) to a commission to sweep existing difficulties out of the way before once more putting the constitution into force. Such a balìa created

Top: LUCA DELLA ROBBIA. MADONNA IN ADORA-
TION. COLORED GLAZED TERRA COTTA. *Bottom:*
GHIBERTI. PANEL FROM HIS SECOND BRONZE GATE
WITH EPISODES FROM THE LIFE OF ABRAHAM

DONATELLO. KING DAVID CALLED LO ZUCCONE. NICHE OF THE CAMPANILLE

DONATELLO. BRONZE EQUESTRIAN STATUE OF GATTAMELATA. PADUA

GHIBERTI. HIS SECOND BRONZE GATE COMMONLY CALLED THE GATE OF PARADIS

by a carefully manipulated parliament in 1387 cut down the participation of the arti minori in the public offices to one-fourth the total, and to make the measure effective ordered the old purses (borse) burned and a new scrutiny (scrutinio) to be carried through conducted on the plan of admitting to the new borse the names of none but accredited supporters of the regime and of rigorously excluding the names of known opponents.

Ever since the adoption of the system of filling the offices by lot the sure way of controlling the government was to control the borse. In the reform of 1387 the oligarchy showed clearly how this could effectively be done. It would seem that the borse thus manipulated might be held to offer a sufficient guaranty against an unpleasant surprise at the recurrent drawings. This was not the view of the anxious oligarchs; and further to guard against an unfavorable signory the balìa charged with correcting the constitution authorized the creation of what came to be called the *borsellino*. Borsellino means little borsa (or purse) and into it were dropped the names of the most devoted and ardent adherents of the oligarchy with the provision that henceforth two of the eight priors must be regularly drawn from this preferred list. While after all these precautions there were still two priors (two being the required one-fourth) hailing from the lesser gilds, these two small tradesmen could be reduced to effective nullity by their six colleagues of the greater gilds headed by a gonfalonier of the same social stratum.

With the oligarchic balìa of 1387 set on clearing obstacles of every sort out of the way it took occasion to banish Benedetto degli Alberti together with some of the members of his family. Benedetto was the richest Florentine of his time and therefore closely bound up with the interests of the ruling clique. But inclined to take an independent stand, he had come under the suspicion of his fellows, who seized the occasion afforded by the balìa to rid themselves of an unreliable and possibly dangerous associate. Besides, a feud existed between the Alberti and the family of that man whose talents had enabled him to become the effective head of the ruling faction. This was the merchant Maso degli Albizzi. Maso was a sane, vigorous, and relatively moderate party leader, but in one respect, in the sacred matter of vendetta, he was as extravagant as every other self-respecting Florentine. It was his opinion that a former head of the house, his uncle Piero degli Albizzi, had been put to death during the democratic period because of an intrigue spun by Benedetto degli Alberti; and when the chance came to even the score, Maso made the most of it without hesitation. Neither at this nor at any other period of Florentine history did motives of a purely personal character fail to play their part in the revolutions and reforms that followed one another in unbroken succession.

A second reform was instituted six years later, in 1393. As soon as it began to take shape it was clear that it was to have the same character as its predecessor, for its instigator was Maso degli Albizzi, who happened at the time to be gonfalonier of Justice. Accordingly, we meet with an exact repetition of the just-recited measures: creation of a balìa, exclusion of opponents from office by a new scrutinio authorized to make new borse, strengthening the party in power by a revised borsellino, and reissue in a more sweeping form of the decree of condemnation and exile against the clan of the Alberti. The new measures signified a further tightening of oligarchic rule, to which same end there was adopted an additional provision of a peculiarly revealing nature. The reigning merchants were rich popolani who by developing the outlook of a privileged class effectively closed the chasm which had opened a century before between them and an upper group of feudalized families designated by the law as magnates or grandi. While under the Ordinances of Justice the magnates were still excluded from office, they had in the course of the trecento, when war became the province of the companies of adventure, completely lost their military character and were now, insofar as they had not through poverty and concomitant social decline sunk to the level of the common people, nothing other than dyed-in-the-wool conservatives. Judging that here was a body of natural allies, the ruling oligarchs resolved to strengthen their cause by drawing these congenital tories to their side. In consequence the ancient clans of the Frescobaldi, Cavalcanti, Ricasoli, Bardi, Rossi, Adimari, and many others besides, constituting in their sum the hated magnates of the trecento, were cleared of their magnate stigma and, by being declared popolani, again became eligible for office. The conversion of status could of course also be made to work the other way. If it was possible to win support from magnates by giving them back their political rights, it was just as easy to get rid of undesirable popolani by stigmatizing them as magnates. This is precisely what happened in the case of the Alberti. Already exiled and therefore financially ruined, they were for good measure and as a final gesture of aversion raised to the magnate dignity.

Engaged in such multiple sleight-of-hand, which, although carried to a very high technical perfection at this time, was by no means new since in one form or another it had been practiced in the city from the earliest days of the republic, the oligarchy was not likely to overlook the device of ammonizione or warning. Invented by the parte Guelfa to serve its attempted control of the government, it had in the revolution of 1378 been struck from the hands of its supporters. But that was no reason why it should not be taken over by the new rulers. They were men without scruple, ready to employ every available means to suppress their antagonists, whether these antagonists were simple folk of the shops or too ambitious members of their own group. The ammonizione was therefore cannily added to the weapons wherewith the government smote its adversaries. Under no circumstances, however, did the new rulers intend to share the resumption of this sharp implement with its inventors of the parte Guelfa. By confirming the act of 1378, which forebade the use of the ammonizione to the party, they let it be known that they were not minded to permit a rival government to function at their side. The once powerful organization obediently accepted the decision; and although it continued its existence for many generations as a distinguished social club housed in a fine palace, from the time of its defeat in 1378 it ceased to figure in any conspicuous way in the political life of the town.

The many secret and open manipulations here indicated made the so-called free republic of Florence a good deal of a travesty. Operating nominally as a democracy of twenty-one gilds, it was in reality a government conducted by, and in the interest of, a small class of the well-to-do. In actual practice, however, even a class government is not run by all its members but rather by a few capable and ambitious individuals prepared, according to their temperamental endowment, to share or to dispute the control among themselves. We have just learned that Maso degli Albizzi had early acquired a leading influence and that, among other ways, he used it to rid himself of the rivalry of the hated Alberti family. When after the fall of the wealthy and personally distinguished Benedetto Alberti, Gino Capponi and Niccolò da Uzzano rose more and more into public view, Maso got along fairly well with these vigorous representatives of the oligarchy and even took them into a kind of political partnership. Like himself, they were both hard-headed business men deeply and sincerely concerned with promoting the welfare of the state according to their light. Besides, all three were so genuinely possessed of the true optimate outlook that, while aspiring to stand in the front rank of the citizens, they entertained no pretensions to exclusive rule. Under these circumstances cooperation was possible among them and in point of fact all important decisions in domestic and foreign affairs alike were taken by them in consultation with such other merchants and friends as from motives of prudence they chose to draw into their counsels. Over each freshly arising issue they would hold an informal session in the mansion of one of the leaders, and as the fiasco of good red Tuscan wine made the rounds, they came to a conclusion which they would then convey by suitable channels to the constituted authorities. The control of the borse had made them the effective masters of the priors and of all the other governing bodies of the state as well. This extra-constitutional procedure could not be kept concealed from a people so alert as the Florentines, and grumbling complaints made themselves heard against a rule exercised "fuori del palazzo" (outside the palace), instead of by the priors within their appointed residence. To be effective a protest would have to swell to the dimensions of a revolution, and a revolution was difficult in the face of the sleepless watch maintained by the masters. In sum, Florence had become an undercover oligarchy which, while secretly asserting its preeminence, found it advantageous to flatter the traditional democratic pretensions of the citizens by an apparent deference to the constituted authorities.

The lively but splenetic contemporary, Cavalcanti, tells a story which illustrates so strikingly how the concealed control worked that it deserves to be quoted. By way of introduction it will be well to remind ourselves that the republic, moved from its inception by fear of individuals likely to become too powerful, had invented a system of checks and balances consisting chiefly of a number of councils, in which opinions might be freely voiced before a final decision was taken. There, for instance, was the council (usually called the collegium or college) constituted by the priors assisted by the Twelve Good Men and the Sixteen Captains of the Companies, thirty-seven individuals in all; and, again, there were the two much larger councils respectively of the captain and the podestà. To most republican societies, no matter how jealous of their liberty, three councils would have seemed sufficient and more than sufficient for the end in view, but not so to the Florentines. They had gradually brought into existence an additional council, which consisted of leading citizens summoned at the pleasure of the priors to advise them in a pressing issue.

Such a council, very informal in character, was called a *pratica,* and the pratica
came more and more into vogue in the oligarchic period because it was found
to lend itself admirably to the purposes of the ruling group. It would be entirely proper for the priors in seeking counsel to invite the secret party heads
to attend the pratica, and it would be equally proper for the party heads to
give their opinion. Their opinion would in reality, however, be a command
and would be understood as such by their puppets in the seats of authority.

Cavalcanti's story introduces us to a pratica called to discuss a question involving nothing less than peace and war. During the very lively and long-
drawn-out debate Niccolò da Uzzano, an outstanding member of the governing
junta, did not utter a single word, in fact he paid his respects to the debaters
by dropping into a deep sleep (*fortemente dormiva*). Aroused at last by a
neighbor to give his opinion, he managed with difficulty to shake himself
awake and, ascending the platform, briefly pronounced for war. No sooner had
he sat down than his view was unanimously approved.[2] Is any other judgment
possible than that the priors may have reigned but that the junta governed?

If in the light of these developments it will have to be agreed that the eclipse
of the old and proud executive, the priors, had begun, we should not fail to
see that their decline was not solely due to their having become the stalking-
horse of a secret governing group. In spite of apparent stability the Florentine
constitution was and had ever been in flux, and already during the recent
democratic period changes had been introduced which, continuing under the
oligarchy, gradually transferred to other bodies some of the powers originally
reserved to the priors. There, for instance, were the Eight, the *Otto di Guardia.*
It had long been the custom to appoint this committee in time of special peril
and to intrust it with the task of ferreting out the local enemies of the government, but in the period under consideration the Eight acquired a character of
permanence. Constituted as a secret police, they undoubtedly signified a measurable reduction of the sovereignty of the priors. A much more serious dimi-
nution, however, flowed from the Ten, the *Dieci di Balìa.* Whenever a war
threatened it became customary to appoint a war committee, the above-mentioned Ten, and to put the complete management of the war into their hands.
That meant the withdrawal of what had once been a leading interest of the
priors from their control. While the Otto and the Dieci, far from signifying a
loss in government efficiency, were probably an improvement on what had
gone before, they establish the contention that the impairment of the city's celebrated chief executive, the priors, had begun, and that it was in part brought
about by the desire to give the services of the state a greater measure of efficiency. A parallel decline may be observed in other characteristic features of the
old constitution. In the great days of the past the vitality of the Arno city had
found its most vigorous expression in the two large councils associated with the
podestà and captain. They continued to be called together as before and their
formal acceptance of a measure was still required ere it could become a law;
but as these councils with their widely representative membership were viewed
with suspicion by the oligarchy, which found it easier to operate with the informal pratica, the councils of podestà and captain imperceptibly lost credit

---

[2] Cavalcanti, *Istorie Fiorentine,* Book II, chap. I. 2 vols. Florence, 1838-39.

and showed it by a diminishing attendance. When, later, under the Medici this single family replaced the power of the oligarchic junta with its own, the enfeeblement of the constitution became so manifest that no one pretended any longer not to see it. But those writers who lay the collapse to the sole charge of the Medici are manifestly in error, since after the developments just detailed it cannot be denied that already under the oligarchy the hollowing-out of the constitution had made considerable headway.[3]

The very capable Maso degli Albizzi, around whom the governing group had chiefly cohered since its seizure of power, died in 1417. He was followed to the grave a few years later (1421) by Gino Capponi, who, another tower of merchant strength, was generally credited with the most popular single achievement of the period, the capture of Pisa, to be treated later on. With the death of Maso and Gino the burden of responsibility came to rest chiefly on the shoulders of Niccolò da Uzzano, one of the most widely respected and cultivated Italians of his generation. A colored terra cotta bust of him by Donatello is one of the great portrait busts of all time and reveals a man of alert and powerful intelligence (see p. 322). As Niccolò, on the passing of his two leading associates, was no longer young, he had no objection to sharing control with Rinaldo degli Albizzi, son of his former colleague, Maso. Rinaldo was endowed with high spirits, bore himself proudly, and possessed a ready and fiery eloquence. From among the practical, hard-headed products of the counting-house who made up the bulk of his party he stood out with the graces of a born gentleman and cavalier. His personal distinction recommended him as the elegant representative oligarch, suitable to be dispatched on embassies to the princes and governments of Italy. Accordingly, from early manhood Rinaldo had been employed on missions that sent him over the length and breadth of the peninsula. His many gifts coupled with his undoubted services tended to make him arrogant and to practice an aristocratic aloofness, than which it would be impossible to imagine a quality less in keeping with the solidity and earthiness of the typical Florentine business man. The brilliant Rinaldo was admired but not loved and his coming more and more to the front after the death of his father did not augur well for his party.[4]

So thoroughly, however, had the reforms carried through by the ruling

---

[3] The chronicler Dati in Book IX of his *Istoria di Firenze* gives an interesting review of all the public offices in his time. Amazing, however, is the circumstance that he never so much as mentions the secret control of the oligarchs and that he ascribes to the institutions he enumerates the free exercise of the functions with which they are endowed by law. It is an excellent example of the common human difficulty of distinguishing between shadow and reality.

[4] This is as good a place as any for a bibliographical note covering the material of this chapter. The most important source publication is *Commissioni di Rinaldo degli Albizzi per il Comune di Firenze dal 1399 al 1433* (Vols. I, II, III of the *Documenti di Storia Italiana*). Of the numerous chroniclers the most important are Morelli (Florence, 1785), Buonaccorso Pitti (Florence, 1720), Gregorio Dati (Florence, 1735), Domenico Boninsegni (Florence, 1637), Giovanni Cavalcanti (Florence, 1838-39). Machiavelli, who in his *History of Florence* treats the oligarchic episode with his unfailing liveliness and piquancy, should be employed with care, as he was content to take his facts without subjecting them to a critical re-examination from the above-mentioned chroniclers, chiefly from Cavalcanti. Ammirato was the first Florentine historian to offer a study of the period not exclusively based on the chroniclers, and his work is therefore still valuable. The general histories of Capponi, Perrens, and Caggese present much new material and are worth consulting not only for their facts but also for their astonishingly divergent estimates of the men and the issues of the period.

group—the great purges of 1387 and 1393 had been followed by further, some-what less vigorous cures—crushed their antagonists that, as we approach the period of Rinaldo's dominance, there was no longer so much as a trace of an organized opposition. But that did not signify that the regime was without enemies. Among the poor and the oppressed the ancient discontent lived on in undiminished energy. It prompted them to hope for a deliverer, and from the beginning of the fifteenth century they began to see in that light a man who was coming more and more to the front as the leading banker of the town. This was Giovanni di Bicci de' Medici. A generation before a Medici, Salvestro by name, for reasons that can no longer be clearly disentangled, had sounded the tocsin that started the famous revolution of 1378; and since that time the common people would not have it other than that Salvestro and his whole clan were warmly enlisted on their side. Giovanni, who was not a descendant of the prosperous Salvestro, belonged to a branch of the family which had only recently in the person of Giovanni's father, Bicci, risen from obscurity. Relying on the gifts with which nature had endowed him, Giovanni had de-voted himself wholeheartedly to business, which still meant, as had always been the case in Florence, the union of money-lending with the purchase and sale of goods. By slow degrees he succeeded in piling up a fortune, which as he entered the middle period of his life equaled and possibly overtopped that of any of his fellow-citizens. Although thus economically identified with the ruling oligarchs, he had so recently risen from the ranks and was so patently a *novus homo* that men of older wealth looked down upon him as an upstart. As he was greatly absorbed by his private affairs and gave no hint of enter-taining any political ambitions, he apparently did not much mind his exclu-sion from the inner circle of the optimates. Added to his being a Medici, a family supposed to nurse democratic sentiments, his marked exclusion from the councils of the mighty confirmed the inclination of the people to look up to him as their leader. On making their attitude known to him, however, they met with no encouragement. We have only to look at Giovanni's picture in the family portrait gallery recently arranged in the palace built by his son Cosimo to have an adequate explanation of his course. We are confronted with the homely visage of a shrewd, unimaginative trader as far removed as possible from the traditional conception of a merchant prince. The most conspicuous feature is the set jaw, the hard effect of which is softened by a general expres-sion of troubled kindliness. We can imagine this commonplace individual moving among the people without the least display of condescension; but we cannot conceive his letting himself be persuaded to stake his hard-won fortune in a hazardous gamble for political power.[5]

The political quietism of Giovanni di Bicci explains why the oligarchs took no protective measures against him. Perhaps as a gesture of appeasement toward his supporters they even admitted him to the honors of office, for he served repeatedly as prior; in 1414 he was a member of the important war committee, the Dieci; and in 1421 he was promoted to the highest office of the state, the gonfalonierat of Justice. When his son Cosimo reached manhood he

[5] The portrait is reproduced in G. Pieraccini, *La Stirpe dei Medici di Caffagiolo* (p. 239), 3 vols. Florence, 1925. This is perhaps the most important single work on the Medici.

was treated with the same consideration. Suspicion no doubt spun its spider web between Giovanni and the ruling junta, a suspicion inseparable from the conditions of his rise to prominence, but that there existed an incurable enmity is a postulate based on developments belonging to the period after Giovanni's death. Nothing proves the absence of an inalterable hostility better than the great issue of taxation which arose toward the end of Giovanni's life in consequence of a fresh and peculiarly grinding war with Milan. By continuing for years the war swallowed up enormous sums and laid a burden of taxation on the people under which they threatened to succumb. We are aware that from the early fourteenth century a financial system was in use which favored the wealthy by raising the ordinary revenues of the state through a mass of indirect taxes called gabelle. On pressing occasions, like war, forced loans or prestanze were voted which were so irregularly and capriciously levied on the propertied classes that they caused the greatest bitterness and indignation. The clamor for a direct tax based on an exact estimate of the wealth of every citizen had never ceased to make itself heard, but the well-to-do had always succeeded in averting the measure.[6]

Thus matters stood when there arose the financial crisis of the twenties caused by a war with Milan, of which we shall presently hear more. After hot and prolonged debates in the various councils the long-desired reform was at last adopted. It was based on what were probably the broadest and most equitable principles of taxation which thus far had been evolved by any European state. Known from the register of the assessments as the *catasto,* the new tax became a law in 1427. Because direct taxation is always associated with democratic tendencies, it will never cease to cause surprise that the catasto was adopted by an oligarchy. For Machiavelli, who loved to reduce history to weighty precepts and epigrams but was averse to the time-robbing occupation of investigating the facts, the problem had little difficulty. He declared that the catasto was favored by Giovanni de' Medici and was carried by pressure from him and his popular following. It was so plausible an explanation that it early became an outstanding item of the accepted Florentine tradition. And it would still be accepted had it not occurred to a nineteenth-century scholar to verify the statement by turning to the record of the original debates.[7] These revealed to him that plausibility was a poor substitute for the facts, for to his amazement he learned that the catasto enjoyed the support of most of the oligarchs themselves and notably of Rinaldo degli Albizzi and Niccolò da Uzzano, whereas the attitude toward it of Giovanni di Bicci was often negative and never better than lukewarm. We cannot get around crediting the catasto in the main to the ruling junta, but we need not be at a loss for an explanation. The Milanese war was their war, the revenues had inescapably to be raised, and in the existing emergency there was no course open but for every man of means to dip into his pocket. Another circumstance may have had a certain weight. Although the new system put an end to many special favors hitherto enjoyed by the well-to-do, it retained a feature of the prestanze

---

[6] See chap. XVI.
[7] The scholar is P. Berti. See "Nuovi Documenti intorno al Catasto Fiorentino," *Giornale Storico degli Archivi Toscani,* Vol. IV, pp. 32-62.

which in the past had accounted for such favor as this levy enjoyed with the upper classes. Exactly as in the case of the prestanze the money paid under the catasto was declared to have the character of a repayable, interest-bearing loan. It was, in the current phrase, "written on the Monte," that is, it was regularly entered in the registers of the National Debt.

According to the law of 1427 every citizen was obliged to make a declaration of his possessions of every kind, gold, silver, jewels, houses, farms, animals, rents, mortgages, and capital employed in commerce. The declaration was subject to review by a tax commission, which after correcting the figures and permitting deductions for debts, house rent, and family maintenance, regarded the remainder as interest-bearing capital. On the assumption that the capital would yield 5 per cent, or five florins for every hundred florins, there was imposed a levy of one-tenth of every five florins of calculated income. Accordingly, while the system was called the catasto, the levy itself was known as the Tenth or *decima*. Precisely like the earlier prestanza, the decima was supposed to be raised only in cases of emergency such as war. While in time of peace it might not be demanded for years, on the other hand with the state engaged in an expensive conflict it might be levied repeatedly within the course of a few months.[8] To sum up: the decima was an income tax marking a vast advance in social justice since it fell substantially on the well-to-do, passed the poor by entirely, and exacted from those whose legitimate expenses were approximately equal to their earnings no more than a nominal sum imposed by the assessors.

Since the catasto was imposed by the oligarchy we cannot escape the view that it must have added to the prestige enjoyed by the rulers among the people. If, notwithstanding, the oligarchy fell only a few years afterward, it was for the commonest reason known for the collapse of governments: it engaged in an unsuccessful war. Therewith we are back in the realm of foreign policy, into the general character of which during the merchant supremacy we looked at the beginning of the chapter. We there learned that great states were taking shape all over Italy, and that Florence itself was aspiring to be a great state founded on the undisputed control of Tuscany. For all these governments alike, war was an accepted tool of policy. In the case of Florence it might be resorted to either for offense in Tuscany or for defense against any other state attempting to get a foothold in that province.

The first war of the oligarchic period was of a defensive order and was directed against Gian Galeazzo Visconti. This astonishing lord of Milan had seized the power in the northern metropolis by an act of unconscionable treachery against members of his own family, and, following up this measure by alternately playing the fox and the lion, he had made himself master of Lombardy up to the barrier of the Apennines. When he next revolved a plan to burst across this impediment into Umbria and Tuscany, Florence became alarmed and challenged his advance. The ensuing war began in the year 1390 and lasted, with trucelike interruptions of often considerable length, for

---

[8] The law regulating the catasto was published by G. F. Pagnini in Vol. I, pp. 214-31, of his work *Della Decima e di Varie Altre Gravezze Imposte dal Comune di Firenze*. 4 vols. Lisbon-Lucca, 1765-66. The author gives a good summary of the law on p. 17.

twelve years. Although frequently checked, Gian Galeazzo, a man of the most stubborn determination, would not be denied. Having at last acquired Perugia, Siena, and Pisa, he drew a ring of iron around Florence which threatened to throttle it into submission. In June, 1402, the Milanese tyrant completely closed the ring by the capture of the city of Bologna. In the face of this situation even the most sanguine citizens hardly dared hope that they would succeed in maintaining their independence. But before the expected disaster occurred Florence was saved by the sudden taking-off of Gian Galeazzo by the pest. At the news of the event the conqueror's vast dominion, held together solely by force, fell violently apart. Gian Galeazzo had left behind him as his heirs two boys who, when the precipitate defections were at last arrested, found their possessions reduced to the original kernel of the Visconti dominion.

The sudden relaxation of Milanese pressure gave Florence the opportunity to resume the construction of its Tuscan empire. Ever since their return to power in 1382 the greater gilds, the original exponents of territorial expansion, had been on the lookout to strengthen their position in the Arno Valley. They had at once directed their attention to Arezzo which, because of irreconcilable local strife, had become the prey of a succession of military adventurers. In the year 1384 the soldier in temporary possession, a Frenchman, De Coucy by name, let himself be persuaded to sell his prize to Florence for 40,000 gold florins. Although repeatedly before this time in Florentine control, Arezzo had always managed to wrest itself free again. On taking renewed possession of the key position on the upper Arno the Florentines turned their eyes more hungrily than ever toward Pisa occupying a corresponding position on the lower Arno. The long crisis connected with Gian Galeazzo had obliged them to control their appetite; but when on Gian Galeazzo's demise Pisa, which he had brought under his scepter, was awarded as a sort of consolation prize to a third son, the illegitimate Gabriele Maria, they thought the opportunity had come to satisfy their desire.

The new lord of Pisa was a young, ill-governed foreigner, who lost the favor of his subjects almost at once by burdening them with exorbitant taxes. When the Florentines judged that his position was becoming precarious, they drew him into secret negotiations with a view to relieving him of his troublesome signory for money paid in hand. On the Pisans getting wind of the treacherous action of their ruler they rose against him as one man and drove him from the city. The old love of independence still burned in their hearts and the blackest fate that could befall them in their eyes was to fall a prey to that town which had been sleeplessly plotting their destruction for two hundred years. But Florence was no less determined than its intended victim. It brought its negotiations with the deposed Gabriele Maria to a close by paying him 200,000 florins for his title, which, on thus being transferred to them, somewhat naïvely for such old hands at the imperialist game they expected the Pisans to honor. The spontaneous rising of the Pisans against Gabriele Maria and the acceptance by the deposed lord of the Florentine bribe belong to the summer of 1405. When the Florentines now sent commissioners to take possession of their purchase, the Pisans naturally refused to receive them; and just as inevitably the truculent imperialists from the middle Arno declared war to enforce what they were pleased stubbornly to call their rights. They began a siege of Pisa which drew so impenetrable a hedge around the city that a terrible famine gripped the population. When it could no longer be borne it brought the exhausted city to its knees. On October 9, 1406, Pisa and its very considerable territory passed into Florentine control. Perrens and other historians of Florence before and after him have indignantly denounced the Pisan war as an immoral enterprise. On the other hand, they have not hesitated to ascribe a sound moral basis to the wars fought against Gian Galeazzo and other ambitious princes. To anyone who lifts himself to a height above the murky atmosphere of Italian statecraft it becomes difficult to classify the wars of the Italian states as either moral or immoral, for none of them were waged on any discoverable ethical principle or for any consideration whatever other than that of power. It must certainly be conceded that Florence at all times shaped its policy with a view to playing an ever larger and larger part in the Italian world. The reception it gave the news that Pisa had passed under its yoke was therefore exactly suited to its power outlook. All the chroniclers are agreed that the much-divided population of greater gilds, lesser gilds, magnates, proletariat, and beggars was converted into a single happy family which literally went mad with joy.

There can be no doubt that the acquisition of Pisa added greatly to the reputation and resources of the Florentine state. The city now enjoyed the long-desired unhampered access to the sea. Enabled to appropriate the ancient Levantine connections of the Pisans, it rose to a distinguished position in many a Mediterranean port and notably at Constantinople. But Pisa itself sickened and shriveled. While its decline was partly owing to the hostile measures of the victors, who had no desire to see the vanquished town recover its strength, it followed partly also from natural causes largely beyond human control. Because of the continued silting of the mouth of the Arno, Pisa was already at the time of its capture some five miles from the coast. The Pisans themselves had attempted to remedy the situation by constructing a harbor farther down stream called Porto Pisano. But Porto Pisano, too, was an unsatisfactory location compared with Livorno directly on the coast a few miles south of the river and therefore safe from the river's vagaries. While the advantages of Livorno were not fully recognized for another hundred years and while therefore Pisa and its harbor remained the chief objective of Florentine ambition, it was already clear that Livorno must under no circumstances be overlooked. However, owing to a succession of accidents too involved to follow here, at the time of Pisa's capture by Florence Livorno was in Genoese hands. In their watchful way the Florentines awaited the auspicious moment and in 1421 acquired Livorno by purchase, the route for which they, as merchants and not warriors, had a natural predilection. Then only did they come into the unconditional possession of the main Tuscan coast.

Our growing town had enjoyed its Pisan laurels only a few years when it was again obliged to defend itself against attack from without. This time the blow threatened not from the north, as had thus far been usually the case, but from the south. A young and vigorous king of Naples, Ladislaus by name, was seized with the desire to imitate Duke Gian Galeazzo and bring as much of Italy as possible under his scepter. His initial advance was relatively easy, for the first opposition to a northward thrust on his part would be offered by the State of the Church. As this was the time of the Great Schism, the church was divided between two popes, one of whom made his capital at Rome, the other at Avignon. It was the Roman pontiff with whom Ladislaus was obliged to deal, and this ruler's position was so feeble that he could offer Ladislaus no serious resistance. It will confirm our view of the papal weakness if we note at this point that the state forged by Cardinal Albornoz a little past the middle of the fourteenth century had again fallen apart into a score of practically independent towns and principalities. King Ladislaus began his aggressions in the year 1408 by occupying the papal capital. From Rome as his base he gradually extended the range of his enterprise until it looked as if the whole of Peter's patrimony was destined to fall into his hands. At this turn Florence, bristling with alarm, bestirred itself to organize a league against the conqueror. The plan cleverly concocted by the league was to support the claim of a rival family to the Neapolitan throne. This family was headed by the duke of Anjou, a Frenchman, and he was put forward in the hope of creating difficulties for Ladislaus which would keep him in the south fighting Anjou and Anjou's partisans.

We shall not follow the Neapolitan war, which, as usual, was made up of a thousand and one confusing minor incidents. As usual, too, it was waged to the accompaniment of treacherous secret negotiations on the part of all the participants. One of these reprehensible arrangements, however, needs to be mentioned, for it led to Florence abandoning its allies and being rewarded for its treachery by the cession of the town of Cortona, which Ladislaus had seized. It was in January, 1411, that Florence was enabled to add Cortona to its dominion; nonetheless the bribe did not stick, since before many months had passed the City of the Red Lily was again in the field against the king. It could hardly do otherwise if it desired to survive as an independent commonwealth, for Ladislaus was a capable soldier and subtle diplomat who had set his heart on dominating Italy. The renewed war exposed Florence to a peril hardly inferior to that which had threatened a decade before from Duke Gian Galeazzo of Milan, and again, as in the earlier case, the city was saved by what patriots of the devouter sort hailed as an act of divine interference. On August 6, 1414, after a brief illness, Ladislaus died in the full flower of manhood.

On this rescue from extreme jeopardy there followed a rare and blessed interval of peace which lasted for eight years and was not terminated until Gian Galeazzo's heir, Duke Filippo Maria, having got his Milanese dominion well in hand, with much of his father's persistence but with little of his skill, resumed his father's policy of conquest. By 1422 his aggressions in the neighboring Romagna had become so dangerous that Florence, no longer able to ignore them, resorted to war. The struggle, which continued for years, went cruelly against the Arno city until in 1426 it succeeded in gaining Venice as an ally. Straightway the theater of war was shifted to the north, where the forces of Venice won such a succession of victories that in April, 1428, Filippo Maria was obliged to come to terms with both his adversaries. By this peace

Florence got no more than the restitution of the strongholds which had been taken away from her, but victorious Venice was enabled to push its boundary westward beyond Brescia, thus giving it control of the whole northeastern section of the peninsula. By far the most memorable incident of the war was the domestic event already recorded, for the prolonged struggle occasioned a financial crisis which in the year 1427 led to the adoption of the famous reform measure of the catasto.

It might be thought that, after the strain and agony of the grinding conflict with Duke Filippo Maria, Florence would have been glad to enjoy a long repose. It was not so. In the very next year, in 1429, without either provocation or excuse the city deliberately set out to conquer Lucca and its territory. Although the oligarchy directed the struggle and must accept responsibility for it, there is no denying that the whole population, eager to round off its Tuscan dominion, clamored for war with such unanimity that there was no resisting the general madness. Shortly before the Lucchese issue arose, on February 20, 1429, death carried off Giovanni di Bicci de' Medici, and his son Cosimo became the head of the house. As he had inherited his father's solid burgher qualities, coupling with them a much more lively interest in politics, he continued to be regarded by the common people as their spokesman. When the question of the Lucchese enterprise arose, Cosimo, perhaps from natural caution, was disinclined to support the war party, but he accepted the war wholeheartedly as soon as he saw the uselessness of standing out against so general a demand. That other prominent Florentines, however, from the very first vehemently egged the citizenry on to war is undeniable. Among them on the Medicean side was Cosimo's influential cousin, Averardo de' Medici, on the side of the oligarchy, Rinaldo degli Albizzi and Neri Capponi, the brilliant son of Gino Capponi, to whom the acquisition of Pisa had been mainly due. With frank admiration we learn, however, that the fine old merchant and statesman, Niccolò da Uzzano, employed all his authority and eloquence to turn his fellow-citizens from their purpose. While he labored to no avail, his courageous stand makes it forever impossible to represent the Lucchese war as an enterprise of the united oligarchs.

The war against Lucca got off to a bad start and was pursued by the most exasperating ill fortune. As happens everywhere and always, the people blamed the failure of the campaign on the government and the government in last analysis meant the oligarchic junta. And without any doubt the successive thrusts against Lucca were attended by a degree of mismanagement which even in Florence, accustomed to mismanaged wars, was unique. However, the maladministration cannot be fairly laid to the exclusive charge of Rinaldo degli Albizzi and his immediate following, for on the Dieci, the Ten, intrusted according to custom with the conduct of the war, oligarchs and Mediceans sat side by side. The capital mistake effectively accounting for all the subsequent ills was made at the outset and was of a political and diplomatic rather than of a military order. It consisted in the assumption that Lucca was weak and small, had no friends, and would fall at the first assault. But owing to the Italian power situation with which we have made ample acquaintance, every neighbor of Florence begrudged it its prospective increase in territory.

The doctrine on this head was (and for that matter still is) that no state entangled with a group of rivals in a struggle for eminence may add as much as a frog pond to its territory without first offering an equivalent frog pond to its competitors. Therefore, no sooner had Florence launched its attack on Lucca than neighboring Siena came to Lucca's aid, although not openly at first in order not unnecessarily to expose itself. Should Lucca fall a prey to Florence, Siena would be the only remaining free town of Tuscany, and it took no prophet to foresee what in that event would happen to the small upland state. In case any Sienese doubters needed to be convinced of what was in store for their city, the street urchins of Florence might have enlightened them, for they went about the city singing: *ave Maria, grazia piena; avuto Lucca, avremo Siena.*[9] They travestied the common prayer to the Virgin to serve notice that with Lucca conquered Siena was next on the list. In its justified alarm Siena communicated with Duke Filippo Maria of Milan, who was nothing loath to make trouble for the hated Red Lily. In short, by wantonly attacking Lucca Florence brought on itself another Milanese war as expensive and far-reaching as the one it had just terminated. It hired unreliable condottieri, although probably as good as any in the market, was defeated before Lucca by an army sent by the Milanese duke to Lucca's relief, had its territory brutally ravaged by the troops of the northern tyrant, and in the end was glad to make peace on the promise faithfully to respect the independence of its little neighbor on the Serchio.

The treaty concluding the Lucchese war was signed on May 10, 1433. While the negotiators were still haggling over its terms, the most respected and authoritative of the oligarchs, Niccolò da Uzzano, had passed from among the living. The event left Rinaldo degli Albizzi to defend the regime against the flood of criticism set in motion by the Lucchese disaster. There would of course be much talk of a change of government, and the opponents of the ruling sect, who had grown vastly in number and daring, would not hesitate to put forward as their candidate Cosimo de' Medici. Apparently Cosimo was not overpleased with the ardor of his followers, for when in June the term of the war committee, the Dieci, of whom he was one, came to an end, he abandoned the turmoil of the city and retired to his country place in the distant Mugello. But Rinaldo's suspicions against his rival were kept alive by the murmurs of the citizens, and he could not but feel the ground quaking under his feet. When the new priors, who entered on office on September 1, were found in their majority to be friendly to him and to have at their head as gonfalonier of Justice a man completely devoted to his interest, he resolved to act. Cosimo was recalled to Florence by a message, equivalent to an order, from the signory, and on being summoned to the palace on September 7 was put under arrest. He was confined in a small stone chamber high in the palace tower, whence through a tiny window he could look down on the central piazza and watch the constitutional comedy which his enemies now proceeded to stage. For with their victim in their hands Rinaldo and his friends took the step which had

[9] Cavalcanti, Libro VI, chap. 18.

long ago become the measure preliminary to every act of juridical violence or governmental change. On September 9 they summoned a parliament of the usual packed order and had it vote supreme power to a balìa of two hundred men. Then the balìa sat down to determine Cosimo's fate.

While some voices were heard that demanded the death of the prisoner, there were others which, in view of his great popularity and the excited state of the public mind, counseled moderation. A few soft-treading politicians, after the nature of their kind through all the ages of the world, were in favor of putting him secretly away. That Cosimo, who may be supposed to have known his countrymen, suspected that this would be the course adopted and that he was about to be removed quietly by poison is proved by the circumstance that he refused to eat the food supplied to him in his cell. Only after his keeper declared his readiness to share his meals with him was he reassured. Meanwhile the debate over his fate went on in the balìa and gradually opinion swung toward exile (confino) as, after all, the more usual sentence following political defeat. The story that Cosimo strengthened the sentiment for moderation by a bribe of money secretly conveyed to the hostile gonfalonier, although only a story, may well be true. In any case when at last on September 29 the verdict was reached, it was to the effect that Cosimo, his brother Lorenzo, and a few of the more outstanding Medicean partisans were to be banished to various cities of Italy. A few days later Cosimo was taken under guard to the frontier. He made his way to Venice which received him more in the manner of a great prince upon his travels than of a discredited and exiled commoner.

On Cosimo's departure it became apparent that the impulsive Rinaldo had not gained very much, since the opposition to him waxed rather than waned in strength. Henceforth his power hinged on the chance of his having a favorable signory; and since the signory was renewed every two months he could never be really at peace. When a year after Cosimo's fall, on September 1, 1434, a body of priors entered office who in their majority were hostile to him, his power collapsed overnight. The new government took steps at once to recall the banished Cosimo. In his desperation Rinaldo resolved to drive his enemies out of the palace and take the government into his own hands. He assembled an armed following, but the signory, warned of his action, occupied the piazza with troops. When the temperamental oligarch, checkmated, permitted himself to be drawn into negotiations, he showed that he lacked the unshaken resolution of the born leader of men. It happened that Pope Eugene IV had taken refuge in Florence at this time and was residing at the Dominican monastery of Santa Maria Novella. Eugene offered to mediate between the factions in order to make peace and at the pope's request Rinaldo paid him a visit in his chambers. At this exhibition of pusillanimity his disgusted followers dispersed to their homes and his cause was lost. Thereupon the scene was re-enacted with which we are familiar to the point of weariness as the customary accompaniment of every political crisis: a parliament was called, the constitution was suspended, and a balìa of three hundred Medicean partisans was empowered to reform the government. On September 29 the balìa decreed Cosimo's recall and in the course of the next few days visited banishment on Rinaldo and his most compromised adherents. In exactly one year to the day the wheel of fortune had come full circle round. On October 5 Cosimo re-entered Florentine territory and was welcomed by his fellow-citizens like a conqueror returning from the wars. The government was in his hands and for the present at least he was free to do with it as he saw fit.

XXI. The Government of Cosimo de' Medici

MPORTANT a landmark as is the return of Cosimo de' Medici from
exile in 1434, it has not quite the significance which has been assigned
to it by many, especially of the older historians of Florence. For them,
instead of a landmark, the event was rather in the nature of a chasm by
which the history of Florence falls sharply into two periods labeled respectively Before and After the Medici. For this clean-cut dichotomy there would
be some justification if, as indeed these same historians generally maintain,
Florence before the Medici had been a free republic and immediately on the
appearance of the Medici had passed under the yoke of a tyrant. Nothing,
however, would be less well founded than such a contention. We have seen
that at no time of its history had Florence made a conspicuous success of the
democratic tendencies which it undoubtedly nourished; and when in the
fourteenth century the lesser gilds had set up the closest approximation to a
democratic government Florence ever achieved, the experiment broke down
in 1382 before the attack of the greater gilds. These thereupon resumed control; or rather, under cover of the authority belonging constitutionally to the
body of twenty-one gilds, a group of associated merchant families created an
alert and jealous oligarchy. So ruthlessly did the oligarchic junta, to which the
family of the Albizzi has lent its name, manipulate the constitution that for the
half-century the junta lasted the constitution functioned not with its own
energy but with that supplied by a sect or party. And if the Albizzeschi had
remained united under firm and, above all, elastic leadership, it is very doubtful that they would have been overthrown when they were.

The governing group of the Albizzi yielded its place in 1434 to Cosimo de'
Medici, who as much under the pressure of circumstances as by reason of his
political ambition had become the head of a group of rival families. These had
in the main only recently acquired their wealth and were for this very reason
more daring and ruthless than the older families which gathered around the
Albizzi. To all appearances it was they, much more than Cosimo, who were
responsible for the orgy of vengeance in which they indulged against their
defeated predecessors on beginning their rule. While the earliest victims of the
Medicean revolution, among them Rinaldo degli Albizzi himself, got off with
the usual sentence of exile, the animosity of the victors grew as they realized
the completeness of their triumph. Thereupon not only did they multiply the
banishments far beyond recent Florentine practice but they gave themselves

the added satisfaction of spilling the blood of a considerable number of their enemies by sending them to the block. The forceful suppression of opponents had been a feature of every successful Florentine revolution and the indispensable concomitant measure was the adoption of constitutional "reforms" calculated to give the victory a desirable permanence. It is when we examine the alterations in the constitution effected by the victors that the chasm reputed to yawn between pre- and post-Medicean history should become visible. But no one has ever succeeded in detecting it nor has any objective observer ever come to any other conclusion than that the new government was the old government operated by a different set of beneficiaries. We must conclude that the Mediceans saw no reason for changing the system of control elaborated by their predecessors; and it is a fact that they took it over and made it their own with but a single important change.

The single change, however, so patly rounded out the inherited system that it must be given close attention. The control which had been elaborated by the oligarchs had, as its central feature, the periodical revision of the borse by means of a new scrutiny. As a new scrutiny was impossible without authorization, this was obtained from a commission or balìa to which a packed assembly of the people held in the public square voted full powers. It looked like an air-tight system and was air-tight, except for the fact that the men whose names went into the purses on the supposition that they could be depended on were liable, especially during a political crisis, to change their opinion. That was what on the occasion of the September drawings of the year 1434 had ruined Rinaldo degli Albizzi, for he found himself confronted with, and helpless before, a signory of Medicean complexion. On Cosimo and his friends taking over the power they were resolved not to be hoist by the same petard. They therefore had the balìa, authorized by the parliament called by them, appoint a subcommittee of ten *accoppiatori* who were to serve for five years with the power to choose the new priorate every two months from among the names in the purses. This process of election, which won the appropriate designation *a mano* (by hand), completely removed the danger inseparable from an election by lot. By the simple device of reappointing the accoppiatori at the expiration of their term for another five-year period, a hand-picked signory was or seemed to be assured for an indefinite time.

To repeat: while the accoppiatori represent the finishing touch applied to an older system of control, it is absurd to maintain that only with their appointment was the Florentine constitution denatured. It had been more or less flagrantly manhandled practically from its birth and indisputably from the time of the adoption of the practice of choosing the signory by lot. From the very start of this system an evil inseparable from a resort to chance as a method of appointing magistrates had made itself felt. This was the elevation to office of a high percentage of the flagrantly incompetent. If to this evil we add the perilous flux imposed on the executive department by the brief two months' term of office, we shall be disposed to agree that anything approaching a considered and consistent governmental policy had become impossible. The plain truth is the constitution did not work; and Florence would have suffered incalculable harm if a group of men of substantially the same outlook and loosely formed into a party had not by variously devised subterfuges brought the recurrent drawings from the purses under control. The surprising thing is not that these practices, already old before the Medici came to power and merely perfected by them, should have been in vogue, but that commentators on Florentine affairs down to our time should have bewailed the trickery employed as an unpardonable crime. From the strict point of view of law it undoubtedly was a crime; but we follow a much more fruitful line of reflection when we take note that a political system, so offensive to the most rudimentary demands of common sense as this of Florence, cannot be maintained and that, if it cannot by legal means be adjusted to the most immediate needs of society, a way will unfailingly be found to circumvent it.

Among the most immediate needs of the Florentine state we can distinguish between a domestic and a foreign need and agree that in regard to either a much greater stability was desirable than the constitution afforded. The ten accoppiatori represent the Medicean contribution to stability in the domestic field. The importance attached to this contribution by its sponsors is made clear when we observe that the leading Mediceans, such men as Agnolo Acciaiuoli, Neri Capponi, and Diotisalvi Neroni, served regularly as accoppiatori. But what is surprising at first blush, Cosimo de' Medici himself was not on this decisive committee. The sufficient reason for this self-effacement was that, although leader of the victorious party, he was regarded by his jealous fellow-oligarchs as their equal and was obliged to tread warily; above all, he had to share the power with them and scrupulously to guard against the impression of being, or even of wanting to be, a tyrant of the type that had come to the top everywhere else in Italy. He therefore left the accoppiatori, the priorate, and most of the other honors of state as their due spoils to his associates. Except for his having been gonfalonier of Justice three times, in 1435, in 1439, and in 1445, thereby serving a total of six months as chief executive during a control of thirty years, he never held a high state office. However, if he was at pains to conciliate his followers, he had not the least intention to surrender control to them or to let them get out of hand and run amuck. First and foremost he was resolved that they should not harden into too close a corporation. It was this congealing into a narrow-minded caste that had been the undoing of the Albizzeschi. In measure as members of the lower ranks of society endowed with intelligence and energy amassed new fortunes they were to be admitted to the ruling circle. While government was to continue to be an affair of the few, it was Cosimo's intention that the reigning body of optimates should be constantly refreshed with new blood. As a result he had the ambitious, and the ambitious meant the alert and dangerous, rising young men of the common people on his side, for he placed no obstacle in the way of their aspiration to join the ruling junta and achieve the honors of office.

If by his readiness to welcome talent into the governing set Cosimo acquired something of the reputation of a democrat, he added to this report in other, still more effective ways. For, wisely, he never forgot that he owed much of his success to his and his family's popularity with the lower orders and that these orders, although their direct share in the government had by now become unimportant, still counted considerably in the general political equation.

Like the typical Florentine burgher he was, Cosimo had always practiced an easy familiarity with his fellow-citizens of high and low degree alike. A manner more removed from social snobbery than that of this most eminent banker of his day could not be imagined. Following his accession to power, he continued to dress, talk, and show himself in street and square exactly as before. Aware of the awed regard in which he was held owing to his great wealth, he had the intelligence to recognize that money by itself does not offer assurance of continued respect, and that in order to win abiding honor with his opulence he would have to spend it generously on enterprises of a public character. Accordingly he devoted immense sums to the building of churches and the founding of monasteries and libraries; and since by these creations he added to the beauty and fame of Florence among Italian cities, the people, to whom the glory of their town meant much, rewarded him with a lively affection. Floated into power on a wave of popular approval, the Medicean party steadily strengthened its hold on the people, and for this invaluable backing by the masses it was exclusively indebted to its calculating, intelligent head.

In view of the influence of Cosimo both over the Florentine masses and his own oligarchical party we will readily concede that his person was a large factor in the domestic stability of Florence after 1434, even though he himself avoided rather than sought office. But when it came to foreign policy he did not dare trust to a system of indirect control to achieve the stability absolutely indispensable in this field; for, since the state of Florence had by Cosimo's time become involved in a perilous power situation, its very existence was momently at stake. So difficult, complicated, and dangerous had its relations with its Italian neighbors become that they could no longer, save at the greatest risk, be intrusted to an ever-changing plural executive like the Florentine signory. Cosimo therefore quietly but unhesitatingly appropriated this all-important department for himself. Of course he preserved appearances as much as possible and did nothing calculated unnecessarily to offend the dignity of the official heads of the state, the priors. But, in effect, he assumed the office of minister of foreign affairs, and his fine new palace in the Via Larga became the unofficial foreign office of the state. It was a delicate situation, for while it was he who shaped the foreign policy of Florence, the policy had to have the support of the constituted authorities, the priors with the gonfalonier of Justice at their head and the numerous councils. The signory, wholly composed of party nominees, was generally easy to manage, but the councils, in which public opinion continued to make itself heard, were frequently a source of embarrassment to the self-appointed foreign minister. In the end the deft and affable but steady and persistent Cosimo always imposed his will and, as long as he lived, both projected and steered the course which Florence followed among the Italian states.

Further to insure the control of the state under his hand Cosimo could not afford to overlook the public finances. They were to an eminent degree centered in the Monte, the administration of the National Debt. Cosimo insisted on serving in person on the board of directors, and as often as his term expired had himself reappointed. This was, therefore, in sharp distinction from his management of foreign policy, a service performed in the open. That Cosimo, whose position in regard to Florence and whose conduct in reference to his party have frequently invited a comparison between him and a modern American city boss, should, in the matter of the Monte, have departed from the secrecy which was his element and still is that of his American counterpart, proves the great importance he attached to an immediate influence over the public monies. Naturally his enemies made his connection with the Monte, the one point at which his carefully concealed association with the state machinery became visible, the main object of their attack. They tried repeatedly to eliminate him from the board, but, never quite succeeding, took revenge by circulating every conceivable slander against his integrity. Cavalcanti reports that they went so far as to spread the whisper that Cosimo treated not only the monies of the Monte but even the ordinary revenues of the state as his personal property, and that he had the gabelle, that is, the receipts from the consumption taxes levied at the gates, deposited every night at his house.[1] While the gossip purveyed by Cavalcanti should not be taken too literally, it has the merit of disclosing the malignant quality of the underground opposition which Cosimo had to face throughout his days.

The foreign policy of Cosimo was determined by considerations, first, of the safety and, second, of the possible enlargement of the Florentine state and was elastically adjusted to the ever-shifting situation within the Italian peninsula. It would be as tedious as it is unnecessary to trace the innumerable oscillations of his policy, especially as, in view of its set central purpose, it can without practicing any violence be reduced to a relatively simple pattern. On Cosimo's taking over the department of foreign affairs the outstanding feature of the Italian situation was the fixed resolution of Duke Filippo Maria of Milan to enlarge his dominions. To meet the threat from Milan Cosimo's predecessors, the Albizzeschi, had allied themselves with Venice, and to this alliance the new ruler gave a ready adherence as it was the only available means for holding the Lombard ruler in check. The duke was a savage and restless tyrant who, served by the most famous condottieri of the age, continually renewed his thrust, on the one hand into Tuscany, and on the other into the Romagna, the exposed northern province of the State of the Church. In consequence, even though the alliance between the two city-republics proved strong enough to repel his aggressions, the peace of Italy was permanently disturbed. The papacy was too weak to contribute greatly to the defense of its territory, which was at the mercy not only of the enterprising duke but also of every impudent leader of mercenaries disposed to invade the patrimony of Peter with the intention of carving out a dominion for himself. Shortly before Cosimo's return from exile Pope Eugene IV, unable any longer to maintain himself in his own capital, had taken up his residence at Florence as the city's guest. Under these painful circumstances the papacy did not, for the time being at least, count for much in the Italian situation. The kingdom of Naples, too, had been temporarily eliminated, owing to the fact that on the death, on February 2, 1435, of the childless Queen Joan the succession to the throne precipitated a contest between King Alfonso of Aragon and the French

---

[1] Cavalcanti, Vol. II, chap. 33 (Seconda Storia).

duke of Anjou, the dead queen's distant relative. War followed between the two claimants which after many years was decided in favor of Alfonso; however, while the civil struggle lasted, the southern kingdom did not and could not make its power felt in the general situation.

Under these circumstances easily the most important event of peninsular scope during the early years of Medicean control was the struggle of the duke of Milan to penetrate the powerful defensive ring drawn about him by Florence and Venice. Battles were won and lost, the hireling condottieri frequently changed sides on the offer of better pay, treaties among the combatants were signed only to be broken—in the agitated succession of trivial events in field and council chamber there is no happening calculated to impress itself on our mind till we come to 1440. In that year Duke Filippo Maria at last lent an ear to the repeated representations made to him by Rinaldo degli Albizzi and the other Florentine exiles and dispatched an army under the famous general Piccinino directly against the Arno city. According to the exiles this army would only have to appear before the walls for the Florentines to rise in a spontaneous movement of rebellion against the hated Medicean tyranny. It was indeed a critical moment for Cosimo when the Milanese host, bursting through the barriers of the Apennines, sifted down the valleys of the Mugello range and appeared on the heights of Fiesole directly over the city. Nonetheless, contrary to the confident boast of Rinaldo and his band, the Florentine population did not so much as lift a finger against its reputed tyrant, and Piccinino, incapable of conducting the siege of so large a town, was compelled to withdraw to the Casentino. In this upper Arno area the Florentine forces caught up with him and on June 29, at Anghiari, beat him roundly. The invaders were obliged to abandon Tuscany and with them went the self-deceived and disconsolate Florentine exiles. When the spirited Rinaldo died two years later, the old oligarchy may be said to have been buried with him, for the Medicean rule was never again challenged from that quarter.

The sweeping victory brought certain territorial advantages in its wake, as it enabled Florence to strengthen its hold on the upper valley of its river. This mountain region had originally been and long remained a typical feudal area. In the course of time, however, most of the castle-owners had been ousted and their possessions taken over by the expanding republic. Up to the Milanese invasion the greatest of all the feudal lords, the counts of Poppi, had escaped this fate, owing to their having sought and obtained the friendship of the republic by formal acknowledgment of Florentine supremacy. Unfortunately for himself the reigning count joined forces with the commander of the invading host, with Piccinino, and when this general was defeated at Anghiari and abandoned the country, the overbold ally had to pay the penalty for his hardihood. The castle of Poppi, which, happily spared by the ravages of time, still overwhelms the visitor with its feudal grandeur, was appropriated by Florence together with its dependent territory and the count himself driven into exile. He was the last representative of the great Guidi family who had inscribed their names on many a page of Tuscan history during the preceding four centuries. The Guidi had now reached the end of their journey. The count Francesco's exit from the scene and descent into an engulfing oblivion is therefore not without the pathos that clings to every completed human destiny. During the Casentino campaign Florence had possessed itself of the mountain town of Borgo San Sepolcro and, in spite of its belonging to the State of the Church, was not minded to give it up again. As the homeless Pope Eugene was in no position to insist on his rights, he finally agreed to leave it in the republic's hands for a cash consideration. Borgo San Sepolcro and the Poppi lands gave Florence the unchallenged command of the upper Arno. They had the additional significance of enabling the Medicean regime to boast that it, too, had met the patriotic obligation laid upon every government, no matter what its nature, to enlarge the Florentine dominion.

By the time of the crisis so happily resolved by the victory of Anghiari a new factor had crept into the general Italian situation which materially changed its aspect. The greatest of all the freebooters of this era of mercenary soldiers was Francesco Sforza. Already before Cosimo's advent to power Sforza had taken advantage of the continued feebleness of the papacy to seize some of its territory and proclaim himself its lord, of course under the nominal suzerainty of the pope, whose ultimate authority was not disputed. But this success did not satisfy his ambition, which gradually directed its aim at nothing less than Filippo Maria Visconti's duchy of Milan. As the leading condottiere of Italy, Sforza had made himself so indispensable to the duke that this ruler could not prosecute his far-reaching military designs without taking Sforza into account. A strong bond therefore tied the duke to the hireling soldier. Now it happened that the Visconti ruler had no children save an illegitimate daughter, Bianca. As the prospective heir of Milan, Bianca was in her day the greatest match in Italy, and to this exalted lady the audacious, low-born Sforza ventured to lift his eyes with a view to acquiring her hand and throne. Although the duke, her father, at first angrily rejected his condottiere's proposal as nothing less than an insult to his birth and grandeur, so long as he persisted in his policy of conquest he remained in an unescapable dependence on the good-will of the powerful freebooter. In order to secure his continued attachment to the ducal cause, gradually and with what inner reluctance may be left to the imagination the Milanese tyrant was obliged to come around to Sforza's view; and, after first tentatively affiancing the general to his daughter, he at last consented to their marriage. The startling event took place in November, 1441. Thenceforward, as the duke's son-in-law, the condottiere might seem to have had smooth sailing, but such was not the case. The duke, who had yielded only to the pressure of necessity, remained instinctively hostile to his daughter's husband, while Venice, desiring to end the ancient quarrel with neighboring Milan once for all, laid its plans to utilize the confusion sure to ensue on the duke's death by seizing Milan for itself.

As soon as the Milanese succession question moved into the focus of political attention, Cosimo resolved to back Francesco Sforza on the ground that the alternative to Sforza was Venice and that Venice enlarged by Milan would completely dominate the peninsula. It was an attitude inspired by intelligible patriotic considerations, but it did not please the Florentines, chiefly because through the long years of waiting for the duke's death they were called upon to finance the Sforza claim to the Milanese succession. In spite of a grumbling, all but universal opposition, Cosimo clung to his purpose and by his unwavering support of Sforza more than by any other single episode connected with his rule, showed that when it came to a crucial issue he was resolved to do what the situation demanded even at the risk of losing his popularity. At last, on August 13, 1447, occurred the long-awaited death of the crafty and unprincipled Filippo Maria. The first effect of the event was that the Milanese in an access of democratic enthusiasm re-established their republic. But no longer possessed of the virtues required for this form of government, they made a miserable showing in their struggle against the two enterprising claimants to the duke's heritage, Venice and Francesco Sforza. In the end the condottiere carried off the honors and in February, 1450, was acclaimed by his new subjects as their duke.

The support, chiefly of a financial order, which Florence had for years uninterruptedly given Francesco Sforza was a big factor in his success, and when he now blossomed forth as the duke of Milan there followed a new alignment of the Italian powers. Deeply resenting the help given the hardy adventurer, Venice indignantly abandoned its long-standing alliance with Florence and sought the friendship of King Alfonso, who, having at length driven the Anjou claimant out of the Neapolitan realm, was now in secure possession of the southern throne. The revised political orientation produced a war, in which Milan and Florence were obliged to meet the attack of Venice and Naples. The new conflict, as wasteful and purposeless as its numerous predecessors, continued until there fell upon the ears of Europe with a sound like the crack of doom the news of the capture of Constantinople by the Turks (1453). The moving event prompted the successor of Eugene IV, Pope Nicholas V, to plead with all the combatants to compose their petty differences and present a united Italian front to the dangerous Moslem enemy. Although the appeal for union under the pope fell on deaf ears, the urgent self-interest of Venice obliged it to seek an accommodation. In order to have its hands free to deal with the situation in the east, a situation so grave that it threatened a complete catastrophe, the republic opened negotiations with Milan at the town of Lodi which on April 11, 1454, were successfully concluded. To the peace of Lodi, Naples, the ally of Venice, and Florence, the ally of Milan, ended by giving their adherence, thereby making it effective for the whole peninsula. In point of fact the treaty, through its acceptance by practically every state of Italy, great or small, assumed something of the character of an Italian confederation, since all the signatories agreed to support the cause of peace and to stand together against any member state that would thereafter commit an unmistakably aggressive act. While it is true that Lodi did not achieve its federative mission and that Italy continued to be torn with rivalries and war, it is undeniable that the political situation registered an improvement, at least for the time being. Florence perhaps benefited more and for a longer time than any other state. The policy incorporated in the Lodi document was an expression of the mature view, to which Cosimo had come after an experience of twenty years as foreign minister of the Arno city. That view was that Florence, a commercial republic, was not constituted so as to be able successfully to carry on a policy of aggression and that its best hope was a mutual guaranty of peace among the Italian powers on the basis of existing boundaries. To be sure, Florence did not, because of Lodi, give up its recently established intimacy with Milan. The union was even strengthened when, before long, King Alfonso of Naples joined it as a third member. The maintenance of a ring within a ring was naturally displeasing to the outsiders, to the pope and Venice. It clearly indicated that all was not well within the league of Lodi and that the old jealousies continued to smoulder under the surface. Nonetheless Florence achieved a peace which lasted for the remainder of Cosimo's life, while the system, of which the peace was an expression, was adopted by his son and, after some fluctuation, by his grandson and was accepted as a basic principle of government guaranteeing the Medici rule. The peace of Lodi was a triumph which constituted a new bright feather in Cosimo's cap and helps explain the ease with which he overcame the revolt in his own ranks—to be presently related.

Having with the peace of Lodi brought Florence to an arrangement with its Italian rivals and neighbors which Cosimo considered, and which probably was, the best attainable under prevailing circumstances, we shall turn to consider the domestic developments in his time, not without once more expressing regret that, in the interest of continuity, we are constrained to present foreign and domestic occurrences as two distinct series of events. Nothing could be farther from the truth than such an assumption; and before we have concluded our renewed domestic survey we shall be provided with at least one excellent opportunity to illustrate the always busy interaction between the happenings outside and inside the Florentine walls. And since events promoting our acquaintance with the tang and quality of Florentine life are no less important to us than strictly political movements, we shall begin our domestic record with the consecration of the cathedral of Santa Maria del Fiore on March 25, 1436. The occasion for the ceremony was the completion by the architect Brunelleschi of the great cupola over the octagonal east end. As Pope Eugene was a resident of the city at the time, he could be utilized as the leading figure in the spectacle and a magnificence could be unfolded in which the citizens, young and old, rich and poor, always took a childlike pleasure. The chroniclers vie with one another in describing the raised board walk which was constructed all the way from Santa Maria Novella, where the pope resided, to the cathedral, and along which, hung with carpets and gay with banners and garlands, Eugene IV attended by seven cardinals, thirty-seven archbishops and bishops, and the nine members of the Florentine signory moved in solemn procession to perform the act of consecration at the altar erected under the newly finished dome.

Three years later Florence became the seat of a General Council of the church, and during a period of six months its citizens enjoyed the spectacle of innumerable ecclesiastical ceremonies as well as the frequent formal entry and departure of exalted personages. Pope Eugene had issued a call for a Council in the hope of bringing about the union of the eastern and the western, the Greek Orthodox and the Roman Catholic churches, which, owing to doctrinal differences defying compromise, had parted company over six hundred years before. He had originally selected Ferrara as the place of meeting for the representatives of the two faiths; but Cosimo by bringing his great financial reserves into play had maneuvered so cleverly that in January, 1439, the assembly was transferred from Ferrara to Florence. In addition to the heads of the two churches, the pope and the patriarch, each attended by a cloud of bishops and learned doctors, a great secular prince, the Greek emperor, graced the Council with his presence. In fact it was really because of him that the Council was held, for, hard pressed by the advancing Turks and fearing the loss of his ancient capital, Constantinople, the emperor had come to the west to ask for help in his desperate struggle. Solely because the Turks were pressing a dagger to his throat, he and his clergy offered the theological concessions which made it possible for the breach between the two churches to be closed. On July 5, 1439, in a final ceremonial session held in the cathedral of Santa Maria del Fiore the union of Christianity was declared to have been happily restored. So important did the event appear to be to the contemporaries that it was resolved to perpetuate its memory by an inscription on one of the vast stone piers supporting Brunelleschi's soaring cupola. There, at the side of the door leading into the sacristy, it may still be read not without ironical amusement in view of the fugitive character of the triumph it celebrated. Hardly had the Greek prelates reached home when they repudiated the agreement; the emperor never received the political support from the west, to obtain which he had bent his knee before the pope; and not much over a decade after the Florentine gathering Constantinople met the tragic fate which the Turks had been preparing for it for more than a generation. The General Council of Florence lingers in the memory as one of the minor futilities of history; but with the coming and going through many months of a pope, a patriarch, an emperor, and innumerable gorgeously costumed prelates, the Council brought to the streets and squares of Florence an unwonted and long-remembered gayety, color, and excitement. A cultural by-product of the assembly should not be overlooked, especially as it shows Cosimo de' Medici in another than the political role with which we have become familiar. The most learned as well as the most venerable of the visiting Greeks was George Gemistos Plethon. A passionate champion of the philosophy of Plato, not only did he attract the attention of the numerous Florentine humanists but he won the special regard of the untitled lord of Florence. It was his contact with Plethon that moved Cosimo to consider the idea of a Platonic academy on the Arno, and as a preparatory measure to its creation to give the alert and promising youth, Marsilio Ficino, the son of his physician, a thoroughgoing education at his expense in the Greek language.

Following the peace of Lodi there occurred a movement within the Medicean party which furnishes a clear indication of the repeatedly asserted interaction between events in the foreign and domestic fields. With the long wars brought to a close and all danger from ambitious neighbors at least temporarily removed, certain associates of Cosimo within the ruling group believed that the time had come to reduce his swollen power and proportionately to increase their own. They hoped, on what grounds it is difficult to understand, to achieve their purpose by giving up the accoppiatori and returning to the older system of electing the priors by lot. Cosimo thought it prudent to let them have their way; and accordingly by successive steps in the latter half of the year 1454 the control exercised for twenty years was surrendered and the signory again drawn from the borse as chance determined. The leaders of the revolt were Luca Pitti, Agnolo Acciauoli, and Diotisalvi Neroni, all three of them men who had filled the highest offices of state. The Florentines, enamored of their "liberty," greeted with delight the elimination of the ten accoppiatori, stigmatized in private conversation as the ten tyrants, and praised to the skies the rebels who had freed them from an abominable yoke. But the satisfaction of the conspirators was of short duration. Before many months had passed they were made aware that if the removal of the accoppiatori weakened Cosimo's control, it weakened also their own. The signories that emerged from the unsupervised purses assumed a more and more independent attitude, and early in the year 1458 the then ruling government roused to indignation the whole body of wealthy Mediceans by resolving to draw up a new catasto. This meant nothing less than a radical reform of the taxation practices identified with the ruling group. The rivals of Cosimo responsible for the return to the older system of electing officials were without exception typical, well-to-do oligarchs. Exactly how they had profited from the taxation they had hitherto imposed must now be told.

Our last contact with Florentine taxation was on the occasion of the adoption in 1427 of the law of the catasto. Again affirming that this legislation was an improvement on everything that had gone before, we have now to note that, notwithstanding its fair appearance, it could be more or less completely nullified by being dishonestly administered. Unfortunately, in the matter of taxation, Florence suffered from an evil tradition, for the ruling groups of the past had never scrupled to levy the municipal imposts as they saw fit, and that means capriciously and without fixed principle. While it may therefore be said that, when the Mediceans on assuming power manipulated the taxes in their own interest, they merely followed a long-established custom, it is also true that they went beyond any of their predecessors by more effectively systematizing their outrageous partisanship. We have already insisted that Cosimo's party, far from inventing political control, merely perfected the inherited regime by adding the accoppiatori feature. To this main string of the bow of Medicean rule a second alternate string of equal strength was joined when it was resolved to manage taxation in such a way that the wealthy Mediceans would be favored and the wealthy opponents mulcted and crushed. From the point of view of the Medicean opposition the accoppiatori were bad enough, but the brutal oppression represented by an arbitrary system of taxation was several times worse, since he whom it selected as its victim was irretrievably ruined.

The falsifying of the provisions of the catasto began with the failure to renew the assessment at regular three-year intervals, as the law in its original form required. Since the leading followers of Cosimo were the new-rich whose wealth was steadily increasing, it was to their advantage to be taxed according to the register in operation on their arrival at power, which was the register of 1431. By refusing to consent to its renewal they escaped the heavier tax to which they were liable on account of their mounting fortunes. Even more profitable to them was the protection they enjoyed at the hands of the purely Medicean commissioners of taxation (*sgravatori*), for these officials had the power to name at their good pleasure the sum each citizen was obliged to pay on the basis of his supposed income. In the forties, owing to the growing need of revenue in order to meet the costs of the uninterrupted wars, the income tax was made progressive. In the light of modern opinion this must be considered an advance, since the low incomes escaped with a low assessment, while the rate increased for the higher brackets until all returns over fifteen hundred florins were subjected, depending on the needs of the public purse, to a rate ranging from 25 to 50 per cent of the taxable total. It constitutes an interesting comment on changing points of view to observe that with practical unanimity the contemporary chroniclers voiced their horror of the new graduated feature. Seeing that they were without exception members of the bourgeoisie, we need not take their outcry too seriously, since every bourgeoisie from the beginning of time has emitted similar moans. We should not fail to note, however, that the small tradesmen, whose favor Cosimo wisely never ceased to court, were pleased with the relief afforded them. Gladly conceding that the revision of the forties, usually referred to as the *scala,* was not without merit, we should not forget that it wrought no change in the intolerable central principle, according to which the taxes were so manipulated that they were a buckler for the friends and a poniard for the enemies of the regime.

It was natural for the signory, as soon as it was free of the accoppiatori control, to try to break the other chain, the chain of taxation, by which the city was held in Medicean bondage. Plainly the way to bring this about was to draw up a new catasto without fear or favor; and no sooner was this proposal broached (January, 1458) than the disgusted conspirators ran to Cosimo for aid. Sadder but wiser men, they now regretted the abolition of the accoppiatori and implored their leader to help them re-establish the lost control. This could not be done without the familiar trick of the parliament, and Cosimo, willing to teach his slippery friends a lesson, kept them whining at his threshold for over half a year. At length in the month of August he gave his consent to proceed. The gonfalonier of Justice of the July-August period was Luca Pitti, and Cosimo may have felt a particular satisfaction in having a leading rival and ex-conspirator assume responsibility for the parliament, thus offering himself as the target for the hatred that the use of this loathsome instrument invariably released. To what a monstrous abuse the so-called assembly of the people had by this time degenerated is handsomely demonstrated by a description of its action some days *before* the projected parliament was held. In 1458 Florence was closely allied with Milan, and in sign of this intimacy a certain Nicodemo resided in the Arno city as the ambassador of Duke Francesco Sforza. Living in the closest intimacy with Cosimo, Nicodemo dispatched to his master a succession of reports which constitute one of the most important sources for our knowledge of the period. The parliament, planned to bring back the system of the ten tyrants, was to be held on August 11. Three days before, on August 8, Nicodemo wrote to his duke as follows:

The lord of Faenza [a condottiere employed by Florence] will arrive tomorrow with three hundred cavalry and fifty footmen; there will also be the troops of Simonetta [another condottiere]. . . . On the morning of the day fixed for the parliament the troops will draw up in battle array on the piazza. The people will arrive without arms. Then the priors will read a list of the citizens to whom balìa shall be given to reform the town and will ask the people whether they agree. The partisans planted in the square will shout "Yes! Yes!" and the common people will join in the cry according to custom.[2]

The comedy of August 11 was acted out exactly as forecast by Cosimo's intimate: the people shouted their approval and the balìa was instituted. There followed the making of new purses and the intrusting of the nomination of the signory to a commission of ten accoppiatori. The brief interlude of the free purses was over. As Luca Pitti, in the capacity of gonfalonier of Justice, had been the visible impresario of the spectacle of August 11 he was regarded by the mass of the Medicean party as the hero of the occasion. This was also his own view and his self-importance expanded proportionately. He was a vain, affable, and vivacious man who held the view that his great wealth entitled him to a larger share of power than Cosimo had seen fit to accord him. With Agnolo Acciaiuoli, Diotisalvi Neroni, and many similar birds of fine feather he was of the opinion, traditional among the leading merchants of Florence, that the rule of the city belonged of right to the optimates. But while detesting the government of the many, these men of means were as little disposed to accept the domination of a tyrant. The signore was to them that intolerable thing: *il governo d'un solo*. It is a fact that, following the successful revolution of 1458, Luca Pitti came to be regarded by many observers as the most important figure in Florence. Cosimo was waxing old and, owing to his growing infirmities, showed himself more and more rarely in public. Under the circumstances it is perhaps not so strange that the whisper should have gone around that Luca had succeeded in wresting the scepter from Cosimo's hands. How superficial and mistaken this judgment was is amply attested by Ambassador Nicodemo's reports to Milan. Not for a moment did this intelligent diplomat, whose business it was to remain in touch with the true source of Florentine authority, turn from Cosimo to Luca. One of the old Medicean fox's most valuable gifts was his ability to read character. We cannot doubt that he saw to the very bottom of Luca Pitti and had arrived at the opinion that he had nothing to fear from this agitated and colorful but inconstant butterfly. When Luca presently undertook to feed his vanity by commencing on the slope of the hill of San Giorgio the construction of a palace twice as large as that of the Medici, we can imagine Cosimo's face wreathing itself in its familiar enigmatic smile. This rival of his was about to spend his energy in idle display. That he estimated Luca correctly is indicated by the fact that Luca did not live to finish the famous Pitti palace and that in due course of time it became the official residence of the dukes of the house of Medici.

It was a very different Florence from that he had known as a boy that Cosimo faced in his old age. Many of the shibboleths and battle-cries of his

---

[2] Perrens, *Histoire de Florence depuis la domination*, etc. Vol. I, pp. 187-88.

youth had lost their significance. Truth to tell, even at that early time many of them had already been long on the wane. What around the year 1400, when Cosimo was a vigorous adolescent, did the terms Guelph and Ghibelline still mean? Was not the empire, the hope of the Ghibellines, a withered plant and the papacy, the protecting arm of the Guelphs, paralyzed by the Great Schism? What was the significance of the Ordinances of Justice, when there were no longer any magnates whose excesses needed to be repressed? True, the oligarchs who preceded Cosimo had found the Ordinances useful as a device to exclude their enemies from the government by stigmatizing them as magnates, but this trickery only helped to bring it home to even the simplest minds that the original magnate class had disappeared. More important even than changes such as these was the fact that the gild system, so closely identified with the city's rise to greatness, was also no longer what it had been. The trecento was without question the great age of the gilds. In the quattrocento they were weakening, and the downward movement may undoubtedly be ascribed to the victory in 1382 of the greater over the lesser gilds and to the subsequent all but complete eclipse of the latter. Ever since their victory the greater gilds, and that, when all is said, meant the great merchants individually, enjoyed an unchallenged ascendancy. More and more they became pure enterprisers of the "putting-out" type, whose function it was to "put out" to the working people the tools and the raw products they needed for the various manufacturing processes. We shall have to conclude that, as soon as its democratic vigor was squeezed out of the gild system by the crushing defeat of the arti minori, the capitalists discovered that they no longer needed the gilds, especially as with their intricate restrictions and regulations they had become a good deal of a nuisance. Not to exaggerate, let us agree that while the gilds retained their full formal importance throughout the quattrocento, their sun was beginning to set. The new economic factor was the enterpriser, pure and simple, who aspired to liberate himself from shackles of every kind and to rule unhampered over a free labor market.

Hesitant as Cosimo was to change political appearances and desirous to give the impression that the inherited institutions operated exactly as before his advent, he could not keep changes from creeping also into the political segment of Florentine existence. Particularly marked was the decline of the podestà. While it is certain that already the generations before Cosimo had busied themselves to clip the wings of this one-time ruler of the commonwealth, not till the Medicean era was he deposed from the formal headship of the state and this honor assigned to the chief of the priors, the gonfalonier of Justice. At the same time the podestà's judicial powers, constituting his very life-blood, were sensibly diminished. Having already under the Albizzeschi suffered a loss of jurisdiction in favor of the police committee, the Otto di Guardia, he was now obliged to transfer to the Otto all cases involving the issue of politics. A judge to deal justly with political offenders was no longer wanted and the Eight were accordingly exalted over the podestà. From them, as strictly partisan nominees, the regime might expect the unqualified condemnations it demanded. It is worth while to call attention to these relatively unimportant changes to remind the reader that, like everything else in Florence, the apparently frozen forms of the constitution were undergoing alterations and that time never stands still.

Taken up with Cosimo's political activity, we have thus far hardly touched an interest of his which in the eyes of some observers still constitutes his greatest distinction. He lived in the quattrocento, a period of the rapidly expanding Renaissance, and took an eager part in its intellectual and artistic manifestations. There have been schools of historiography in the past which, aesthetically oriented and disposed to regard the Renaissance as one of the summits of human development, have celebrated Cosimo, because of his association with art and literature, as a hero of the world-cause of culture. Occasional encomiasts have even gone so far as to make it appear that he was the magician, by the waving of whose wand the Renaissance rose as a finished product from the void. The opinion is so absurd that it hardly needs to be expressly refuted. All serious students agree that the Renaissance is an epoch of European history which unfolded slowly under the action of innumerable forces and that it constitutes a definite link in the chain of western civilization. The idea that Cosimo or any other individual could have produced this era is simply laughable. Far from being the creator, Cosimo was the creature of the Renaissance. And because undeniably he was from his birth steeped in its spirit, he presents himself to view, exactly like the whole upper stratum of his Florentine fellow-citizens, as a Renaissance man: as a man of the *early* Renaissance, let it be observed, for the Middle Ages had not yet spent their vigor, and in the first half of the fifteenth century the medieval influences still counted greatly in the outlook of even such individuals as may have thought they had cast them off.

Since Cosimo was brought up as a banker and throughout his life gave his time and attention chiefly to business and politics, he was not, and could not be, in a professional sense either a humanist or an artist. However, endowed with a keen mind, he interested himself in all that the humanists and artists were doing and, possessed of vast means, he was pleased to encourage their activities by his patronage. This defines his historic role in the field of culture: he was a patron, a Maecenas. What this signified in respect to humanism, although already touched upon elsewhere,[3] may be briefly summarized at this point for the sake of the complete picture of the man. Apart from his assembling three libraries, on which he expended immense sums, he cultivated the acquaintance of a large number of leading humanists such as Leonardo Bruni, Carlo Marsuppini, and Poggio Bracciolini, all of them chancellors of Florence in Cosimo's day. When as the result of his contact with Platonic philosophy at the General Council of 1439 he resolved to bring up at his expense the promising youth, Marsilio Ficino, as the western interpreter of the great Athenian's message, he made what may perhaps be called his most important single contribution to Renaissance thought. For from this resolution emerged the Platonic academy, center of one of several movements by which philosophy attempted to steer its course among the uncharted speculative seas which confronted it as soon as it had abandoned the safe medieval moorings.

Much more widely noticed, because affecting a larger human circle, was Cosimo's patronage of the arts. Besides building himself the great palace, which

[3] Chap. XIX.

still stands and which in our own day has again very properly been given the Medicean name, he erected a villa at Careggi, another at Fiesole, and still another at Cafaggiolo in the Mugello, the original home of his race. For the city palace as well as for the convent buildings of San Marco, which he presented to the Dominican order, he employed the architect Michelozzo. But he by no means overlooked Brunelleschi, the most famous architect of his day. To Brunelleschi he intrusted the two very notable structures, the church of San Lorenzo and the Badia (abbey) of San Domenico below Fiesole. In sculpture Cosimo linked his name with that of Donatello, who became and remained his devoted friend. Among the painters he was particularly close to Fra Filippo Lippi, Fra Angelico, and Benozzo Gozzoli. The question so often discussed whether he practiced his lavish patronage of scholars and artists out of love of learning and the creative skills or from a selfish desire to increase his reputation is idle and unfruitful. His enemies said one thing, his friends another. To anyone raising himself above the battle of partisan opinion it is clear that Cosimo shared the tastes of his time and social class and easily and naturally slipped into the patronage, which was an all but universally recognized obligation of the rich and powerful men of the age.

Like every man whose character unfolded in the storm and stress of circumstance Cosimo exhibited many contradictory traits. In the main he was moderate, disciplined, and magnanimous; and if it is possible to charge him with occasional cruel and vindictive acts, he was nonetheless essentially humane and forgiving. Most characteristic of him was the hard, practical outlook of the Florentine man of affairs and, like this well-established type, he was not given to unnecessary words. Deficient in natural eloquence and avoiding speech-making as much as possible, he owed his authority in the state preeminently to his tact and skill as a party leader and to his great and unusual administrative talents. His habitual reticence did not keep him, however, from manifesting a remarkable power of terse comment, of which it is very much worth while to take note, as it permits us to penetrate to the very core of his being. His compact utterances, much cited in his own and still remembered in our day, have been used by his opponents to prove his cold and calculating cynicism. Cynical they no doubt are, but they have a pungency and bite that makes them entirely admirable on their level. States are not maintained by pater nosters; two yards of red cloth suffice to make an honorable citizen; envy is a plant that should not be watered; better a city ruined than a city lost: such are some of his sayings that went the rounds among his half-resentful, half-admiring countrymen. They have an epigrammatic edge which explains why they were incorporated in the local folk-lore and have persisted through the ages.[4] His personal appearance accorded perfectly with his words and actions. He was of medium height, spare of figure, of olive complexion with large rude features. His carriage as he moved about the city was dignified, his aspect benign. He spoke familiarly with merchant and market woman and

---

[4] A full collection of the sayings attributed to Cosimo will be found in Note 136 of A. Fabroni, *Vita Magni Cosmi Medicei*. Pisa, 1789. This is still the fundamental biography. See also Cosimo's life in Vespasiano da Bisticci, *Vite di Uomini Illustri del Secolo XV*. An English translation by William George and Emily Waters was published at London in 1926. The best biography of Cosimo in English is by K. D. Ewart, *Cosimo de' Medici*. London, 1889.

declined to underscore his position with such trappings of lordship as palace guards and a lavish household. His piety, as evidenced by his many ecclesiastical endowments, was represented by his enemies as pure hypocrisy. They adduced his patronage of humanism in proof of his religious skepticism, but the point cannot be said to have been well taken, for in his case, as in that of most of the leading spirits of the age, the old and the new managed somehow to lie down together without a disturbing inner conflict. In the monastery of St. Mark may still be seen a cell which he reserved for himself as an occasional quiet retreat from the clamor of the world. There is no reason to assume that he engaged in periodic prayer and penance except to satisfy a genuine need of his heart.

Cosimo was spared neither the cruel private losses nor the gradual impairment of health which are the common human lot. His son Giovanni died without offspring in 1463; his only other son, Piero, was afflicted with gout to such a degree that he had to keep to his bed often for prolonged periods. Piero had two promising boys, Lorenzo and Giuliano, but it would be some years before they could be charged with any public or private responsibility. To leave behind a large and prosperous family was the outstanding ambition of every true son of Florence: how much more then of a man like Cosimo who had carried his family to the headship of the city. After Giovanni's death he had himself, already bedridden, carried through the empty rooms of his city residence. We catch the intimate sorrow in his muttered words: "Too large a house for so small a family." Following the passing of this beloved second son, he sank rapidly. On August 1, 1464, at the age of seventy-five, he died at his villa of Careggi. He was buried without special pomp amidst a vast concourse of his fellow-citizens before the high altar of the church of San Lorenzo, which owed its existence to his munificence. The plain slab over his tomb carries his name and under it the simple legend *Pater Patriae*. This was the honorable title which, under the sharp impression of the loss they had suffered, his sorrowing countrymen united in officially bestowing on him.

XXII. The Government of Piero de' Medici and of Lorenzo the Magnificent to the End of the War with the Pope and Naples (1480)

WHEN Cosimo died on August 1, 1464, the question that sprang spontaneously to every tongue was whether the dominant position acquired by the dead statesman could be maintained by his heir and only surviving son, Piero. For, towering as Cosimo's authority was, it was a cloaked and extra-constitutional authority and would in all probability collapse if exercised by a political talent conspicuously inferior to his own. Now that Piero was the son but not the spiritual replica of his father was manifest to all observers, and particularly to Cosimo's jealous intimates who shared with him the control of the Medicean party. Already during the last years of their chief they had indicated in no uncertain manner that they refused any longer to be regarded as subordinates. In this connection it is proper once again to remind ourselves that it is the incurable weakness of every regime of optimates that, in measure as it becomes secure against outsiders, it is threatened by revolt within its ranks. We have had occasion in the previous chapter to touch upon the subterranean activity of three prominent Mediceans who, on being brought face to face with the ruinous consequences of their revolt, humbled themselves to petition Cosimo to have its effects undone, but who did not on this account abandon their secret hostility to their leader. These three rivals, thenceforth gnawed by an inner rage, were Luca Pitti, Diotisalvi Neroni, and Agnolo Acciaiuoli. Each had his own particular list of grievances against Cosimo, but private complaints, no matter how huge the mass of them may be on being heaped together, are not easily converted into a viable program of common action.

It is evidence of the decline of political principle among the oligarchs that only a single member of the ruling ring, Niccolò Soderini, was opposed to Cosimo on other than purely selfish grounds. This Niccolò was an idealist of the childlike, ingenuous kind that, instead of doing himself or anyone else any good by his agitation, gets no farther than to deepen the existing confusion by his failure to grasp the simple actualities staring him and everyone else in the face. We thus have a sum of four disgruntled Medicean subleaders, each one of whom was minded not to let slip by unused the opportunity afforded by the assumption of the shrewd Cosimo's succession by his feebler son, but who, prompted by diverse motives, found it difficult to agree on a plan of attack. When after some months an action was at length inaugurated, it was on the sole responsibility of the impetuous Niccolò, honestly but fatuously resolved to rouse the people in an effort by legal means to restore the constitution—the miraculous original constitution, which had made an impressive show on paper for almost two hundred years but which had always been manipulated by shrewd cliques in their own interest. Planning a return to the lost "liberty" of the Florentines, Niccolò could not under the most favorable circumstances have done more than overthrow the Medici in order to replace them with another tyranny, probably his own.

The first hurdle encountered by Niccolò Soderini on beginning action against the ruling system was taken without any difficulty. On September 6, 1465, a proposal was made and carried to return to the system of choosing the signory by lot; and when the first group of priors under the new dispensation issued from the supposedly unmanipulated borse, lo and behold, the name drawn for banner-bearer of Justice was none other than that of Niccolò, the impassioned champion of free elections. It was an excellent example of the "liberty" habitual to the Florentine system. On entering the palace for the term beginning November 1, the new gonfalonier was attended on the way by a wildly cheering multitude, whose acclamations reached a climax when an olive wreath was placed upon the hero's brow. This first was also the last of poor, sap-headed Niccolò's triumphs. Before large assemblies of his fellow-citizens called together by him, he delivered ringing addresses, which everybody agreed were magnificent but in which intelligent observers regretfully remarked the absence of anything that by any stretch of the imagination could be called a coherent program. Whenever the noble orator and patriot came forward with something even a trifle definite, it was buried in the councils under an avalanche of contrary votes cast by the followers of Piero de' Medici and the other leading merchants. For, as soon as the oligarchic system as such was threatened, Piero and most of his enemies within the optimate group stood together as one man. When at the end of his two months' service Soderini again abandoned the palace, he presented the usual sorry spectacle of the deflated reformer. His deep chagrin made him an embittered man prepared henceforth to employ almost any method which might rid the city of the Medici. Disappointed by the meager results attained by constitutional methods, he no longer scrupled to travel the path of violence. This altered attitude drove him into the arms of the three fellow-oligarchs, whose discontent was of an older date than his and who, on being strengthened by the accession of Soderini, felt encouraged to resort to direct action to unseat the hated Piero.

The new revolt against the Medici was favored by an event at Milan: on March 8, 1466, Duke Francesco Sforza passed away. His successor was his son, Galeazzo Maria, a young man of twenty without a particle of either the military or the governing talents of his rude, self-made father. It was uncertain whether the youthful heir would succeed in imposing his authority; and in the most favorable case it was probable that he would for a long time to come be so much concerned with affairs close at home that he would not be in a position to lend his distant Medicean ally support. The Sforza alliance, we must always keep in mind, had been made by Cosimo the very fulcrum of his policy; and just as Francesco Sforza had counted at every turn on the instant help of the Medici, so the Medici had been strong in their confidence of the ever ready succor of the Milanese duke. But now the duke was dead, the stability of his state to all appearances threatened, and Piero de' Medici deprived of the foreign support which was an important factor of his strength. The plot promptly hatched by the four conspirators was to induce the enemies of Florence, such as the duke of Ferrara and the republic of Venice, to lend them a body of troops on the understanding that their crossing of the border would serve as the signal for the domestic rising having as its goal the overthrow and attendant murder of Piero.

The plot, perfected in the course of the summer following the change of ruler at Milan, was brought to a sudden head by the threatened Piero's taking the offensive. This took his enemies by surprise, for they were persuaded that Cosimo's son, for whom they had nothing but contempt, would weakly suffer himself to be crushed. Physically incapacitated by gout, Piero was familiarly known as *Il Gottoso,* and perhaps because of his infirmity had developed the habit of avoiding open, uncompromising conflict as much as he possibly could. Nevertheless, on his becoming aware that his rule and life were jeopardized by the conspiracy hatched by his rivals, a hidden fire burst into flame and caused him to act with unfaltering resolution. While staying at his villa at Careggi, he was warned in a letter from the friendly ruler of Bologna that Ferrarese troops were being moved toward the Florentine border. The fuse was therefore about to be lighted. Without delay and bedridden as he was, he had himself carried in a litter to the city in order to inform the signory of the threatened invasion and to rouse them to defensive action. It was on August 27, 1466, that he made his unexpected appearance in the town and challenged the conspirators to strike the first blow. Whether it was the consternation caused by the premature revelation of the plot, or the small agreement among the four principals, or the settled Florentine burgher preference for political rather than for military action, the conspirators permitted the favorable moment to slip by. Their cardinal mistake no doubt was to let themselves be drawn into negotiations. These were proposed by the signory, and Piero, the avowed defender of the country's peace, was of course more than willing to engage in them. A few days passed amidst excitement and severe tension until with the elections for the September signory, which proved favorable to the Medici, the attack was beaten off, leaving control securely with Piero.

The upshot of the August commotion was the familiar parliament, which, called on September 2, conferred extraordinary power on the familiar commission or balìa. The balìa in its turn authorized the renewed abandonment of election by lot in favor of officials hand-picked by a committee of accoppiatori, the constitutional device identified with Medicean rule since the return of Cosimo from exile. Thus lifted to the saddle, Piero rode roughshod over his enemies. Niccolò Soderini, Agnolo Acciaiuoli, and Diotisalvi Neroni were banished from the city and its territory. To his greater shame Luca Pitti, the fourth head of the conspirators and generally considered their biggest figure, was suffered to remain. At the height of the crisis he had betrayed his associates and by visiting the stricken Piero in his sickroom had effected a reconciliation with that mild-tempered chief. Whether it was Luca s natural flightiness, or his enfeebled mind (he was over seventy years old), or his great riches which he was reluctant to jeopardize, or the vast Pitti palace, which, still incomplete, he wished to leave behind as his enduring monument, his courage failed him at the crucial moment and, renouncing the risk of war, like a panicky animal at the approach of danger, he ran to cover. He passed the few remaining years of his existence in the deepening obscurity that overtakes a man who has become morally discredited and universally despised.

Unfortunately there was an aftermath of foreign war. The exiled conspirators gathered at Venice and tirelessly spurred on to action against Florence the republic of St. Mark and certain minor states of the Romagna, which had been in guilty collusion with them from the start. They engaged as their commander-in-chief the Venetian condottiere, Bartolommeo Colleone. This is the same Colleone whose equestrian statue, wrought by Verrocchio's masterhand, still dominates one of the minor squares of the City of the Lagoons. Colleone was at the head of the wretched Italian mercenary business at this time, and the deluded Florentine exiles nursed the hope that he would lead them back to their lost paradise. The hireling soldier received enough support from the states openly or secretly hostile to Florence to threaten Tuscany with invasion from his base in the Romagna, but as Florence remained firmly joined with Milan and Naples, constituting with them the well-proved triple alliance, the danger passed and in April, 1468, the rather trifling struggle, usually called the Colleonic war but more readily identified if labeled the war of the exiles against the Medici, came to an end. The peace, which still further raised Piero's steadily mounting prestige, buried his opponents in oblivion.

The chief support of Piero in these trials was his young son Lorenzo. Indeed so constantly was Lorenzo at his father's side and so conspicuous was his part in all the negotiations conducted within and without the city that there were many who believed that he already was the head of the state. While this was an exaggeration, as Piero without doubt kept the threads of policy in his hands and Lorenzo never fell from the role of the dutiful son, it is true that Lorenzo was pushed into an early acquaintance with affairs of state which made him a master of all their intricacies by the time his father's mantle fell upon his shoulders. As Lorenzo was born on January 1, 1449, he was but fifteen years old at the death of his grandfather Cosimo; and he had not yet celebrated his twenty-first birthday when the long-expected death of the sorely stricken Piero put the full responsibility for the Florentine state into his hands. The character and career of this most brilliant ruler of the house have elicited the admiration of the succeeding generations of men down to our own time. Without any doubt the Medicean family tradition was the animating core of his being. Throughout the European world the family was still a more authoritative institution than the state, and all the movement and change imported into Florence by the vast network of its commercial relations had proved unable to weaken the grip of the family on its members. Even when the gild system had been at its height in the fourteenth century, the family had continued to count for more than the gild; and the gild system had no sooner been enfeebled by the rise of the enterpriser than the family completely overshadowed the gild as a social and political determinant. The obligation impressed on the youthful Lorenzo until it became the mainspring of his being was his duty to uphold and strengthen the position achieved by his forebears. An influence different in kind and yet of a like emotional pull can be ascribed without hesitation to his mother. She was Lucrezia Tornabuoni, a member of one of the oldest and most distinguished families of the city. While her sterling intelligence made her a valuable helpmeet of her husband Piero in all his concerns, her significance for Lorenzo, and for her other children as well, lay chiefly in her being a well-nigh perfect example of the woman type formed by many centuries of Florentine teaching and experience. On the one hand, she was the embodiment of common sense and a busy practicality, like the woman commended in the Bible arising betimes and looking well after the ways of her household; on the other hand, she was the robed priestess charged with the preservation of the ancient pieties of the hearth and altar. From his childhood she so steeped Lorenzo in the practices and folkways of Catholicism that, in spite of the overwhelming pagan influences to which he was afterward exposed, he never quite broke away from his Christian moorings. Together with the forceful family inheritance the never resolved residuum of faith at the bottom of his heart constituted the invaluable steadying element in his often stormy career.

After the home came the school, and the school for Lorenzo, as for every Florentine boy of his class and period, signified a prolonged bath in the Pierian spring. In the second half of the fifteenth century the last conservative resistance to the mounting tide of humanistic enthusiasm had broken down, and the curriculum of the new age took the form of the transmission to the young of the wisdom of the ancients as embodied in Greek and Latin literature. Accordingly, Lorenzo was given the best available tutors in Latin and Greek, and by the gracious Marsilio Ficino, central figure of the Platonic academy, he was inducted into the noble mysteries of Ficino's revered master of ancient philosophic thought. From the prolonged feast of alien learning many of Lorenzo's contemporaries arose as insufferable prigs, a fate that might also have befallen the young Medici had it not been for certain rival influences which enabled him to bring his manhood to a rich and natural maturity. In spite of the inculcated preference for the dead languages and literatures, Lorenzo had an unconquerable natural predilection for the living Tuscan speech and its great literary monuments and at a very early age developed the habit of setting forth his thoughts and feelings in the many available forms of native verse. To such eminence did he attain in the field of poetry that, short as his life was destined to be and incessantly concerned with the public interest, he is now generally held to rank as the leading Tuscan singer of his day. A second influence corrective of the excessive scholarly emphasis of humanism was his devotion to physical exercise and sport. He became an expert at football and at the vigorous form of handball known locally as *pallone;* he had an enthusiasm for horses, dogs, and falcons which converted him into a passionate follower of the hunt. In short, spiritual, intellectual, and physical elements of training were brought to bear on him in such perfect balance that in an age abounding in eminent personalities he stands forth as perhaps its best-rounded product. His personal appearance, however, was far from pre-possessing. He had a vigorous frame of more than average height, but his face was almost repulsively ugly with its sallow complexion, its strained, myopic eyes, its flat and spreading nose. Nor was Nature, which had so opulently endowed him in heart and mind, content to balance the account with these facial liabilities. It is strange to reflect that this man so conspicuous for inner harmony should have had a harsh and croaking voice and should have been almost completely lacking in the sense of smell.

The other children of Piero and Lucrezia de' Medici were a boy, Giuliano, five years younger than Lorenzo, and two sisters, Bianca and Nannina. We have a letter of their mother which affirms that her two daughters were ex-tremely beautiful. In the absence of any other opinion on the subject, we may cautiously write her evidence into the record. According to Florentine custom the two girls were given in marriage at an early age to members of distin-guished local families, Bianca being wed to Guglielmo Pazzi and Nannina to Bernardo Rucellai. Marriage as the life-blood of the institution of the family was of course the undisputed province of the head of the house. Al-though in successive brilliant ceremonies Bianca was married to her Gu-glielmo and Nannina to her Bernardo, the four principals had nothing to do with the preliminary arrangements, since these were the result of negotiations among the respective family heads, each exclusively concerned with advancing the fortunes of his particular group. In the case of Lorenzo's brother, Giuli-ano, the evidence regarding his good looks is so abundant and comes to us from so many sources that we may say without any reservation that he grew up to be an extremely handsome young man. As strong and tall as his brother, he had a greater natural grace of body and a far more harmonious assortment of features. He did not yield to Lorenzo in his addiction to games and pageants, but, while gladly consorting with scholars and artists, he had none of his brother's literary gifts. Nor did he boast Lorenzo's clear intelli-gence and swift energy but, modest, lively, and gentle, he was singularly cherished by all the town. His ingenuous spirit led him to subordinate him-self with spontaneous deference to Lorenzo's authoritative leadership.

Long before Lorenzo reached his twentieth birthday his marriage had be-come the engrossing concern of his parents. After a careful survey of the scene they decided to negotiate for the hand of a daughter of the great Roman baronial house of Orsini. This was a startling departure from tradition, for hitherto the Medici had regularly contracted marriage among the other burgher families of their native town. But they were now virtually a reigning dynasty, and a family connection capable of strengthening their general position in Italy was undoubtedly desirable. No greater uncrowned house than the Orsini was to be found in the peninsula, innumerable members having for many generations past figured in the country's politics and wars. What particularly impressed the close observer was that the house had proved itself a veritable nursery of those two specialties of the Italian climate—cardinals and condot-tieri. By tieing themselves to a great feudal race the Medici ran some risk of offending Florentine republican sentiment; but the advantages were consid-ered to outweigh the disadvantages, and on June 4, 1469, the wedding of the

Medici heir with Clarice Orsini was celebrated amidst a great burst of pomp. The splendor which was unfolded expressed the more firmly established Medicean rule quite as much as the exuberant disposition of the young bridegroom. Gone was the cautious self-concealment of old Cosimo for which there was no longer any need. For by this time the common people, if not yet the representatives of the substantial burgherdom, had come round to viewing the Medici as the native dynasty from which, somewhat in the manner of the public games offered to the Romans by their emperors, they had a right to expect a steady succession of free entertainments. Already in 1468 Lorenzo with his ailing father's consent had given a tournament in the Piazza Santa Croce in honor of the reigning local beauty, Lucrezia Donati. Doubtless he was prompted to stage this spectacle, the fame of which made its way to the four corners of Italy, by the still lingering ideals of medieval chivalry as well as by his own inborn zest for pleasure; but it is not improbable that even at that early age he was not inaccessible to the purely political consideration that splendor was an attribute of royalty and that nothing has delighted the multitude of every age so much as a good show. A year after the tournament offered to Lucrezia Donati, Lorenzo's union with the handsome copper-haired Clarice Orsini served as another occasion for dining friends and entertaining the masses on a lavish scale; and what was probably the climax in a long train of public pageants was touched in 1475 when Giuliano followed his brother's example by giving a tournament, again on the Piazza Santa Croce well suited to this kind of exhibition, which dazzled all beholders with its unnrivaled display of brocaded costumes strewn with pearls and precious stones. It was characteristic of the unwarlike, spectacle-loving Italy of the Renaissance that these Florentine tournaments no longer bore any resemblance to their medieval exemplars with their hard knocks, their abundant blood and dirt; they were more in the nature of ably directed theatrical shows, in which make-believe knights tried to outdo one another not so much in skill of arms as in picturesqueness of holiday costume and in the size and splendor of their retinues of squires, pages, and musicians. Tournaments or not in the true sense, these displays aroused keen delight, and the young brothers who presided at them with such unaffected gusto rose higher and higher in the public favor.

Six months after the wedding gayeties of Lorenzo and Clarice, Piero de' Medici at last made good his oft-repeated threat and departed this world in earnest (December 2, 1469). He was laid to rest in the sacristy of San Lorenzo, where a magnificent porphyry sarcophagus fashioned by Verrocchio received his mortal remains together with those of his younger brother Giovanni, who had preceded him in death by six years. And now Lorenzo ruled in his father's stead in nominal partnership with Giuliano, although the latter's youth and willing self-effacement left the power exclusively in the older brother's hands. The ease with which Lorenzo succeeded to the still unofficial Medicean rule of Florence measures the extent to which life had gone out of the old republican constitution. The leader of the Medicean party under Piero had been Tommaso Soderini. It is well to consider him for a moment, for, although a brother of Niccolò Soderini, he had not lost his credit with Piero when Niccolò had lent his strength to the revolt of 1466. The case of the brothers

Soderini shows that, despite the customary familial solidarity, there were instances, and some of them take us as far back as the early Middle Ages, when individuals of the same clan attached themselves to the fortunes of opposed factions. As Tommaso Soderini's loyalty was above suspicion, he was not molested by Piero after Niccolò's exile, and immediately after Piero's death he rewarded the trust put in him by assembling some six hundred leading citizens, whom he persuaded to petition Lorenzo to assume the place vacated by his father. In a diary-like record from Lorenzo's hand which has come down to us, Lorenzo voices a certain reluctance, which he declares he felt when the citizen committee headed by Tommaso Soderini requested him to take over the invisible Medicean scepter. The many historians of the city who have written as convinced and often embittered republicans unanimously cry out at this example of the familiar Medicean hypocrisy. But why the young Lorenzo with his strong attachment to literature and sport should not have felt a passing regret at irretrievably sentencing himself to the galley-slavery of politics is not clear. However, one of the reasons given by the young man for his acceptance of the position offered him is so revealing touching the character of Florentine politics that it must not be passed over. "In Florence," says Lorenzo, "one can ill live in the possession of wealth without control of the government." [1] For many generations past the party in power had been in the habit of oppressing its opponents with excessive taxation, and this ancient practice the Medici, as we are aware, had brought to an iniquitous perfection. From Lorenzo's frank avowal we learn that for him and his partisans the local issue reduced itself to the question of rule or ruin.

Everything considered, in no long established monarchy could the heir apparent have mounted the throne much more easily and securely than Lorenzo succeeded Piero on the latter's demise. It was probably on this account that he made no immediate move to trim the constitution still further to suit his figure. Its operations had been adequately controlled by his father and grandfather by means of the election supervisors called accoppiatori, and for the present this device sufficed also for Lorenzo. As the new ruler no more than his father and grandfather held an office by which he could be designated in public, it became customary to refer to him as Il Magnifico (The Magnificent). It was a purely honorary title never expressly authorized by a constitutional enactment. However, some slight constitutional tinkering in the manner sanctioned by long custom did take place at Lorenzo's accession. It effected no change demanding attention. We may therefore, following Virgil's excellent advice to Dante in the matter of merely bewildering details, be content to look and pass on (guarda e passa). [2]

Lorenzo's early familiarity with the government had made him aware that the Medici rule owed much of its vigor to the close association it maintained with Milan and Naples, and he took over this policy without change. Follow-

---

[1] "A Firenze si può mal viver ricco senza lo stato." Fabroni, Vol. II, Adnotationes, 21. The full title is: A. Fabroni, Laurentii Magnifici Vita. 2 vols. Pisa, 1784. Other biographies worth consulting are: W. Roscoe, The Life of Lorenzo de' Medici. 10th ed. London, 1895. A. Reumont, Lorenzo de' Medici. 2 vols. 2d ed. Leipzig, 1883. E. Armstrong, Lorenzo de' Medici. London, 1927. E. L. S. Horsburgh, Lorenzo the Magnificent and Florence in Her Golden Age. London, 1909.

[2] Inferno, III, 51.

Top left: VERROCCHIO. POR-
TRAIT BUST IN MARBLE
OF AN UNKNOWN WOMAN.
MUSEO NAZIONALE. *Top
right:* DESIDERIO DA SET-
TIGNANO. PORTRAIT BUST
IN MARBLE OF AN UN-
KNOWN WOMAN. MUSEO
NAZIONALE. *Bottom:* VER-
ROCCHIO. BRONZE EQUES-
TRIAN STATUE OF BARTO-
LOMMEO COLLEONI. VENICE.

Top right: POLLAIUOLO. HERCULES SUFFOCATES ANTAEUS. BRONZE. MUSEO NAZIONALE. *Bottom left:* ROSSELLINO. TOMB OF THE HUMANIST LEONARDO BRUNI OF AREZZO. SANTA CROCE. *Bottom right:* VERROCCHIO. DAVID. BRONZE. MUSEO NAZIONALE

ing the Colleonic war the peace of Tuscany remained undisturbed for almost a decade, and peace brought a welcome renewal of prosperity. The only disturbing event of Lorenzo's early years was the revolt of Volterra and, as it was quickly suppressed, it cannot be said to have struck the country a heavy blow. That the revolt nonetheless was a disaster in both a physical and a moral sense cannot be denied. Nor is it possible to free Lorenzo from blame, because, owing no doubt to the newness of his rule, he championed the use of strong measures against Volterra in order to impress the whole body of Florentine subject towns with his unshaken resolution.

Like every other subject town, Volterra accepted from Florence its two leading officials, the podestà, who acted as chief executive, and the capitano, who commanded a small occupying force. Under these two agents of the suzerain power the old local government retained considerable authority over both the town itself and the surrounding territory. In the year 1471 there arose a dispute between the local government and a private company organized to exploit the limited and relatively worthless alum mines within the Volterran dominion. Alum, we should remember, was an astringent mineral indispensable for dyeing; however, into the contest between town and company we need not go farther than to say that each party to the controversy was convinced that the law was on its side. When Florence interfered in behalf of the company, there was a popular upflare in Volterra which developed into a tumultuous demonstration against the Florentine representative on the ground, the podestà. The Arno citizens had always been nervous about their subject towns, all of which continued to nurse dreams of liberty; and spurred on to precipitate measures by Lorenzo de' Medici, the signory levied war on its rebellious dependency without first offering to negotiate. That, besides on the patent political ground, Lorenzo was inclined to take action also for private financial reasons is impossible to prove and very difficult to believe. As he was the sole lessee of the immensely more profitable alum mines at Tolfa in the State of the Church, he cannot very well be charged with acting in his selfish interest when he lent his support to a rival company operating at Volterra. A mercenary army was assembled and the recalcitrant town besieged until, recognizing the futility of further resistance, it signed an agreement with the Florentine commissioners accompanying the troops to surrender on the assurance that the inhabitants were to be secure in life and goods. But when on June 17, 1472, the Florentine condottiere, Federigo of Montefeltro, rode into the town at the head of his bands a terrible thing happened. Once within the walls the mercenaries broke rank, threw themselves on the inhabitants and their possessions, and could not be brought under control until they had put the ancient stronghold to a devastating sack. It is impossible to exaggerate the misery and despair into which the hideous excesses perpetrated by the troops plunged the poor people of Volterra. The sack supplied evidence, although additional evidence on this head was certainly not needed, that the mercenary armies of the day, always eager to avoid shedding each other's blood on the field of battle, were no better than organized robber bands. Conceding that the monstrous event is referable, in the main, to the revolting military system which prevailed throughout the peninsula, we cannot wholly free Lorenzo from responsibility. While he cannot be charged with the sack, as his enemies have clamorously done ever since the event, he was the author of the needlessly aggressive policy, which, getting out of hand, subjected the old Etruscan hill town to an unspeakable degradation.

Apart from the, after all, local character of the Volterran siege and sack, peace continued to prevail and the sky over Tuscany remained blue and hopeful until dark clouds began to rear their thunderheads along the Romagna border. Therewith we are obliged to turn to the papacy, to the honors of which, in the year 1471, the cardinals elevated a Franciscan friar, who took the title of Sixtus IV. As soon as the Great Schism had been healed over half a century before, a main object of the popes had come to be to establish themselves as the unchallenged civil rulers of their considerable dominions embracing a large part of central and north-central Italy. In measure as the four great states of Venice, Milan, Florence, and Naples emerged out of the Italian chaos, it became desirable and even necessary for the papacy to acquire a commensurate political power if it was not to fall into galling dependence on its stronger neighbors. However, the post-schism popes up to the accession of Sixtus IV had not made much headway with this program. In the country around Rome the great feudal families, such as the Orsini and the Colonna, exercised an undiminished authority, while in Umbria, the Marches of Ancona, and the Romagna a vast number of petty tyrants had established themselves in the various towns, who, in return for the formal acknowledgment of the papal suzerainty and the payment of a small tribute, expected to be left in undisturbed possession of the territory they had illegally appropriated. On his first mounting the papal throne Sixtus IV did not depart from the policy of his predecessors, for he accepted the situation as he found it. Then a savage energy, native to his rude blood, made him revolt against the merely decorative power which he found himself exercising and persuaded him to undertake measures calculated to bring at least Umbria and the Romagna under his more direct control. With this policy went hand in hand an illicit but ungovernable passion to push his family into prominence by endowing individual members thereof with papal lands in order to establish them as hereditary rulers at the side of the many other dynasts who were lording it over a divided Italy. Sixtus had many nephews, some belonging to his own, the della Rovere family, others, the sons of his sister, bearing the husband's name of Riario. In his early years the pope directed the main stream of his favors to Pietro Riario, who, being like himself a Franciscan friar, had benefice on benefice bestowed on him until it looked as if all the riches of the church were to be dropped bit by bit into his lap. But Pietro died in the year 1473, the victim of his own excesses, whereupon the pope picked as the new object of his extravagant family affection Pietro's brother, Girolamo. Before the papal favor drew the obscure Girolamo into the light of history, he had been either a small customs' clerk or an equally unimportant grocer's assistant. The momentous question never having been authoritatively settled must remain undecided. What is certain and alone matters is that the pope resolved to transform the customs' clerk (or grocer's assistant) into an Italian princeling by making the most of an opportunity afforded in 1474 of establishing him as lord of the Romagnole town of Imola.

That move completely reversed the friendly relations which had hitherto obtained between Sixtus IV and Lorenzo de' Medici. Lorenzo had inherited one of the great states of Italy, which his father and grandfather had labored to consolidate within and without. The state of Florence was enveloped on the south, east, and north by the State of the Church, than which moreover it was much smaller in extent. The political weakness of its papal neighbor was therefore an advantage for Florence, and this was so instinctively recognized that when, a hundred years before, the papacy had for the first time in its history been territorially consolidated by Cardinal Albornoz, the Florentines felt so deeply aggrieved that they waged the famous War of the Eight Saints against the Supreme Pontiff. However, the work of Albornoz proved ephemeral, the papal state again fell into scores of substantially independent principalities, and Florence breathed more easily on being freed from the nightmare of a powerful, enveloping neighbor. Since, owing to its dominantly commercial character, Florence found it impossible to engage in an undisguised career of conquest, it was content to perpetuate the chaos at its border and provide the needed security against the frequent Umbrian and Romagnole disturbances spilling over into Tuscany by a cordon of petty border states under Florentine influence. Communities of this kind were Bologna, Faenza, Città di Castello, and Perugia. Nominally papal, they hovered under the Florentine wing. Among these dependencies figured also Imola, the little city which in 1474 the pope determined to acquire for his nephew, Girolamo Riario.

In this first political clash between Lorenzo and Sixtus IV the latter was victorious and Imola, lying in the plain of the Romagna at the foot of the Tuscan Apennines, became the prize of Girolamo. Aware that this was but a first step, the alarmed Lorenzo cast about for means to hinder the extension of Girolamo's power over Faenza and Forlì, to which nearby towns it was known his ambition was directed. As Venice and Milan were as much interested as himself in keeping the pope from becoming too firmly established in the Romagna, the Magnificent entered into negotiations with them, and in November, 1474, perfected a new triple alliance dedicated, according to the dishonest verbiage of such documents, to the safeguarding of the peninsula's peace. To calm the alarm which the pope and the king of Naples might be expected to feel, an article was added inviting their participation in the new arrangements. Notwithstanding, these two powers took offense and answered the provocation with an alliance of their own. It can hardly be doubted, and later, after the disastrous outcome, Lorenzo himself did not doubt that it had been a grave error on his part to arouse the wrath of the pope by spinning an intrigue against him, especially as the new turn of Florentine diplomacy involved an abandonment of the old triple alliance, Milan-Florence-Naples, which had served as the solid rock of the city's foreign policy since the days of his grandfather. And once committed to a false program, Lorenzo got himself more and more entangled. When at about the time of the Imola affair the pope had trouble with the Vitelli family, which had usurped the power over Città di Castello, he discovered that Lorenzo was giving support to the enemy, and Lorenzo's disingenuous denial of the fact did not make his case any better. Despite these serious clashes over fundamental matters of policy, the differences between the two rulers might have been ironed out had it not been for the pope's inflammable temper and his brutal resolve to have his undisputed way. To his mind Lorenzo had become an implacable enemy, whom it was his business to injure in any and every manner he could. It was in this spirit that he seized the opportunity to appoint a Florentine enemy of Lorenzo's, Francesco Salviati, to the archbishopric of Pisa. What made the papal action worse, it occurred in the face of a solemn undertaking by Sixtus not to nominate any bishops or archbishops of Tuscany without previous consultation with the Florentine government. Deeply offended in his turn, Lorenzo revenged himself by forcibly preventing Salviati from taking possession of his see for three years. This enraged the archbishop, who was a member of a powerful Florentine clan, as much as the pope, and did not exactly strengthen the Magnificent's hold on the city.

The unfortunate conflict failing to be brought to a settlement tended in the manner of such personal issues to be exacerbated by every passing incident. How much more, then, by such a capital event as took place at Milan on December 26, 1476. On that day three Milanese youths, incited to their deed by the encomiums lavished by the classical authors on tyrannicide, murdered the Duke Galeazzo Maria as he was entering the church of St. Stephen. He was one of the most infamous representatives of the current political type of the despot, on whose bier it is not likely that there fell so much as a single tear. However, politically his disappearance had disastrous consequences not only for Milan and Italy but also for Florence. His heir was a three-year-old boy, for whom his mother assumed the regency. As her rule was challenged by the four restless and ambitious brothers of the deceased duke, Milan was threatened with a long period of disturbances, during which it would not count for much in the Italian parallelogram of forces. For Lorenzo this signified the enfeeblement and possible collapse of his leading ally and the consequent weakening of his own position. It followed from this blow to his prestige that his many enemies were encouraged to assume the offensive; and since they were desperate men, who had lost their moral scruples in an Italy which, cut loose from its medieval anchorage, had become the scene of every form of violence, they resolved to resort to murder and, after the manner of the Milanese assassins, to exalt their crime by representing it to themselves and to the world as an instance of the honorable practice of tyrannicide.

Therewith we have arrived at the Pazzi plot, which merits a close scrutiny, not only because it is the outstanding event of Lorenzo's political career, but also because it affords an unequaled opportunity for familiarizing ourselves with some of the less admirable manners of Renaissance Italy. The origin of the plot takes us to Rome, where, in the shadow of the papacy, most of Lorenzo's envenomed personal enemies were in the habit of congregating for the exchange of views. The plan to murder Lorenzo and his brother Giuliano, coupled with the design to seize the Florentine government, was in the first instance hatched by two equally unprincipled young men, Girolamo Riario and Francesco Pazzi. The ex-customs' clerk was inspired by a hatred of

Lorenzo as uncontrolled as that of his uncle, the pope, to which was added the ever-present fear that he would be dispossessed of his precious Imola by the resentful Florentine ruler as soon as the protecting hand of his aged uncle should have been withdrawn by death. A much more important figure, considered by himself, was Francesco Pazzi, member of the great Florentine clan which has given to the conspiracy its historical name. The Pazzi were a more ancient family than the Medici and had accordingly been stigmatized as nobles or, more properly, as magnates, by the Ordinances of Justice. In Cosimo's day they had, as a special favor, been stricken off the magnate list, thereby becoming eligible once more for all the offices of state. A certain intimacy between Medici and Pazzi had followed, of which one bit of evidence was that Lorenzo's sister, Bianca, had been married to young Guglielmo Pazzi, brother of the above-mentioned Francesco. But the spirit of family rivalry persisted, intensified by the circumstance that the bank representing the leading business enterprise of the Pazzi was in sharp competition with the bank of the Medici. Moreover, owing to the rift between Lorenzo and the pope, the Pazzi bank had recently scored a great victory over its Medici competitor. Following the example of his immediate predecessors, Sixtus IV on his accession continued to deposit the papal monies in the Roman branch of the Medicean firm until, angered by the conflict over Imola, he transferred his account to the Roman branch of the Pazzi. Now of that prospering Roman branch young Francesco Pazzi was the resident head, and by becoming the leading financial adviser of the pope and the pope's nephew was thrown into intimate personal relations with them. He is described as a small, thin, restless man, who had persuaded himself that the Medici had usurped a position in Florence which properly belonged to the more ancient and distinguished Pazzi and, kindling his enmity to Lorenzo at the wrathful fires of the upstart lord of Imola, he gradually prepared his mind for extreme measures to rid himself of his foe and the city of Florence of its tyrant.

To these two violent young men was added the sinister figure of Francesco Salviati, archbishop of Pisa, savagely averse to Lorenzo ever since the latter had attempted to block his appointment to the Pisan prelacy. The active participation in the plot by one of the most exalted officials of the Catholic church is a Renaissance touch one would not care to miss from the resulting blood-curdling drama. Better than anything else it helps us to realize how far the corruption of morals had gone under the dissolution of medieval culture and the reign of a fashionable paganism. And the murder charge, from which for the archbishop there is no escape, at least brushes the figure of none other than the vicar of Christ, the pope himself. When, after the plot had been well advanced by its three main promoters, Girolamo Riario, Francesco Pazzi, and the archbishop Salviati, Sixtus IV was informed of its character and objectives, he approved heartily insofar as the overthrow of the Medici brothers was concerned, but at the same time he salved his conscience by insisting that there must be no bloodshed. He might as well have ordered the brothers drowned but not in water! Giving the pope the benefit of every doubt, we cannot, unless we wish deliberately to bury our heads in the sand, exonerate him from the charge of having been at least an accessory before the fact. In spite of the papal warning, the conspirators went on with their murder plans exactly as if the pope had not spoken, and presently picked a daring captain in the lord of Imola's employ, a certain Gian Batista da Montesecco (a name any grand opera brigand might envy) as the man to do the deed. Montesecco accepted the invitation and, making all the necessary arrangements, carried them to the very threshold of fulfilment, when he withdrew on learning that it had been arranged for him to dispatch Lorenzo in church during the celebration of the mass. Owing to his superstitious reluctance to shed blood in a Christian temple, Montesecco had almost at the last minute to be replaced by less scrupulous assassins, but as he did not leave town, he was captured after the event. This is distinctly important, since before he was executed as an accomplice he wrote out a full confession, which is our main source for the plot.[3]

After many changes of program due to the difficulty of putting both the intended victims simultaneously, in modern gangland language, "on the spot," it was agreed that the murder was to take place in the great cathedral of Florence during the celebration of High Mass on Sunday, April 26, 1478. Because of Montesecco's default, substitutes had to be found without delay, and the dispatch with which this was done indicates that the Medici were surrounded by a host of deadly enemies. Two disaffected priests volunteered to replace Montesecco and to account for Lorenzo, while Francesco Pazzi and another oligarch with a personal grievance against the Magnificent, Baroncelli by name, agreed without hesitation to attend to Giuliano. The role which the archbishop Salviati assigned to himself was to occupy the palace and take over the government. In this undertaking he was to be aided by old Jacopo Pazzi, the head of the house and uncle of Francesco. Jacopo had at first refused to be drawn into the conspiracy, but as soon as he became persuaded that it could not fail, he joined the others, accepting as his particular task the rousing of the masses in support of the archbishop's action at the Palazzo Pubblico. Owing to the many interlocking divisions of the plot, so large a number of people had to be drawn into the secret that it will always remain a marvel that it was not prematurely divulged. Girolamo Riario, in all probability the original deviser of the conspiracy, chose not to endanger his precious life by direct participation, but he magnanimously conceded the honor of representing the Riario name to a young nephew of his and grand-nephew of the pope. Although this papal grand-nephew was only seventeen years old and was still attending classes at the university, he had already been named a cardinal, and his coming to Florence to pay the Medici rulers a visit was arranged in the expectation that they would be obliged to honor him with a succession of public entertainments. One of these occasions was the mass of April 26, which it is not likely the brothers would have attended, except to show respect for the city's guest. While young Cardinal Riario thus took an important part in the day's proceedings, his was almost certainly the role of the innocent decoy, since his elders considered him too young to be initiated into the bloody business about to be launched.

The signal agreed on for the simultaneous assassination of the brothers was

---

[3] Montesecco's confession will be found among the documents printed by Capponi, *Storia di Firenze*, at the end of his second volume.

that most solemn moment of the Catholic service, the elevation of the host; and no sooner, to the tinkling of the mass bell, was the host elevated by the officiating priest standing before the high altar under Brunelleschi's majestic cupola than the murderers leaped upon their victims. Francesco Pazzi and Baroncelli quickly dispatched the young and handsome Giuliano. When he was later laid out for burial, it was discovered that he had poured out his life's blood by nineteen gaping wounds. In such blind rage did Francesco Pazzi continue to hack at the prostrate form of his enemy that he wounded himself in the thigh so severely that it was only with the greatest difficulty that he made his escape from the scene. The two priests allotted to Lorenzo proved themselves less expert in the art of murder than the two civilians, and Lorenzo, alertly turning on his assailants, was able with drawn sword to hold them at bay until with the help of some friends he could take refuge in the sacristy. The vast concourse of worshipers, unable to grasp what was going on, filled the echoing vaults of the great cathedral with a clamor of confused cries and sped away in every direction. When after some moments of breathless waiting behind the doors of the sacristy (the north sacristy with the fine bronze doors of Luca della Robbia), loud knocking was heard to the accompaniment of voices assuring the group within that the newcomers were friends, the slender stripling, Sigismondo della Stufa, one of the devoted band who had helped Lorenzo make his escape, climbed agilely to the organ gallery over the sacristy door, from where he had a view of the whole spacious interior of the great edifice. It had been completely emptied by the panic of its worshipers, the men demanding admission at the sacristy doors were recognized as friends come to carry Lorenzo in safety to his house, and in the aisle just beyond the great octagon of the choir the startled eyes of young Sigismondo saw what they remembered till their light went out: the crumpled figure of Giuliano lying in a pool of blood.

While this only half-successful man-hunt was being conducted around the principal altar of one of the great temples of Christendom, the archbishop Salviati and old Jacopo Pazzi attempted to fulfil their part of the plot by seizing the government and inciting the masses to revolt against the lordship of the Medici. They failed miserably for the reason that the government and citizens sided with practical unanimity with their reputed tyrants. On invading the palace the archbishop and his troop of thirty helpers were promptly arrested; and when the pale and haggard figure of old Jacopo, armed and mounted on his war horse, passed through the streets hoarsely shouting *Popolo* and *Libertà*, the ancient rallying-cry of the Florentine masses, the people answered with a lusty, *Palle, Palle*, to signify their devotion to their present rulers. The shout referred to the six red pellets or balls constituting the Medicean coat of arms. Meanwhile the news of the assault in the cathedral had spread with the rapidity of lightning through the town, drawing the whole excited population into the streets and squares. Before the hostility of the constantly waxing crowds the routed Jacopo retreated to his palace and fled thence without delay into the mountains. And now there was no longer any possibility of restraining the maddened people. They became that murderous thing, a mob, which clamored for revenge and blood and would not

be denied. Obedient to its raucous summons, the officials of the Palazzo Pubblico tossed one after the other of the archbishop's captured attendants through
the windows to the pavement, much as a keeper might toss meat into a pit
of hunger-crazed bears; and finally they followed up this gesture of appeasement by swinging the archbishop himself, with a rope tied around his neck,
out of one of the Gothic windows, there to hang clad in his ornate vestments
till he was dead. In another part of the town the crowd invaded the Pazzi
residence and, dragging the murderer Francesco from the bed where he lay
writhing with his self-inflicted wound, insisted on rushing him to the palace
in order that, suspended by the neck from a mullioned window, he might
serve as a companion piece to that arch traitor, the archbishop. Not till every
individual even remotely connected with the plot had been captured and
been either murdered outright by the mob or executed by the authorities
in a manner indistinguishable from murder was, and then only after many
days, an approximate tranquillity restored to the tumultuous town. Young
and innocent Cardinal Riario was fortunately spared by the government's
taking him into its safekeeping. Even the hate-blinded multitude seemed to
have sensed that he was no more than the dupe of his criminal elders and
desisted from its original intention to have his blood. If among so many grue-
some acts of vengeance, there is an act of superlative gruesomeness, it befell
old Jacopo, head of his house. Captured by peasants while he was threading
his way through the hills of the Mugello, he was brought back to Florence to
be tortured and hanged. Servants then laid him to rest in the beautiful chapel
of his family at Santa Croce. But the populace was unwilling that he should
enjoy so honorable an interment. Once and then again his body was dragged
from its grave. On the second occasion it was a company of street urchins
who took the matter in hand. The horrible mockery to which these children
of the Florentine slums subjected the half-decayed corpse is too repulsive to
relate. Suffice it that they at last tossed the mangled remains into the Arno
and that they slowly floated down the stream until, after many days, they
cleared the bridge at Pisa and passed out into the sea.

Thus amidst an orgy of violence and bloodshed expired the Pazzi conspiracy. Although the assassins had disposed of Giuliano, the far more important Lorenzo had made his escape and drew from an outraged people such
extravagant expressions of loyalty that his rule, instead of being shaken, was
more firmly established than before. But the threat to his life and state was
by no means ended. In a sense it may even be said to have only begun. For
the pope who, baulked of his prey, refused to consider any feature of the terrible Florentine drama save the enforced detention of his grand-nephew and
the indignities heaped upon the sacred person of an archbishop, excommuni-
cated Lorenzo and threatened to put the city and all Tuscany under interdict
if the malefactor was not delivered into his hands to be punished as he deserved. As Florence steadfastly refused to do the papal bidding, the interdict
was duly pronounced and immediately after was followed by war. Shoulder
to shoulder with the pope stood his ally, the king of Naples; and when these
two powers took the field against Lorenzo, the Florentine allies, Milan and
Venice, automatically armed in Lorenzo's support. By the summer of 1478 all

Italy in the Age of
Lorenzo the Magnificent

Scale of Miles

0 20 40 60 80 100

D stands for Duchy
M stands for Marquisate
REP. stands for Republic
R. stands for River

ITALY IN THE AGE OF LORENZO THE MAGNIFICENT

Italy was in arms, as most of the numerous small states joined one or the other of the two major combinations. However, the turmoil was not quite so devastating as the wide extent of the struggle would suggest. The wretched Italian military system made swift and vigorous action in the field impossible. To be sure, the evil worked both ways, but in the end it favored Florence since, if the enemy had commanded a more effective system, the Red Lily could hardly have escaped destruction. Never since the city had turned to the use of mercenaries had it had luck with them, and the new occasion proved no exception to the rule. What made a bad situation worse was that the help Florence expected to get from its two allies was insufficiently furnished. Venice was involved in a war with the Turks which called for the expenditure of all its strength, and Milan was so disturbed by the interminable struggle between the duchess regent and her intriguing brothers-in-law that the government was often completely paralyzed.

Under these circumstances King Ferrante of Naples and Sixtus IV, who assumed the offensive and invaded Tuscany on a common plan from the south and southeast, might have swiftly overwhelmed Lorenzo if their warfare had not been under the same curse as that of their opponents. Even so, in the course of the second campaign, fought in 1479, they came within a hair of achieving their purpose. At Poggio Imperiale, near Poggibonsi, the Florentines had constructed a fortified camp in order to block the advance of the enemy into the Arno Valley. On September 7, King Ferrante's son, Alfonso, duke of Calabria, made a surprise attack on the Florentine camp, captured it, and drove the enemy in headlong flight toward Florence. Not till the panic-stricken fugitives had reached San Casciano, some eight miles from the Tuscan capital, could they be regathered into even the semblance of a fighting force. It is probable that if Calabria had pushed gallantly on, he might have driven right through San Casciano to the gates of the city. But such determination was not in the military style of the day. Instead of pursuing his advantage, the duke returned on his track to lay siege to the little town of Colle; and on November 24, on the approach of winter, he proposed the usual seasonal truce, which the Florentines eagerly accepted.

When, on the signing of the truce, the clear-sighted Lorenzo reviewed his situation, he had to admit it was desperate. True, the Florentines had made their ruler's cause their own to a degree almost unparalleled in the history of Italy. But how much longer would they resist the grinding pressure of circumstance? To the heavy taxation necessitated by the war was added a wide destruction of crops, for the conflict had been waged largely on Tuscan soil. The diminished supplies brought famine and famine brought pestilence, famine's hideous twin brother. Finally, there was the interdict, which for the mass of the still deeply religious population was a very heavy trial. From the ever-deepening gloom suspended over Florence and its ruler there was no possible escape except through peace and the only avenue to peace was surrender. In measure as the pope, who had started the war in the spirit and with the aim of revenge, was cheered with the prospect of victory, he became increasingly implacable. It was impossible to surrender to him till every other resource had failed. Luckily for Lorenzo the king of Naples was not equally adamant.

For his own part the Magnificent was firmly persuaded that it was directly against the interest of Naples to weaken Florence and tip the always precarious balance of Italy in the pope's favor, If only he could present his arguments to King Ferrante in person, he might yet win his case. Distractedly revolving these thoughts, he resolved to appeal to his Milanese ally to intervene at Naples in his behalf. In that Lombard state the situation had recently achieved a certain clarification through the definite replacement of the duchess regent by one of her brothers-in-law, Lodovico. This is the complex, typically Renaissance personage, who, called from his dark complexion *Il Moro* (the Moor), was destined hereafter to play a sinister part in unbarring the gates of Italy to the foreigner who had long been waiting for the opportunity to enter. In spite of the traitor he became, Lodovico was a man of distinct gifts and from 1479 on the government of Milan rested exclusively in his hands as regent for his young nephew, the duke. His answer to Lorenzo's appeal was to assure him of Milanese support at Naples if he would frankly put his destiny into the hands of King Ferrante. When, following the Moor's advice, Lorenzo was unofficially assured that he would be honorably received by the Neapolitan court, he no longer hesitated. Early in December he secretly left Florence for the Tuscan coast, took ship at a small Maremma port, and set sail for the southern capital. It was a dramatic step which once more fanned to a blaze the waning devotion of his fellow-countrymen. In their eyes he was risking his person to obtain the peace, for the lack of which they were slowly perishing; and a feature that may have appealed to their volatile nature even more than his patriotism was that he boldly took the gambler's chance of staking his all on a single throw.

While the diplomatic correspondence in our possession [4] proves that Lorenzo's famous voyage was carefully prepared by him and was not the sudden improvisation he wished to have it appear, it nonetheless had about it an element of risk and sacrifice which could not but enthrall the imagination. There was always the chance that he might not be released if he did not sign the treaty which the victor dictated or that the treaty he finally accepted would be so ignominious that his angered fellow-citizens would reject the document and the negotiator along with it. Arrived at Naples, Lorenzo, although handsomely welcomed, trod anything but a path of roses. King Ferrante, and more especially his son, the duke of Calabria, had no idea of letting Florence escape without paying at least some of the usual penalties of defeat. For three months the Magnificent with cogent eloquence and ever-gracious manners argued the terms of peace with his victorious hosts until in February, 1480, the document was at last perfected. That the Florentines were mulcted in considerable sums of money and had to make some slight cessions of territory goes without saying; but only an intemperate enemy would have the effrontery to affirm that Lorenzo, on re-entering his city, had not brought back peace with honor. The vast majority of the Florentines accordingly overflowed with gratitude and greeted as their deliverer the man who had terminated the war which had pushed them to the edge of the abyss.

Even with Naples pacified the war was not terminated altogether. There

[4] Fabroni, Vol. II, *Adnotationes,* 99, 104.

was still the pope to be placated, and the pope was not converted to a kindlier attitude by what to him was the base desertion of their common cause by his ally of Naples. At this point the hidden rulers of the universe came to Lorenzo's aid; at least what happened must have seemed to him like a divine intervention, even though its human instrument was the hated infidel Turk. On a hot August day of the year 1480 a Turkish flotilla made a sudden descent on the Neapolitan coast town of Otranto and captured it. The Moslem enemy had established a foothold in Italy and an apprehensive tremor passed through the length of the peninsula. The duke of Calabria, who had lingered on in Sienese territory unwilling, in spite of the peace treaty, to surrender the Florentine fortresses he had taken in the war, was obliged to return to the south with all possible speed. In the following year he recaptured Otranto from the Turks, certainly the most notable achievement of his undistinguished career. The enforced withdrawal of the Neapolitan garrisons from the Florentine towns they had hesitated to evacuate was a pure windfall for the Red Lily, but it was not the only advantage accruing to it from the Turkish menace. In the face of the Moslem invasion Sixtus IV was prompted to remember his responsibilities as shepherd of the Christian flock and, moved to proclaim the need of common action on the part of all Italians, he could no longer with any show of decency prosecute his private grudge against Lorenzo. He let himself be drawn into negotiations, which on December 3, 1480, were concluded with a remarkable act of reconciliation. Before the middle door of St. Peter's church a body of Florentine commissioners were received by him wearing the triple crown and seated on his chair of state upholstered in purple silk, and with the magnanimity becoming a supreme pontiff he granted the penitents his pardon for having attacked them. The commissioners, grave, elderly men, played the role of submission assigned to them with the same high regard for the proprieties; and after the pope had touched each in turn with his staff, thus cleansing them of their taint, they humbly kissed his foot and, in sign of their readmission to the Christian flock, followed him into the church to participate in a solemn mass of thanksgiving. Thus closed the dark chapter of the Pazzi conspiracy. Rescued as by a miracle from an infinity of perils, Lorenzo was henceforth regarded as fortune's darling and became the leading figure of the Italian political world.

XXIII. The Magnificent Lorenzo (1480-92)

ATROCIOUS as was the plot from which Lorenzo had barely escaped with his life and hardly less atrocious as was the subsequent war, he was too prudent and level-headed a man not to recognize that in a political sense he was himself not free from blame for the recent events. For, in order to create difficulties for the pope in his attempt to establish his relatives in the Romagna, he had abandoned the proved alliance with Naples and Milan, substituting therefor a union with Milan and Venice. But when the war waged against him by Sixtus IV and King Ferrante threatened him with ruin, he had been obliged by means of his hazardous voyage to Naples to find his way back to the earlier combination, from which, in sign that he had learned his lesson, he never again departed. For the remainder of his life he regarded the triple alliance of Milan-Florence-Naples as the anchor of his foreign policy and the best guaranty of the peace of the peninsula. At the same time he very substantially altered his attitude toward the papacy. If he continued to believe that it was to the interest of Florence that the State of the Church should not become consolidated at the expense of the many semi-independent lordlings established on its soil, he was no longer prepared to block every papal move in the direction of better control but rather to concede something to the pope in the hope of not again falling into that ruler's disfavor. For Lorenzo had been made aware of the enormous reserve strength of the papacy and was resolved, so far as lay in his power, not again to enter the lists against it. Without therefore wavering in his attachment to the triple alliance, he used his best skill to draw the pope within its orbit. That was difficult, however, as long as Sixtus IV lived, since Sixtus, having attacked the problem of the temporal power, neither would nor could recede from a course which kept his neighbors in a perpetual state of alarm. Even when the virile Sixtus was followed by the weakly vacillating Innocent VIII (1484-92), the situation was not materially changed, for the conversion of the loose dominion of the church into an effective civil state had by now become a papal obligation which no successor of Sixtus, whether bold or faint-hearted, could avoid assuming.

The policy of Lorenzo in the second and concluding period of his rule has been correctly described as the attempt to preserve the peace of Italy by maintaining a judicious equilibrium among the five leading states of the peninsula. Entirely contrary to the facts however, he is often credited with having achieved his purpose; and to clinch the argument it is pointed out that he had hardly disappeared from the scene when the whole delicate system of balance, which none but his extraordinary skill could operate, collapsed like a house of cards. Now while it is true that the invasion of the French of 1494, which totally disrupted the Italian state system and inaugurated the enslavement of the peninsula, did not take place till two years after Lorenzo's death, a French intervention had periodically threatened ever since the days of Lorenzo's grandfather, Cosimo. In fact, Cosimo and his ally, Francesco Sforza, as early as 1452 had signed an alliance with the then king of France, Charles VII, by which that sovereign agreed to aid them in their struggle against Naples and Venice. While the treaty did not on that occasion result in direct French action, Florence and Milan had threatened their Italian enemies with a foreign sovereign, and the example thus set was certain to be imitated. In the course of the following decades ambassadors from every Italian state at one time or another found their way to Paris to curry favor with the French king and invite his participation in peninsular affairs; and if Charles VII and his successor, Louis XI (1461–83), had, in spite of repeatedly renewed temptation, never crossed the Alps, it was solely because, deeply involved in domestic troubles, they were unable to embark on a perilous venture beyond their border. However, as this condition was not likely to last forever, the descent of the French was for many decades suspended like a portent over the peninsula, filling all its states, large and small alike, with alarm, but at the same time exercising a curious, hypnotic fascination. To appreciate the full significance of the half-dreaded, half-desired event, we must not forget that the ancient claim of the house of Anjou to the kingdom of Naples had by the recent extinction of the Angevin line (1481) passed to the French crown, and that therefore Louis XI's successor, Charles VIII, might readily persuade himself that in attacking King Ferrante he was doing no more than making an honorable effort to recover stolen goods. Moreover, in addition to the Neapolitan claim, there was the claim of another branch of the royal line, the house of Orléans, to the duchy of Milan based on its descent from a princess of the former ruling family of the Visconti; and with this claim the king, as head of his house, could also identify himself if he so desired. Every discussion of Italian politics in Lorenzo's time that does not assign a central position to the continued French threat of intervention based on either the Neapolitan or the Milanese claim is beside the mark. Indeed to understand Lorenzo's policy at all, it is necessary to see that it was governed by the aim to omit no measure calculated to cut off military action from beyond the Alps. That he had only a limited success is undeniable, since he had hardly departed this life when the long-threatened invasion took place, drawing down unspeakable calamities on Florence and all Italy. While we must admit that Lorenzo did not succeed in staving off the French avalanche, we may confidently assert that of all the Italian rulers he was the least guilty in connection with that dire event.

Only in case the French threat is conceded its due weight can it be clearly understood what is meant by describing Lorenzo's Italian endeavors as dedicated to the maintenance of peace. It required no particular insight on his part to arrive at the view which was the substance of his policy. This core and kernel was that if the five Italian powers continued their traditional quarrels, they would sooner or later with mathematical certainty draw the French into their conflicts, and that the measure alone capable of keeping the northern monarch from crossing the Alps was the solid peace front of Milan, Naples, Florence, Venice, and the pope. Toward this end the triple alliance of the first three, which, with interruptions, had been in existence since the days of Cosimo, was regarded by Lorenzo as a happy, preparatory measure; and after his one lapse, productive of the war of 1478-80, which had brought him to the verge of extinction, Lorenzo, as already said, faithfully based his Italian policy on this league. Furthermore, he attempted to extend its action by drawing the pope within its fold; and he would not have been averse to having it include also the Venetians, had it not been a matter of common knowledge that these islanders so doggedly pursued their exclusive advantage that they could never be trusted to follow a policy that took account of any other interest than their own. Had Lorenzo been able to expand the triple into a quintuple alliance, it would have been an achievement of absolutely capital import, as a sincerely conceived quintuple alliance would have been, in effect, an Italian confederation. In the light of subsequent events it is easy to see that nothing less than the unbroken front presented by such a confederation would have saved the peninsula from the French invasion of 1494 and from all the subsequent invasions, for which that first action served as precedent. But so impossible of fulfilment was the confederation program that, even in its most soaring flight, Lorenzo's thought no more than casually brushed the idea. For an effective federation the one indispensable prerequisite was the sentiment of nationality. Unfortunately for Italy this sentiment had not yet been born among the residents of the land or else was cherished by such small and scattered numbers that it possessed no collective vigor. The mainspring of the competitive Italian states was naked self-interest, and every government, having for generations pursued as its leading concern the widening of its boundaries at the expense of its neighbors, looked upon every contiguous government as an obstacle in its path and viewed it, if not always openly, at least secretly, with envy, suspicion, fear, and hatred.

Such was the monstrous situation to which Lorenzo, a realistic statesman, as he had to be, and not an empty daydreamer, was obliged to accommodate his policy. He therefore set himself no higher goal than peace, knowing full well that even peace was so considerable an innovation in war-torn Italy that he could do no more than strive with all his might to create a sentiment in its favor. The simplest measure to secure peace would have been the renunciation on the part of one and all of the states of their hitherto hotly pursued policy of expansion, but Lorenzo entertained no illusions regarding the possibility of having such a course adopted. The best and only pressure he could bring to bear in behalf of his cherished measure was perpetually to remind the Italian governments that a foreign power once admitted to the peninsula would enslave them all in turn, and that the very self-interest which each government accepted as its law dictated the avoidance of upheavals calculated to convey the impression that divided Italy would fall an easy prey to an enterprising invader.

It does not impugn Lorenzo's statesmanship to declare that he was unable to impose on his fellow-rulers the peace policy in which he believed. He plied them with his powers of persuasion and they, hardening their minds against his arguments, with a stupid and criminal blindness persisted in the traditional pursuit of a narrowly selfish advantage. The peace of Italy was therefore as uninterruptedly disturbed after 1480 as had been the case before that date. Let the facts speak for themselves. In 1482 Pope Sixtus IV, still bent on improving his personal control in the Romagna, made an alliance with Venice for the purpose of partitioning Ferrara, thereby plunging Italy into a general war, since the triple alliance rushed promptly to Ferrara's aid. Although the Ferrarese war came to very little—what Italian war ever came to much?—it created disturbances that were not quieted for two years and freshly embittered the relations among the Italian powers. Besides, it revived the interest of France in the situation since France was urged by several reckless participants in the struggle to lend help and take sides. Hardly had this conflict been terminated when another war broke out (1485), this time between Naples and the pope. Each state thought it had good reasons to resort to arms, but it could easily be shown that the reasons were trivial and that essentially the outbreak was caused by nothing other than the savage ill feeling with which the Italian governments periodically overflowed. Again the other states were sucked into the vortex and again France began to loom, a shadowy giant clad in steel, across the summit of the Alps. Even after an accommodation had been arranged (1486) between Pope Innocent VIII and King Ferrante, a real pacification did not follow since the Neapolitan sovereign failed to comply with the terms of peace and the pope, filling the ears of all Europe with his protests, threatened every moment to renew the struggle. Lorenzo never ceased to pour water on the dangerous embers and to plead for a definitive settlement, but it was not till January, 1492, that the cantankerous recriminations between Rome and Naples, which an intriguing foreign power like France made it its business to keep alive, were brought to a mutually satisfactory adjustment.

Without taking the time to enumerate the countless minor disturbances of the Italian peace, chiefly in the ever-volcanic province of Romagna, the facts just recorded serve to show that, contrary to some encomiasts, who assign to Lorenzo the role of pacifier of his country, there was no peace in his day in passion-riven Italy. And again let it be said that his failure single-handedly to impose a policy, for which the other governments had neither sympathy nor understanding, draws no discredit on his head. It cannot even be fairly reckoned as an inconsistency on his part that, with the political competition continuing about him unabated, he should have utilized an occasional opportunity to strengthen himself territorially. As the head of the Florentine state he had a plain duty to improve its security, provided he could do so without turning the peninsula topsyturvy. This attitude will explain his action in regard to Sarzana. The important fortress of that name, which commanded the coast road leading southward from Liguria, had been acquired through purchase (1468) by his father Piero and ten years later had been seized by the original owners, the

Genoese, on the occasion of the threatening collapse of Florence toward the close of the war of the Pazzi conspiracy. The indignant Lorenzo was resolved to have Sarzana back as soon as the auspices were favorable. In 1484 he believed the moment had come, but he succeeded only in capturing Pietrasanta, some fifteen miles to the south of Sarzana and almost equally important as a defense against an enemy advancing on Tuscany from the north. Not till 1487 did Lorenzo retake Sarzana, and that the capture was effected under his personal direction and without precipitating a general war added greatly to his satisfaction. The Florentine people were no less narrowly patriotic than the inhabitants of the other Italian states and would not have given continued support to a ruler who did not make it a leading point of his policy to strain every nerve to maintain the integrity of their territory.

Nonetheless there was an ambiguous element in Lorenzo's pursuit of peace, of which he was himself well aware but which he was incapable of remedying. The Magnificent had made himself the advocate of peace largely in the hope of thus thwarting any ambition France might entertain to invade the peninsula. At the same time he maintained closer relations with the French court than any other Italian ruler and in and out of season protested that he was the devoted servant of the king. A number of pressing reasons imposed this course on him as unavoidable. For so many generations had the Florentines looked to the kings of France as the guardians of the sacred Guelph tradition that an attachment had sprung up, shared on the Arno by high and low alike and heartily reciprocated on the Seine. By Lorenzo's time the sentiment had acquired an independent life and, like the fabled chameleon, lived apparently on air. Notwithstanding, a close examination will reveal that it sucked its uninterrupted nourishment from the material advantages accruing to Florence from its commercial activities in the French kingdom. As far back as the thirteenth century it had been the French market which yielded the great mercantile companies of the Arno town their handsomest profits, and two hundred years later, in Lorenzo's time, the situation was still substantially unchanged. Moreover, the Florentines had ever been and still were in a highly vulnerable position, for their presence across the Alps was resented by the native traders and could be terminated at a moment's notice by the withdrawal of the special protection of the monarch. With Arno merchant prosperity hanging on the thread of the king's favor no Florentine government had ever been able to maintain any other attitude toward the Parisian court than one of a rather abject humility. To this general submission consecrated by long custom should be added the particular subjection into which the banking house of the Medici had slipped. Having already under Cosimo extended its operations into France, the firm had on the usual business score fallen into the royal dependence. Louis XI, to whom both Cosimo and his son Piero had shown themselves consistently devoted, in 1465 rewarded their zeal by an unusual concession. He permitted the Medici to stamp the lilies of France on one of the balls or *palle* of their coat-of-arms. Since that day a blue ball carrying three golden lilies stood out from the other five unadorned red balls in perpetual testimony of the grace conferred by a French king. As the heir of so honorable a royal friendship Lorenzo could do nothing but nurse it, especially as in his day the

Lyons branch of his bank rose to great eminence and served as the depository of the funds of innumerable French courtiers and noblemen.

The elements constituting Lorenzo's French problem were many and complicated but they are perfectly intelligible. While his political insight warned him of the peril threatening his own and every other Italian state from across the Alps, proper regard for the Gallic sentiments of his fellow-countrymen and important considerations involving their commercial interests as well as his own obliged him to cultivate an intimacy with the French court which caused the Arno republic to be regarded at Paris as a French protégé ready, whenever the call went forth, to smooth the king's way into the Promised Land beyond the Alps. Lorenzo was obliged to be deftly double-faced not to be found out at the Valois court as its secret antagonist. That he succeeded is clearly indicated by the unbroken good relations between himself and Paris to the end of his days. However, when two years after his death the French at length made their long-expected appearance on the scene and Lorenzo's son, Piero, came out into the open against them, their indignation flamed to heaven over what was to them his abominable treachery. This is not the place to enlarge on the incapable Piero's mistakes and puerilities; unquestionably they contributed to the disaster which overtook him and his state. Nonetheless, it is impossible to subscribe to the opinion voiced by many writers on Florentine history that, had Lorenzo been still alive, the catastrophe might have been averted. We may go so far as to grant that the resourceful Lorenzo would have found a way to avoid some of the worst consequences of the French invasion, but that he could have hindered the event and the many evils that flowed therefrom is a wholly unjustified assumption. It is to speak darkly and cryptically to declare that the invasion of 1494 was writ in the stars. However, the statement becomes defensible and even irrefutable if it intends to convey no more than that the grave event resulted from forces which were prepared in the womb of time and which no individual, not even one of such unusual talents as the lord of Florence, could have annulled. On the other hand, whoever is wont to weigh historical events in purely human scales will be disinclined to free Lorenzo from blame, in spite of his having been the only Italian who had a correct understanding of what foreign intervention signified. To such an interpreter of history Lorenzo's intimacy with and silent encouragement of France will constitute his tragic guilt, which, though dooming him to ultimate defeat, involved him in a heroic conflict with forces which he helped release and which proved stronger than himself.[1]

The domestic policy of Lorenzo was the product of the same subtle mind that conceived his foreign policy and it suffered, though not in the same degree, from a similar weakness. This was that, although dictated by essentially sound considerations, it did not enjoy the support of those immediately concerned and was imposed on unwilling citizens by a mixture of authority and sleight of hand. On succeeding his father he had, as we have seen, taken over the system of veiled control which had been in force since 1434. While it left

---

[1] For Lorenzo's relations to France see Buser, *Die Beziehungen der Mediceer zu Frankreich,* etc. Zweiter Abschnitt. For a recent appreciation of his peace policy see R. Palmarocchi, *La Politica Italiana di Lorenzo de' Medici.* Florence, 1933.

the old constitution of the priors apparently intact, it brought it under Medicean management by abolishing election by lot in favor of a hand-picked system operated by a board of accoppiatori. The constitution thus manipulated had, to put it moderately, at the very least worked as well as during any earlier period. Better control had, above all, greatly reduced the amount of domestic disturbance. Nonetheless, no sooner did the state become involved in war with its unescapable reverses and heavy costs, than the opposition, which normally remained in hiding, took heart and voiced its criticism in the councils. Not only were the councils still, as they had ever been, the outstanding popular feature of the Florentine system, but they were also composed of so many members that many individuals had found a seat in them who were not proved and tested Mediceans. During the disastrous war of the Pazzi conspiracy largely waged on Tuscan soil, a certain amount of opposition sprang to life in the councils, reasonably responsive as they would be to the trends of popular opinion. The repeated manifestations filled Lorenzo with alarm, and as soon as he had overcome the immediate crisis in his affairs by his surprise visit to Naples, he resolved on constitutional changes which would further weaken the popular elements still imbedded in the system.

If the Magnificent had not been a Florentine faced with a republican tradition of long standing, he might have considered that the time at length had come to replace the patchwork constitution inherited from the past with his open and confessed tyranny. All around him tyrants flourished, not because, though the thought must have occurred to many an indignant and suffering contemporary, that the time, long foretold, of Antichrist and the Day of Judgment had arrived, but because tyrants were the unattractive but solely available instruments for the reorganization of society following its medieval collapse. However, the powerful sentiments of his fellow-townsmen and doubtless, to a certain extent, his own sentiments forbade him openly to adopt the tyrannical solution. He would have to continue to respect republican appearances, while at the same time reducing the surviving liberal elements of the constitution and concentrating the power more effectively in his own hands. Only a few weeks after his return from Naples, on April 8, 1480, he attacked the problem by the measure which in Florence regularly initiated a "reform," a balìa endowed with sweeping powers. Without delay this balìa began its conventional, elaborate legerdemain, which we will deliberately ignore in order to fasten our attention on the rabbit it finally drew from its magical hat. This surprise animal was a new council, the council of Seventy, intended to supersede all the existing councils without, however, definitely and finally replacing them. In constitutionally conservative Florence nothing old was ever replaced, even though it no longer functioned in any effective sense.

Undeniably the council of Seventy was meant to become and became the core of the government. Its members sat for life, they filled vacancies in their ranks by co-optation, and all power in the state was concentrated in their hands. Moreover, as even seventy men more or less devoted to the Medicean interest were too many-headed a government to act efficiently and speedily, the Seventy delegated their most essential powers to two permanent committees. One of these was the *Otto di Pratica,* the Eight, intrusted with foreign and military matters; the other was a group of twelve set over finance, credit, and trade. The Otto di Pratica are not to be confused with the Otto di Guardia, a committee for police and criminal matters dating from the Albizzi era and left undisturbed by the latest reorganization. It is permissible to think of the Seventy as a self-perpetuating senate served by two working committees appointed from its membership. As already stated, the old councils continued to meet in order to approve the measures prepared by the Seventy, while the priors and gonfalonier of Justice, henceforth nominated by the Seventy acting as accoppiatori, continued their existence with no other significance than that of an ornamental figurehead of the still nominally republican ship of state. Lorenzo himself sat among the Seventy and was directly or indirectly represented on the two committees charged with the most important functions of government. In the gradual breakdown of the old constitution as well as in the complementary emergence of a Medicean monarchy the Seventy may be taken to mark a decisive step. There can be no doubt that the government became more responsive to a single guiding will; but the fact that the old forms, as hollowed out as a forest of dead oaks, were nonetheless left standing, testifies to a public state of mind which obliged the cautious Lorenzo substantially to continue the inherited Medicean anonymity and to refrain from too visibly playing the signore.

Probably it was the shaky public finances more than any other single governmental difficulty that prompted Lorenzo to strengthen his personal control. The finances were the feeblest feature of the Florentine and every other contemporary state; and the income tax of 1427, called the catasto, had not proved the cure-all that was hoped. Lorenzo clung to the commendable progressive feature added to the original system by Cosimo, while to his credit, be it said, he largely abandoned his grandfather's hateful practice of ruining his opponents by an excessive assessment. In spite of the complaints the income tax continued to elicit in Lorenzo's day, a modern student will find it difficult to disagree with its central principle. Still, the catasto was far from perfect since, for one thing, it was often levied many times in a single year, and again, because, though carried on the books of the Monte as an interest-bearing loan, the Monte, in periods of financial stress, arbitrarily reduced the interest or defaulted altogether. Deeply considered, the root of the trouble was that Florence wanted to play its part in the human drama as a great state but had no stomach for the increased costs which wars, frequent embassies, and a regulated administration of affairs entailed. Lorenzo could under no circumstances give up the income tax, but he could make concessions in regard to it to his main supporters, the merchants, who, like their kind through all the ages, were stiffly opposed to an examination of their ledgers to determine their profits. Besides, by various tricks of bookkeeping best known to themselves, the merchants could easily lead the tax authorities by the nose. In view of these circumstances, Lorenzo consented on the occasion of the reforms of 1480 to a bifurcation of the income tax. Henceforth the main burden of direct taxation fell on the returns from land and houses, while commercial profits, without being exactly made tax-exempt, escaped close governmental scrutiny by the imposition on the citizens of a progressive poll-tax.

While these changes in applying the income tax may from a purely administrative angle have been an improvement, they did not put an end to the irregularities which had always characterized the Florentine financial department. Indeed these irregularities increased through Lorenzo's direct interference and particularly owing to his permitting his personal finances to become inextricably tied up with those of the state. The beginning of this confusion went back to the days of Cosimo, to the possible advantage at that time of the public treasury, as Cosimo frequently came to its relief with advances from his private purse. This Lorenzo was no longer able to do, since, lacking the time and inclination to attend to business, he was penalized for his neglect with a shrinking income. At the same time his living expenses experienced a considerable increase, in large part no doubt owing to the obligations resting upon him as head of the state. He entertained visiting princes and their suites in the great palace in the Via Larga often for many days, and the display characteristic of this age of upstarts required him to practice a prodigal hospitality. Neither for this nor for the embassies he dispatched to the courts of his fellow-rulers nor for any other of the public services he rendered did he receive compensation; and if, on discovering that the inherited Fortunatus purse no longer automatically dropped gold florins into his palm, he argued that he had impoverished himself for the good of the state, he was not entirely in the wrong. His difficulty was that since his tyranny was unofficial, there could be no regular accounting between him and the government, and that if he dipped his hand into the public treasury, he was, regardless of his private convictions, formally guilty of theft. How far he went in the appropriation of public funds, especially to stave off the crises, which repeatedly threatened his bank with shipwreck and of which we shall presently hear, will never be known, but that there were irregularities is, to put it as mildly as possible, not improbable. On the other hand, it is fair to remember that the allegations against him emanate from disgruntled and hostile contemporaries who in no single instance have adduced the proof of their charges. When these same whispering opponents refer to the disorder, already mentioned, in the management of the National Debt (*Il Monte*) or to the scandalous manipulations of the dower fund for girls called *Il Monte delle Doti,* they do not hesitate, again without supplying any evidence, to lay the alleged malfeasance at Lorenzo's door. This must make us hesitate to put too much faith in their accusations, especially if we recall that there never was a time when the Florentine finances were not at loose ends and that at the bottom of the trouble, in Lorenzo's day as in the past, was the power politics of the Florentine republic. While it is possible and even probable that Lorenzo made a bad situation worse by diverting public funds to his private use, his enemies defeat themselves in ascribing all the financial embarrassments of an over-ambitious state to his personal wrong-doing.[2]

As it was the troubles of the Medici bank which gave rise to the rumors of Lorenzo's dishonesty, this is the place to review the fortunes of that institu-

[2] Reumont, Vol. II, pp. 405 ff., lists the charges of such contemporaries and near-contemporaries as Rinuccini, Cambi, Guicciardini, and Nardi, and apparently believes every one of them to be true. A much more judicial attitude is adopted by Armstrong, pp. 267-69.

tion in his day. It is often stated that the bank had passed its meridian even before Lorenzo assumed control.[3] Conclusive figures are not available and the matter must remain undecided. The bank still did business in every country of Europe and the Levant, it still received deposits and made loans, it still dealt in every known article of merchandise, more particularly in wool, cloth, silk, dyes, alum, spices, and furs. If it had got its start under Giovanni di Bicci through his connection with the papacy, it continued to profit from this association under the direction of all of Giovanni's successors. Even the mortal feud between Lorenzo and Pope Sixtus IV caused no enduring breach, since a year before he died Sixtus, who needed the bank as much as the bank needed him, received it back into favor. Nor was the value of the connection for the Medici family limited to the role of the pope as a leading depositor and borrower. Shortly after the middle of the fifteenth century great beds of alum were discovered at Tolfa in the papal state and presently their exploitation was intrusted by the pontiff to a company organized by the Medici interests. Alum, a mineral indispensable in the dyeing process, had hitherto been supplied chiefly from Asia Minor and other countries of the east. With the discovery of the Tolfa deposits not only did the importation of alum from abroad become unnecessary, but the Medici company acquired a practical monopoly in the Italian market, netting it considerable profits.

Failure of the papal favor cannot therefore be alleged as even a contributory cause of Lorenzo's business difficulties. The most plausible explanation of the decline of the bank lies in Lorenzo's insufficient training in trade and the necessity he was under, owing to his absorption in matters he held to be more important, of intrusting his material interests to agents whose choice was often extremely unfortunate. Another evil was the merging of business with politics. This practice had already begun under Cosimo and followed inevitably from the head of the firm becoming also the head of the state. However, both Cosimo and Piero after him, as trained, professional traders, employed a restraint which Lorenzo no longer observed. An examination of some of the worst crises of Lorenzo's time will show these various influences at work. It was the London house which first sent up signals of distress. The London and every other branch of the great Medici bank was in effect a separate firm which reported to Florence for orders but which was conducted with a large measure of independence by the partners on the ground. When the London house advanced the huge sum of 120,000 gold florins to Edward IV, and the king was obliged (1470) to flee from his realm, the investment had to be written to profit and loss. The blame attached to the London agents looking for speculative profits from a political gamble, but, in spite of warnings issued from Florence, the practice continued to flourish. A leading Medici branch was that of Bruges, where Tommaso Portinari, member of a family already highly regarded at Florence in Dante's day, was in control. The thirteenth-century ancestor of Tommaso was the father of Dante's Beatrice and founder of the great hospital of Santa Maria Nuova, expanded in our day to a vast and flourishing medical center. Tommaso, ill advised by his hunger for gain and under lax restraint on the part of Lorenzo, backed Charles the Bold of Burgundy,

[3] Meltzing, *Das Bankhaus der Mediceer*, etc., Part II.

and when in 1477 Charles perished in battle and his extravagant adventures came to an abrupt end, the Bruges office could be saved from disaster only by Lorenzo's coming to its aid. It was on this occasion that the rumors first became insistent that Lorenzo had abused his position as head of the state by diverting its funds into his pocket. The Lyons branch, which reached a high eminence through the intimacy between Lorenzo and King Louis XI, repeated the story of London and Bruges, for, when the death of Louis in 1483 occasioned a run of the French depositors, the bank had to suspend payments and did not become liquid till Lorenzo replenished its coffers. His liberality of course occasioned renewed whispers that he had saved himself at the expense of the state. Luckily not all of the Medici ventures were equally unfortunate and, so far as known, the banks at Rome, Milan, Naples, and Constantinople never gave Lorenzo any anxiety. Nevertheless it is clear that his enterprises owed their continued existence in his day less to his business acumen than to his political standing and prestige. As soon therefore as his son Piero lost his authority by being driven out of Florence (1494), the great bank with its network of connections throughout the known world collapsed over night. The history of the Medici as bankers had come to an end.

It is the more reasonable to ascribe the decline of the Medici bank to bad management of one sort or another, as Florentine business in general flourished and a prosperity reigned suggesting that, in commercial enterprise and industrial activity, Florence in the quattrocento did not fall below the trecento level. However, certain changes in the town's economic life had taken place which are interesting in themselves and merit attention. The manufacture of woolen cloth, on which throughout the fourteenth century the prosperity of the town had largely rested, with the beginning of the fifteenth century entered on a decline which became more marked with every decade. Nations, such as the French and the English, which had hitherto absorbed great quantities of the excellent Florentine product, undertook, often by importing Florentine artisans, to manufacture an approximately equivalent cloth, and then, by means of protective tariffs, to shut out the foreign supply. As Florence was at a disadvantage in the matter of raw wool, which it had to import to a large extent from Spain and England, there was no reason why its cloth should continue to command the world-markets as soon as the artisans of the other countries had taken over the taste, skill, and technical processes of their Florentine rivals. That the energy which had carried the Arno town to its great eminence was not yet spent was proved by the citizens promptly finding a substitute for the waning wool trade. This was the trade in silk which rose in measure as the trade in wool declined.

At the time of the revival of commerce in the eleventh century, silk fabrics were eastern luxuries imported by the Italian coastal cities, and only very slowly did the manufacture of these gorgeous stuffs, much desired by the clergy and nobility, acquire a foothold in the west. So far as Tuscany is concerned the earliest center of the silk industry was Lucca, and the Lucchese looms long retained their reputation even after other Tuscan towns, and Florence among them, had inaugurated a silk trade of their own. It is certain that an *arte di seta* was in existence by the middle of the dugento, at which time, or immediately afterward, it was incorporated as a membrum in the Por Santa Maria gild.[4] When in 1314 Lucca suffered an inhuman sack at the hands of its Pisan enemies, Florence by offering prompt, if not wholly disinterested, hospitality to the distressed weavers of the pillaged neighbor was enabled greatly to boost its production. While the advance of the industry continued steadily through the fourteenth century, it was not till the fifteenth century that it equaled and finally outstripped in importance the older textile craft. Exactly as had once been the case with its woolen cloth, Florence owed the vogue of its silk stuffs to the special skills developed by its artisans. They turned out light and heavy silks, taffetas, velvets, damasks, brocades, all without exception of outstanding excellence. The enriching of brocades with interwoven threads of gold and silver was a technique not mastered till around 1420, but was quickly carried to such a pitch of perfection that these costly, shimmering stuffs were in demand by the upper classes throughout Europe. When we learn that the Arno merchants disposed of their silk goods not only in all the countries of the west but also in the Levant, where the art had been practiced for centuries before it had spread to the occident, we find it easy to agree that the Florentine silk merchant uttered no idle boast who declared that his countrymen's *panni serici* surpassed those of all the countries of the world.[5]

It was in the fifteenth century, too, that the Florentines gradually overcame the disadvantage of being dependent on the orient for the raw product required by their looms. The mulberry tree was planted among the vineyards and wheat fields to a constantly increasing extent and by their yield of good silk fiber the imported silkworms intimated their satisfaction with the Tuscan climate. However, throughout the fifteenth century importation from the east of raw silk and dyestuffs continued, greatly facilitated by the development of Florence as a sea power. This event, a result of the conquest of Pisa, was the proudest achievement of the Albizzi period. Florence at once set vigorously about reviving the long-failing Pisan trade and met, on the whole, with considerable success. On the capture of Constantinople by the Turks (1453), representatives of the Arno government signed a favorable trade treaty with the sultan, who, out of enmity toward his maritime rivals, the Venetians, was pleased to favor their Italian competitors. Even before being made welcome at the Turkish capital the Florentines had established contact with the Moslem ruler of Egypt and in the course of time proved as much of a thorn in the Venetian flesh at Alexandria as on the Bosporus.

The expanding Levantine trade probably counted no whit less than the prosperous silk industry in keeping Florence to the fore among the leading cities of the world. Commercial statistics of the full and accurate modern type are of course not available, but we learn from a well-informed trader that in 1469 fifty-one Florentine firms did business in the Constantinopolitan area. As at the same time thirty-seven Florentine merchant companies were represented at Naples and twenty-four in France, we seem to be justified in concluding that by the second half of the fifteenth century the Levantine connection had

[4] Davidsohn, Vol. IV², pp. 71 ff.
[5] Davidsohn, Vol. IV², p. 73.

acquired a greater importance than belonged to either of the two markets which, during the two previous centuries, had stood out as the leading sources of Florentine wealth. We owe the above-quoted figures to a certain Benedetto Dei, who, early in Lorenzo's reign, was moved to discharge a thunderous broadside against *cierti Vinitiani gentilomini* who had had the impudence to speak slightingly of the economic position of his beloved fatherland.[6] To crush them utterly he added a number of other data illustrative of the material grandeur of Florence around the year 1470. He mentions eighty-three *botteghe d'arte di seta* and lists the markets from Turkey to Antwerp and London to which the finished goods were dispatched. Florence had thirty-three banks, in which connection we must remember that by Dei's time the smaller trading firms no longer dealt in money and therefore were not listed as banks. That there still were two hundred and seventy woolen shops (*botteghe di arte di lana*) would indicate that woolen goods were still being manufactured in considerable quantity, although, since nothing is said of the size of the shops, we have no way of telling what their actual output may have been. Further items declaring the splendor of *Florentia bella* are sixty-six apothecary shops, fifty-four establishments of stone-cutters who practice both *intaglio* and *rilievo,* forty-four mastergoldsmiths and jewelers, and so on for two bewildering quarto pages. It is clear that to Benedetto Dei, a typical Florentine burgher, who spent his life circulating among all the countries of the Mediterranean in pursuit of gain, the thought never occurred that his city had begun to decline or had ceased to be what to his mind it had been for generations past, the hub of the universe.

No more than the bourgeois trader was the Medicean ruler of this busy community persuaded that its path had begun to slope downhill, nor did he believe, in spite of the heavy seas which his own business venture had encountered, that the twilight of Florence, even as one of the world's financial centers, was at hand. In addition to having a sufficiently open mind to ascribe his commercial difficulties to his own mistakes, Lorenzo was blessed with the optimism which permitted him to look upon every gathering of clouds as a passing event. His most conspicuous and attractive trait, his special gift from the gods, was his immense zest for life. A large section of his fellow-citizens must have been animated with an identical vitality or they would not have been so sympathetically affected by his activities. The Renaissance movement, fast mounting to its climax, was engaged in releasing enormous energies directed upon every conceivable form of human endeavor. There was a joyousness abroad which is the natural accompaniment of creative effort in a community untouched, or at least as yet not greatly disturbed, by paralyzing doubt. So far were the upper classes from distrusting the secular outlook championed by humanism that, in taking it over, neither were they agitated by any moral scruples nor did it occur to them that they had sharply divorced themselves from their religious past. As for the Florentine masses they had hardly so much as been brushed by the semi-paganism that had taken possession of the ruling group. This fact the episode carrying the name of Savonarola and only just be-

[6] Benedetto Dei's "Lettera per Difesa della Mercatura dei Fiorentini" was incorporated by Pagnini, *Della Decima,* etc., Vol. II, pp. 235 ff., in his still valuable essay, "Sul Commercio dei Fiorentini."

ginning to show its face during Lorenzo's last years was destined before long to bring to the startled attention of Italy and the western world. The life-span of the Magnificent, however, was not darkened by this shadow and owes its special flavor to the hopes and dreams, the attitudes and achievements of the poets, artists, and scholars who were lifted up as on wings by the spirit of their age and who, gathering around Lorenzo, hailed him as the captain of their band.

It was this precious zest of Piero's son that explains the many interests to which he gave himself with all his might from early manhood. Brought up by humanist scholars, he continued to live in their company on easy give-and-take terms to the end of his days. His most constant attendant and most intimate friend was Poliziano, the foremost classical scholar of his age and also its foremost poet, unless we confer this latter distinction on Lorenzo himself. His early and sincere devotion to Italian letters was followed up, in what could not have been other than rare moments of relaxation, with many kinds of poetic composition. Not particularly regarded in the writer's day, they have evoked a steadily increasing admiration with the passing of the years. While Lorenzo's verses were in the main addressed to the cultivated circle of his equals, in his Carnival songs he presented himself as purveyor to the ribald fun with which the common people in their traditional pre-lenten processions and masquerades sought compensation for the rigors of the coming season of penitence. It is characteristic of the age and also of the unchecked exuberance of the poet that many of his Carnival pieces are of a shocking indecency. He associated freely with painters, sculptors, and architects and helped them with commissions, although, owing to his straitened finances, he was far from practicing the lavish patronage of his grandfather. It is a tribute to his fastidious taste that among the sculptors he chiefly favored Verrocchio, among the painters, Botticelli. Nor should it be forgotten that he was the first to recognize the talent of Michelangelo, whom he befriended in his impecunious youth by generously assigning to him a room in his palace and a place at his table. Throughout his life he tirelessly enlarged the famous family collection of manuscripts, gems, cameos, and medals. In the immediately succeeding chapters, devoted to the intellectual and aesthetic developments during the quattrocento, Lorenzo's activity as a humanist, poet, and patron will receive further attention. Our purpose at this point is attained if we succeed in conveying an impression of the unrivaled versatility which enabled him actively and fruitfully to share in all the mental movements of the day. He had the happy gift, more characteristic of the fleet southern races than of the heavier northern breeds, to give himself, with entire surrender of his mind and senses and in swift succession, to the dictation of instructions to an ambassador departing on an important mission, to the examination of a newly discovered manuscript, to a discussion among experts of a mooted doctrine of Greek philosophy, and to the arrangements for a happy hunting expedition with a group of friends. Like his countrymen generally, he was not inhibited by an awkward self-consciousness but was of an open nature, courteous, and accessible to everyone he met. Thus easily and graciously identified with all that his fellow-citizens dreamt, thought, and did, he well deserves, much more by reason of his radiant personality than of his authority and position as a statesman, to have his period called the Laurentian age.

Lorenzo had hardly reached early manhood when he began to suffer from the inroads of a disease hereditary in his family and identified by the medical science of his age as gout. Probably it was something much more devastating than what we understand by that name; but whatever it was, it obliged him frequently to seek relief at one of the many warm baths dotting the neighborhood of Siena and Volterra. Before he was forty years old his illness had got to the point of obliging him to withdraw from public view for prolonged periods. The alarming condition of his health unescapably turned his thoughts to the future and the problem of transmitting his authority to his heir. Although no one was more anxiously aware than himself that his oldest son, Piero, whom he was bringing up as his successor, could maintain himself as lord of Florence only by that sum of gifts, for which the Italians of the Renaissance employed the word *virtù,* nonetheless as the head of the house, he considered it his duty to take every precaution to leave to Piero as solid as possible an edifice of power. There being no more effective means at hand to buttress the Medicean position than the tried device of matrimonial alliances, Lorenzo was on the lookout for the most valuable available consorts for his children as soon as they should reach the age of puberty. He married his oldest daughter, Lucrezia, to Giacopo Salviati, a relative of the infamous archbishop who had figured in so prominent a manner among the Pazzi conspirators. He wanted by-gones to be by-gones and the breach which had opened between him and another great Florentine clan to be closed. With a like view to multiplying his local adherents another daughter, Contessina, was wed to Piero Ridolfi. When the question was posed of the family connection most advantageous to his prospective heir, Piero the Magnificent adopted the course which had been followed in his own case and arranged a union with Alfonsina, of the great Roman clan of the Orsini. The marriage took place by proxy in March, 1487, and a year later, when the bridegroom was seventeen years old, the bride took up her residence in Florence. For his third and last daughter, Maddalena, Lorenzo developed a very ambitious plan. Ever since his disastrous quarrel with Sixtus IV he had been brought to an appreciation of the value of a close papal connection; and when, on surrounding Sixtus's successor, Innocent VIII, with flattering attentions, he found his regard reciprocated, he resolved to confirm the intimacy by means of a family tie. The result was that Maddalena was married (1488) to Francesco Cibò, a son whom the pope, with a candor exceptional in the succession of Roman pontiffs, frankly acknowledged as his offspring.

Much more important, however, in Lorenzo's eyes and so important historically for the Medici family as to prove decisive for its later fortunes, was the advantage Lorenzo was able to take of his intimate association with Pope Innocent to propose his second son, Giovanni (known afterward as Pope Leo X), for the college of cardinals. There was a third and last son, Giuliano, who was still so young that the father did not live to form any plans for his worldly advancement. We may therefore conclude our tale of the political bargains the Magnificent struck for his children with the memorable case of Giovanni. As his second son was a prudent, studious youth, Lorenzo may have felt a normal paternal pride in directing him toward an ecclesiastical career; however, his primary purpose in so doing was to promote him to a position of influence enabling him to be of service to what Lorenzo, already employing the royal manner, proudly called *la casa nostra*. Since nothing less than a cardinalate would meet this end, it was a cardinalate to which Lorenzo aspired. Rendered anxious by the increasing severity of his illness, he began to work on Innocent's sympathies while Giovanni was still a boy, and so stubbornly did he press the matter that finally, in 1489, when Giovanni was fourteen years old, the pope yielded. Giovanni was promised a cardinal's hat on the understanding that he was not to be endowed with the authority it conferred till three years later. Accordingly, in March, 1492, amidst festivities of an unexampled splendor, all Flòrence joined in acclaiming the newest prince of the church, whose youth, although it gave no offense in that callous age, constituted a scandal of the first order. The father of the seventeen-year-old cardinal was already too far stricken to take part in the celebration. On setting out for Rome to assume his exalted seat Giovanni bade the bedridden Lorenzo an affectionate farewell and, shortly after his arrival in the Eternal City, received from him a remarkable letter of instructions.[7] It has been extravagantly praised in some quarters as a model of its kind. While it may be a model, it is so far from being fresh and original that it differs in no respect from what solicitous fathers have counseled their sons from the beginning of time with a view to holding them to a line of conduct calculated to secure their worldly success. The most impressive feature of the letter for whoever is interested in the quality of Lorenzo's mind is its uncompromising realism. This reveals itself in the writer's exact knowledge of the contemporary Roman cesspool and in his careful prescriptions to his young son for escaping its contamination.

A few weeks after Giovanni's departure from Florence Lorenzo, in expectation of the end, had himself carried to his country seat at Careggi. He wished to die where his father and grandfather had died before him. So rapidly, as the ecstatic Tuscan spring once again took possession of the land, did his strength wane that, early in April, his sister Bianca was obliged to inform him that his last hour was drawing near. Owing to the death of Clarice Orsini some four years before, the household was without a competent head and this favorite sister had come to Careggi to assume control. On a priest being summoned the dying man confessed, was shriven, and received the Holy Sacrament. His closest friend, Poliziano, was in constant attendance, the young and handsome scholar, Pico della Mirandola, paid him a moving visit of farewell. There was a constant coming and going of friends and weeping members of the family, from all of whom in the manner becoming a great gentleman he took courteous leave. With his son and heir, Piero, he had a long last interview conducted without witnesses. Suddenly the Dominican friar, Savonarola, appeared and was ushered into the chamber. According to Poliziano, a bystander and eye-witness, the visitor summoned Lorenzo to repentance, and before taking his departure, at the dying man's request, with raised hand gave him his bless-

[7] Fabroni, Vol. II, *Adnotationes,* 178. An English translation in Roscoe, pp. 285-88.

ing. Poliziano's account of his friend and patron's last days was written in Latin six weeks after the event, and there is no reason to challenge its facts, unless it be to say that they received a certain artificial inflation by reason of the detestable practice of the contemporary humanists never to set pen to paper save with the intention to produce "literature."

If Savonarola had left his own account of the death-bed scene, in view of his impeccable character it would have to be given a much weightier consideration than that of the poet-scholar who was also a Medicean dependent and courtier. Unfortunately Savonarola did nothing of the sort; but when in the years following his tragic death, his sorrowing disciples began to assemble the materials suited to making a cult of his memory, they gave currency to a version of the meeting at Careggi which sharply contradicts that of Poliziano at every point. Their story took the form of drama, of drama moreover of the traditional religious kind, for it presented the trembling but insufficiently repentant sinner faced in the person of Savonarola with the personified Divine Wrath. With the instinctive preference mankind has always felt for irreconcilable opposites to be brought to an open breach, writers were persuaded before long to declare for the Savonarolist version, until by sheer force of repetition through the ages Poliziano, the eye-witness, has been discredited in favor of the visionaries and miracle-mongers who strove to honor their martyred leader by exhibiting him as a towering Old Testament prophet, through whom God delivers his judgments. Like every great religious teacher before or since, Savonarola was by his devoted adherents built up into a myth, and of this myth the death-bed episode at Careggi became an inseparable part. Its culmination has passed into every history of Florence, into every book dealing with either Savonarola or Lorenzo. That culmination came when, after Lorenzo had conceded two of the demands made upon him by the friar, his stern inquisitor confronted him with the third and crowning demand to restore the liberty of Florence. How this miracle was to be effected with Lorenzo lying at the point of death the story prudently refrains from telling. It contents itself with recounting the tyrant's refusal which he signified by turning his face to the wall. Here ended the tale; but the reader or hearer, familiar with the literature of edification, was invited to supply the conclusion, which could only be that, when the friar on his rebuff took his departure, the soul of the wicked tyrant went straight to its reward in Everlasting Fire. If history is to be constructed from the critical examination of documents, it cannot, in the matter of this much-mooted incident, do other than accept Poliziano's version even while freely admitting that the poet may have altered the facts in one or another particular in the interest of friendship. It cannot, however, under any circumstances reject Poliziano's for the Savonarolist version, for the latter, first circulated as hearsay at two or three removes from its source, did not make an appearance in print till after many years of incubation on the part of a group of honest but mentally unbalanced enthusiasts.[8]

Lorenzo died in the early night hours of April 8, 1492, and after simple ceremonies was buried in the ancestral church of San Lorenzo. If life is reck-

[8] Poliziano's testimony, in the form of a letter to a friend, is printed by Fabroni, Vol. I, pp. 199-212. For a temperate review of the evidence see Reumont, Vol. II, pp. 556 ff., 590-92.

oned by fulness of experience and not by length of days, he must, in spite of his death at the early age of forty-three, be considered to have had an enviable existence. As to the affection and admiration of his fellow-citizens throughout his life there can be no doubt, although a stubborn opposition never ceased to gnaw at his regime, intrusting to its secret journals the facts and comments which have ever since served as the chief ammunition of his detractors. Only rarely, however, has the favorable opinion of the contemporary generation been dissipated more rapidly. When Piero was driven out of Florence two years after his father's death, the new republican rulers knew not Lorenzo, and never afterward did his reputation experience a sufficient revival for his country-men to have felt moved to raise a monument to him adequately expressive of his worth.

XXIV. Intellectual Change: The Humanism of the Laurentian Age

IN AGAIN picking up the thread of Florentine intellectual development it will be a help to recall the outstanding features which humanism had presented to view up to approximately the middle of the fifteenth century. Enamored with classical antiquity, the early humanists inaugurated a group of attitudes and activities which may be summarized under four heads. (1) They founded classical philology and undertook by a critical sifting of the manuscripts to make available, in as correct a form as possible, the whole corpus of ancient literature both Greek and Latin. (2) By imposing this material on the curriculum of the schools they attempted to transform the educational system of the Middle Ages with its emphasis on dialectics into a humanistic education based on classical literature. (3) They favored the multiplication of books and the creation of libraries for the advancement of learning. (4) By immersing themselves in pagan thought they became more or less consciously divorced from Christianity and more or less openly converted to a religious attitude definable as neo-paganism.

In the second half of the fifteenth century dominated, so far as our town of Florence is concerned, by the name of the Medici and, more particularly, by that of the family's most brilliant representative, Lorenzo the Magnificent, all of the above-listed features experienced a steady, uninterrupted development. However, a full and ordered presentation of this expansion is not the function of this book, since by the fifteenth century humanism had extended its empire over the intelligentsia of all Italy. Boasting everywhere the same confident energy, it was everywhere the same movement with just those minor variations from town to town inevitable in so diversified a mental atmosphere as that of the peninsula. We have not pretended that humanism even at the beginning was an exclusively Florentine product, although it is undoubtedly true that the Tuscan capital contributed so largely to humanistic origins that its historian is in a position to do justice to its early phases without particularly encroaching on neighboring Italian territory. In measure as the quattrocento unrolls its scroll this becomes more and more impossible, and the Florentine historian is obliged to recognize that much or most of the material lies beyond his reach. In view of this situation the most feasible plan for presenting the leading elements of later humanism without bursting through the framework of this book would seem to be, first, to indicate the changes effected at Florence in the above-listed four outstanding features of early humanism, and second and far more important, to trace whatever new tendencies made their appearance within the range of the city which take rank as fresh and original growths.

Although the early humanists aspired to be Latin authors and turned out copious works belonging to every literary category known to the revered ancients, they were so greatly inhibited by the use of a dead language that they produced a progeny either stillborn or destined for an early demise by a fatal lack of vitality. All the energy of the imitators went into the effort to be "correct" in diction, grammar, form, and meter, and to stick so closely to their models that they would be able at need to justify every slightest turn of phrase by reference to a classical source. This lamentable literary mode underwent no change in the Laurentian age unless it be for the worse; for the worse in the case of such soulless counterfeiting would be the apparent better, when success has at last crowned the long effort to make the copy in every purely external respect so like the model as to be indistinguishable from it. All the rhetorical fluency and the finally achieved "correctness" of form and speech would merely serve to make more painfully evident the tragic hollowness of the reproduction.

To proceed at once to the humanist who represents the apex of this slavish development, let us glance at Poliziano, the housemate of Lorenzo the Magnificent and tutor of his children. His life-span is practically identical with that of his patron, for, a little younger than Lorenzo, he died two years after him at the early age of forty. Poliziano was admired during his life as being, and is still frequently declared to have been, the greatest poet the humanistic movement produced on the ground that he was the most perfect ape of antiquity. An amazing memory added to tireless industry enabled him to write Latin with a mastery no humanist before him had ever attained, to write it indeed almost as though it were his mother-tongue. The result, as manifested in a succession of odes, elegies, and epigrams, constitutes a surface of polish, glitter, dexterity, and charm, behind which there stirs not so much as a trace of individual thought and sentiment, the invariable substance of all true poetry. But this facile and, because facile, negligible poet was also a scholar, and as a scholar he moved on a high and constructive level. In moments when he manifested the clearest perception of his powers, he modestly called himself a grammarian. To this expert philologist Lorenzo assigned the professorship of Greek and Latin eloquence at the university; and Poliziano could not have been better employed than in putting his vast erudition, covering texts, medals, and inscriptions, at the service of ambitious students. In his lectures, his translations from the Greek (of course into Latin), and his editions of classical authors he maintained a critical standard that put philology on a definitely scientific basis. While Poliziano is but a single instance taken at the topmost level of achievement, he serves to bring out the fact that Laurentian humanism still closely resembled early humanism in that, while failing to produce an original literature, it registered an uninterrupted advance in learning and scholarly method.

On turning to the innovations the quattrocento introduced into the second of the above-listed fields, the field of education, we are obliged to begin by admitting that the most incisive experiments originated outside of Florence. Without any doubt the two schools for boys, organized respectively by Guarino at Ferrara and by Vittorino da Feltre at Mantua, went farther toward putting the training of the young on a new foundation than any attempt made anywhere else in Italy. While both of these great educators anchored their curriculum in the classics, they did not for that reason toss overboard the ethical and spiritual values of Christianity but attempted rather to fuse them with the rediscovered wisdom of the ancients. Their program was to utilize the classical authors for the enrichment of the mind without sacrificing the invaluable tradition of Christian conduct. We may think of the two schoolmasters as conservative innovators who did not believe, as did so many of their fellow-humanists, that to profit adequately from the ancients it was necessary to revert to paganism. If it is added that both Guarino and Vittorino placed great faith in games and bodily exercise, and that they upheld and put in practice the principle enshrined in the old apothegm, *mens sana in corpore sano,* we arrive at some notion of the extent of their departure from the ascetic ideal of the monastery school, against which their bright and gallant venture represented a reaction. It deserves at least passing notice that the influence of the two schools at Mantua and Ferrara spread far over Europe, and that they supplied the inspiration for the most notable foundations for boys called to life in the immediately following generations in France, England, and Germany.

In Florence no humanist arose to launch an educational experiment of equal scope, but that does not signify that Florence developed no interest in this particular aspect of humanism. In the hope of retaining for his city the intellectual primacy it had held for a hundred years, Lorenzo was at pains to have the professorships allotted to the new studia humaniora at the local university filled by the best scholars to be found in Italy. We have already heard that the most brilliant luminary of the humanist sky, Poliziano, was appointed to the chair of Greek and Latin eloquence. Cristoforo Landino, one of Lorenzo's tutors, had from as far back as 1457 lectured on rhetoric and poetry; other professors of equal caliber were the Platonist, Marsilio Ficino, and the Hellenist, Demetrius Chalcondylas. While with representatives such as these the university remained an authoritative center for classical studies, Lorenzo weakened it in other respects from very valid considerations of a political nature. Ever since its capture in the early years of the fifteenth century Pisa had been a moribund city, whose dwindling inhabitants looked upon their conquerors with a fixed and unalterable aversion. This situation perturbed the statesman in Lorenzo and very early in his reign he undertook to remedy it. He began by buying a house in Pisa and sought to win the favor of the citizens by going to dwell for extended periods in their midst; above all, somewhat to heal their wounded self-respect he resolved to revive their ancient university. At the same time, because two universities would be one too many for so small a state as his, the Magnificent worked out a division of the existing university at Florence in such a manner that, while Florence would retain its humanistic endowments, the faculties of law, medicine, and theology should be established at Pisa. This signified an enfeeblement of Florence for the benefit of Pisa, but the wisdom of the measure was so manifest that it was accepted without notable protest. By the last decade of Lorenzo's life the university of Pisa had become a flourishing institution drawing its matriculants not only from Tus-

FRA ANGELICO. ANNUNCIATION. FRESCO. SAN MARCO

FRA ANGELICO. CORONATION OF THE VIRGIN. ALTARPIECE
NOW IN THE MUSEO DI SAN MARCO

Top: MASACCIO. THE TRIBUTE MONEY. FRESCO
IN THE BRANCACCI CHAPEL OF THE CHURCH
OF THE CARMINE. Bottom left: MASACCIO.
ADAM AND EVE DRIVEN FROM PARADISE. BRAN-
CACCI CHAPEL. Bottom right: FRA FILIPPO
LIPPI. MADONNA. UFFIZI GALLERY

cany but also from many sections of Italy and even from foreign parts. They were in the main students of the professions and prospective careerists, while the devotees of philology and philosophy continued to congregate at Florence, thus maintaining the city's long-established eminence as a humanist center. In no case, however, must the university be regarded as exhausting the Florentine contribution to the advance of contemporary thought. At its side there flourished an institution destined to exercise a novel and even revolutionary influence in the mental realm. Of this we shall presently hear with some detail: it is the Platonic academy.

The library problem which had given such deep concern to Petrarch and his immediate followers, a little past the middle of the quattrocento met with a solution that struck contemporaries, and with the help of a little imagination on our part might still strike us, as hardly short of miraculous. Printing with movable types, invented in the Rhine Valley at the mid-century, spread rapidly over all Europe, and almost overnight put an end to the long-lamented scarcity and costliness of books. It was in 1465 that the first book printed in Italy made its appearance. It dropped from the press at Subiaco near Rome, the handiwork of two German journeymen. Native Italians quickly acquired the art, and before the close of the century practically every Italian city of any importance boasted a press of its own. The first book printed at Florence bore the date 1471 and was, characteristically enough for this hearth of classical scholarship, a commentary on Virgil. However, Florence never acquired the standing of certain other publishing centers and was notably outstripped by its ancient commercial rival, Venice. In the cutting and founding of type the Italians throughout the peninsula displayed such skill and taste that their first editions, largely of the writers of antiquity, take rank to this day among the most precious products of the new art. The impulse given to humanism by the revolutionary invention can hardly be exaggerated. Obviously the multiplication and cheapening of books made possible their acquisition by people of relatively restricted means, while the well-to-do were stimulated to add them in large numbers to their stock of manuscripts and either to found public libraries for the convenience of their fellow-citizens or else to enrich the libraries already in existence with liberal donations. From the narrow viewpoint of scholarship the printed texts represented a vast improvement over the written copies with their innumerable and unavoidable errors of transcription. Nor should it be overlooked that the publishers in the interest of accuracy were obliged to employ trained editors and proofreaders, and that editing and proofreading became professions by which scores of humanists, hitherto dependent on the bounty of princes, were enabled to earn an honest livelihood by their individual effort.

Contrary to a still too prevalent opinion, the humanists did not all slip into paganism, although it is undeniable that they inclined to adopt a skeptical attitude toward Christianity and in some extreme cases became, even if they did not openly profess themselves to be, outright agnostics. In a general way it may be said that those followers of antiquity who most completely withdrew from their fellow-men and lived as a scholarly coterie in the rarefied upper air were most disposed to adopt the pagan outlook. If their separation from the *vulgus,* the common herd, became the strength of their erudition, it was also the cause of their failure to achieve distinction as poets. Neither in the fifteenth nor in any other century have erudition and poetry lived harmoniously together. A group in touch with, but also distinct from, the scholars pure and simple were those humanists who specialized in philosophy and ethics. Generally speaking, they were not moved to divorce themselves from the society in which they lived nor did they deny the traditions on which that society rested. Members of this very important group were the projectors of fresh adventures in education already mentioned, Guarino and Vittorino da Feltre; and to this group belonged the two Florentines, Cristoforo Landino and Marsilio Ficino. With them may be collocated also Pico della Mirandola, for, although not a Florentine by birth, he settled in Florence and with Landino and Ficino made up the strength of the Platonic academy. Not offering any formal instruction and not concerned with developing a following, the academy nonetheless radiated an influence over Italy greater than that of any established school or university. It represents by far the most important contribution made by Florence to Laurentian humanism and must needs come in for a close examination.

The first thing to get in mind about the Platonic academy is that it bore no resemblance whatever to what we moderns understand by the term, for neither did it have an organization, officers, and revenues, nor did it give instruction or issue an official literature. It was nothing other than an occasional, informal gathering of men with a common interest in the Greek philosopher, Plato, and with a common faith in the guidance of a scholar who had been devoted to Plato from his youth, Marsilio Ficino. A further bond among the members was their attachment to Lorenzo de' Medici, who, besides revering Ficino as his teacher, shared the current curiosity which Plato, overshadowed throughout the Middle Ages by his foremost pupil and critic, Aristotle, had recently aroused. The devotees of Plato at Florence were Lorenzo's most intimate associates, and to be invited to hear Ficino expound a Platonic dialogue was to become a hall-marked member of the Medicean social circle.

It was not, however, Lorenzo but his grandfather, Cosimo, to whom the Platonic academy owed its inception. When on the occasion of the General Council of the church held at Florence in 1439 Cosimo met the philosopher, Gemistos Plethon, he was so deeply moved by the fiery enthusiasm of the venerable Greek for the great Athenian that he discussed with Plethon the creation of an academy dedicated to Platonic studies. Nothing came of the plan at the time and Cosimo might have dismissed it entirely from his mind, had he not learned some years later that the young son of his physician had been seized with a passion for the ancient sage like unto that of Plethon, but that he could only partially satisfy it, owing to his ignorance of Greek. The young man was Marsilio Ficino, whose modesty, lovable disposition, and rare zeal for learning quickly won Cosimo's favor. Accordingly, he resolved to supply Marsilio with the means necessary to complete his education on the understanding that his client would devote himself not only to making Plato accessible to the curious in Latin dress, but also to serving faithfully throughout his days as the master's apostle to the occident. Shortly before his death in

1464 Cosimo had the pleasure of receiving from the hands of Ficino the first-fruits of his labors; and under Piero, his son, and Lorenzo, his grandson, the work of translation continued without interruption until by 1477 or there-abouts the whole majestic roll call of the Platonic dialogues had been rendered into the recovered Latin of the humanists. Some fourteen years later, in 1491, advantage was taken of the new mechanical process of bookmaking to offer Plato's complete works in translation to the public. As an indication that Florence had missed the opportunity to put itself at the head of the publishing business we may note the circumstance that Ficino intrusted his monumental edition to a Venetian printer. However, old Cosimo's faith had been justified, for at last Italy and Europe had at their command the information enabling them to travel with assurance a philosophic path other than that traced by Aristotle and the scholastics.

In giving their philosophy its characteristic development the schoolmen of the Middle Ages had had recourse to Aristotle, and in order to put the intellectual system they elaborated beyond the reach of attack they had ascribed to the Stagirite an unassailable authority. Consequently, not the least important task of the humanists, who saw in scholasticism their chief enemy, was somehow to undermine Aristotle; and when Plato was rediscovered, first by the mediation of his occasional admirers among the Latin classical writers, the opportunity seemed to have come to hand. While the humanistic enthusiasm for Plato, which continued to make headway throughout the quattrocento, may be largely explained on this ground, there was no lack of other reasons for the Athenian's growing vogue. Plato propounded a transcendental philosophy; at least on the strength of his central doctrine, the doctrine of ideas, he could be called a transcendentalist who affirmed the most clean-cut separation imaginable between soul and flesh, spirit and matter. Long after his time, at Alexandria in Egypt, this sharp dualism of his was, with the aid of oriental mysticism, elaborated into one of the most fantastic systems of philosophy that have ever been spun by mortal mind. It was this revised Platonism, usually called Neoplatonism, which had captured the imagination of the Christian Fathers and had greatly influenced the shaping of Christian doctrine. In the course of the Middle Ages the early nexus between Christianity and Platonism or, more properly, Neoplatonism, had been gradually forgotten; and when Aristotle was adopted as the philosopher of scholasticism, as the one and only philosopher and its authoritative guide, Platonism inevitably fell into neglect and ultimately even into disrepute. However, when with the help of fifteenth-century humanism Plato rose once more into view, the close kinship of his dualism with Christianity was at once revealed. In ever-growing numbers the humanists gave him their allegiance because with him as their leader not only might they succeed in destroying the hated tyranny of Aristotle and the scholastics but also, persistently Christian beneath a mere veneer of paganism, they would be free to indulge the hope of bringing religion and philosophy into a new and stimulating harmony.

Under these circumstances Marsilio Ficino (1433–99) becomes a completely intelligible phenomenon. He occupied himself for many decades with translating Plato, and in the explanatory commentaries issued by him doubtless thought he was expounding the Hellenic master. However, as he approached Plato, on the one hand, through Christianity and, on the other, through the perverted doctrines of his Alexandrian followers, he saw him through an interpretative haze and read him in the colorful terms of expositors born hundreds of years after the great age of Greece. As Ficino's fellow-members of the academy and, later, his readers throughout Italy adopted exactly the same approach, he was not challenged from any quarter, and during his lifetime and for some generations afterward was regarded with as much reverence as though he were himself the ancient Athenian come again to life. His friend Lorenzo had presented him with an antique marble bust of Plato which, installed in Ficino's study, majestically presided over his labors. Let the setting up of this grave and uncompromising *genius loci* convince us of the utter sincerity of his Florentine disciple. Nonetheless, instead of a strict Platonist, he was an Alexandrian eclectic and expounded a philosophy which, although not unrelated to Plato, stemmed in the main from Neoplatonic mysticism.

What the high priest of the Platonic academy offered his friends under the name of Platonism will in its most succinct form be found in his Italian treatise *Sopra lo Amore* and reduces itself to what became current at the height of the Renaissance under the name of Platonic Love. This doctrine teaches that Love is the sustaining and ordering principle of the universe, and that it is identical with Beauty since Beauty is its visible emanation. The function of the individual soul, temporarily estranged from the Good by being imbedded in matter, which is Evil, is by laddered stages to find its way back to its source and to end, as it began, in the ecstatic contemplation of God. Unhappily there is a false, a lower love, the love of the flesh, which plagues us in our mortal span and which it is our duty to repress and overcome. The higher love is spiritual: it is the force that holds the universe together. The choice the individual soul caught in the web of flesh has to make is between animal and spiritual love and, as it chooses, it is lost or saved. It is clear that this exaltation of Love and Beauty was bound to appeal most strongly to the sensitive souls of artists and writers. In the case of the impressionable Botticelli we may see its effect in the two well-known allegorical presentations of Love, called respectively the Birth of Venus and the Realm of Venus, although the latter passes under the popular misnomer of Spring.[1] Platonic Love is the sustaining fire of Michelangelo's sonnets, as it is the peroration and climax of Castiglione's treatise on the gentleman, the famous *Il Cortigiano*. In brief, much of the painting, sculpture, and letters of the first half of the sixteenth century carries as its core and marrow the love doctrine of the Platonic academy.

A hardly less exalted philosophic figure than Ficino was Pico della Mirandola, who died in 1494 at the early age of thirty-one. He departed this life in the same year as Poliziano, whose close friend he was, although Poliziano, a grammarian steeped in letters, never pretended to be either a real philosopher or a real Platonist. In general outlook Pico was much closer to his other friend, Ficino, whose doctrine of Platonic Love he shared, carrying it, if possible, to

---

[1] On this matter see A. Warburg, *Sandro Botticelli's Geburt der Venus und Frühling*. Hamburg, 1893.

still more mystical and unscalable heights. If we add Lorenzo de' Medici as fourth to this inmost circle of the academy, it is not because he was either primarily a scholar like Poliziano, or a philosopher like Ficino and Pico. He was as, in spite of his many sympathies, we must never forget, primarily a statesman; but with his elastic nature he responded in turn to all the aspects of humanism and without any doubt satisfied some need of his complex soul by his intimacy with the chosen spirits of the academy. Next after his statesmanship his most important achievement lies in the realm of poetry; and since by his verses he rendered Tuscany and Italy the incomparable service of ending the learned boycott conducted by the humanists against the Italian language, we may fittingly close this brief sketch of the mental changes in his day by defining the literary contribution of the man, whose name is for many the sum and essence of his age.

Lorenzo was so frankly a follower of the Italian and not of the Latin muse that he never expressed himself except in his native tongue in all the many forms of poetry at which he tried his hand. That does not mean, however, that he sounded an original note throughout the body of his verse. As was the case with his contemporaries without exception the past possessed such authority for him that, whether it was a question of the metrical practice of his Tuscan predecessors, Dante and Petrarch, or of the literary forms sanctioned by the ancient writers, he felt constrained humbly to bow down before the dead. Thus it came about that, when he sang of love, as he did in many sonnets and in a much-admired work called *Selve d'Amore*,[2] he adopted the attitude and imitated the manner of Dante and Petrarch; and if he added anything not traceable to them, it was likely to be a borrowing from still another source, most probably from the modish and equally authoritative Platonism of his day. His love poetry is conventional, fictive, and unreal, as to its misfortune Italian love poetry continued to be to the very threshold of the nineteenth century. Not till Lorenzo turned to nature, did he succeed in shaking off the deadweight of the past and feel encouraged to express immediate experiences unmistakably involving his own lively senses and imagination. In his *Caccia col Falcone,* which is not easy to classify but which may be called a country idyll, he tells of a day spent at hawking and is so charged with the impressions of a happy outing, with the first flush of dawn, with the baying of the hounds assembled for the hunt, with the bold flight of the birds, that he thoroughly succeeds in transmitting his own animation to his reader. The realistic vein here revealed received its happiest expression in his *Nencia da Barberino.* In this rustic poem a young peasant tells of his love for a village girl, describing her charms and singing his woes with such simplicity and truth to nature that all the old hampering conventionalities drop away like broken fetters. The fact is that the attitudes imposed by Dante, Petrarch, and the Platonic mysteries were pure literary poses for this man of alert senses and active mind. His most constant purpose was to enjoy life to the full, for the night was coming followed by no morning of which he could be sure. By reason of this immediacy of sentiment he is particularly fresh and most emphatically himself in many of the *ballate*

[2] The standard edition of Lorenzo's works is by Attilio Simioni. Of Lorenzo's English biographers Roscoe and Horsburgh are most enlightening on his poetry.

and carnival songs which he composed, without an eye to literature, to be
sung in their spontaneous merrymakings by the common folk of the town.
Often as the most celebrated quatrain of his carnival literature has been quoted,
it has such an infectious lilt that it can stand reprinting in this place:

> Quant' è bella giovinezza,
> Che si fugge tuttavia!
> Chi vuol esser lieto, sia:
> Di doman non c'è certezza.

> (Fair is youth and free of sorrow,
> Yet how soon its joys we bury!
> Let who would be now be merry:
> Sure is no one of tomorrow.) [3]

In these tripping lines we have the expression of a fleeting, but true and ever-
renewed mood of the poet. And into their small compass he has packed so much
of the spirit of the age that they have appealed to all the following generations
as a kind of marching song of the Renaissance.

It cannot be doubted that the fifteenth-century Florentines of the upper
social stratum confidently believed that they were living in a great cultural
epoch and that the future held the promise of still greater achievements. "I
wish to thank God," wrote Giovanni Rucellai, "for permitting me to live in
the present age, which those competent to judge of such matters call the greatest age our city has ever experienced." And Marsilio Ficino sounded the following paean: "This is an age of gold, which has brought back to life the
almost extinguished liberal disciplines of poetry, eloquence, painting, architecture, sculpture, music, and singing to the Orphic lyre. And all this at Florence!" [4] Notwithstanding this acclaim, scarcely two years after Lorenzo's death
in 1492, a shock that was like an earthquake overtook this high-piled and
splendid cultural structure, damaging it so radically that all the subsequent
patching could never quite put it together again. For this sudden catastrophe,
connected with the name of Savonarola and not even remotely divined by the
self-centered champions of humanism, many explanations have been offered.
As is always the case with significant social movements the Florentine crisis resulted from a vast complex of circumstances and defies the simplified explanation to which our mind is prone. However, a factor of peculiar pertinence to
this chapter figured powerfully in the anti-intellectual rising championed by
the Dominican friar. The new mental world, projected by the humanists and
inhabited by writers and scholars and, fortunately for their own and their city's
fame, to a much smaller extent by painters and sculptors, was the walled-off
garden of a small upper class which prided itself on its clean separation from
the untutored mass of the population. Under Savonarola's leadership this despised mass asserted its viewpoint and power, and the consequent despoiling of
the garden was the penalty paid by an intellectual aristocracy for having lost
contact with its humbler fellow-men.

[3] Translation by Fletcher, *Literature of the Italian Renaissance*, p. 132.
[4] Monnier, *Le Quattrocento*, Vol. II, pp. 52-53.

XXV. The Fine Arts: The Second or Quattrocento Phase

THE term Fine Arts invites so much misunderstanding that, before taking it up once more, a few words of explanation will be in order. The expression did not gain currency till some two or three hundred years ago, when architects, sculptors, and painters were, to their own grave misfortune, considered to be a race apart and designated as artists, while the practitioners of the humbler crafts, such as goldsmiths, carvers of wood and ivory, furniture-makers, and makers of other articles of common use, were classified as artificers or craftsmen. During the Middle Ages no such distinction was recognized in any country of Europe. In that period all shapers of any object whatever requiring the mastery of a special skill were indistinguishably called craftsmen, and while they were considered to have the character of artists, the term artist, at least as we employ it today, had not come into use. Consequently the arts in the medieval period were closely interrelated and the individual artificer often practiced two or three arts without any sense of exceeding either his rights or his powers. Instead of an attempt to set up a hierarchy among the arts, the only issue that counted was that of good or bad workmanship. This healthy attitude gave a noble unity to the whole range of artistic expression and explains why textiles, manuscripts, wood-carving, and metal-work are as much a part of the aesthetic inheritance of the Middle Ages as churches, statuary, and painted altar pieces.

It would have been well for both artists and craftsmen if their early intimacy had never been interrupted and the custom had persisted of applying an identical standard of perfection to every kind of handiwork. Genuine as such regrets are, they do not alter the historical fact that in the later Renaissance centuries, but not yet in the quattrocento to be treated in this chapter, a distinction came gradually to be made among artificers and also among their creations. And however deplorable, in view of the consequences, the distinction may be considered to be, it was not, let us admit, without a certain justification. For we do not have to do violence to our judgment to concede that since architecture, sculpture, and painting require for their practice a lifetime of preparation as well as high personal endowment, they are not misnamed when we classify them as Major or Fine Arts. By the same tests the other artistic practices may without impropriety be called Minor Arts or handicrafts. While such a division recommends itself on the ground of convenience, what we must strictly avoid is the assumption that ideally the arts are ever other than one and that with the passing of the Middle Ages they ceased being referable to a single unifying principle of excellence.

In turning in this chapter to the quattrocento phase of expression the reader is urged to keep in mind that there was as yet no sharply drawn line either between artists and craftsmen or between Major and Minor Arts. It follows that every thoroughly conducted review of the artistic activity of this age should cover the whole field. If this course will not be followed in the present instance, our excuse is the purely illustrative character of this book in the several sections ancillary to our main theme of political history. Deliberately omitting the Minor Arts in order to save space, we shall concentrate attention on the Major or Fine Arts on the ground that, exhibiting, as they undoubtedly do, a higher measure of training and imagination, they adequately meet our limited purpose of opening an avenue to the aesthetic world of the quattrocento Florentines.

When during the communal revolution the rapidly multiplying contacts of men with the world and one another led to that gradual change of mental attitude which we have agreed to call humanism, the immediate effect of this shift of attention on the intellectual élite of the Italian towns was to inspire them not only to cultivate classical literature but also, as far as possible, to revive the whole ancient world. Having in the previous chapter dealing with the fifteenth century looked into the consequences of this devotion for scholarship and letters, we shall now examine them for the same period in the field of the Fine Arts. As the artificers were uneducated in the pedagogical sense of that term and only in rare instances knew more than the rudiments of Latin, the enthusiasm for antiquity was rather slow in reaching them. However, they could not escape it, since, if themselves unlettered, they lived among the lettered and shared the view generally current that the Romans were their ancestors and had set a mark in every field of thought and action which it was desirable to reach again, even though the hope was bold to the point of folly. But in no case would mere enthusiasm suffice to effect a return to antiquity in the arts. For, handed down from the Middle Ages, a solid body of theory and practice held sway in every *bottega* of the city, and this mass of honorable tradition was certain not to give up the ghost without stubborn resistance.

No sooner therefore had the champions of antiquity sounded their trumpets than the battle was engaged all along the line with consequences of great but varying importance in each of the three fields claiming our attention. In architecture the innovators won a sweeping victory, although it was by no means so complete as some historians would have us believe. In sculpture the classical preachment exercised an important effect without depriving the art of its native impulses or impairing its essential autonomy. Finally, in painting, in which field, fortunately for the independence of the painters, there existed no ancient remains inviting imitation, the influence of the propagandists of antiquity was almost negligible. In all three fields the quattrocento endowed Florence with such an abundance of notable works that the period will always rank as one of the greatest epochs not alone of Florentine but of European art in general. However, discerning critics have never failed to insist that the products of the several arts do not stand on the same level of merit. It is their

BENOZZO GOZZOLI. SECTION FROM THE PROCESSION OF THE KINGS. FRESCO. CHAPEL OF THE MEDICI PALACE

DOMENICO·GHIRLANDAIO. BIRTH OF THE VIRGIN. FRESCO. TORNABUONI CHAPEL. SANTA MARIA NOVELLA

BOTTICELLI. BIRTH OF VENUS. UFFIZI GALLERY

opinion that the Florentines attained the greatest vigor and refinement of expression in painting; that after painting, and not very far behind it, came sculpture; and that architecture, because practiced with much less originality than the two sister-arts, brought up the rear. It will not escape the attention of the reader that this order of importance is in each instance in inverse proportion to the domination exercised by the classical fetish. But let each art rehearse its own facts and tell its own story.

The pathfinder in architecture was Filippo Brunelleschi (1377–1446). In the manner usual among gifted apprentices he began to practice several arts without distinction and might have ended by devoting himself primarily to sculpture if he had not been defeated in a public competition of the year 1401 for a bronze gate of the baptistery projected as the northern counterpart to the famous South Gate created by Andrea Pisano almost a hundred years before. When the prize in this competition was attributed to Lorenzo Ghiberti, Brunelleschi, a high-spirited artist content with nothing less than supremacy in everything he undertook, resolved to devote himself to architecture, and, setting out for Rome in company with a younger friend, Donatello by name, spent a number of years studying the still plentiful remains of buildings to be found within the compass of the City of the Seven Hills. So little at that time did anybody at Rome grasp the purport of the intensive sketching and measuring among the ruins conducted by the two strangers that for the perplexed natives they became the treasure-hunters (*quelli del tesoro*).[1] After a long apprenticeship involving the most severe self-discipline, Brunelleschi repossessed himself of the columnar principle of classical construction varied according to the three established orders of Doric, Ionian, and Corinthian. He also mastered the elements of classical decoration with its stylized motives of egg and dart, bead and reel, meander, and honeysuckle. However, on his return to his native city he did not become the spokesman of an architecture based exclusively on his recovered knowledge of antiquity. Even if he had been inclined to such stark dogmatism, he could not do other than graft the new learning on the medieval stem, for the moment he undertook the practice of his art, he had to reckon not with temples, baths, theaters, and aqueducts, but with churches, chapels, town halls, and private residences, and for these modern structures the classical tradition offered no precedent. The circumstance that behind the still dominant Gothic lay the older Romanesque, and that Romanesque was nothing other than a barbarized offspring of classicism, considerably eased Brunelleschi's problem. By abolishing Gothicism as a northern intrusion, which it was, he came face to face with the Romanesque, which he found it reasonably simple to yoke with the more elegant parent forms of which he was the rediscoverer. It is not improper to think of the changes effected by him as being essentially a return to the national tradition. Nonetheless his work so distinctly marks a departure from what went immediately before that we need not hesitate to regard him as the inventor of a new manner identified ever since as the Renaissance style.

It is not our purpose to name more than a few of the structures which serve to describe Brunelleschi's pioneership. In the Loggia degli Innocenti (Found-

[1] Vasari's *Lives* under Brunelleschi.

lings' Hospital) he employed a row of classic columns of such slenderness joined by round arches of such bold leap that we receive an impression of energy combined with elegance for which there is nothing in the Florentine record to prepare us. That his contemporaries were similarly impressed is proved by the fact that the loggias and cloisters built after this achievement invariably follow the Innocenti pattern. Brunelleschi did much work for Cosimo de' Medici, the most outstanding being the church and sacristy of San Lorenzo. Employing and ingeniously varying in the two buildings the structural elements of column (or pilaster) and round arch, which he again made basic, he achieved in each instance an attractive whole of harmonious proportions and balanced parts heightened by the application of perfectly executed ornament. The massive strength and towering majesty characteristic of good Gothic have been banished in favor of the lost ideal of urbanity, the goal of which is the avoidance of excess and the satisfaction of a cultivated taste.

By far the most famous of Brunelleschi's achievements is the cupola of Santa Maria del Fiore, with which he at last brought to completion an edifice begun one hundred and fifty years before by Arnolfo di Cambio.[2] It is probable that the octagon, into which the nave expands to the east and which was to be crowned with a dome, was a part of Arnolfo's original plan. When, toward the end of the fourteenth century, the nave and aisles had been at length completed as we see them today, the building commission, called the opera del duomo, attacked the problem of the east end and found itself for a time completely baffled. For, although innumerable consulting architects presented plans for the key feature, the cupola, none offered a solution which was adequate either from an engineering or an aesthetic angle. The single exception was Filippo Brunelleschi, whose project was so daring and brought so many novel structural features into play that it encountered even more vigorous objections than the rival projects assailable on the ground of calculable error. Only gradually did Filippo manage to infuse the commission with his own never-failing confidence and, hesitatingly installed as chief architect, between 1420 and 1434 he raised the magnificent cupola which, with Giotto's campanile, is still the far-seen landmark of the city.

By nothing which he did more than by this cupola did Brunelleschi prove that, if he drew his inspiration from the ancients, he still maintained his independence as an artistic personality. The only comparable cupola the Romans had erected was the Pantheon, which still stands, and on the score of scale the Pantheon is not really comparable since in neither elevation nor width of span does it approach the cupola of the Florentine cathedral. Besides, the Roman cupola was projected with sole regard to interior effect, while the cathedral dome was planned to make its chief impression from the outside and to dominate the urban unit, illustrious Florence, and proclaim its greatness to the enfolding hills. An examination of the soaring structure will reveal the leading steps by which the architect solved his problem. The octagonal substructure was heavily buttressed by means of a ring of apse chapels crowned by half-domes. From them the eye travels easily to the drum, which is

2 See chap. XV.

penetrated on each of its eight sides with a circular opening to provide the interior with light. Eight powerful ribs of stone leap upward from the drum in curves of great power and beauty. They constitute the bony framework of the cupola and at their point of convergence are crowned by a magnificent lantern. This last feature Brunelleschi did not live to complete, although it was added (1462) in accordance with his plans. That all the domes built afterward in Europe were made possible by Brunelleschi's masterpiece, and that with the single exception of St. Peter's at Rome, the work of Michelangelo, another Florentine, no subsequent cupola ever achieved the majesty and power of Santa Maria del Fiore should serve to inscribe Brunelleschi's name high on the tablets of his art.

At least two young contemporaries of Brunelleschi require notice, Michelozzo Michelozzi (1396–1472) and Leon Battista Alberti (1404–72). The degree in which Michelozzi derived his inspiration from Brunelleschi can be readily divined by throwing a glance at the charming cloister of San Marco. Its graceful arches resting on slender columns were raised at the orders of Cosimo de' Medici but owe their finished artistry to the example furnished by the older master in the Loggia degli Innocenti. Also at Cosimo's command, but this time in complete independence from Brunelleschi, Michelozzi erected the great Medici palace in the Via Larga. It rises directly from the street in three stories, of which the first story bristles with rough-trimmed blocks of stone, while the other two, indicated by their smooth surfaces as the living quarters, are set with round-arched windows at regular intervals and terminate in a heavily accented cornice. By its rectangular massiveness and air of defiance the structure asserts its kinship with the medieval towers, the earliest residences of the town nobility. On passing through the portal, which reiterates the round-arch motive of the windows, we enter a handsome inner court where the more civil spirit of the new age disclosed itself in an open arcade supported on rows of vigorous columns. The Medici palace furnished the model for numerous mansions with which the prosperous merchants attempted to emulate their rulers. Such later and even more imposing structures as the Pitti and the Strozzi palaces make no secret of their affinity with the great house Michelozzi reared for Cosimo.

Alberti gained a vast reputation in his day because of his eminence in a great variety of fields. He is esteemed by many as the first of the universal personalities or supermen, whose genius lent a special luster to the Renaissance. In addition to winning renown as an athlete, a mathematician, a writer on the arts, a musician, and a painter, Alberti was acclaimed as an architect. However, a temperate modern judgment will not concede him a high place in this field. He permitted himself to be overwhelmed to such a degree by the accomplishments of antiquity that, in distinction from the more balanced Brunelleschi and Michelozzi, he tried to effect a complete breach with the medieval past. The result may be seen in two contributions made at the order of his patrons, the Rucellai family. One is the façade of the Rucellai palace, in which he abandoned without qualification the medieval fortress conception and gave his frontispiece a classical articulation by means of rows of superimposed pilasters. His other fabric is the façade of Santa Maria Novella, where his particular problem was to complete the front elevation of a great Gothic house of worship. A weakness from which Florentine churches of all ages suffer is that their façades, if provided at all, were added as an afterthought. When Alberti was requested to supply the missing front for Santa Maria Novella, he drew a design that had no relation to the structure behind it. The pedants of the Renaissance, an innumerable tribe, have rapturously eulogized both the church and the palace façade of Alberti's devising. Whosoever conceives of architecture primarily as structure and demands that every structure be a unified composition, will find it difficult to give to Alberti any other rating than that of a clever draughtsman. Since he indicates a trend in favor of unconditional surrender to antiquity, a trend which in the following generations completely gained the upper hand, he cannot be omitted from even the most compressed quattrocento record of the art of architecture.

When Lorenzo Ghiberti (1378–1455) won the competition of the year 1401 for the North Doors of the baptistery, he established himself as the leading sculptor of Florence. Not till twenty years had passed did he complete his design, which, patterned so far as its external form is concerned, on the older South Doors of Andrea Pisano, told in thirty-two panels the story of the life of Christ. In this impressive work Ghiberti reveals himself as an artist stemming from the Middle Ages, but also as alertly aware that a new day has dawned upon the world. While he has been affected by classical examples, he feels no strong naturalistic urge and achieves his attractive compositions by ordering each panel in flowing lines which fall into a pleasant pattern of animated movement. When, following this success, the third or East Doors of the baptistery were also committed to him, he was an older man who had not remained unaffected by the technical conquests recently achieved by the graphic arts, such as perspective, landscape, and anatomy. His new assignment obliged him to present scenes from the Old Testament; and in order to exhibit his freshly acquired professional powers he abandoned the Gothic frame employed by Andrea Pisano and followed in his own earlier gate, and divided his space into ten large square panels. Into each of these he crowded so many figures arranged in a deepening perspective that, as against a certain pictorial vivacity duly achieved, the monumental effect we normally demand of sculpture is completely lost. The easy graceful line, the essence of Ghiberti's genius, again dominates, providing Ghiberti's second gate, like his first, with a subtle witchery; but both gates alike declare that the artist was a gracious feminine spirit and not a virile innovator.

Virile innovation was the part reserved to Donatello (1386–1466), the indisputable fountainhead of all that is truly significant in fifteenth-century sculpture. As we are aware, Donatello was a close friend of Brunelleschi and, sharing the latter's enthusiasm for classical remains, went with him on his treasure hunt to Rome. From ancient coins and cameos, for the ancient statues were still largely buried in the earth, Donatello acquired an acquaintance with the spirit of antiquity, for which he ever afterward exhibited the most sincere admiration. Nonetheless he never permitted his zeal to divert him from the medieval tradition, from which he sprang, and from his instinctive love for the forms of nature, among which he was placed. Without fear of contradiction it may be asserted that, except for his taking over into his work occasional classical motives, he was not a classicist at all, but a product of the tradition native to his city revitalized by absorption in, and study of, the creature world about him. To bring the sculpture of the quattrocento into juxtaposition with that of antiquity is to be made startlingly aware of their wide divergence and to be readily persuaded of the complete spiritual independence of the later school.[3]

The unusually prolific art of Donatello covers so many varieties of work that it will not be possible to illustrate each category even by description of a single instance. His finest early work and one of the finest works of the whole range of sculpture is the St. George, hewn of marble for an exterior niche of Or San Michele but now withdrawn for safekeeping to the Museo Nazionale (Bargello). The St. George constitutes an excellent starting-point for any consideration of Donatello, as it reveals the master's rootedness in the Christian idealism of the Middle Ages to which he has communicated the incomparable vivacity of his freshened senses. The erect body of the young soldier of the Lord is aglow with life, and the head, an amazing realization of gracious youth, rises from the slim neck like a tulip from its stem. In many of his works both in the round and in relief Donatello gave himself with such passion to the exact rendering of the human figure that, in respect of these creations, we might be moved to set him down as an uncompromising naturalist. Such a realistic work is the Magdalen carved in wood in the baptistery, another, the *Zuccone* (meaning the pumpkin head) of marble high in a niche of Giotto's campanile. Purporting to be an Old Testament prophet, the Zuccone is nothing other than a close portrait study of a Florentine contemporary with a bald head, a dragging walk, and a dozen other details indicative of advancing decrepitude. That Donatello when he thought of himself as having a mission preached nature in the raw is indicated by the fact that his favorite oath was: "By the faith I put in my Zuccone."[4] Less headstrong and consequently more genial realism is encountered in his many portrait busts. Of these perhaps the foremost example is the representation in colored terra cotta of the sharp-featured pre-Medicean oligarch, Niccolò da Uzzano. It is difficult to conceive how the unfathomable complex we call personality could be more unerringly rendered.

It is Donatello's zest for life that explains his many works presenting children laughing and at play. To illustrate this particular class the *cantorìa* (or organ loft) he did for the cathedral will serve, especially as it embodies also his unflagging interest in movement. A procession of children have joined a dance, weaving in and out as they raise their voices and toss their limbs about in riotous abandon to the spirit of the moment. The artist's last great work is in a class by itself since it is a bronze equestrian statue and bronze equestrian statues had not been attempted in Italy since the fall of Rome. The rider he was asked to immortalize was a condottiere familiar under the nickname of Gattamelata, and the completed work was set up in the cathedral square of Padua. It will at once strike the beholder that the condottiere wears ancient

[3] W. Bode, *Florentine Sculpture of the Renaissance*. New York, 1909.
[4] See Vasari's *Lives* under Donatello.

armor and that the horse is not unrelated to the sculptured horses of antiquity. These are touches in which it would be a mistake to see more than a superficial concession to a fashion from which it was impossible wholly to escape. The horse is a massive war steed, which moves deliberately forward as the general with bared head and an authoritative sweep of the truncheon held in his right hand makes the necessary dispositions for the coming battle. Horse and rider are molded into a compact unit of controlled power. They remain with us as the expression of a genius who, though deriving from the near past and borrowing at his pleasure from the far past, received his main impulses from life itself, and who by directing his successors to this ever-bubbling fountain of renewal inaugurated the first great age of modern sculpture.

It is a tribute to the greatness of the age that, indebted to Donatello as were all who took up sculpture after him, they present themselves to view as highly individual artists. An effect, on the one hand, of the breakdown of medieval society, and, on the other, of the secular outlook we have called humanism, was for men to become more and more differentiated and for each one to develop his personality to its greatest potentiality. In the artists this bent becomes particularly marked, as a roll call of the sculptors will clearly bring to light. Luca della Robbia (1400–1482) was molded by the new realism, but he mixed it with something so uniquely his own that it is impossible ever to confuse his work with that of the realist Donatello. Look at the cathedral organ loft which he did (1437) as a counterpart to that of Donatello: it consists of ten panels exhibiting groups of children praising the Lord with dance and song. Some are in motion, others at rest, and all alike tell us with a startling immediacy that life in its Maytime is fresh and fragrant. But, although this is precisely what Donatello said in his organ loft and in a score of other pieces as well, he said it with an intonation which can never be confused with that of Luca. A sculptor of more narrow range was Desiderio da Settignano (1428–64), who in his portraits of the women of the upper social stratum achieved a delicacy and refinement which have never been surpassed. A girl's bust conveniently placed for comparison in the Donatello room of the Museo Nazionale shows an exquisite finish, which the older master never attained and to which, let us add, he did not aspire. A vigorous and restless experimenter in movement was Antonio Pollaiuolo (1429–98). His small bronze group of Hercules wrestling with Antaeus could not more superlatively convey an impression of energy, were it of heroic size.

In concluding our sculptural review let us throw a glance at Andrea Verrocchio (1435–88), than whom no quattrocentist of them all had a more personal savor. A boyish David (bronze) with drawn sword and the head of Goliath at his feet breathes the freshness with which everything the age produced is touched and at the same time renders charmingly the embarrassment of the young hero before the evidence of his own heroism. In a marble bust of a young woman, who with her left hand clasps a spray of daisies to her bosom, Verrocchio has combined the vitality of Donatello with the delicacy of Desiderio into a work which one need not hesitate to proclaim a supreme achievement in its field. The individually treated features and hands, which never belonged to any but to a single woman among all those that have ever lived, are rescued from every suggestion of the commonplace by the almost religious hush of the pose, the elegant lines of the closely clinging garment, and the elaborately stylized hair with its soft parallel waves broken at the temples into a storm of curls framing the tranquil face. Compared with this triumph of restraint, the sculptor's most celebrated work, the equestrian statue of Bartolommeo Colleone at Venice, is but an empty boast. Or let us call it an expression, perfect of its kind, of the frenzied energy that was a characteristic of the age. The alert and rigidly erect rider sits his proudly pacing steed as though he were the very god of war. It is absurd to suppose that we have here a portrait of the insignificant condottiere, whose name the figure bears and who died some twenty years before the work was undertaken. Rather than on any narrowly representative ground the monumental horse and rider have won the world's acclaim as a symbol of the glamorous Italian Renaissance.

A peril connected with periodization, be it of history, civilization, or art, is that the periods will be taken literally and the unbroken continuity of all human unfolding be forgotten. Often as a *caveat* has already been entered against this danger, it may profitably be repeated on turning to quattrocento painting. At the very outset we encounter a number of figures whom the official record of their life classifies as quattrocentist, but who by the evidence of their work occupy the border line between two ages and who should therefore be classified as men of the transition. Quite the most important member of this group is Fra Angelico (1387–1455). He sprang of peasant stock in the Mugello, became a Dominican friar at the age of twenty, and specialized, as many monks and friars had done before him, as a painter. After practicing his art in the Dominican monastery under Fiesole, he was transferred to San Marco shortly after the architect Michelozzi had begun to make headway with the reconstruction of that dilapidated foundation ordered by Cosimo de' Medici. At San Marco Fra Angelico painted in fresco in the cloister, the chapter house, and the cells of the brothers some fifty pictures which, well preserved on the whole, tell us of him today as directly as though he were still alive. And what they tell us is that, more important than his being a painter, Fra Angelico was a dedicated soul of such simplicity and candor that every work of his hand becomes a hymn addressed to God, giver of life and joy. Broadly speaking, we may call him a belated son of the Middle Ages, but on better acquaintance with his particular religious quality we will be struck with his failing to follow the beaten highway of the medieval Doctors of the church in order to take the less traveled path traced by St. Francis of Assisi. The argument that his membership in the rival order of St. Dominic makes such a spiritual relationship improbable is unconvincing. St. Francis distributed his inheritance among all men of a like disposition, and it is a fact that it became a calculable element of general medieval culture after his time. Now the essence of the faith of the *poverello* of Assisi was the goodness of God and the goodness of his creation. It was of course a mystic faith unrelated to the searching processes of the human reason, and its rewards for the believer were that he was flooded with joy and uplifted with ecstatic visions. Fra Angelico affects us like St. Francis come again to manifest his spirit in another field. Such an avatar is in itself less surprising than that it should have occurred at Florence, which more than any other city of Italy was hard, sharp-witted, disciplined, and earthy. Certainly Fra Angelico has no forerunner among Florentine painters, and though the mystic Botticelli is among his successors, Botticelli's mysticism is of so different an order that it constitutes an entirely separate world.

While Fra Angelico is a mystic and has endeared himself to the world as a rapturous visionary, he is professionally a painter who took over the practices of his predecessors and, with a vigor proving that he was after all a Florentine, added much of the new Renaissance knowledge to his medieval stock. To praise Fra Angelico's soul and belittle his hand, as is not uncommon, is to be blind to his honorable, uninterrupted striving as a craftsman. At San Marco at the head of the dormitory stairs leading to the double row of monastic cubicles is an Annunciation which shows Mary under a carefully drawn quattrocento portico in a smiling garden which deceptively recedes in exact accordance with the recently demonstrated laws of perspective. The Annunciation should scatter every doubt that the painter was not moving forward with his time. Of course these fashionable novelties of landscape and architecture do not make the picture. They remain subordinate elements so manipulated that they serve no other purpose than to heighten the hush and gladness of the central theme, which is the meek, surprised Madonna receiving the salutation of the Angel. One of the friar's leading resources in this and all his pictures is the use of transparent, high-keyed color. Than his bright palette nothing was better calculated to enforce the element of joy in which all his renderings of the acts of Christ and of Christ's soldiery are steeped. Nor should we overlook that the remarkable state of preservation of his frescos is convincing evidence of his high technical proficiency.

Equally capable in panel painting, Fra Angelico has endowed us with numerous altar pieces scattered at present through all the museums of the world. A large number have been brought together recently in a special room within the San Marco compound, where they may be studied in happy fellowship with their fresco kin. The Coronation of the Virgin, which is in no way exceptional, may be selected from the mass to illustrate the wonders of his brush. What we behold reveals itself at once as pure vision, wherein the subject matter is much less important than the emotion of the artist. And yet the ineffable scene is marvelously realized. Christ and his Mother are seated upon a cloud, the rapturous angels gather close, singing and sounding trumpets, and beyond them reaching to the very edge of the frame stands or floats the company of the saints in marshaled row on row. It is by these rows organized as concentric circles meeting in the heads of the Virgin and her Son that the picture gets its unity and pattern. Each saintly face is beautiful with a celestial beauty, and the pinks, blues, violets, and greens spread a veil of delicate hue that ravishes the eye. If this is not Giotto's art, which, like Florence itself, is concerned with subduing and possessing the world, still it is art, which in rendering our insubstantial dreams directs us from the necessary earth to the equally necessary sky.

That it was Giotto who was the true father of Florentine painting was made plain by a younger contemporary of Fra Angelico. Unseduced by the friar's blissful raptures, this man took Giotto for his teacher and with little more than his own genius as a guide discovered a new continent. In Masaccio, who was born in 1401 and died at the age of twenty-seven, we encounter one of the most vital and transforming agencies ever manifested in the field of art. We cannot imagine him other than as a youth aglow with energy and resolved, like his leading contemporaries in every field, on excellence and mastery. His development began with the very moment he was apprenticed to a painter; but as painting was slow to shake off the medieval lethargy and was lagging behind the more adventurous sister-skills of architecture and sculpture, it was by these latter rather than by his immediate master that he was introduced to the new spirit and the new knowledge. It was the sculptor, Donatello, who referred him to nature as the inexhaustible mother of forms, and it was the architect, Brunelleschi, who showed him the possibilities of the new science of perspective. All else he owed solely to himself. It is one of the many amazements connected with Masaccio that he lived to complete only a single important work, the frescos of the Brancacci chapel in the church of the Carmine. And not even all of these are by his hand. Nonetheless shortly after his death the modest chapel became a shrine of pilgrimage for his followers, and among his followers it is not an exaggeration to reckon the whole body of Florentine painters after his time. As for the historians and critics of art, beginning with Vasari they have set themselves to analyze Masaccio's revolutionary contribution and have not yet arrived at the end of the tale.

We shall have to rest content with the examination of a single picture of the Brancacci group. It is called the Tribute Money and presents Christ among his disciples confronted by the publican who has come to collect the head-tax levied by Caesar. At the left Peter is seen stooping to extract the coin from the mouth of the fish, and at the right he appears again, this time handing the penny to the tax collector. The great central group has in its single figures the fine dignity of Giotto, while the way the figures are brought together to tell their story suggests the older master's clarity and calculated order. The mind travels easily from Masaccio's Tribute Money to Giotto's Raising of Drusiana in the Peruzzi chapel at Santa Croce and back from Drusiana to the Tribute Money. Nonetheless, while the descent of the younger from the older man is undeniable, how much he has added to his inheritance! His figures have acquired a depth giving the illusion of being truly three-dimensional. At the same time each body underneath its robe has gained an articulation such as no merely painted body ever had before. Although this particular picture shows only clothed figures, there are nudes in some of the other frescos of the Carmine group which prove that Masaccio has dared to ignore the ecclesiastical tabu against nakedness and in his ardent pursuit of reality has arrived at the undraped human form. Had he not taken this forward step, he could not have given us the solidly constructed figures of the apostles and, above all, he could not have achieved the vivacious movement of the athletic young publican. Added to real bodies with dignified or lively carriage according to the character of their owner, we have besides and for the first time a background which is a real landscape of plain and mountain with the gradual recession that only the command of aerial perspective is able to supply. Finally, there is an abandonment of the old linear draughtsmanship and, in place of it, such a distribution of dark and light tones touched with color as to give a much more faithful representation of mass and distance than was possible with the traditional means of expression. Technically this chiaroscuro, as we may call it, was the discovery of Masaccio which was fraught with the greatest consequences for Italy and Europe. For, when his tonal invention was at last comprehended by his puzzled followers, it was so generally accepted as valid that it became the basis of all modern painting down to the threshold of the twentieth century.

It took the successors of Masaccio almost the remainder of the century before they had mastered his novel contributions. These successors fall in the main under two heads, the experimenters or scientists who tried to gain command of some new element of technical expressiveness considered by them to be important, and the traditionalists, who took over from Masaccio what they could understand and employed it in pictorial story-telling in the guileless manner of the age. Among the scientists, an unpopular but interesting group, belong such men as Paolo Uccello (1397–1475), Andrea del Castagno (1396–1457), and Domenico Veneziano (1400–1461). Not particularly regarded in their day, each made an important contribution to the mass of technical knowledge on which Florentine painting at its culmination came to rest. Paolo Uccello occupied himself tirelessly with the mysteries of perspective, Andrea del Castagno struggled as passionately with anatomy, and Domenico Veneziano, who was a Florentine by adoption only, exhibited for the first time the new richness that resulted from supplementing, but not yet supplanting, the old tempera technique with the use of oil.

Although the traditionalists made a much greater stir in the world, we are obliged to dismiss them, too, with a bare mention. Their leader is Fra Filippo Lippi (1400–1465). He was the first painter to tell the gospel stories in terms of Florentine everyday life. This gave his work a familiar and homely quality which would quickly have degenerated to vulgarity, had he not been saved by his ingenuous acceptance of the belief, common to that age of hope, that spring had come to the world and that in spring the earth was a goodly habitation. Certainly not a great artist in the sense of Giotto and Masaccio, he should not be grudged the popularity he owed to his love of existence on the plane familiar to himself and the commoner sort of his fellow-citizens. Benozzo Gozzoli (1420–98) lived equally close to the pulse beat of his time, but instead of picturing the men of the shops and the children of the streets, he took his cue from the pageants that featured the frequent Florentine holidays. An example of his work capable of affording the rarest pleasure, in part owing to its remarkable state of preservation, is the Procession of the Three Kings to the Christ Child's Manger in the chapel of the Medici palace. It is packed with details from the actual pageants of which Gozzoli had been the delighted witness. You see a procession winding around three walls of the rectangular chapel over hillsides, through forests, in leisurely haste to reach the Mother kneeling before her Son over the altar constituting the fourth wall. Eternal summer rules in the world disclosed by Gozzoli, a world of children untroubled by reflection and persuaded that the spectacle of today will be followed by a no less engaging show tomorrow.

The painter representing the culmination of this school of broad and genial narrative is Domenico Ghirlandaio (1449-94). In him Fra Filippo Lippi's honest love of commonplace sentiment joins hands with Benozzo Gozzoli's exquisite feeling for fine people in fine clothes making an appropriate display. Ghirlandaio must have found that life in his native city during the rule of Lorenzo the Magnificent, with whom his own years almost exactly tallied, fell little short of perfection. He became the household painter of families like the Sassetti and the Tornabuoni, who, adherents of the Medici and leading beneficiaries of their sway, accepted the painter's cheerful optimism as a delicate personal tribute. At the command of Francesco Sassetti, one of Lorenzo's numerous business agents, the artist decorated the family chapel at Santa Trinità with pictures from the life of St. Francis; and some years later, on order from Giovanni Tornabuoni, head of the Roman branch of the Medici bank, he covered the choir of Santa Maria Novella with scenes, on one wall, from the life of Mary and, on the opposite wall, from the life of St. John the Baptist. These frescos enjoy an immense reputation, which they fully deserve if taken on their own superficial terms. That means that we must not expect, for Ghirlandaio does not offer, representations in which there survives as much as a trace of the old religious feeling, wherein Florentine and all European art whatever had had its origin. We have here a completely mundane attitude toward the ancient stories of the Christian faith, which did not consider it an offense to transform the sacred personages into contemporary prosperous burghers dressed in their best finery, paying each other ceremonious visits in their houses, or meeting with mannerly exchange of greetings on city square or amidst pastoral delights. As Ghirlandaio was a minutely realistic observer of the house furnishings and clothes characteristic of every class of citizens but particularly of the well-to-do, his frescos constitute a uniquely valuable volume on the private life of the Florentines of quality. Since he was also a portraitist with an instinctive feeling for the elements constituting individuality, he utilized for his scenes the figures of the leading citizens, both men and women, thus making his unique treatise on manners an equally unique contemporary portrait gallery.

In view of the flashy accessories, which completely mask the essence, it can be readily understood that many sincerely religious people regard these elegant versions of sacred history as a blasphemous mockery. However, such critics constitute a vanishing minority, and in our time, as on the day when the frescos were first uncovered, they have enjoyed the unstinted admiration of the general public. In the light of this uninterrupted popularity two deductions may be safely ventured. They are, first, that, in spite of continued lip service in the churches, the secular attitude, which had been pushing to the front in Florence for several hundred years, in Lorenzo's day ruled the hearts and minds; and, second, that this secular attitude has maintained an unbroken domination to the present day.

In the very years in which Ghirlandaio was giving inimitable expression to the material well-being and naïve self-satisfaction of the ruling classes Sandro

Botticelli (1444–1510) produced work which mirrored very different facets of the age. As we are already aware that Botticelli was in touch with the inmost circle of Lorenzo's friends, we should from the outset be inclined to expect from him a much more specialized communication regarding Laurentian Florence than the rather generalized version offered by the creator of the choir pictures of Santa Maria Novella. Not only is this expectation realized, but Botticelli's work further tells us that its creator, who began his career with characteristic Florentine strenuosity, in his young manhood aspired to nothing less than to the conquest of all the technical means and styles of expression which painting had amassed since the dawn of a new day in the Brancacci chapel. His first master was Fra Filippo Lippi. Having learned all the genial friar had to offer, he roamed at will among his fellow-craftsmen, gathering a little here, a little there, and a great deal from such particularly vigorous contemporaries as Verrocchio and Pollaiuolo. It seemed reasonable to expect that the broad and systematic training the young painter gave himself would culminate in a fulfilment associating his name with the starry names of Giotto and Masaccio, when something happened and the bubble burst.

This puzzling event figures in the history of painting as the Botticelli problem. It has given rise to a stream of conjecture which, beginning with Walter Pater half a century ago, has gathered volume with each new decade.[5] Whoever is interested in the issue will have to turn to the considerable literature on the subject. For the general student it will suffice to note that Botticelli was from his birth the victim of an exaggerated sensitiveness. His naturally vigorous physique and his normal Florentine appetite for power kept it for a long time under control. To this healthy, balanced period covering his youth and early manhood belong the works indicative of his triumphant assimilation of the skills distributed through all the *botteghe* of the town. An Adoration of the Magi in the Uffizi with a costumed display of the members of the house of Medici in the role of worshiping kings supplies evidence that, in his zeal to absorb the lesson of every school, he even fell into the pretentious vein of Domenico Ghirlandaio. However, try as he might, against his inner voices, which became more imperious with every advancing year, he could not persist in his course. It is likely the first break occurred when, through contact with the humanistic circle of Lorenzo, he became acquainted with the world of antiquity and had disclosed before his amazed eyes the Love doctrine of Neoplatonism. To this phase of intense self-realization belong the Birth of Venus and the so-called Spring, more properly the Realm of Venus, the serene kingdom over which Love rules. Later, nourished undoubtedly by the esoteric doctrines spread by Ficino and Pico, a vein of Christian mysticism gained an increasing empire over him; and somewhat later still, he was so overwhelmed by the visions and prophecies of Savonarola that they ended by taking complete possession of his being. It is well known that Botticelli in his last period became a devoted *Piagnone* and that, following Savonarola's martyrdom, he gradually ceased to practice painting, dropping completely from the sight of men many years before he died.

Heaven forbid that any reader should take this telescoped analysis of a com-

---

[5] Essay on Botticelli by W. Pater in his volume, *The Renaissance*.

plicated destiny literally and conclude that Botticelli lived in three or four or six successive phases as in so many air-tight compartments. The thought suggested is rather that he was subject to many moods and worked in many manners, all of which persisted even when one happened temporarily to predominate, and that the year in which a picture can be proved to have been completed is not an infallible index of its ruling character. One point, however, is capital and must be reiterated. After following for years a line of development normal for a healthy Florentine and giving rise to the hope that painting would be carried to a new culmination, Botticelli abandoned the broad highway he had been traveling for a tortuous by-path, of which no one had knowledge save himself and which had been calling to him in seductive whispers since his boyhood. Yielding to an inner urge, which until he entered middle life he had managed to keep in subjugation, he became an eccentric, gave up the traditional Florentine view that art was a social function, and thereafter painted to no other end than to please himself alone. Had he been more resolute and less sensitive and fragile, he might have reached the heights to which Leonardo afterward mounted. He made another choice, leaving behind a range of works which proclaim him as one of the most individual and fascinatingly elusive artists of all time.

As it is impossible to pursue Botticelli through the wide gamut of his moods, and as it is equally impossible to take no account whatever of his individual works, we shall make the very halting compromise of examining two pictures, which derive from the later, the eccentric artist and which, although very different in subject matter, carry the same haunting message. The Birth of Venus belongs to what may be called his classicizing period, but perhaps never has there been produced a work farther removed from the true classical spirit. Indeed except that the subject is Venus, there is nothing whatever in the picture having the slightest bearing on antiquity. This Venus is love, the prime mover of the universe, and she comes in her cockleshell driven by the Winds (two male figures at the left) across the sea to the garlanded Earth (female figure at the right) aflutter with welcome on the shore. The Venus, a nude figure of indescribable loveliness, instead of expressing delight and joy, is enveloped in mute tragedy. She seems profoundly conscious that in bringing life to the generation of men she must needs bring also sorrow and heartbreak. This is no more than a feebly approximate statement of her import which, like all mystic communications, defies formulation in insubstantial words. It is much easier and critically sounder to speak of the technical means by which the coming of the sea-born goddess is impressed on the mind and senses. The magnificent swirling movement beginning in the agitated Winds on the left is moderated in the undulating body and blown hair of Venus, to be taken up once more with its original vehemence in the gesture and garments of the welcoming Earth. The tremulous motion is at last gratifyingly arrested by the three stiffly vertical trees at the extreme right. In analyzing Botticelli's command of movement Berenson declares him to be a lineal symphonist of a refinement of harmony beyond the achievement of any European artist before or since.

The other picture to which attention is invited is an altar piece in the

Uffizi showing the Madonna and the Divine Child surrounded by six angels. It is in the round, a shape for which Botticelli had a peculiar liking. It would be pleasant to linger over the reappearance in this picture of the artist's singing line, but we shall limit ourselves to the most immediately arresting feature. It is that this Holy Virgin is the identical Venus we have just seen wafted across the sea. In the altar piece she is of course not nude but amply garmented, and her sad face shows a certain softening through the veil fastened in her hair. But called the Virgin, she is none other than the Venus of the allegory and carries the same burden of unfathomable grief. Let who will unravel the mystery that troubled Botticelli's soul. Certain it is that as he grew older and dared to be, cost what it might, his sensitive and individual self, he had a very different communication to make from Benozzo Gozzoli and the pleasant narrative painters, Botticelli's predecessors and contemporaries, to whom life was a perpetual holiday.

When Botticelli by choosing the solitary path made the great refusal, it was as good as certain that someone else would undertake the task of gathering together the diverse knowledge and experience of the quattrocento into a magnificent synthesis. This man was Leonardo da Vinci. With him we reach the culminating, the cinquecento phase of Florentine art.

XXVI. The Savonarola Episode (1494–98)

IN THE year 1494, two years after the death of Lorenzo the Magnificent, King Charles VIII carried out the long-threatened French invasion of Italy. It completely shattered the delicately balanced peninsular relations with which we are familiar and inaugurated a new period of Italian history. In its further consequences it revolutionized the whole European situation by inaugurating that ferocious rivalry among nationally organized states which is a leading characteristic of Modern as distinct from Medieval History. Owing to these effects, many historians are inclined to accept 1494 as a convenient date for the beginning of Modern History; and if periodization is to be determined in the main by changes in the realm of politics, there is much to be said for this decision. It is clear, however, that to historians of religion or art or economics other dates will present themselves associated with happenings of greater significance in the field in which they are interested. We do not conceive ourselves as quarreling with these other historians, if, concerned in this book with a political unit, the republic of Florence, we accept the absolutely determining character of the great event of 1494. We have followed the successive stages by which Florence disengaged itself from the octopus embrace of feudalism and, becoming an independent city-state, developed into a commonwealth of notable political power and unique cultural creativeness. That age of struggle, the great age of the Red Lily, covering almost five hundred years, was now drawing to a close. Toward the end of the fifteenth century the peoples of Europe overcoming in their turn the conditions of the Middle Ages, which in their altered frame of mind they came to regard as barriers to their free development, had come to assemble their strength in great national monarchies; or rather, to state the case with greater historical sweep, they had gropingly inaugurated a movement of enlargement and unification which has continued uninterruptedly down to our day.

In this enormously significant development three peoples took the lead, bringing about at approximately the same time the rise of the national monarchies of France, Spain, and England. Acquiring a power hitherto unknown over taxes, the army, and the administration, the sovereigns of these three countries gained an immense advantage over their neighbors, whether republics or principalities, which for one reason or another had failed to bring themselves to the same size and concentrated might. This was the case of each and every one of the Italian states. It was therefore also the case of the republic

of Florence, which, constrained from 1494 onward, to deal first with France
and then with France and Spain, found itself completely outclassed by these
great monarchies, a pigmy among giants. As will become presently apparent,
from the moment the French set foot in the peninsula the republic was no
longer free to formulate its own policy. It fell into a dependence on France,
and afterward on France and Spain alternately, from which it struggled desperately to escape. The struggle went on without respite till 1530, when, having
summoned its remaining strength and having clasped to itself its noblest traditions, it went down in final defeat. In the remainder of this work we shall treat
this last phase of the republic covering some thirty-six years. Already shadowed
by an implacably advancing doom, they constitute a not unworthy conclusion
to the story of human ingenuity and heroism unfolded in this book.

Although the French invasion came as a surprise to most Italians, an occasional statesman had woven it into his calculations and had correctly estimated
its absolutely fatal consequences. Such a statesman was Lorenzo de' Medici,
who, as we have seen, had directed his main effort in the latter part of his
life to the maintenance of peace among the Italian states as the surest available means for persuading the French not to embark on their transalpine adventure. Regardless of all that Lorenzo could do, the direct claim of the
French crown to Naples and its indirect claim, through the younger or Orléans
branch, to Milan kept the monarch interested in Italy at all times and on
occasion aroused his cupidity to the danger point. In shaping their policy the
rulers of Italy took no account of patriotism, which was a sentiment as yet
unknown in the peninsula, and did not scruple about intriguing at Paris in
the hope of scoring some petty advantage close at home with the aid of the
distant but powerful king of France. Lorenzo himself had played at this
dangerous game until, ripened by experience, he came to regard the French
intervention as an event incapable of bringing its local abettors more than a
temporary advantage and sure to end by putting the whole peninsula under a
foreign yoke. His policy was therefore to close every break in the peace front
of the Italian states as fast as it appeared; and he may be credited with having
maintained a hazardous amity among the contentious peninsular neighbors sufficient to discourage the French from taking the offensive in his day.

Hardly had Lorenzo died in the spring of 1492, when the delicate Italian balance he had made it his business to maintain began to show signs of violent
agitation. A leading culprit was none other than his own son and heir, Piero.
A handsome, arrogant young man of twenty-two, Piero spurned his father's
cautious policy in favor of bolder measures suggested by nothing more valid
than his foolish, juvenile preferences. For some time an issue had existed between the king of Naples and the *de facto* ruler of Milan, which, owing
mainly to the efforts of Lorenzo the Magnificent, had been kept under fair
control. The *de facto* ruler of Milan was Lodovico, called the Moor, and he
had acquired his authority as guardian of the titular duke, his nephew and
a minor. At the death of Lorenzo the young duke had reached the age of
twenty and was considered by his partisans to be ripe for rule. Sickly and
docile, he made no personal disturbance, but his beautiful wife, who was a
granddaughter of Ferrante, king of Naples, was a spirited creature resolved

BOTTICELLI. ADORATION OF THE MAGI. UFFIZI GALLERY

BOTTICELLI. VIRGIN WITH CHRIST-CHILD AND SIX
ANGELS. UFFIZI GALLERY

Left: POPE LEO X. RAPHAEL. PITTI GALLERY. *Right:* POPE CLEMENT VII. BRON-
ZINO. MEDICI PALACE

Left: SAVONAROLA. PORTRAIT BY FRA BARTOLOMMEO. SAN MARCO. *Right:*
MACHIAVELLI. BUST IN TERRA COTTA BY AN UNKNOWN ARTIST. PROPERTY OF
THE SOCIETÀ COLOMBARIA OF FLORENCE

to have her rights. Accordingly, she stormed at her southern relatives to bring pressure to bear on the Moor with a view to having him put an end to his long regency. Lodovico, pricked by ambition and utterly unscrupulous, was greatly chagrined by the representations of the court of Naples. In his heart he had long ago decided never to yield his place, and to secure himself against a sudden stroke by the aggrieved husband and wife kept them under close watch.

Murder, as the confidential agent of every Italian tyrant, would doubtless have been brought into the situation at this juncture if the Moor had not been obliged to reckon with an immediate declaration of war on the part of the king of Naples. Carefully pondering the problem, Lodovico came to the conclusion that his own safety demanded the overthrow of the interfering dynasty. This was not so difficult as it might seem, since all it required was to induce the king of France to undertake the long-threatened campaign to vindicate his right to the Neapolitan crown. Of course Lodovico himself, through such an invasion, would be running a certain risk, for there was no assurance that the northern sovereign, once in the peninsula, would not recall that, in addition to a Neapolitan, his house had also a Milanese claim. Persuaded, as oversubtle plotters often are, that he could make a clown of another man by using him as a tool, the Milanese regent began to play upon the ambition of the French king by offering him help in the Italian undertaking and by teasing him with the prospect that, thus seconded, the conquest of Naples would cease to be much of a hazard. It was in connection with the growing friction between Naples and Milan that Piero de' Medici abandoned his father's mediatory role. Instead of insisting on an adjudication, he put himself unreservedly on the side of the king of Naples, thereby filling the Moor with the panic fear of peninsular isolation and prompting him to redouble his effort to bring the French across the Alps.[1] The French king was a young man, Charles VIII by name, who lent a fascinated ear to Lodovico's siren call. Deformed and feeble physically, and mentally in no better case, the royal youth was the very antipodes of his cunning father, Louis XI. He had a pathetic passion for old tales of derring-do and under the flattery of his courtiers readily persuaded himself that he was called to renew the glory of his medieval namesake, the half-fabulous Charlemagne. Of the five states reckoned as Italian powers, Venice as usual stood to one side, Naples, Florence, and the pope leagued themselves together to resist the French invasion, and only Milan offered active help. Nevertheless, in the spring of 1494 Charles assembled an army at Lyons near the passes of the Alps, and after much uncertainty due to the battering effect on his weak mind of the opposed opinions of his councillors, in the late summer he led his army unmolested over the mountains and emerged upon Italian soil.

[1] The relations of Piero with Charles VIII, as well as those of the republic after him, are revealed by the documents published by A. Desjardins and G. Canestrini, *Négociations Diplomatiques de la France avec la Toscane*. Paris, 1859. Invaluable sidelights on Franco-Tuscan relations are offered by the Memoirs of the French courtier and statesman, Philippe de Commines. A conspicuous place among the innumerable presentations of the Italian invasions, beginning with that of 1494, must still be conceded to the earliest of them all by F. Guicciardini, *La Storia d'Italia* (on which see Introduction).

At Asti the young sovereign was met by his ally, the treacherous Lodovico the Moor. There were the usual receptions and parades, but only after another attack of indecision had been overcome did the king give the order to resume the march. The army at the head of which he proceeded southward in the direction of the Apennines was of a size and efficiency whereof the peninsula, accustomed to the trifling and treacherous warfare conducted by relatively small bands of hireling condottieri, had absolutely no experience. Not only did the French forces amount to sixty thousand men, but they were armed and disciplined to a degree far beyond the Italian standard. Furthermore, at the side of the panoplied cavalry, constituting the arm on which the Italians exclusively relied for success in the field, there operated an effective infantry, among which figured a select body of Swiss mercenaries capable of withstanding the most determined charge of horse and just then at the height of their reputation. Finally, the French had developed the artillery service far beyond any other European nation, and with an abundance of light, mobile cannons discharging iron instead of stone balls were able to work havoc among the dense enemy lines before they could be brought into action. Under these circumstances it is not surprising that the campaign of the three Italian allies collapsed before it began. To begin with, the usual jealousies kept them from joining their forces into a single unit; and when, in addition, Alfonso, king of Naples, who had just succeeded his father Ferrante and who alone among Italian leaders commanded a halfway impressive body of troops, withdrew them from central Italy resolved to confine his defense to his own kingdom, Tuscany and the State of the Church were at the mercy of the invader. When the hesitating Charles at length crossed the Apennines and prepared in his march through Tuscany to treat it as enemy territory, the stupidly proud Piero de' Medici, who, firmly committed to the house of Aragon, had rejected the numerous friendly advances of the French court, suddenly and pitifully lost heart. Stealthily departing from Florence on a late October day, he made his way in a panic to the camp of the French king, and without waiting to give his fears a chance to subside signed a treaty by which he completely reversed himself. Not only did he go over to the side of the invader, but in sign of good faith he delivered over to the French the fortresses of Sarzana, Sarzanella, Pietrasanta, Pisa, and Livorno, constituting in their sum the key positions of his state.

When this precipitate and disgraceful surrender became known in Florence, a fierce resentment took possession of the whole population. Traditionally attached to France, the Florentines had never viewed with other than antipathy Piero's alliance with the house of Aragon; but they failed just as completely to understand why it was necessary to mollify the angered French king by terms so injurious to the power and dignity of the state. Ominous murmurs among all classes required only the return of the discredited Piero from the French camp to occasion a general uprising. When, on the morning of November 9, the unhappy young man presented himself at the palace to report on his visit to the French king, he was refused admission. Boiling with indignation at the rebuff, he returned to his residence to assemble his partisans and take the

Palazzo Pubblico by storm, but before he could carry out his plans, the rebellious signory had rung the great bell accustomed to summon the citizens to the piazza. Recognizing that he could not make headway against the aroused masses, Piero pusillanimously gave up the struggle, made his way to the Porta San Gallo, and, attended by his brothers Giovanni (the later Pope Leo X) and Giuliano, rode hurriedly across the Apennines into safety. After exactly sixty years of an unusually secure rule the domination of the Medici had come to an end and the Florentines once again took their destiny into their own hands. Aside from plundering from cellar to garret the great Medicean palace with its invaluable treasures and doing the same mischief to the houses of a few of Piero's favored henchmen, no grave excesses were committed. In the face of the perilous crisis confronting the city the signory was moved to maintain as united a front as possible and resolutely suppressed all further public disorder.

What chiefly troubled and perplexed the government was that Tuscany had passed into the hands of a foreign power, which, although no longer officially at war with Florence, was the unquestioned master of the situation. On November 9, the very day on which Piero had been expelled from the city, the French, pushing southward, had entered Pisa. This was all the encouragement the Pisans needed to rise in revolt against Florence and to appeal for the protection of their recovered liberty to Charles VIII. More from lack of understanding than from political malice the king accepted the honor conferred on him, thus giving his royal support to an act which deprived the Florentines of a possession hardly less dear to them than life itself. When Charles next moved up the Arno Valley toward Florence the hectic situation reached a climax. Did he come as a friend or as an enemy? To the anxious commissioners sent by the signory to his camp to press for an immediate agreement he returned the stock answer that he would negotiate when once inside what in his muddled Italian he called the *gran villa*. On November 17, amidst feverish excitement, he entered the city in triumph at the head of his army. On that day the Florentines witnessed the greatest military spectacle of their history. They greeted the finely disciplined and magnificently appareled troops with cordial shouts of *Francia, Francia,* but the leading actor of the show proved a strangely disconcerting sight. For what met their eyes was a little solemn-faced monkey of a man, who, clad in steel and bestriding a great war horse, sat impassively holding his lance at rest, the conventional gesture of conquest.

Making his entry in this fashion, the king divulged that in his view he had captured the city and could dictate whatever conditions he pleased. When he had taken his residence in the Medici palace, lately sacked by the mob but lavishly refurnished for the occasion by the government, negotiations began that did not get far in the face of the lively protest of the Florentine representatives. Refusing to accede to the king's opinion that theirs was a captured town, they indignantly rejected the treaty submitted by the putative conqueror. On Charles insisting on his document, Piero Capponi, the boldest of the commissioners and the worthy scion of one of the city's greatest families, snatched it from the king's hands and, tearing it to bits, tossed the pieces on the floor.

"We shall sound our trumpets," threatened the miffed little man. At which Piero, rising to the occasion, thundered: "And we our bells!" The dramatic exchange deservedly became famous among the Florentines, for it was the king and not the spokesman of the citizens that gave way. The narrow winding streets of a populous town were not suited for the unfolding of the might of a great army; and Charles thought twice before exposing himself to the risk of having his Neapolitan venture die prematurely on the banks of the Arno. In a chastened state of mind he agreed to return the fortresses surrendered by Piero de' Medici as soon as the war was over and to be content with a subsidy of 120,000 gold florins. The crucial Pisan matter was wrapped up in a bundle of inconclusive phrases. Plainly if the Florentines wanted Pisa back, they would have to send an army and conquer it.

The citizens heaved a sigh of relief when, ten days after their entrance, the French at length evacuated the town. It is not our business to follow the army on its southward march further than to note its amazing triumph. Rome, like Florence, was occupied without resistance and the pope obliged to abandon King Alfonso of Naples and to enrol himself on the side of the invader. The pontiff whom the French thus humiliated was Alexander VI, a Spaniard with the family name of Borgia. Elevated to the papal throne in 1492, he inaugurated a reign of ten years which constitutes one of the most amazing chapters of Christian history and which, owing to its impact on our city of Florence, will hereafter repeatedly invite our attention. Moving ever southward, the French army entered the city of Naples on February 22, 1495, without striking a single blow. Before the wind raised by the tremendous reputation of the Ultramontanes the cowardly Neapolitan forces scattered like dry autumn leaves. The despairing Alfonso resigned his crown to enter a monastery, and his youthful successor, Ferrante II, threw away his sword and fled for his life. By crowning himself king of Naples victorious Charles certified to the world that he had attained his goal. Almost before the cheering was over, he was fated to learn that he had made the frailest of conquests.

As soon as the French king had evacuated Florence, the citizens set about the business, adjourned by them in the presence of danger, of providing themselves with a new constitution. In this process the first traditional step was to call a parliament. On December 2 it assembled in the usual manner on the piazza and unanimously acclaimed the proposal of the signory to give power to a body of twenty accoppiatori to appoint the magistracies for the length of a year. With the most pressing necessities thus provided for the deliberations touching the new form of the constitution might proceed with some measure of security. In view of the excitement attending the fall of the Medici it was inevitable that the whole population should wish to share in the argument. The opinion most commonly heard when men gathered at street-corners was that the old constitution must under no circumstances be re-enacted without change, since it was with the aid of that instrument that the Medici had succeeded in imposing their tyranny. The exiled and active Piero still had numerous followers within the town, and for the anti-Medicean majority the main issue was to close every possible avenue to the deposed family's return.

It was this frame of mind that caused the general attention to swing to Venice. Here was a republic which had suffered no major change for two hundred years, and which, besides, had never been tyrant-ridden. Before long the general discussion concentrated more and more on two features of the Venetian republic, which, it was argued, not only explained its extraordinary stability but which also might, with no more than a few slight changes, be taken over by Florence. The first feature was the Grand Council, which in its Florentine version it was proposed to make up of a large body of citizens empowered to elect the leading officials and to vote the laws; the second feature was a smaller council or senate to be consulted by the executive on all matters of policy whatever. With these two stabilizing importations was to be combined the traditional system of a rapidly revolving signory of nine members (eight priors and a gonfalonier of Justice) with their advisory colleges of sixteen gonfaloniers of companies and twelve Buoni Uomini. The affection felt for this familiar executive, amounting almost to obsession, sprang in part from the fact that it was native, in larger part still from its enabling over a hundred citizens to achieve the much-prized honors of office in a single year. It did not escape the intelligent inquisition of the Florentines that whatever the Venetian Grand Council may have been in the beginning, it had long ago congealed into an hereditary chamber of nobles. As there no longer were any nobles in Florence and the very concept of nobility was unpopular, the necessity made itself felt of adjusting the Venetian borrowing to Florentine conditions. Accordingly, it was proposed that the Grand Council should be made up of all those who boasted among their ancestors for three generations back as much as a single occupant of one of the three major magistracies, that is, signory, gonfaloniers of companies, and Buoni Uomini. As it presently appeared that there were over three thousand citizens who on these terms might qualify for the Grand Council, and as so large a body was more in the nature of a mob than of a deliberative assembly, it was further proposed to divide the eligibles into three groups, each called to serve in turn for a period of three months.

Once again the relativity of all political concepts is startlingly brought home to us by the conflict of opinion that arose in the late autumn of the year 1494 over the Grand Council. The Florentines who favored an institution establishing a body of three thousand electors in a population close to one hundred thousand people were considered to be extremely democratic and were opposed by the great merchant families which, having traditionally exercised the power, were stubbornly averse to giving it up. Compared with these favorers of oligarchy, the supporters of the Grand Council were unquestionably democratic, regardless of their inability to qualify as democrats under a twentieth-century definition of the term. The clash of opinion over the Grand Council filled the town and, long continued, might have led to civil war, if a democratic champion had not put in an appearance who brought the issue to a quick and generally satisfactory close.

The democratic champion was Girolamo Savonarola, but before we consider his intervention in the Grand Council debate we must briefly sketch his career as it had unfolded up to the moment of his plunge into politics.

Girolamo was born at Ferrara on September 21, 1452.[2] His people were respectable middle-class folk loosely attached to the court of the ancient ruling family of Este. There is nothing in the known circumstances of Girolamo's family and upbringing that accounts for the preference he showed from his early years for solitude and prayer. We have to conclude that here was that phenomenon, much less common in our time than was once the case, of a soul naturally religious, for which life had no other purpose than earnestly to look for and, after finding, to hold fast to the road to heaven. Under the direction of his father he occupied himself with scholastic philosophy and its most eminent exponent, St. Thomas Aquinas, until at the age of twenty-three, unable any longer to support the burden of living in the world, he abandoned home and family and knocked for admission at the gate of the great Dominican monastery at Bologna. There followed a probationary period of privations, prayer, and ardent study, during which he strove with all his mind and will to make himself a worthy follower of the great founder of his order. By calling themselves Preaching Friars the Dominicans had indicated from the start that they regarded the preaching of the faith as their highest function. Not till he was sent to Florence in 1482 was Fra Girolamo put to the test in regard to this central feature of his training. However, on this first exhibition of his powers he scored an unqualified fiasco. He had taken his residence in the convent of San Marco, of which the Medici were patrons and where, some decades earlier, Michelozzo had built the fine cloister and library and Fra Angelico had painted his ecstatic visions. To the entrancing memories which to this day hang like a luminous halo above the place, Fra Girolamo was destined to make a notable contribution; but nothing that he did during his first residence of some four years figures in the record. The elegant Florentine humanists set the tone for platform and pulpit oratory alike, and with their purely rhetorical standards the rude sincerity of the Ferrarese visitor was in hopeless disaccord. He must have felt relieved on being recalled to Lombardy, where the humanist influence was much more feeble. Sent on a preaching round to many towns, he gradually got his magnificent resources of heart and mind so effectively in hand that the memory of his Tuscan failure was forgotten as his reputation mounted till its echoes filled the most remote corners of the peninsula. At the instance of Lorenzo de' Medici himself he was in the summer of 1490 recalled to San Marco, and on this second occasion, beginning with his very first pulpit address, he fairly brought the town to his feet.

It was now seen that the aping of ancient literature and the adoption of pagan manners were fashions which flourished among a limited upper class and that the Florentine masses still retained their medieval attachment to religion and the church. To be sure, the spontaneous sentiments associated with worship had been largely buried under the dead weight of elaborate,

[2] There are two outstanding biographies of Savonarola: P. Villari, *La Storia di Girolamo Savonarola*. 2 vols. Florence, 1859 (2d ed. 1887; latest ed. 1926). English translation published by Scribner's, New York, 1893. The other biography is by J. Schnitzer, *Savonarola: Ein Kulturbild aus der Zeit der Renaissance*. 2 vols. Munich, 1924. Both Villari and Schnitzer offer an illuminating and exhaustive discussion of the sources. In recent years Savonarola's *ipsissima verba* have been made accessible in excellent editions. His *Prediche Italiane ai Fiorentini* appeared in three volumes in the years 1930-33 under the editorship of F. Cognasso; and his *Lettere* appeared in a single volume in 1933 edited by R. Ridolfi.

multiplied ceremonies, but under the impact of the convictions which poured from Savonarola's mouth like molten metal, the superimposed forms were consumed like tinder and the fountains of faith again unsealed. The friar preached nothing new, for what he offered his crowded congregation was the gospel of Life Eternal to be won by wholehearted surrender to God and his commandments. He based his sermons strictly on the Bible, especially on the Old Testament and the exhortations and warnings of the prophets. Macerated by fasting and other privations, he became, as is not unusual with the progress of physical enfeeblement, subject to hallucinations and heavenly visions. Although he himself long doubted their validity, they ended by persuading him that he was the latest member in the long succession of the Lord's chosen vessels and that he had the double mission from on high to free men of their evil habits and to reform the church. As his self-confidence increased, the promises and threats he uttered from the pulpit become more definite and culminated at last in three ever-repeated declarations. The first was that the church will be scourged; the second, that it will be renewed; and the third, that the time was at hand. There had been no prophets, his awed followers whispered to one another, since the far days of John the Baptist, and now after hundreds of years God in his goodness had been moved again to send an inspired messenger to his erring children. When San Marco proved too small to hold the crowd of listeners, Savonarola uttered his warnings and prophecies to dense gatherings in the duomo, and to all these reawakened Christians his fiery eloquence and reiterated affirmation of what the future had in store certified him as the veritable man of God.

Even before Lorenzo the Magnificent's death the friar had acquired so large a following in Florence that the suspicious tyrant became filled with misgivings. Nor was his state of mind improved by the obstinate aloofness of the Dominican. In 1491 the brothers of San Marco elected Girolamo prior, and custom required that the new head pay a visit of respect to Lorenzo as patron of the establishment. This the new prior firmly refused to do on the ground that he owed his elevation to no one but to God. Like the great gentleman he was, Lorenzo overlooked the social lapse. In fact in his heart he could not help being deeply impressed with so much sterling independence; and when, in the very next year, death knocked at his door calling on him to prepare his soul for its uncertain journey, he summoned the prior of San Marco to his bedside. While the story that Savonarola's disciples afterward circulated as to what passed between the two men must be dismissed as apocryphal,[3] the fact that Lorenzo, the pagan-minded, pleasure-loving tyrant in the last hours of his earthly sojourn felt impelled to consult the unbending champion of the Christian way of living fixes a moment in the life of both these great men and of their contentious age as well which must remain forever memorable.

In the two years intervening between Lorenzo's death and Piero's expulsion from the city Savonarola's influence grew steadily until a large portion of the population looked to him for guidance in all matters pertaining to morals and religion. And when on the liberation of the city from the Medicean yoke

[3] See chap. XXIII, pp. 405-06.

the debate began to rage about the political system to be adopted, it was inevitable that his followers should turn for direction also in this matter to their
celestially illuminated guide. A sharp struggle followed in Savonarola's own
breast, for he never doubted that he was sent to labor in the vineyards of the
Lord and not in order to waste himself in the petty quarrels of the market
place. However, on recognizing the danger to the newly won civil freedom
of an indefinitely prolonged agitation, he resolutely stepped into the political
arena and in a succession of fiery sermons delivered in the cathedral declared
in favor of the democratic principle as represented by the Grand Council.
At once public opinion rallied behind him with such irresistible vigor that
the necessary measures were passed with a minimum of delay and the new
constitution completed before the end of the year. Its novel features, as already
noted, were the Grand Council of approximately one thousand members and
a small council or senate of eighty (the *Ottanta*); the features retained from
the traditional system were the priors and gonfalonier of Justice with their
two advisory colleges. By January, 1495, the new government was set agoing
amidst extraordinary rejoicings. For the time being the *Popolari* or democratic
party swept everything before it. That the Popolari were never called other
than *Frateschi* (Friarists) or, more derisively still, *Piagnoni* (Weepers, Sniv-
elers) by their opponents proves that they were confronted from the first with
a very active ill-will. These opponents were well represented in the Grand
Council and might, under favorable circumstances, achieve control of the commonwealth by being elected to the signory which, as in the past, was changed
every two months. Luckily for the democrats their opponents were far from
united. The most powerful group were the optimates, who because of their
rabid antagonism to the ruling system were currently called *Arrabbiati*. Certain young men of the upper circles, not numerous but spectacularly active,
were prepared at any moment to descend into the piazza and demonstrate
against the puritanical friar; from their evil habits of life they were called
Compagnacci. Although the Medici had suffered expulsion, they could still
boast many followers, who, because they prudently avoided the light of day,
were picturesquely called *Bigi* or Greys. Admitting that these enemies alone or
in combination constituted a potential threat to the reconstituted republic, for
the present at least they were harmless, owing to the general favor enjoyed by
the new government. However, so great were the difficulties of that government that before long something was bound to go wrong and, as soon as that
happened, the watchful opposition would be sure to leap into action.

The greatest peril to the government lay in the foreign field, for Florence
lacked the power to play an independent role and was more or less at the
mercy of all its neighbors. Ever since the invasion of Tuscany by the French
it was very definitely at the mercy of Charles VIII, who to bind the Florentines to his side had planted garrisons in Pisa and in all the strongholds surrendered by Piero de' Medici. To make matters worse, Pisa had revolted, and other
subject communities, such as Arezzo and Montepulciano, were preparing to
follow suit. While the city owed these humiliations to the French sovereign and
manifested great ill humor toward him, it was obliged to cling to the recently

concluded alliance, if for no other reason than that it expected to be rewarded for its faithfulness with an early return of the occupied fortresses.

It must therefore be clear that the immediate destiny of Florence was indissolubly tied up with the destiny of the French expedition. We have followed Charles VIII to his occupation of Naples, up to which point he had been the very darling of Dame Fortune. But now the ever capricious lady suddenly deserted his banner. The first mishap was that, alarmed at the immense growth of French might, almost the whole European world combined together to deprive the king of the fruits of his victory. Spain and the emperor Maximilian of Germany were the heart of the movement, but three Italian states, Venice, the pope, and the shifty Lodovico of Milan gave an eager support to the cause. It was Lodovico on whom more than on any other Italian rested the responsibility for the French invasion. He had been, alas, only too successful in his purpose, and, filled with mounting fear of the ally who had waxed too great, he now completely reversed himself. The League, as the members of the anti-French combination called themselves for short, planned to raise an army in the rear of the French and thus shut off their retreat. One and all members of the League eagerly pleaded with the Florentines to join their ranks, for with Tuscany on their side they would have closed to Charles every avenue of escape. But the Arno folk could not be dissuaded from their view of the invincibility of the forces they had seen parade through their city a few months before. Consequently when Charles, obliged to beat a quick retreat from Naples in order to secure his communications with his homeland, passed again through Tuscany, he encountered a friendly reception from his faithful ally. Not till he attempted to cross the Apennines did the army of the League undertake to bar the way. On July 6, at Fornovo, the French king was obliged to attack a numerically superior foe who lay across his path. His desperate charges gave him the victory, and he continued his northward journey without further molestation until he reached home and safety. Almost as soon as he had left Naples behind, his Aragonese rival, young Ferrante II, reoccupied the kingdom and again set up his throne in its capital. A year after Charles VIII had entered Italy to turn the peninsula topsyturvy, he was back again on French soil, and Italy, relieved of his presence, to all superficial appearances resumed its former aspect.

So to its inner core, however, had Italy been shaken by the French incursion that it never again recovered from the shock. Let Florence, our immediate interest, illustrate the new risks that had been introduced into an already highly unstable situation. Before recrossing the Alps Charles VIII signed a new treaty with ambassadors of the republic, in which, in accordance with his earlier promise, he reassigned the Tuscan strongholds to the Red Lily. But whether the fault was the king's or that of his self-willed subordinates, the commandant of the Pisan fort surrendered it not to the Florentines but to the Pisans, while the commandants of Sarzana and Sarzanella surrendered to Genoa and the commandant of Pietrasanta to Lucca, in each case for the vulgar lucre of which no contemporary commandant could ever have enough. Of all its lost possessions Florence at this time reacquired only Livorno; and Livorno passed again into Florentine hands not owing to the loyal execution of their treaty by the French but in consequence of its resolute seizure by a Florentine captain.

No patriotic son of Arno doubted that trust and fidelity had been repaid by the French king with callous treachery. All this high-piled resentment, however, did not avail to bring about an abandonment of the French alliance. In Florentine eyes France led Europe in military might and would only have to reappear on the scene, as Charles VIII on leaving Italy had volubly promised to do the very next year, to scatter its enemies like chaff before the wind. Another reason for avoiding a rupture with the northern kingdom was of economic origin. France was still a leading market for Florentine goods and enterprise, which the government at Paris could destroy over night by directing the expulsion of the Florentine merchants from the kingdom. Finally, there was Savonarola. We have seen that he had from the time of his second sojourn at San Marco authenticated himself with the Florentines as a prophet sent by God by solemnly announcing the approaching punishment and reform of the church. When, following the death of Lorenzo de' Medici, the expedition of Charles VIII began dimly to take shape across the Alps, the friar became more definite in his language and proclaimed the French king as the tool by which God would effect the needed reformation. During the passage of the French through Tuscany, Savonarola repeatedly had speech with Charles and on these occasions never failed to utter the hortatory words his solemn faith imposed. "O most Christian king," he would say, "you are an instrument in the hand of the Lord who has sent you to cure the ills of Italy, as I have long since predicted. He sends you also to reform the church which lies prostrate on the ground. . . . Should you forget the work for which you are sent, the Lord will choose another to carry it out and will punish you with terrible scourgings. I say this to you in the name of the Lord." [4]

When we recall that these and similar words were addressed to a half-witted dwarf, whom an accident of birth had invested with the purple and who had come to Italy not to cure the country's ills but to take advantage of them for his selfish ends, we receive an impression of the immense gulf yawning between the substance of Savonarola's dreams and the realities of life from which there is no escape. Intent upon his inner voices, Savonarola completely overlooked the palpable insufficiency of the sovereign whom he summoned to great deeds. Had he employed his native shrewdness, which was excellent, he would quickly have reduced this imaginary Charlemagne to the simpleton he was. But native shrewdness enjoys no credit among prophets exalted by heavenly visions and commands. Being what he was, the friar went the narrow road traced by his convictions. It led unescapably to that martyrdom which he predicted for himself and which he craved. Every solemn commitment of his spirit, and not least among them his visionary misapprehension of the character of Charles VIII, contributed to the pre-ordained catharsis. For even after steadily increasing numbers of Florentines had become disillusioned about Charles, Savonarola clung to him as the savior designate of both Florence and the corrupt church and used his immense

[4] Villari, Vol. I, Book II, chap. 2.

influence over the common people to maintain the French alliance. For his well-born enemies, the Arrabbiati, he had been ever since the revolution the man responsible for the new constitution and the democratic trend of the successive signories. As the years rolled by, with constantly increasing vehemence they charged him also with shaping the city's foreign policy. They raged at him as the secret ruler of the state, as that abhorrent thing, the hypocritical priest with an unslaked thirst for political power.

Although the charge of political ambition is still occasionally lodged against Savonarola in our day, it is undoubtedly based on a complete misconception. Fra Girolamo was a son of the Middle Ages, a logical product of the faith that the individual's leading concern on earth is the issue of life eternal, the issue of salvation. Not to leave bewildered man without guidance, God in his mercy has established the great institution of the church and committed to it the authority to save or to destroy. Never for a moment throughout his life did Savonarola doubt the divine power conferred upon the church. To his sorrow, however, and to the sorrow of all true believers, under a succession of worldly popes culminating in the abominable Borgia, Alexander VI, the church had grown so profoundly corrupt that it was threatened with estrangement from its mission. For a dedicated spirit like the friar, it was not difficult to become persuaded that the degenerate church must imperatively be renewed and that he was the man appointed by God to that end. To this central purpose, as wide as Christianity itself, was joined a purpose of more local import which grew out of his residence in Florence and his identification with the weal and woe of that particular community. On the immense following he had acquired on the Arno he made it his business to inculcate the need of daily living in the love and fear of God. This implied a reform of morals, which he regarded as the logical and unescapable concomitant to the reform of the church. It is possible that since the reform of morals could be inaugurated on the reformer's own initiative and without vexatious delays, it received at times greater attention in his sermons than the reform of the church. Essentially, however, Savonarola regarded the two reforms as inseparable and entertained no preference for one as against the other. Yet the fact stands out that, a minor and feeble member of the Catholic hierarchy, he made no headway with the reform of the vast institution of the church, while his attack on the evil customs of the Florentines brought him a notable success. Granted that it was ephemeral, as successes in this field have always been, still it constituted a seven-day wonder in his time and may not be passed over without notice.

A perusal of the friar's sermons will show that in attacking the evil daily practices of his Florentine fellow-citizens he unfolds the picture of a society essentially identical with that disclosed by puritanical preachers of every degree before and since his day. The Florentine men were reckless gamblers and blasphemers; their women decked themselves out in finery, painted their faces, and shamelessly displayed their physical charms. It would be absurd to maintain that these were novel transgressions or that it was a phenomenon of recent origin that the streets were infested with courtesans and that sodomy and other sexual perversities flourished. When and wherever men have built towns

and developed an urban civilization, excrescences of the kind scourged in the
friar's sermons have put in an appearance and have obstinately resisted eradi-
cation. Undiscouraged by past failures, Savonarola resolved to attack the reek-
ing corruption of Florence with a view to creating a truly religious community
fit to serve as a model for the rest of the evil world. Once upon a time, according to the official Christian doctrine, the Jews had been such a community ruled by the invisible Jehovah and led and admonished by his prophets. In Savonarola's ambitious design the Florentines were to be the chosen
people of the modern world, acknowledging Christ as their king and the
lowly prior of San Marco as Christ's prime minister.

Admitting again that never in history have the preachers of moral perfection made other than a temporary impression, we may fairly marvel at the
measure of success achieved at Florence in his heyday by the Dominican friar.
Courtesans and gamblers went into hiding; ribald street songs were replaced
by pious hymns; men and women alike adopted a plain and modest dress and
were untiring in their attendance at mass and sermon. Particularly remarked
was the way the religious fervor took hold of the youths and children. Under
the direction of the prior's most devoted follower, Fra Domenico da Pescia,
they formed themselves into volunteer bands organized according to the parish
in which they resided. They proclaimed themselves guardians of the town's
morality and, roaming the streets of their quarter, induced gamblers to hand
over the tools of their trade and women too fashionably attired to renounce
their scandalous display. The plentiful, year-round merrymaking of the town
had been wont to mount to a climax during carnival, which was characterized
by a succession of disgraceful public orgies. Lorenzo de' Medici had fostered
these practices, although to refer them to him as their author is a wildly partisan
perversion of the truth. The cleansing of the city of its carnival excesses became a cardinal point in Savonarola's program of moral reform and in attempting to uproot them he wisely looked about for an equivalent. What
were the usual sportive masquerades other than an indulgence of the flesh
and a triumph of Satan? He, too, would have the people range the streets
with songs upon their lips. But the songs would be religious lauds, and what
had hitherto been a season of secular folly would be transformed into a joyous
festival of the Lord. Then, on the last, the culminating day of the carnival
he would send the whole population, men, women, and children, in religious
procession through the streets to gather them at last in the duomo to receive
the divine blessing delivered by the prophet's mouth.

In the year 1497 the friar added a feature to this carnival program, the
rumor of which is loud in the world to this day. He ordered the children to
make a house to house canvass to the end of persuading the occupants to
surrender some small possession to which their heart was unduly attached.
These "vanities" were piled together in a vast pyramid in the central piazza
and the concluding act of the carnival, converted under the new dispensation
into a season of penance, was the setting on fire of the inflammable heap,
while trumpeters sounded a fanfare that made itself heard above the roar
of the flames. This is the famous Burning of the Vanities, which was repeated
the following year (1498), the last of Savonarola's life, when, in sign of the

prophet's waning power, it was almost broken up by his enemies. There is little to recommend the ceremony to the sober judgment of mankind, and subsequent champions of moral reform have not seen fit to imitate it. But misrepresentations of the event fathered by the Dominican's enemies must be rejected. There is no proof whatever that valuable books and irreplacable works of art were sacrificed to the flames. The surrendered vanities were conceived as symbols of the worldly life, and there is good reason to believe that the bonfire, which, like all bonfires, delighted the hosts of children, consumed nothing more valuable than carnival masques, dice, obscene books, and lascivious pictures together with innumerable trivialities of dress and furniture.

To charge a man so exclusively set on creating an austere Christian society with political ambition is, let it be said again, flatly to misunderstand his type. Savonarola never sat in the Grand Council or the signory, he participated in no elections or party caucuses. Undeniably, however, these surface facts are not the whole story. For, though not a direct political agent, indirectly he figured in all the acts of government through his moral influence over the supporters of the democratic system, the Popolari. To this system he had committed himself at a critical moment with no idea of pleasing anyone other than the God in whom he put his faith. Fiercely hating tyranny because of its secret crimes and moral laxity, he wanted in the interest of the religious society which was his aim to close the gates forever on the Medici and justly concluded that the most effective way of achieving that result was a broadly based popular regime. In the same way his unwavering support of Charles VIII, in spite of its purely religious motivation, had unavoidable political implications. With every honorable intention to limit himself to the part of friar and prophet he was pushed into the arena of politics to sustain the cause for which he believed he was sent by God. As a result, although not intentionally a politician, he succeeded in offending powerful political forces, which by finally combining against him proved his undoing.

The undoing of Savonarola constitutes an intrigue so extraordinarily involved that full justice cannot be done it under many chapters. It will therefore have to suffice to assemble its leading elements and carry them forward to their tragic climax. The foremost as well as the most constant plotters against the friar were the great Florentine families, the optimates, loosely associated in the party of the Arrabbiati. They were well represented in the Grand Council and occasionally placed representatives in the signory, but for the first two years of the new government they were in such general disfavor that they were unable to injure Savonarola directly. Their impotence in their own community led them to resort to Rome, where, because of their wealth and social position, they had no difficulty in getting a hearing. Their plan was to work upon Pope Alexander VI and by filling him with alarm regarding the friar's program of ecclesiastical reform to persuade him, by virtue of the authority vested in him, to remove the offender from Florence or at the very least to condemn him to silence. In this early and still relatively harmless stage of the conflict there was as yet no desire to take Savonarola's life. Since, to their disgust, the plotters had but a doubtful success with Alexander, it will be necessary before going any farther to examine this celebrated personage somewhat more closely. Undeniably one of the most infamous pontiffs of history, he was not just that sum of all conceivable infamy as he has been often described and, taken as which, he becomes a devil incarnate and is no longer a man. Where there are so many proved iniquities we should not find it difficult to dispense with figments. Let it suffice that Alexander Borgia was addicted to all the lusts of the flesh; that he had many children into whose lap he did not scruple to pour the riches of the church; that he purchased his elevation to the papacy by open and scandalous bribery; and that, enthroned on St. Peter's chair, he sold, as it were under the hammer, all the dispensations, pardons, bishoprics, and cardinalates at his disposal. These abominations notwithstanding, he was a man of good intelligence and a capable administrator. It does not help our understanding of the papal policy toward Savonarola to conceive of its author as an ogre bent on indiscriminate mischief.

We bring Alexander into correct historical focus if we say of him that, like many other men of the culminating Renaissance, he had lost both his religion and his morals by his too exclusive pursuit of purely selfish advantage. With his grossly material outlook on the world he had no immediate interest in the friar who was making such a stir in nearby Florence by preaching the reform of morals and the church. Of course Alexander did not believe in either of these reforms; but what, versed in the cynic wisdom of the world, he did believe was that the Dominican's enthusiasm would soon evaporate and that, as in a score of similar cases of which he had had personal experience, in the end the forces of social inertia, than which there was nothing stronger in the world, would win the day. The feature of Savonarola's activity the pope liked least was the friar's assigning the role of reformer of the church to the powerful king of France. However, now that Charles had come and gone, even this dangerous vagary of the Ferrarese need not be taken too seriously.

Unable greatly to excite the Holy Father about the religious agitation of the Dominican, the Arrabbiati agents at Rome turned next to his political activity and at once met with a much livelier response. For politics, whether of the church or state, constituted Alexander's only genuine interest. In forcing his way during his recent campaign through the State of the Church the irresistible king of France had deeply humiliated the pope; and when the great league was formed to oblige the French to relinquish their Neapolitan prey, Alexander had not hesitated to join it. Since then his policy in regard to Charles VIII was clearly mapped out. He must hold with the anti-French combination in order by a solid front to dissuade the French sovereign from repeating his Italian adventure. And in regard to Florence, the one Italian state which by clinging obstinately to the French alliance extended a perpetual invitation to the northern invader to return to the assault, it was Alexander's opinion, which his neighbors of Venice, Naples, and Milan shared, that every available ounce of diplomatic pressure must be brought to bear on the Arno government to draw it into the anti-French league. We have already examined the situation and listed the reasons why Florence stubbornly refused to give up the French connection. While they may be said to have been inspired in the main by the public interest, indubitably one reason not of a public nature was Savonarola. In his capacity of missionary and prophet the friar inclined violently toward France and by his support made the French party in the government invincible.

As soon as Alexander was persuaded that Savonarola was a factor in the hateful foreign policy of Florence he was much more ready to consider taking measures against him. But as the information that reached him from his private agents in Florence revealed that even without the friar the government would persist in its pro-French attitude, he refused to commit himself to the Arrabbiati and handled the problem created by the inconvenient reformer after his own judgment. He tried repeatedly to draw Savonarola to Rome. However, when the Dominican, suspecting a trap, urgently but politely excused himself, the pope showed no particular resentment and let the matter drop. For almost two years the best efforts of the Arrabbiati to get Alexander to use his ecclesiastical power against Savonarola produced no appreciable result. Nonetheless, in these two years the friar was becoming increasingly outspoken in his denunciation of the church and its servants, priests and prelates alike; and although he carefully avoided mentioning names, he was sufficiently precise to leave no doubt in the mind of his hearers that he regarded the Holy Father as the greatest sinner of them all. Constantly annoyed by and frequently enraged against his merciless critic, the pope at last resolved on reprisals and on November 7, 1496, issued a brief by which he deprived the convent of San Marco of its independence and subordinated it to the provincial of the Tusco-Roman congregation. What lent the order a directly punitive character was that the independence of San Marco was a gift which Alexander himself had made to Savonarola only three years before. Had the new decree become effective, the friar could have been lifted out of San Marco and transferred from Florence to some small provincial town by the stroke of the pen of his new Dominican chief. This was of course the purpose of the order, which Fra Girolamo so clearly understood that he was resolved in his heart never to accept it. His dispatch of a remonstrance to Alexander was interpreted as open recalcitrancy and for the first time persuaded the pope that, unless he was prepared to surrender the leadership of the church to the friar, he must bring him to heel. But even though he was the omnipotent head of the Christian congregation, there were precautions to be observed in view of the attachment the Florentines manifested for their prophet and of the wisdom of not unnecessarily offending a civil government the pope and the other Italian powers were attempting to lure away from the French. Not till a change of popular sentiment had been effected and a gonfalonier of Justice headed the signory who was not of the Savonarolist persuasion would it be safe to proceed against the friar with the vigor to be expected from an authoritative pontiff.

To the pope's chagrin the signories of the winter of 1496–97 were as devoted to the prior as any that had gone before. During the January-February term of 1497 the tide seemed to run even more strongly in Savonarola's favor, inasmuch as Francesco Valori was elected to the post of gonfalonier of Justice. Valori was the most energetic statesman of the democratic party and so completely under the friar's spell that he held the prophet's divine inspiration to be no less sure than the Day of Judgment. It was under his gonfalonierat that the inverted carnival of 1497 culminated in the first Burning of the Vanities. However, because of a natural reaction to these excesses, the next signory (of the March-April term) was of Bigi or Medicean complexion; and the signory after that was of even worse augury for the Piagnoni, for it was strongly Arrabbiati. As in every republic, the mass of Florentine voters was subject to these sudden fluctuations, which did not necessarily signify a change of fundamental opinion. Still the successive enemy signories were dangerous, since Bigi and Arrabbiati, although hostile to each other, agreed in hating the democratic regime and its leading sponsor, the friar. By dispatching his November brief against him Alexander had again drawn close to the Arrabbiati; and when, early in the following May, certain extremists in the Arrabbiati ranks started a riot in the crowded cathedral during one of Fra Girolamo's sermons, the pope was delighted. The outburst was happily suppressed before it became general, but with an Arrabbiati signory in the seat of power and a hostile demonstration conducted under the very nose of the prophet, Alexander VI persuaded himself that the time had come for a more energetic offensive. Consequently he now hurled his long-threatened decree of excommunication at the friar, justifying his act on the ground of Savonarola's flagrant disregard of the papal rescript of the previous November. On June 18, 1497, the document was read with the usual impressive ceremonies in the leading churches of Florence. Henceforth retreat on the part of the pope was not possible. It was war between the head of the church and his rebellious subject, a distressingly unequal war, which the friar might sustain for a period but in which he would be disastrously defeated the moment the Florentine people no longer lent him their enthusiastic support.

While the events just recounted had occurred during an Arrabbiati signory, that signory did not feel strong enough as yet to employ its ascendancy for a final stroke against its enemy. In fact the aroused Piagnoni rallied their forces so successfully in the Grand Council that the signories following that of the May-June period were again favorable to the friar. Cheered by this renewed support, his indomitable spirit now resolved to scale the last height and to defy and ultimately to depose his enemy, the pope, with the machinery supplied by ecclesiastical tradition. On Christmas Day he administered communion to the brothers of San Marco and, shortly after, he resumed his public preaching. A more flagrant offense against age-old Catholic practice was not conceivable, for by the renewed exercise of his ecclesiastical functions he boldly set the papal excommunication at nought. At the same time he took a step even more offensive to the pope in that he opened negotiations with the princes of Christendom with a view to persuading them to call a General Council. The papal sinner and criminal was to be brought to trial before the supreme bar of the church. To be sure, this latter action of the friar's, which proceeded under cover of the greatest secrecy, did not become generally known till long afterward; but the flouting of the excommunication was a demonstration conducted in the public view and for this open defiance of the ancient ordinances of Christianity conservative Florentine opinion was not prepared. Again and again in the past the city had on one ground or another resisted the Holy Father, but it had never

dreamt of challenging his ecclesiastical supremacy. With opinions clashing in
the streets and squares more vehemently than ever, the timid and lukewarm
among the citizenry began to leave the friar's camp; and when the elections
for the March-April signory of 1498 took place the victory went in a decisive
manner to Savonarola's enemies.

The pope could now play his last card. He declared that unless his diso-
bedient subject be delivered into his hands for punishment, he would put the
whole city under interdict. While in some ways the surrender of the friar's
person might appeal to his local enemies as a convenient way of washing their
hands of him, they had too keen an understanding of their countrymen to believe in its practicality. For, should they hand over the prophet to his Roman
executioner, not only would his popularity flare up afresh but they would put
such a stigma on their own name as would quickly bring their regime to an
inglorious fall. They would have to take the matter of ridding the city of the
fanatic into their own hands; and before taking his life they would have to
bring him into discredit and, more particularly, they would have to deprive him
of his halo as a prophet. While with vacillating thoughts they were pondering
the thorny problem, an incident was created by the San Marco brotherhood
itself, which with the sharp clairvoyance of hate they foresaw could, if skilfully
manipulated, be made to bring about the desired result.

In speaking of the organized bands of children we had occasion to mention
a disciple, Fra Domenico da Pescia, who stood next in authority at San Marco
after Savonarola and who by his utter devotion to his chief had come to be
regarded almost as his other self. To him the prophet character of Fra Girolamo was so incontrovertible that he was ready to prove it by going through
fire. As the city was full of scoffers, Brother Domenico had been moved to
repeat from time to time his offer of the fire test without any immediate effect
until a friar of the rival Franciscan order took the matter up. It is highly probable that the Franciscan was persuaded to come to the front by a group of
Savonarola's enemies, from whom he received a secret promise of protection
from the consequences of his hardihood. The plan of the plotters was to have
the current Arrabbiati signory take the affair in hand, go through with all the
preparations for an old-fashioned ordeal by fire, work up the miracle-loving
masses to the highest pitch of excitement, and then let them down abruptly
by an adjournment which would be dishonestly laid to the door of Savonarola
and his friars. In view of the blind and unsuspecting zeal of Fra Domenico, a
zeal which he shared with the whole San Marco brotherhood, it was easy to
get the intrigue under way. Not one of the two hundred and fifty brothers but
envied Fra Domenico the honor of bearing witness before assembled Florence to the divine mission of their beloved master. For that the prior was the
authentic messenger of God had by now become the basic article of their renewed Christian faith. Since he had prophesied again and again and the proph-
ecy had always been fulfilled, it could not be other than that on this supreme
occasion the Father Omnipotent would cool the ardor of the flames and permit
the prophet's champion to walk through them unscathed. Although Savonarola
had had nothing to do with the affair in its initial stages and apparently dis-
approved of it, he saw no way of breaking off negotiations after they had

begun, as he could not possibly exhibit less faith in supernatural intervention in his behalf than did his followers. By the end of March there was talk in Florence of nothing else but the ordeal, until to appease the constantly waxing excitement the plotting signory, assuming the willing role of impresario, proclaimed that it should take place on Saturday, April 7.

On the afternoon of that day the great piazza before the palace of the priors presented an extraordinary sight. Opposite what is now called the Loggia dei Lanzi stretched a long rectangular heap of firewood with a passage in the middle through which, when the match had been applied, Fra Domenico da Pescia and his Franciscan challenger were supposed to walk to prove or disprove the prophetic claim of the prior of San Marco. The two champions, each surrounded by the chanting and praying members of his order, were gathered under the great stone vaults of the Loggia; the lordly signory, in its role of umpire, occupied the platform in front of the palace; and in the piazza pressed and from the windows and house roofs hung suspended a vast and wildly agitated mass of citizens. We call the period the Renaissance and glibly speak of it as pagan. Yet we should have to go back four hundred years in Florentine history, into the deep Middle Ages, to encounter a comparable spectacle. It was in the year 1068 that a Vallombrosan monk, celebrated after the event as Petrus Igneus, walked through the flames in nearby Settimo to attest the truthfulness of the charge of simony lodged against the bishop of Florence.[5] Gazing at the spectacle afforded on that April day of the closing quattrocento by the Florentine piazza a pessimistic philosopher might have been moved to affirm that life perpetually repeats itself and that there is nothing new under the sun. And yet, compared with the earlier ordeal, there was something new which, could our putative philosopher have known of it, might only have deepened his pessimism. This novelty was that the show that met his eye was a pure hoax arranged by a skeptical signory for selfish political purposes, and that this exalted body had no intention whatever of going through with the game. Accordingly, they welcomed one trivial objection after another presented by the Franciscans until the afternoon wore away with futile negotiations between the contesting parties. The packed and perspiring multitude was already showing signs of impatience when a heavy shower descended soaking everyone to the skin. More negotiations were followed by more delays until, as the day died, the signory announced that, owing to the lateness of the hour, the ordeal would have to be adjourned.

It did not require the whispers of the enemies of the friar to put the blame for the fiasco on his shoulders. Even his ardent followers were inclined to find fault with him, for they had worked themselves up to such a frenzy of faith that in their opinion Fra Domenico da Pescia should, if necessary, have been sent into the flames alone to provoke the confidently expected miracle. The first effect of the plotters had been achieved in the sudden decline of Fra Girolamo's favor following the disappointments of the day. To pursue their advantage they organized demonstrations around San Marco and by the evening of the next day (April 8), a Sunday, they had succeeded in assembling a mob which surged in frenzied excitement around the place, threatening to

[5] See chap. IV, p. 48.

set it on fire and level it with the ground. The first mood of the brothers, heartened by the crowding to their aid of numerous adherents from among the citizens, was to meet force with force. However, when commissioners from the signory appeared with a warrant for Savonarola's arrest, he promptly agreed to surrender in order to avoid bloodshed and civil war. Together with Brothers Domenico and Silvestro, his two closest associates, he was led through the seething, howling mob, which cuffed and spat upon him to vent its hideous spite, and thrown into prison.

Filled with rejoicing, the Arrabbiati pressed the signory to complete its triumph without delay. Composed as it was of the friar's enemies, that body needed no urging to pursue its advantage. It appointed a commission of the most ferocious opponents of Savonarola to subject him and his two fellow-prisoners to a criminal inquisition. The one certain statement this commission was determined from the start to get from its victim was the confession that he was an impostor. To this position the friar's enemies were forced by the fact that nothing less than the friar bearing witness against himself would serve to destroy the legend which had grown up around him. Accordingly, for several days in succession he was put to horrible, bone-racking torture after the monstrous criminal procedure of the day. Not till, unable any longer to support his sufferings, he left the path of truth and gave ambiguous answers to the questions put to him were his tormentors satisfied. On handing over the pathetic evidence they had thus secured to a notary for "editing," the unscrupulous scribe converted it into a clear confession of fraud and in this form published it to the world. The effect for the moment at least was overwhelming. Not only Christian Florence but Christian Italy as well, if it is permissible, at the turn of the century, to speak of such an entity, was stunned into silence and sorrow. The prophet was a confessed deceiver, the light that had risen over the land had gone out.

All that remained now was to put the friar out of the way before a reaction should set in in his favor. However, as he belonged to the clerical order, it was impossible to proceed with his execution without the consent of the pope. Alexander at first took the position that his honor required that the offender be delivered into his hands for trial at Rome; but when the signory made it clear that they would under no circumstances surrender their prey, he yielded and agreed to dispatch two commissioners to Florence to review the case in behalf of the church. When they arrived on May 20, the torture began all over again till a fresh body of incriminating admissions had been wrung from the three anguished victims. They were then declared guilty of heresy and handed over for punishment to the secular arm in accordance with the ancient, hypocritical pretense that the church never spills blood. The verdict of heresy was precisely what the signory needed in connection with its campaign of destroying the reputation of its victim before crushing his life. No sooner had the church spoken than the government named the following day, which was May 23, as the day of execution. As the custom ran in such instances, the wretched men were to be first hanged and immediately afterward to be destroyed by fire.

Six weeks after the great spectacle which had proved such a sorry failure, the Florentines were offered another spectacle, which it was certain would not be a failure because the government that stage-managed both events was as firmly resolved to make a success of the one as it had been determined to ruin the other. Again the center of interest was a wooden pyre, from which, an unbroken mass of brush and logs, there reared itself with an ominous gesture a tall gallows with three arms, from each of which dangled a stout rope. The pyre in the center of the piazza was connected with the palace by an elevated wooden walk, over which the three victims were to proceed on their last journey. Against the gallows rested a ladder, on which stood the expectant executioner. At the appointed hour the three friars were conducted slowly from the palace across the platform to the foot of the ladder. They had recovered their courage and bore themselves with the dignified humility demanded by their faith. Fra Silvestro was the first to mount the ladder and have the noose adjusted to his throat. Fra Domenico came next; the last was Fra Girolamo. They could not yet have been dead as the hangman leaped to his torch and set his inflammable pile ablaze. When, some hours later, the fierce fire had spent itself, the charred scraps of what had once been men and pious Christians were gathered up by the city scavengers and tossed into the Arno to be carried away to oblivion and the sea.

Owing to two remarkable portraits by which the painter, Bartolommeo della Porta, has preserved the appearance of Fra Girolamo Savonarola, his features have been so often reproduced that they are perhaps better known than those of any man of his age. Carried away as a young man by the friar's call to repentance, Bartolommeo joined the Dominican order after the tragic end of his spiritual guide and ended his days in the hallowed precincts of San Marco. One of his pictures now hangs in the cell which Savonarola occupied as prior and which retains its simple, solemn character unchanged to this day. The painting, showing the friar in profile, displays a powerful hooked nose, a heavy, drooping lower lip, and a firm-set jaw. The deep hollow under the high cheek bone speaks of fasting and privations; the dark cowl drawn over the head almost to the eyes reveals a spirit withdrawn from the world, intent on the eternities. If Savonarola's sermons and writings had been swallowed up by Time and the most immediate remaining item of evidence regarding the man were this strangely haunting face, we should find it easy to convince ourselves that the charge launched against him by his enemies that he was an impostor is absurd. On this face are stamped austerity, truthfulness, and an uncompromising sincerity. It belongs to one who, having earnestly sought and found God, as earnestly preached him to his countrymen in the resolute hope of bringing them to the foot of the Cross. The owner of this face authenticates himself without effort as one of the long succession of the saints and martyrs constituting the church militant of Christianity.

On turning from the man to his mission an equally conclusive judgment is not possible. His two leading modern biographers, Villari and Schnitzer, while recognizing his radical antagonism to the main trends of his period, nonetheless concede him a considerable relevance in its general moral, religious, and political set-up. This view the present author is unable to share. Regardless of the depth, the sincerity, the rarely unified character of the friar, he sees him, in the language of modern biology, as a throw-back or, in terms more immediately relevant to history, as an anachronism. The plain and undeniable fact is that Savonarola lived his life among strictly medieval thoughts and feelings, and that with a vigor worthy of unstinted admiration he tried to revitalize them in an age, into the altered conditions of which they could no longer be fitted. To have had something more than the brief sensational success that attended his revivalist preaching it would have been necessary for Florence not merely to rid itself, as the reformer perpetually urged, of its gamblers and courtesans, of its wastrels and usurers, but also to close its banks and warehouses, to surrender its Tuscan conquests, to reduce itself once more to the dimensions of a country market, and, as a final measure, to wreck its Palazzo Pubblico and tear down its cathedral. Like the uncompromising heir of the Middle Ages he was, Savonarola preached that nothing mattered but the life beyond the grave and that the only proper concern of the sinful son of Adam during his mundane sojourn was salvation. In spite of the advance during recent generations of a civilization opposed to these ideals and energetically bent on taking possession of the earth and its fruits, there was still so large a residuum of medieval thought and feeling in the average Florentine that a large proportion of the citizens instinctively responded to Savonarola's impassioned call to repentance. No one, in view of the friar's failure and end, will doubt that he lit in their hearts a mere fire of straw. At the same time it is indisputable that his leading opponents, well-to-do merchants and religious skeptics, fell far below him in integrity of character and moral worth. If nonetheless they won the victory, it was because, accepting the new day which had arisen over Europe and which it was not in their power to turn back, they fought on the side of destiny for an expanding as against a stationary or a retreating civilization. In final historical analysis the issue between two contending individuals or groups does not and cannot reduce itself to the simple question of the moral worth of each, for in every such issue are involved also innumerable social and intellectual forces, whose strength and incidence are an inseparable part of the problem. It was the verdict of these latter forces that Savonarola was an impediment in their path. Therefore they swept him aside; but as he stood his ground unyieldingly, heroically, until the advancing hostile flood poured over him, he will always live in the memory of mankind as a soul that, refusing commerce with corruption, kept the faith.

XXVII. The Revived Republic: The Story of a Living Corpse (1498–1512)

S O COMPLETELY was Savonarola identified with Florence and so domi-
natingly did his figure for a period of almost four years rise above the
turmoil of Italian politics that his individual eminence concealed from
the general view the fact that the revived republic was woefully without power
and authority. And yet such was the unchallengeable truth. Ever since that
November day of the year 1494 when Charles VIII made a triumphant entry
into the city, Florence had become a client of France and owed such security
among its neighbors as it enjoyed to the distant French protector enforced by
the nervous expectation of his early return to the scene of his meteoric glory.
From a narrowly territorial angle the leading event of the passage of the
French army through Tuscany had been the revolt of Pisa. Violently as Piagnoni, Arrabbiati, and Bigi might quarrel with each other as to the kind of
government best suited to the city, in regard to the Pisan rebellion they were
of a single mind and prepared unitedly to forswear liberty and life itself rather
than to accept Pisan independence. But in the span of almost four years since
Charles's expedition nothing of any consequence had been done to realize the
purpose with which everybody declared he was animated. Calling loudly on
Heaven to witness their violated integrity, when it came to action the Florentines had shown themselves feeble to the point of impotence. With all their
spiteful neighbors lending open or secret support to Pisa, the rebel city had thus
far mocked at the threats of the Red Lily to bring it again under its yoke.

As soon, however, as the distracting issues raised by Savonarola had been
disposed of, at least temporarily, by his death, the government resolved to
prosecute the Pisan matter with greater energy and intrusted a celebrated
Italian condottiere, Pagolo Vitelli, with the commission to lay siege to Pisa till
it was captured. Doubtless the death of Charles VIII, which by a curious coin-
cidence took place on the very day of the famous ordeal by fire that did not
come off, was a factor in the heartening spurt of governmental vigor. For
Charles was morally pledged to turn Pisa over to Florence, and as long as he
lived his Tuscan dependents were free to indulge themselves in the hope that
he would some day become conscious of his responsibility and utter the Olym-
pian word that would cow Pisa into surrender. With his death that dream was
dispelled and, cheated of its French hopes, the government felt prompted for
the first time to rely on itself alone. In choosing Vitelli as commander-in-chief
of its forces it probably made as good a choice as the circumstances permitted.

In the approved manner of his hireling tribe Vitelli went about his task with such deliberation that months passed before Pisa was invested. Then, when after new delays, his cannon had made a breach in the walls and all Florence was joyously expecting from moment to moment to hear that the town had been taken by storm, the lame news reached the city that Vitelli had withdrawn to a safe distance in order to rest his exhausted troops. It was too much for the disappointed government and citizens. Commissioners were dispatched to the camp with orders to arrest Vitelli and bring him in chains to Florence. The condottiere, whose sole guilt probably was that he conducted war in strict accordance with the principles in which he had been reared, was tried on the charge of treason and executed (October, 1499).

At the very time the first assault on Pisa worthy of the name came to this lamentable end, the whole Italian situation was undergoing one of its frequent kaleidoscopic changes in the wake of a new French invasion. It was conducted by Louis XII (1498-1515), head of the Orléans branch of the royal line, who succeeded Charles VIII on the latter's demise without direct heirs. More a humdrum burgher than a victim, like his predecessor, of the glamorous romances of chivalry, Louis was nonetheless a king with a tradition to uphold; and no sooner had the crown been placed upon his head than he began preparations for a new invasion of Italy. In correction of his predecessor's mistaken strategy directed solely at the conquest of Naples, he resolved as a necessary preliminary measure on the seizure of Milan. This state lay just across the Alps from France and was the logical base for any military action conducted in the peninsula by an invader from the north. Should we assume that the geographical argument did not of itself suffice to direct the sovereign against Milan, there was the additional circumstance that, as duke of Orléans, Louis had been brought up in the tradition that the Lombard duchy belonged of right to him, since he was the heir of the Visconti predecessor of the upstart and usurping Sforza. Nor, in making his preliminary survey of the situation, did the king overlook the advisability of operating in Italy with Italian allies. While Florence could no doubt be counted on morally, the amount of calculable physical aid the badly shaken republic might give was highly problematical. It therefore greatly cheered Louis to receive an offer of help from another and far more important quarter.

Immediately on mounting the throne Louis XII had approached Pope Alexander VI in a strictly private issue, in which he required papal support. He wished to divorce his wife and marry Anne, the widow of his predecessor, in order to make sure that the province of Brittany, of which she was duchess, would remain merged with the royal domain. Save by special dispensation from the pope the desired divorce was impossible. Accordingly, Louis presented himself as a petitioner at Rome and found Alexander unexpectedly well disposed because that sharp bargainer, who never in his life gave anything for nothing, desired a return favor. He had a young son, Caesar, to whom, as to all his children, he was passionately devoted, and whom he wished to establish in the world as an independent prince. In theory this was not difficult, since he would be doing no more than following the example set by his immediate predecessors if he made over to Caesar one or another of the many territories belonging to the State of the Church. A practical obstacle to this procedure, however, lay in the circumstance that the papal lands were already held by rulers, euphemistically called vicars but really independent sovereigns, whose formal acknowledgment of the papal suzerainty did not hinder them from doing very much as they pleased. If the pope wished to set up his son as a ruler in Umbria or the Romagna, he could only do so by displacing an existent tyrant; and in order to effect such a displacement he could not dispense with military power. As soon as Louis XII approached the pope with the request to grant him the dispensation, which would cut the bonds tieing him to his queen, Alexander declared himself ready to strike a bargain. Completely reversing himself in regard to the French, whom to keep out of Italy he had thus far been unintermittently busy, he affirmed his willingness not only to promote the divorce, but also to support the king's projected campaign against Milan if, in exchange, Louis would marry Caesar to a lady related, no matter how remotely, to the royal house and if, further, he would lend young Borgia the French troops necessary to effect a lodgment by force of arms in the State of the Church.

The bargain, advantageous to both sides, was struck with the result that when in the late summer of the year 1499 the French again crossed the Alps, the young and darkly handsome Caesar Borgia, recently married to a royal relative and created, as an added favor, duke of Valentinois, rode proudly in the train of the French monarch. So weak was the Milanese state that it required no more than the presence of the French army to produce its collapse. Lodovico the Moor escaped capture by hurriedly crossing the Alps into Germany, and King Louis, after entering the capital as conqueror and planting a garrison in its citadel, ended a pleasant, sight-seeing tour of northern Italy by going home to receive the congratulations of his court. Taking advantage of the opportunity afforded by the king's withdrawal, in February, 1500, the ever-adventurous Lodovico staged a sudden return from Germany and for a few days flattered himself that he had recaptured his duchy. It was a gross miscalculation, for, as soon as the surprised French had assembled their scattered forces, the Moor's unpaid Swiss mercenaries deserted him and, unable this time to escape the net flung about him, he was captured and transported for safekeeping to France. There, some ten years later, he ended his life in a dungeon. No contemporary Italian with as much as a touch of patriotism can have viewed the catastrophe of the Moor with any other feeling than that a traitor had received his reward.

No sooner had the French effected the conquest of Milan than Caesar Borgia, in command of a body of royal troops, proceeded southward into the Romagna in adventurous quest of a kingdom. He began with the towns of Imola and Forlì, which did not yield to him without offering rather more resistance than Caesar had expected. Having organized their government, he carefully scanned the scene with a view to deciding where and whom to strike next. Already his first swift action had drawn the eyes of the peninsula on himself. Instinctively the country sensed a political portent, and as the months and years passed by, disclosing fresh and ever bolder aggressions committed by the young condottiere, who had behind him both the pope and the king of

France, his figure gained in stature till it dwarfed all the other actors on the Italian stage. It does not fall within the scope of this book to trace the steps, by which young Borgia, usually called Valentino by his countrymen from his French ducal title, consolidated his successive brutal seizures and bloody conquests. Let it suffice to mention that in the course of little more than three years he succeeded in uprooting a score of petty tyrants planted in papal territory and in assembling his whirlwind gains into a single political unit. Technically, even after his conquests had been consolidated, they constituted not his personal realm but the State of the Church and owned the pope as their ruler. No one doubted, however, that Caesar was firmly resolved to keep as his property what he had seized, as it was also universally assumed that the pope, his father, was so completely under the son's domination that he was fully prepared to commit the monstrous felony of alienating the patrimony of St. Peter in order to supply his bastard with the territorial basis required for a self-perpetuating dynasty.

While all Italy followed these astonishing developments with a mind fluctuating between terror and fascination, even more than with Caesar Borgia's actions the country was intrigued by the personality of this latest military adventurer sprung from its fertile loins. For here surely was the summit, the super-condottiere, to whom his numerous lawless predecessors beginning with Ezzelino da Romagna were but stepping-stones. This suddenly risen Valentino was tall, handsome of feature, powerfully built. Although he had not been brought up to arms, he showed himself to have been born to them from the first moment that he assumed command. He had also the rare executive gift enabling him to penetrate at a glance to the core of a problem. Finally, hard as flint and pitiless as a beast of the jungle, he subordinated every human consideration to his dream of grandeur and was prepared to go through fire and wade through blood to reach his goal. Since there seemed to be no limit to Valentino's ambition, he spread an alarm through the small states of the peninsula which in the case of his most immediate neighbors, the Florentines, rose intermittently to panic. When we recall that the sons of the Red Lily had recently established a republic of a democratic pattern and that in their public conduct since that event they had exhibited a painful lack of self-assurance, we should not be surprised to learn that Duke Valentino's activities along the unprotected line of their eastern border gave them the gravest concern.

In the spring of the year 1501 the Borgian activities precipitated the first active crisis. Caesar suddenly crossed into Florentine territory with the ostensible purpose of passing through it in order to reach Piombino on the western coast. As eventually he actually arrived at that seaport, his avowal was not contradicted by the facts; nonetheless it is plain that in entering Tuscany on a seemingly harmless errand, his real plan was to test the military resistance of the Florentine state. He moved his forces down the Arno Valley with deplorable deliberation, permitted them to plunder at will the villages through which they passed, and closed his eyes to the monstrous acts of cruelty with which they punished the occasional reprisals of the tormented peasantry. To the indignant protests of the Florentine signory he responded with the cool offer to serve as their general for a modest annual return; and it was not till he had extorted a portion of his proposed salary from his anguished hosts that he finally took his departure. He might not have left at all if the Florentines had not, like himself, been allies of the king of France, and if they had not directed a clamorous appeal to that sovereign for protection.

No comment of Caesar's on his Tuscan transit of 1501 has come down to us, but that thenceforth he held the republic in contempt is proved by what happened a year later. In June, 1502, Arezzo followed the example of Pisa and revolted against Florentine supremacy. Montepulciano to the south had already done the same, and Pistoia, torn by bloody factions, was trembling in the balance. Only a strong Florence could succeed in holding its conquests together; the revived and hopelessly feeble republic was visibly dissolving into its constituent elements. No sooner had Arezzo proclaimed its independence than a number of Duke Valentino's subcommanders appeared upon the scene and fanned the flames of revolt till the whole upper Arno Valley seemed lost to the republic. Valentino himself lurked watchfully in the background awaiting developments. It was an immensely critical moment with nothing less than the very existence of the state hanging in the balance. And again, having no stomach for action, the only coin of courage, the pusillanimous government offered the sorry spectacle of going on its knees to the French monarch to save it from destruction. Thereupon Louis XII, happy to play the part of Italian Jove, gave orders to his Borgian ally to cease molesting his other ally, the equally beloved Florentines. To make it quite plain to Valentino that, while ready to support his original adventure in state-building, the king drew a line beyond which he did not intend to let his protégé go, he dispatched French troops into the upper Arno Valley, under whose authoritative direction the whole territory was restored to his faithful Florentine servants.

While this last-minute rescue released great demonstrations of joy at Florence, many thoughtful citizens, filled with apprehension by every phase of the outrageous Arezzo incident, were stirred to demand a change of system. The French king might not always be prepared to launch his august veto against a trespasser on Tuscan soil and, besides, it was a disgraceful derogation from the dignity of a free state to live by a monarch's favor, and he a foreigner. The trouble lay with the new constitution, perhaps with its main democratic feature, the Grand Council, perhaps with its swiftly changing executive and the consequent lack of continuity and firmness. That the butchers, bakers, and candlestickmakers constituting the majority of the Grand Council would ever be moved to decree its abolition or that they would agree to even the slightest curtailment of its authority was out of the question. However, the continued misfortunes of the state had gradually brought them around to the view that a new signory every two months, totaling six distinct governments for each calendar year, undermined the sense of responsibility and was the sufficient reason for the paralysis that overtook the rulers every time there was need of vigor. In the face of recent events and of the all but certain prospect of an early resumption by Caesar Borgia of his wanton aggressions, a majority came around to the view that a more steady executive was indispensable. Prolonged constitutional debates, which, as in 1494, were greatly influenced by the example of Venice, resulted in at least one capital change. In imitation of the Venetian doge, the gonfalonier of Justice was given an appointment for life. The new life appointee was to exercise substantially the same functions as the old gonfalonier, while to meet the undiminished Florentine thirst for office eight priors serving for two months, exactly as in the past, were to be associated with him in the signory.

When the election for the new head of the state took place in the Grand Council, the victory went to Piero Soderini, who entered on his duties on November 1, 1502. Soderini belonged to an old family of optimates and doubtless owed some of the votes that fell to his lot to the prestige of his name. But as the optimates, as a rule, were greatly feared and hated by the democratic majority, in the main his success was probably owing to his consistent defense of democratic principles. Not only had he never missed an occasion to show his respect for the Grand Council, but throughout his prolonged participation in public life he had always proved himself a stickler for strict constitutional forms. The sum, besides, in his private life of all the conventional virtues, he was just the man a body of small tradesmen and property-owners never fails to look up to as its ideal and to pick as its spokesman. That an executive of Soderini's type can render an important service to the commonwealth in ordinary, quiet times is certain. Unfortunately the times were neither quiet nor ordinary with the result that Piero Soderini's burgher virtues became a contributory factor in the ruin of the state.[1]

It is undeniable that the Florentine government gained in stability at home and in authority abroad with the assumption by Soderini of the gonfalonierat for life. For one thing, one man now held all the threads of policy continuously in his hands. A second advantage was that since Soderini was a capable administrator and hated slovenly finances, he succeeded in a surprisingly short time in putting the Florentine house in better order. It may even be said that the city entered on a period of improved security, although this blessing cannot by any stretch of the imagination be attributed to the new head in person, since it flowed from events with which he had nothing to do. The first of these events occurred some nine months after the gonfalonier's advent to power. On August 18, 1503, Pope Alexander VI died of the malarial fever which was endemic in Rome and annually levied an enormous toll on the population.[2] The doting father departed this life before the son had been solidly established in his conquered dominion. Even more destructive of Caesar's plans was the circumstance that, stricken by the racking fever at the same time as the pope, he lay for many critical weeks at the point of death. When he finally recovered, a man who was his match in energy, if not in his defiance of the moral

[1] Among the many diarists of the period Luca Landini perhaps offers most of that precious quality called local color. See his *Diario Fiorentino* published by I. del Badia (Florence, 1883). Luca was an apothecary and a Piagnone with a typical small shopkeeper outlook. When Piero Soderini was elected gonfalonier for life Luca was of course delighted and piously commented: "Veramente fu da Dio tale opera!"

Invaluable for this period is F. Guicciardini's youthful work, the *Storia Fiorentina,* published as Vol. III of the *Opere Inedite* (Florence, 1859).

[2] The piquant tale of the banquet at which the pope accidentally drank the poisoned wine intended for his guests has absolutely no basis in fact. That small defect will not keep it from being handed down from author to author to all eternity.

law, sat upon St. Peter's chair. This was Giuliano della Rovere, raised to the cardinalate over a generation ago by that other Rovere, his uncle, the fourth Sixtus. Having at last reached the goal of his ambition, the new pope, Julius II, was not minded to let the State of the Church slip out of his hands into those of a hated predecessor's despised bastard. He dispossessed Caesar of his conquests, and although after some hesitation he released Caesar's person, the condottiere's fickle goddess, Fortune, had turned her back on him and, slowly pushed into oblivion, he died a few years later (1507) in an obscure skirmish in the Pyrenees.

A relative calm succeeded in the ever-troubled State of the Church as Julius II directed his powerful energy to the task of appropriating Caesar's conquests for himself and the papacy. At the same time the political storm which had been raging ever since Louis XII had occupied Lombardy was temporarily calmed by developments in the south of Italy. When Louis seized Milan in 1499, he looked upon his action as no more than the initial step toward the total subjugation of the peninsula. The next step was to be the conquest of Naples, to which his immediate predecessor had pointed the way. When Charles VIII had been obliged to withdraw from that kingdom, the displaced Aragonese dynasty had effected a quick return with the aid of its Spanish relatives. On pondering the Neapolitan problem after his Milanese success Louis came to the conclusion that he was not strong enough permanently to hold the southern territory against the will of the king of Aragon and entered into negotiations with him with a view to a peaceful settlement of their opposed claims. The king of Aragon was Ferdinand, husband of Isabella, queen of Castile, and one of the most cunning and grasping sovereigns of his century. Ever ready to extend his sway, Ferdinand received his French rival's overtures with the greatest alacrity. The result was a treaty signed at Granada in November, 1500, by the terms of which Louis, in return for the northern half of the kingdom of Naples, conceded the southern half to his rival. The rights of the actual ruler received the consideration the strong are in the habit of giving the weak, and he was coolly dropped on the ash heap of history by being declared deposed.

There followed the occupation of the kingdom of Naples by French and Spanish armies, with everything passing according to plan until the agents of the two powers intrusted with the partition disagreed regarding the boundary between their respective shares. From harsh words they passed to blows with such precipitation that already by 1503 the two jealous partners were openly at war. In the very months when Rome was disturbed by the death of Pope Alexander and the election of his successor, the armies of France and Spain were engaged in bringing their Neapolitan differences to a decision in the field. It came with extraordinary swiftness, owing to the amazing military talents of the Spanish commander, the famous Gonsalvo of Cordova. In the month of December, on the banks of the Garigliano River, Gonsalvo all but destroyed the French army and followed up his victory by taking possession of the whole of the Neapolitan kingdom in behalf of his sovereign. As Louis XII, involved in manifold difficulties with such neighbors close at hand as Maximilian I of Germany and Henry VII of England, was unable to continue the war in southern Italy, he came to terms with Ferdinand of Aragon, by which he surrendered his claim to Naples to his triumphant rival. Accordingly, the reduction of Italy by foreign powers begun in 1494 came to a temporary halt. France at Milan dominated the north; Spain at Naples ruled the south. Held as in a vise between them were the as yet unconquered states of Venice, Florence, and the papacy, together with such minor historical accidents as Siena, Lucca, Mantua, and Ferrara. The situation remained dangerously unstable; however, as long as France and Spain, exhausted by their recent efforts, kept the peace, the doomed peninsula might hope to enjoy a welcome temporary lull.

The general situation needed to be put before the reader in order to explain the improved position of the Florentine republic in the years immediately following Piero Soderini's assumption of power. In view of the narrated facts no further proof is required that the improvement did not follow from any contribution immediately ascribable to the gonfalonier. We put his case in a nutshell, when we say that he enjoyed beginner's luck; and he enjoyed the same luck also in another matter. In the precipitate retreat of the French following Don Gonsalvo's victory, Piero de' Medici, who was serving in the French ranks, met his death in the waters of the swift Garigliano. The worthless Piero had never ceased to harass the republic either by joining with its enemies or by plots of his own devising. Now that he was gone the Medici interests came into the safekeeping of Piero's two younger brothers, Giovanni, the cardinal, and Giuliano. Both of them were men of kindly disposition and superior intelligence, who saw the futility of trying to win their way back to the city they had lost by antagonizing its inhabitants. Not only did they cease from plotting against the government but more especially the cardinal, who was a great personage at Rome, went out of his way to extend a gracious hospitality to every Florentine who for one reason or another paid a visit to the papal capital. With the outlawed Medici giving no immediate anxiety, with Duke Valentino no longer rampant along the eastern border, with France and Spain at least temporarily quiescent, the problem which since its renewal the republic had never ceased to regard as its leading concern again came automatically to the front. This was the problem of rebellious Pisa. Soderini was aware that what the Florentines to a man expected of their new executive was the reduction of that port; and, eager to please them, he went about the business in the familiar way by hiring mercenary troops. Although he got the usual unsatisfactory returns, since there was nothing else to do he persisted in his efforts until one day a slight, studious-looking, ingratiating official in his employ let fall the arresting remark that he knew of a far more effective way of levying war.

The man whom our story now brings to the front is one of the most strikingly individual figures in the long panorama of Florentine political agents from Farinata degli Uberti and Giano della Bella to Rinaldo degli Albizzi and Lorenzo the Magnificent. He is Niccolò Machiavelli, descendant of an old but impoverished family, who in the year 1498, one month after the tragic end of the prophet Savonarola, received the appointment as head of the second chancellery and secretary of the war committee called the Ten. He was an alert and clever young man, twenty-nine years old, whose leading intellectual attribute was an inexhaustible interest in all the concerns of the state. Since in his double capacity of chancellor and secretary of the Ten all papers relating to both domestic and foreign affairs henceforth passed through his hands, he was free to indulge his peculiar taste to the limit. Before many months had elapsed he had gained an unrivaled insight into all the problems vexing the city. Even before Florence provided itself with a gonfalonier for life the secretary's special talents had won recognition and he had been enabled to enlarge his political experience by being sent on important missions to neighboring states. When Piero Soderini took over the executive, he was so greatly drawn to the official who was always primed with the decisive information on every subject that arose that he made use of him more than ever. In the autumn of 1502 Machiavelli was sent to spy out the plans of Duke Valentino, just then at the height of his career; and after the death of Pope Alexander in the following August the shrewd secretary was dispatched to Rome to study and report on the now fast sinking fortunes of the great adventurer. So satisfactorily did he perform these services that, on Soderini's express orders, he was sent repeatedly to Louis XII and Emperor Maximilian, and at least once to every Italian ruler, great or small, who in any way affected the Florentine destiny. Naturally Soderini consulted him also in the matter of the interminable Pisan war. Having pondered the problem closely for years, the secretary had come to the opinion that a radical change in Florentine military methods was unavoidable. His deliberate view was that it was pure folly to continue to trust the welfare of the state to mercenary troops. While freely consuming the substance of the citizens, not only did the hired condottieri fail to give wholehearted service, but on sufficient inducement they were always ready to betray their employers.

The condottiere system had long been a stench in the nostrils of every Florentine, but until Machiavelli came forward no one had ever proposed a remedy. When he first divulged his plan confidentially to his subordinates and cronies of the chancellery, they burst into amused laughter. When the gonfalonier heard of it, he, too, was convinced that it was utterly impracticable for the unanswerable reason that the Florentines of the beginning cinquecento no longer bore any resemblance to their medieval forebears. This was indeed the core of the issue; for what Machiavelli proposed was to return to the military system of the early republic, which was, as everyone was aware, that the citizens themselves, including the residents of the contado, supplied the army required for the protection of the state. It was almost two hundred years ago that the national army had expired to be replaced by the mercenary system which, whatever its early effectiveness may have been, had latterly become an intolerable burden. Only reluctantly and because of the desperateness of the situation was the gonfalonier persuaded to give the secretary's proposal a trial; and conscious of the certain opposition to the measure of the substantial burgher element, he turned by way of experiment to the more tractable countryside. First in one village and then in another the peasants were called together to undergo a brief period of military training. So promising were these beginnings that they did not fail to make an impression in the city and, spurred by the tireless secretary, Soderini at last ventured to bring the issue before the councils.

It was accounted a notable victory for the gonfalonier and his ingenious subordinate when, on December 6, 1506, a bill authorizing the establishment of a national militia was formally enacted. Owing as much to the fear of putting weapons in the hands of citizens, who might use them to levy civil war, as to the settled burgher dislike for military service, the bill limited the obligation to serve, at least for the time being, to the country residents. This was a serious flaw. Not only did it cut down the new militia to approximately ten thousand men, but it excused from a primary obligation of patriotism the very people who were the masters of the state and its leading beneficiaries. Machiavelli was aware of these and other drawbacks imposed by the existing frame of mind, but he persuaded himself that they did not count as against the capital advantage of providing the government with a reliable force capable of being brought into action with a minimum of expense and delay. Of course there remained such weighty questions as whether the necessary discipline and courage could be instilled into bands of unwilling peasant lads, and how the indispensable corps of devoted native officers was to be obtained. On the answer hung the success or failure of the new institution. As always in novel experiments, much would have to be left to time; and till time had spoken there was nothing an energetic statesman like Machiavelli could do but to labor incessantly in behalf of his plan. It was a great help that the organization of the new force fell into his hands. By the terms of the law of 1506 the national militia was put in charge of a commission of Nine; but as the Nine made Machiavelli their secretary, he became to all intents the civil head of the native forces, from which he expected the salvation of the republic.[3]

When elements of the new national militia were first employed in connection with the siege of Pisa, it was found that they were serviceable at less exposed points but that they could by no means be rated as the fighting equivalent of professional troops. The state had therefore to continue to employ mercenaries, although it was considered a cause for congratulation that from year to year their numbers could be reduced and the national units increased proportionately without imperiling the enterprise. We thus come to the spring of the year 1509 when, in connection with the latest developments in the general Italian situation, it became apparent that Pisa was about to fall. The general situation had by that year taken a new and, as usual, an unexpected turn. In view of the Franco-Spanish settlement of 1504 a reasonable forecast would have run to the effect that the peace of Italy would not be again disturbed until France and Spain should resume their struggle for peninsular control. For reasons having to do with events engrossing each of them at home, they adjourned the inevitable breach, each power contenting itself with the Italian territory in its possession. As a result, for the four years during which the

[3] The fundamental biography of Machiavelli is still that of P. Villari, *Niccolò Machiavelli e i Suoi Tempi*. 3 vols. Florence, 1877-82. The English translation is by Linda Villari, *The Life and Times of Niccolò Machiavelli*. 2 vols. London, 1898. The leading source for Machiavelli are his collected works (*Opere*) of which there are many editions. It would require a footnote of essay proportions to discuss even the recent literature on Machiavelli. An unusually illuminating character sketch will be found in R. Roeder, *The Man of the Renaissance*. New York, 1933.

truce between France and Spain continued, the leading disturber of Italy's always precarious peace was a native ruler, the new pope.

In Pope Julius II (1503–13) we encounter one of the most masterful of the great Renaissance personalities. On mounting the thror e of St. Peter he at once identified himself with the purely secular policy which had distinguished his immediate predecessors, but he put behind it an impersonal majesty, of which they with their petty aims of family aggrandizement had not shown so much as a trace. As soon as he was able to rid himself of the incubus of Caesar Borgia, his single purpose came to be to bring the territories the duke had conquered under the control of the church, to which they rightfully belonged. The task was rendered difficult by the chaos precipitated in Umbria and the Romagna following the collapse of Caesar's power. Some of the dispossessed tyrants took advantage of the confusion to return to the towns from which they had been driven, while the republic of Venice, always recklessly eager to make up for its loss of sea power since the coming to the near east of the Turks by its expansion on *terra firma,* seized a considerable section of the adjoining Romagna. Julius II was not the man meekly to bear this succession of effronts. By breaking Caesar's power he had broken the immediately available sword of the church and he would have to put off action until he had succeeded in forging a new weapon. It was characteristic of his essentially military temper that he never thought of letting anyone but himself exercise the supreme command; and when at length he was ready to resume the interrupted task of consolidating the papal state, he took the field in person, armed beneath his flowing pontifical vestments from head to foot in flashing steel.

Although the warrior-pope enjoyed considerable success against the petty usurpers of his dominion, when it came to rich and arrogant Venice he was helpless. His frustration caused the mighty man to erupt like a volcano. He was a son of the Ligurian littoral, and just as characteristic of him as his sailor-like bluffness and honesty, was an impulsiveness that often hurled him forward on a path which he had no desire to travel. Blocked in the Romagna by the republic of St. Mark, he readily joined in a plot for the partition of the Venetian possessions on the mainland hatched out by the three towering sovereigns of France, Spain, and Germany. Grasping Venice, although certainly no more grasping than the rulers who combined against her, had made the mistake of giving offense to all three of them at the same time. The result was the league of Cambray of December, 1508, by which they revenged themselves on Venice by agreeing to blot the ancient republic from the map. It was this callous arrangement, to which the hate-blinded Julius II gave his consent on being promised the alienated Romagna lands as his share of the spoils. Hardly, however, had the campaign of the Cambray allies been inaugurated in the spring of 1509, when the pope was visited by compunctions. The overwhelming might of the league had in a first concerted rush all but suffocated the Venetians, thus enabling Julius to repossess himself of the lands he considered his own. Then, as his passions cooled and his judgment reasserted its empire, he was reduced to the role of spectator while three great foreign powers proceeded to divide among them the strongest of the few remaining independent states of the peninsula. His patriotic gorge rose at the sight until he could hardly wait to undo the mischief he had himself helped to wreak. He made a separate peace with the republic, of course prudently retaining what he had already seized. Immediately after, he went boldly over to the side of his threatened fellow-countrymen. It is certain that his action was a large factor in the recovery that the Venetians presently effected and by which they extricated themselves from the deadly net of Cambray. Not content with this contribution, with characteristic initiative the pope next attempted to give the war an entirely new turn by transforming it into a national struggle for the liberation of Italy from its foreign oppressors.

Before we follow the fortunes of the new struggle we shall have to return to the Florentine siege of Pisa. That the impoverished, desperate, and starving seaport had been able to resist its more powerful neighbor for so many years was nothing short of a miracle, partially explained by the disguised or open assistance afforded it by the many enemies of Florence. When the spring of 1509 arrived, Niccolò Machiavelli, who, although only a lesser official, was substantially in charge of the siege, recognized that the preoccupation of Italy with the attack on Venice by four great sovereigns furnished Florence an unequaled opportunity to push the siege without the probability of serious interference from any quarter. Accordingly, he drew his lines closer and closer around the miserable town, making more and more use of his national militia, until on June 8 the Pisans gave up their stubborn struggle of fifteen years' duration by opening their gates to the enemy. It was the greatest moment in the life of the revived republic. Its divided citizens forgot their hatreds as they gave themselves up to unrestrained manifestations of joy. Incoherent with rapture, one of his chancellery assistants dashed off a congratulatory note to his "honored Niccolò" at Pisa: "Everyone without exception has gone mad with exultation. There are bonfires all through the city, although it is still afternoon. Think what it will be like at night! . . . If I were not afraid of making you overproud, I would say that with your battalions you have conducted the work so well that it was none other than you who have re-established the Florentine state." [4] If on that June day of the year 1509, when Pisa surrendered, the struggling Florentine republic touched its apogee, the statement applies with equal force to the public career of Niccolò Machiavelli.

From these heights the descent was tragically precipitate for both. In the course of the following year (1510) the pope, as we have already noted, succeeded in converting the war of the league of Cambray into a struggle for the liberation of Italy. He naturally appealed to Florence to join the national movement. As the ever-fluctuating Emperor Maximilian before long declared his willingness to come to terms with Venice, and as Spain, although associated diplomatically with the league of Cambray, had not sent a single soldier into Lombardy from its south Italian listening-post, the liberation of Italy, as viewed by Julius II, might be effected by a union of Italian states against the original invader, France. However, to join in a struggle against France ran violently counter to Florentine tradition as well as against the settled predilections of the Gonfalonier Soderini. In regard to the problem presented by the pope's invitation the gonfalonier and his favorite man of affairs were perhaps for the

[4] Machiavelli, *Opere* (Passerini-Milanesi), Vol. V, p. 431, note.

first time since their association in the government of different minds. Machiavelli argued in favor of an opportunist policy, such as since his day has with a wholly unjustified implication of malignancy been called Machiavellian. The position of the secretary was that since Florence was a feeble republic confronted by more powerful states, it must not once and for all commit itself to any one of them but must be prepared to act according to circumstances. This view was not shared by Soderini, who was inflexibly resolved to keep Florence under the protecting wing of France. He argued that Florence had always been associated with France, that in the past France had regularly come out on top in the long run, and that to turn against France now in the interest of an Italian independence, for which nobody really cared, would be both folly and perfidy.

When the impulsive Julius first inaugurated his liberation campaign to the ringing nationalist cry *Fuori i Barbari!* (Put the barbarians out!) the refusal of Soderini and his democratic supporters in Florence to join hands with the pope brought no immediate injury to the city. The pope's original plan was to expel the French by means of a union of peninsular governments, that is, by an action limited to the nationally aroused Italians. It need hardly to be pointed out that the flaw in this plan was that it was based on something that did not exist, on an Italian national sentiment. Therefore the war that resulted in 1510 and continued through 1511 simmered down to a struggle of Venice and the State of the Church against Louis XII; and in such a struggle Florence could without running any grave risks decline the invitation to join the Italian cause. In fact, on narrow considerations of immediate safety it may even be said to have made the correct decision, for the best efforts of which the liberators were capable failed to shake the grip of the French on the fertile plains of Lombardy. Pope Julius filled his contemporaries with amazement as at the head of an army he swept across the area of conflict like a pagan Mars or heathen Thor. But the French had the heavier artillery and the more mobile troops, and sadly Julius had to admit to himself that with his countrymen refusing to participate in his great national undertaking his program for putting the barbarians out would have to be revised.

With his habitual lack of reflection the pope now invited Spain to come to his aid and concluded with it and Venice what he was pleased to call the Holy League (1511). It might much more appropriately have been called the Unholy League, since its purpose was to drive out the devil with Beelzebub. The allies renewed the invitation to the other Italian states to share in the great work; and now that the two great powers of France and Spain faced each other to determine, regardless of the pope's private expectations, which one of them was to be supreme in Italy, the choice Florence might make between them became a matter of the gravest import. However, the issue was not even debated on the Arno, for, hypnotized by its French tradition, the republic decided for Louis XII. A single campaign decided the new conflict. In April, 1512, there occurred a desperately fought battle between the French and the Spanish armies at Ravenna, and although it was finally won by the French, it brought them no advantage. Owing to pressure from many sides, the French troops were obliged to retreat from the Adriatic coast toward their base at

Milan, which, when their quarreling generals could agree on no plan, they were unable to hold. Withdrawing more and more precipitately, they ended by giving up Italy altogether.

When summer came the Holy League was in complete control of the peninsula. Thereupon the delegates of the victor states held a congress at Mantua, at which, after the son of the Moor, Maximilian Sforza, had been restored to the recovered duchy of Milan, the fate of Florence was made the order of the day. The unanimous verdict was to the effect that the republic, identified with the defeated French cause, should be abolished and the Medici brought back to the city. The leading member of the banished family was Cardinal Giovanni. He had vigorously co-operated with the pope in the affairs of the Holy League and might not improperly look upon the restoration voted by the congress as his personal reward. To carry out the judgment against Florence the victorious Spanish army under the viceroy of Naples, Raymond of Cardona, was ordered to cross the Apennines into Tuscany.

It would be an exaggeration, and therefore fallacious, to declare categorically that the republic might have been saved if it had possessed the foresight to have switched in good time from France to Spain. While it is true that in that case its existence might have been prolonged, it should by now be plain beyond dispute that in the altered circumstances of Italy an independent Florentine state, regardless of the constitution under which it might be operating, was no longer possible. Florence had become the helpless shuttlecock of France and Spain. Should by some chance the republic have escaped the doom pronounced at Mantua in 1512, it would irretrievably have met its end under different auspices a little later. Agreeing therefore that its demise was fated, we may nonetheless regret the manner of its passing, since it took place amidst manifestations of pusillanimity, cowardice, and base betrayal calculated to wreck the faith in human nature of the stoutest optimist. When the approach of the Spanish army was reported on the Arno, the councils on being summoned by the gonfalonier pledged themselves spiritedly and to a man to defend the popular government. Hardly had this courageous stand been taken, when the Spaniards were reported at Prato some ten miles away; and shortly after, on August 29, came the message that they had taken the little town by storm and were putting it to a murderous sack. The defense of Prato had been intrusted to the new militia re-enforced by a small band of mercenaries. Confronted by the Spanish veterans, the militia made a miserable showing by scattering in headlong flight as soon as the enemy, who possessed only two small, almost useless cannons, had made an inconsiderable breach in the walls. Poor Machiavelli! A single touch of war as conducted by foreign soldiers revealed the flimsiness of the national instrument he had forged with such high hopes for his country. The sharp disappointment caused by the militia added to the terror struck to the hearts of all by the merciless plunder of Prato produced a precipitate change of sentiment. A commission was hurriedly dispatched to Raymond of Cardona with instructions at all costs to come to terms with the general. It was a panic such as every people is liable to in similar circumstances and which only a resolute leader can stem. In Piero Soderini Florence had given itself an official head but that he was not even remotely a leader was now revealed to every jabbering shopkeeper. It sufficed for five impertinent young men to appear (August 31) in the gonfalonier's suite of rooms in the palace with the demand that he resign to overcome his resistance. Not only did he obediently evacuate the palace, but he fled from Florence with such haste that he did not again draw a quiet breath till he had set foot in the town of Ragusa on the farther shore of the Adriatic Sea. When he died some ten years later, still an exile whom papal charity permitted to reside at Rome, his one-time henchman and collaborator, Machiavelli, composed an epitaph for him which breathes such withering contempt that it must have scorched the dead man in his grave:

> La notte che morì Pier Soderini,
> L'alma n'andò dell' Inferno alla bocca;
> E Pluto le gridò: anima sciocca,
> Che Inferno! va' nel Limbo dei bambini.[5]

It did not require long negotiations on the part of the commissioners sent to the Spanish camp at Prato to come to a settlement with their unbidden guests. On the payment to them of 140,000 ducats and the readmission of the Medici to Florence as private citizens the guests agreed to take their departure. Since it was now the end of August and the signory was on the point of expiring, the Grand Council elected a new signory and appointed a new gonfalonier in place of the fugitive Soderini. Evidently the official view was that, save for the reintegration of the Medici, the government would go on much as before. With these matters settled, the Medici brothers, first Giuliano, and, some days later, Cardinal Giovanni, entered the city, the latter with appropriate pomp under escort of four hundred lances. According to the treaty the Medici were to have the position and rights of simple citizens. Undeniably, however, they had been brought back by Spanish bayonets and were protected in the city against violence by mercenaries smuggled into the palace and piazza. Under these circumstances could it be pretended with any show of reason that they were citizens on the same basis as the rest of the Florentines?

[5] On the night when Piero Soderini died, his soul descended to the mouth of hell; at which Pluto snorted: Silly soul, hell is no place for you; your place is in the limbo of babies.

XXVIII. Florence an Annex of the Papacy (1512–27)

THE status of the repatriated Medici was not long left undecided. It has already been pointed out that the two younger brothers of Piero had broken with his policy of violence not only because they recognized the folly of systematically antagonizing the Florentines, but also because, as men of peace, they were reluctant to resort to force and bloodshed. This was particularly true of the younger of the two brothers, Giuliano. Indeed Giuliano was unfitted by temperament to play a political role in a country so chaotic as Italy; and except for the fact that he was a gracious aristocrat with many friends in the literary and artistic circles of his country, he cannot be said to have been much of an asset to his family. The responsibility for the Medici fortunes therefore devolved exclusively on Cardinal Giovanni; and while he, too, was averse to unnecessary violence, he possessed a sufficiently robust nature to take action whenever a crisis arose and especially when the interests of his house were at stake. For Giovanni never forgot that he owed his cardinalate to his father, who had secured the son's appointment to the single end that the young prince of the church might use his ecclesiastical dignity to advance the family fortunes.

Cardinal Giovanni made a ceremonial entrance into Florence on September 14, 1512. Although, for safety's sake, he was attended by troops, he tried to give his homecoming an ecclesiastical rather than a political character. However, there was no escaping politics, for hardly had he taken his residence in the great palace of his family, which had stood empty and bare since the sack of 1494, when he was importuned by his friends to change the government. These partisans insisted that neither they nor the family to which they were pledged had any security under the existing regime. It required no long urging on their part to win over the cardinal. Two days later, on September 16, a parliament was called, and with Medicean mercenaries holding all the entrances to the piazza and letting only Medicean adherents pass, the proposal of the intimidated signory to the assembled people to appoint a balìa to "reform" the state was accepted by acclamation. It was the familiar device long practiced by the oligarchic cliques of the past and so thoroughly detested by the advocates of a free regime that the parliament had been solemnly outlawed in the days of Savonarola. The resort to the banished institution was made possible only by the threat to use force, and the same threat constituted the sanction behind the balìa. This all-powerful committee consisted of forty-five members (later increased to sixty-five), all trusty Mediceans hand-picked by the cardinal. It went about its business of destroying the republic with the greatest good will. Not only did it expressly abolish the numerous characteristic features of the constitution, more particularly the democratic Grand Council, but yielding to the spirit of blind partisanship, it even canceled the outstanding institutional creation of the period just closed, Machiavelli's militia. The offense of the militia was not that it had proved a poor prop of the state, but that it represented a concession to popular principles.

This wreckage effected, the balìa at a somewhat more leisurely pace reestablished the Medicean system as it had operated in the days of Lorenzo the Magnificent. Florence again acquired a senate of the Seventy, a council of the Hundred, a signory of eight priors and a gonfalonier of Justice, in short, an elaborate visible apparatus serving no other purpose than to mask a hidden control. Actual authority lay with the Medicean balìa, which was made a permanent institution. It named the signory for each two months' period and determined the foreign and domestic policy of the state. However, as the balìa took its orders from the cardinal, Florence in effect again had a single ruler and with some show of reason Lorenzo's son might persuade himself that his father's age had returned.

Although the Medici on again entering Florence had no more than a feeble following, it grew steadily under the cardinal's skilful nursing until his elevation to the papacy released such popular enthusiasm that opposition, or at least all visible opposition, completely disappeared. Once more we must return to Rome to take note of the position of Pope Julius II after the sweeping triumph of the Holy League. The terrible old man, as his harassed and overworked dependents called him, had actually achieved his purpose, for in fulfillment of his slogan, *Fuori i Barbari,* he had driven the barbarian French out of Italy. In so doing, however, he had greatly strengthened the hold on Italy of those other barbarians, the Spaniards. Profoundly dissatisfied with this result, he let it be growlingly known to whoever succeeded in catching him off his guard that his next move would be to throw out the Spaniards after the French; but before he got under way with this new and far more difficult undertaking, he was cut short by death (February 13, 1513). Immediately on receiving the news Cardinal Giovanni left Florence to join the conclave, from which he himself, in spite of his youthful age of thirty-seven, on March 11 issued as pope. He took the title Leo X.

Rarely has the election of a pope been attended by such high expectations. Leo's fellow-townsmen on the Arno gave themselves up to wild demonstrations of joy, partly on personal, partly on patriotic, grounds, for the young Medici was the first Florentine ever to achieve the papal honors. The last endearing memories of the republic were forgotten, as all eyes turned toward Rome, from which the common people confidently expected valuable favors for their city and innumerable ambitious and selfish members of the ruling class liberal benefits for themselves. Hardly less keen were the hopes aroused by the new pope in the general body of the Italian literati. They saw in him the embodiment of the culture of the age, a friend of the humanists, a patron of the artists, and that rarity among recent occupants of St. Peter's chair, a high churchman who was not soiled with the common vices of his age and who had never failed to show a scrupulous respect for ecclesiastical decorum. Leo promptly met these expectations of the publicists by casting himself for the role of Maecenas. Innumerable scholars, musicians, architects, and painters found employment at his hands. Although they constituted in the main a vulgar horde of sycophants and mediocrities, it will always be remembered in his favor that, included in his patronage, were also Raphael and Michelangelo. The fact is Leo X was a soft, genial personality, who loved movement and gayety and who, even when he glimpsed a high goal, lacked the moral fiber to pursue it for long. An examination of the striking portrait done of him by Raphael reveals the man more unerringly than the most searching words. The Leo of the famous canvas is a large, flabby man, whose native intelligence and cultivated taste have been all but destroyed by habitual self-indulgence.

It is impossible to take leave of the republic without paying our respects to the man who, although he never rose above a dependent political office, in the eyes of posterity looms as the most important figure in its employ between the death of Savonarola and the flight of Piero Soderini. Niccolò Machiavelli had worked hand-in-glove with the gonfalonier, and although he lamented his chief's pitiable collapse in the crisis of 1512, he never denied the obligations resulting from their long and close association. To their credit the Medici on their return did not practice a mean revenge, and, in the main, were inclined to let by-gones be by-gones. That they did not feel safe, however, with the sworn supporters of the past regime was natural, and accordingly they gradually pushed most of them out of office. Among the dismissed servants of the republic was the chancellor and secretary, Machiavelli, who two months after the Medicean triumph was deprived of all his functions. It was a terrible blow, for, as already noted, not in all probability since the world began has there been a man more interested in the state *per se* and more bent on finding out the procedures and measures that promote or hamper its welfare. Life to Niccolò was politics and outside of politics there was no life. To his mind, therefore, it was neither inconsistent nor unfaithful to tender his services to the Medici. They now represented the state, his ever-worshipful master, and he was as ready and anxious to serve that master under the new lords as he had been to serve him under Piero Soderini. Not impossibly Machiavelli might have succeeded in making himself acceptable to the restored rulers, had he not, while waiting for their suspicions to lose their first sharp edge, become the victim of a blind mischance. A young Florentine who, seduced by the revived pagan doctrine of tyrannicide, was engaged in evolving a plot for the murder of Giuliano and the cardinal, had written the names of possible supporters on a slip of paper and had afterward accidentally dropped it from his pocket. When the paper was picked up, the conspirator and his one accomplice were promptly arrested and executed. Unfortunately the name of Machiavelli figured in the list of sympathizers. He was taken into custody and, after the practice of the day, cruelly tortured in order to bring him to confession. As there was nothing to confess, nothing was elicited with the result that it was conceded by all, except the most rabid Mediceans, that he was not guilty.

The planned assassination was discovered in February, 1513, just as Cardinal Giovanni was preparing to hurry to Rome to the conclave. On his elevation to the papacy, he was inspired to publish an amnesty, by which Machiavelli and all the other suspects were set free. Thus was the ex-secretary officially cleared of specific charges but his person remained under a cloud. Influential friends did their best to plead his cause and to make his great talents once again available for the state; but his enemies were stronger than his friends and always succeeded in hindering his re-employment. Only very reluctantly did he persuade himself that his days of office-holding were over. Well, then, if fate blocked the path of active public service he would devote himself to a theoretic study of the state. He became a writer, one of the most distinguished in his chosen field in the long succession of the ages. Although his second life, as one may call it, was a second choice, it is in reality far more important than his first life, but it no longer belongs to Florentine political history. To this new Machiavelli, to Machiavelli the writer, we shall return when we take up the literary developments of the age.

When Leo X, the acknowledged and hardly any longer veiled ruler of Florence, became pope, he made the Arno city an annex of the papacy. Henceforth whatever foreign policy he would find it desirable to adopt as pope, he would impose on Florence as its own policy. No longer able, however, to exercise direct rule on the Arno, he was obliged to choose a Medici to serve as the visible head of the city. He may possibly at first have thought of Giuliano in this capacity. If so, he very soon changed his mind, for he permitted Giuliano to follow him to Rome and, apart from occasionally evolving an ambitious plan for his brother, he permitted Giuliano to live the obscure existence he preferred. The nearest Leo ever came to pushing his brother to the front was to have the French king give him a French princess to wife together with the title of duke of Nemours. Always in delicate health, the duke of Nemours died in 1516, and by this closing act leaped into an immortality for which no achievement of his active period offered the slightest warrant. The immortality was conferred by Michelangelo. On being commanded by Leo X to carve Giuliano's idealized figure for his tomb, Michelangelo wrought the seated warrior, who with lifted head eternally searches the horizon in the New Sacristy of San Lorenzo.

It is probable that Pope Leo never seriously considered any other Medici for the Florentine post than his nephew Lorenzo, only son of his brother Piero. Young Lorenzo was twenty years old on the repatriation of his family, a handsome, alert young man who, quite apart from any preference Leo may have had for him, was designated as the head of the state by the unwritten law of succession. So it was Lorenzo who was put in charge, although Leo, reluctant to trust the state to his nephew's inexperience, kept in the closest possible touch with Florentine affairs by an almost daily exchange of news and instructions through the mediation of Lorenzo's secretary. At the same time he never ceased plying the young man himself with counsel. "You must," he says in his earliest letter of advice, "introduce your own men as far as possible into all the principal magistracies. Seek to keep well informed as to what goes on among the members of the signory, making use to this end of Niccolò

LEONARDO DA VINCI AND VERROCCHIO. ANNUNCIATION. UFFIZI GALLERY

LEONARDO DA VINCI. THE LAST SUPPER. FRESCO AT MILAN IN THE CONVENT OF
SANTA MARIA DELLE GRAZIE

Left: LEONARDO DA VINCI. ADORATION OF THE KINGS. UFFIZI GALLERY. *Right:* LEONARDO DA VINCI. MONA LISA OR LA GIOCONDA. LOUVRE GALLERY. PARIS

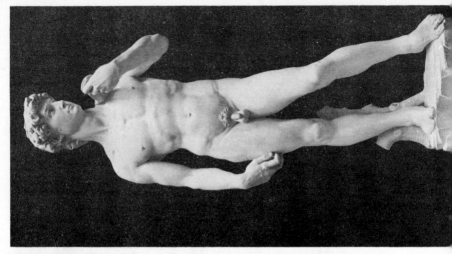

Left: MICHELANGELO. PIETÀ. MARBLE. ST. PETER'S. ROME. *Right*: MICHEL-
ANGELO. DAVID. MARBLE. GALLERY OF THE ACADEMY OF FINE ARTS. FLORENCE

Michelozzi" (Machiavelli's successor, by the way, whom we thus see cast for the role of spy). "Above all, you must be sure of the Otto di Pratica and the balìa." [1] The Otto di Pratica were in control of foreign affairs and the balìa in control of everything. There is more to the same tenor, all of it interesting as an exposition of the Medicean system by a Medici, but not requiring reproduction in detail since we have long since become familiar with all the secrets the document lays bare.

Since, beginning with the year 1494, the history of Florence became inextricably tied up with the attempted conquest of Italy, we are obliged to take note of every capital move among the European powers affecting this issue. On Louis XII's being ejected from the peninsula in 1512 by the Holy League of Pope Julius II, he refused to abide by the consequences, and in the very next year renewed the attempt to gain a foothold in the plains of the Po. Although again defeated, he would again have returned to the attack, had he not died on January 1, 1515. His successor was Francis I (1515-47), a young man twenty-one years old, handsome, intelligent, and deeply persuaded that war was the only true business of a king. Without hesitation he made ready for still another invasion of Italy which, owing more to his undaunted spirit than to any other single factor, led to a dramatic overturn. By winning the battle of Marignano (September 13, 1515), Francis was able to oust young Duke Maximilian Sforza from Milan and repossess himself of the Milanese state. As Pope Leo X had maintained the political system inherited from his predecessor, he suddenly found himself at a disadvantage. He promptly sought an accommodation with the victor. The papacy, strengthened though it was at this time by the addition of Florence, was a feeble power compared with France or Spain and was obliged to steer its course carefully between them if it wished to avoid destruction. The frequent change of sides of Leo X (and of his predecessors and successors as well) was not so much due to the shiftiness of character charged against him by moralistic historians as to the need of every weaker organism to be watchfully alert in order not to be crushed by its stronger neighbors. Confronted with French predominance in northern Italy, Leo X quickly adjusted himself to the new situation and for the moment at least succeeded in doing so without giving offense to Spain. Spain was as determined as France to dominate Italy, but was less headlong than France, and frequently for several years in succession desisted from the pursuit of its Italian aims. Following the victory of Francis of 1515, the two countries actually signed a peace by which each acknowledged the other's position in the peninsula. This made it relatively easy for Pope Leo to maintain good relations with both powers; and, free under the circumstances to attend to matters close at hand, he took up plans to advance the fortunes of both the states intrusted to his care, the State of the Church and Florence.

A study of Leo's actions throughout his reign makes it perfectly clear that, as pope, he desired to continue his predecessor's policy of unifying the papal rule and that, as head of his house, he hoped to enlarge the Medicean state. The two aims were not necessarily incompatible, but they proved incompatible in Leo's case. For, precisely as with most of his recent predecessors, his family

[1] Villari, *Niccolò Machiavelli*, Vol. II, p. 204.

meant more to him than the crown of St. Peter. In spite of the stout besom wielded by Caesar Borgia and Julius II, there were still some petty tyrants left in Umbria and the Romagna. Some of these Leo dutifully got rid of, not hesitating to employ violence when milder measures failed. It is therefore possible to say of him that he contributed his bit to the consolidation of the State of the Church. In the crucial matter of the duchy of Urbino, however, he egregiously violated his papal obligations. This little mountain dominion was ruled by Francesco Maria della Rovere, a nephew of Pope Julius II. Sincere and honorable as Julius had proved himself on the whole to be, he was sufficiently touched with the nepotism he despised to find it impossible to brush Francesco Maria aside and bring Urbino directly under his rule. The problem evaded by Julius devolved on Leo, and Leo to his shame undertook to solve it in the interest of his house. In the year 1516 he declared Francesco Maria deposed in favor of his nephew Lorenzo, who, thus far no more than a citizen of Florence, now entered the high-titled world as duke of Urbino. The dethroned duke possessed enough of the energy of his stock to offer vigorous resistance to the papal army sent by Leo to establish his nephew in the disputed dominion, but in the end he had to yield possession to Lorenzo.

Embarked on the policy of raising his nephew to a higher eminence, Leo X next procured a French princess for him. Already Leo's brother Giuliano, who had died just before the launching of the Urbino venture, had been married to a woman related to the French ruling house. There had been a time when the Medici were considered audacious to look for spouses as high as the Roman house of Orsini. Under the guidance of Leo they became affiliated with the oldest royalty of Europe, the royalty of France. Young Lorenzo received a magnificent welcome on entering Florence with his foreign princess; and the rejoicings were repeated the following year (1519) when the princess gave birth to a daughter. This daughter was destined to reach the highest rung in the ladder of·earthly honors, for she is the famous Catherine de' Medici, afterward queen of France and mother of three kings. To her parents, however, she was far from a bringer of good fortune. Her French mother died in childbed and her father on May 4, less than a month after her birth. His enemies affirmed young Lorenzo perished prematurely, the victim of his numerous vices, while his friends maintained just as positively that he was a man of promise, and that his death resulted from the ill health which was the aftermath of the strenuous Urbino campaign.

Whatever be the truth regarding Lorenzo's character and death, he was gone and with him went the fine plans spun by his papal uncle for his aggrandizement. Leo was not only saddened but deeply perplexed, for there was no legitimate male of his family left on whom to confer the rule of his native city. To win time for the consideration of the problem he dispatched his cousin, Cardinal Giulio de' Medici, to Florence to take over the government. This Giulio was the illegitimate son of the Giuliano, who had died in 1478 from nineteen dagger thrusts administered by the Pazzi conspirators. Born some months before his father's death, Giulio had been received into the Medici family by Lorenzo the Magnificent. He was destined for the church and, owing to his pleasant manners and lively intelligence almost as much as to the potent

Medici influence, he rose rapidly in his profession. His cousin Leo, who never let an opportunity pass to advance his family, made him a cardinal and found him so useful a personal agent that he intrusted the most important business of the papacy to his hands. No wonder that when the question of the Florentine succession arose, Leo should have sent Cardinal Giulio to the Arno as a sort of interim ruler. Giulio made a great success of this critical mission. He avoided the lordly airs with which young Lorenzo had latterly given offense, he lived in simple burgher style in the family palace, he conferred with the leading citizens on the conduct of affairs, and by taking pains not to over-burden the budget of the city he won a very general approval.

At the very moment at which Leo was confronted with this latest phase of the Florentine problem, the Franco-Spanish relations entered a fresh period of disturbance. The first jolt to the recent truce was administered by the death in January, 1519, of Emperor Maximilian. When the seven German electors were called together to choose, according to custom, Maximilian's successor, they conferred the honor on the king of Spain. This was Charles, a youth of nineteen, who had entered on the rule of Spain three years before (1516) on the demise of his maternal grandfather Ferdinand. Charles, to be sure, did not owe his promotion to the empire to his being the king of Spain. He owed it to the fact that his father Philip, who died young, was the son of Emperor Maximilian, head of the house of Hapsburg and archduke of Austria. In other words, through the marriage of Joan, who, as the daughter of Ferdinand and Isabella, was the heiress of Spain, to Philip, who was the heir of Maximilian, their oldest son, Charles, brought the enormous possessions of both houses into his single hand. While at the time of Maximilian's death young Charles was already king of Spain, king of Naples, and lord of the Netherlands, what weighed with the German electors and German people was his being also a German prince, and he won the imperial election owing solely to this circumstance. In 1520 the new sovereign came from Spain to Germany to receive the crown and incidentally to look into the revolt against the rule of the Catholic church which had recently taken place, championed by an Augustinian friar by the name of Martin Luther. While the Lutheran movement is no affair of ours, we must not fail to bring it into our reckoning henceforth whenever we treat of international affairs. Inevitably it caused grave concern to Emperor Charles V, the new civil head of Germany; and while it occasionally troubled Leo X, the head of the church, owing to his care-free, secular nature he refused to let it distract him from the pursuit of the personal ends on which his attention was concentrated. Young Charles was a self-contained, taciturn youth of remarkable talents, as yet undisclosed either to himself or to others. Even before coming to Germany, he had resolved to reopen the Italian question. That signified war with France; and in preparation for that event he wished to secure for himself the help of the pope. Leo for his part was willing to accommodate Charles, in case the emperor would yield to him a share of the prospective Italian conquests. After the usual haggling, in May, 1521, an alliance was signed on this basis. While the pope was to receive a small territorial increase, the Milanese state, the hotly disputed apple of discord between France and Spain, was to revert to the emperor.

The new war between France and Spain began at once and led to still another of the dramatic reversals which had characterized the struggle of the two powers over Italy from the beginning. Merely by clever maneuvering and without having to fight a single pitched battle, the Imperialists, as the many kinds of troops in the employ of Emperor Charles V were henceforth called, forced the French to abandon Milan and retreat in complete disarray toward the passes of the Alps. When the news of the triumph was brought to Pope Leo, he ordered a joyful celebration at which, extended far into a November night, he was seized with chills and fever. As he had never possessed great physical stamina, the attack made such rapid headway that in three days he was dead (December 1, 1521).

To the surprise of the whole world, the conclave elected a foreigner, a Fleming, as Leo's successor. The new pope owed his election to the influence among the cardinals of Emperor Charles, whose tutor he had been and with whom he was still closely associated. He took the name of Hadrian VI. He was an honest, austere, and learned cleric steeped in medieval conceptions so out of harmony with the semi-pagan ideas prevailing at Rome that he quickly became an object of general contempt and ridicule. It was his dream to reform the church; but before he had even begun to break down the resistance of his hostile environment, he was carried away by the fatal Roman fever, not much more than a year after mounting the papal throne.

The new conclave gave its vote to Giulio de' Medici, who adopted the title of Clement VII (1523–34). His recent successful conduct of the Florentine government had won him golden opinions, and because of his earlier service under Leo X at Rome no one was better acquainted with the diverse business of the papacy. In spite of personal and administrative merits considerably above those of his average predecessor, he was destined to be overwhelmed with such a succession of calamities as to make his reign one of the most disastrous in the long history of his office. Without any doubt these calamities were in large part the mere mounting to a peak of difficulties, which had been gathering momentum for generations past and for which his predecessors rather than himself were responsible; unquestionably, however, they fell upon him more crushingly than would have been the case had he not suffered from a fatal flaw of indecision. He had the habit, in the case of every issue that arose, of listening to many opinions; whereupon, after cautiously moving forward, he would hurriedly retrace his steps with the net result that he was back at his point of departure. We are aware that in his day the papacy was perilously suspended between the two aggressive powers of France and Spain. Clearly the interest of Clement VII was to maintain such a balance between them that, courted by both, he would not be obliged to become the dependent of either. He understood this perfectly, but his method of reaching his goal was to threaten to act without ever acting. While action, in the case of such a feeble power as the pope, will always involve risks, constitutional inaction and perpetual subterfuge lead to catastrophe with mathematical certainty. It is a curious circumstance that at the climax of his misfortunes Clement had among his advisers the two wisest political heads of Italy, his two Florentine fellow-countrymen, Francesco Guicciardini and Niccolò Machiavelli. After the Medici had permitted Machiavelli's talents to rust for ten years, this particular Medici, while still a cardinal, had added to his other merits the recognition that it was desirable by gradual stages to draw the former secretary back into the public service. But no good came to him from his two exceptional counselors. They urged with passionate and finally with frenzied insistence that a definite, virile stand be taken. They could not overcome the mental seesaw, for which the pope had a fatal preference and which ended by casting him for that least attractive of human roles, the deceived deceiver, the universal scapegoat.

Before following Clement to his downfall, we shall have to look into his handling of the Florentine problem. He was thoroughly familiar with the situation on the Arno, since from the death of the second Lorenzo to his own elevation to the papacy, that is, for a period of four years, he had exercised the rule in the city to the apparent satisfaction of most of the inhabitants. On withdrawing from Florence to take up his residence at Rome, he was obliged either to name another Medici in his place or to give the city back to the citizens by inviting them to re-establish the republic. He played with the latter solution, possibly to convey to the Florentines an impression of his great liberality. Considering that he was both a product of the individualistic Italian cinquecento and a typical Medici, it is much more likely that he never seriously entertained any other thought than to preserve the Florentine dominion for his family. The household situation that confronted him, however, was almost desperate. While there were some Medici females still alive, among them the little Catherine born in 1519, females had never counted in the Medici succession. With Leo X had expired the last legitimate male, and Clement VII, admittedly illegitimate, was generally regarded as the very last masculine shoot of the stock. There was indeed a younger branch of the family descended from old Cosimo's brother Lorenzo, but the two lines had quarreled and, like Leo before him, Clement VII did not view the younger branch other than as a house of strangers.

Faced with this situation, the pope disclosed the existence of two young Medici bastards, of whom till this moment the Florentines had had only the vaguest knowledge. One was Ippolito, supposed to be the son of Giuliano, duke of Nemours, by a woman of Pesaro, the other, Alessandro, putative son of Lorenzo, duke of Urbino, by a mulatto slave. Ippolito, about fourteen years old, was an exceedingly handsome and promising youth, but Alessandro, who was a year older than Ippolito and who had inherited the dusky skin, thick lips, and crisp hair of his mother, was regarded as almost a monster. After much dubitation, probably feigned, Clement VII sent these two youths to Florence to represent the house. While they were growing to manhood, Cardinal Passerini was set over them with authority to conduct the government in their name. The cardinal was as unhappy a choice as the two young men with the blot on their scutcheon. It irked the Florentines greatly to have a pair of dubious Medici suddenly dropped on them out of nowhere, while the boorishness, avarice, and small intelligence of Cardinal Passerini aroused an opposition which steadily gained in volume. Had it not been, however, for the catastrophe that overtook Pope Clement, it is not likely that the Floren-

tines would have been encouraged once more to remedy the situation by rising
in revolt.

Clement's catastrophe, as already said, was precipitated by the Franco-
Spanish struggle over Italy, which had in 1521 entered a new phase when
Emperor Charles V resolved to challenge the French occupation of Milan
effected by King Francis I six years before. We have learned that Leo X
had allied himself with Charles and had died in consequence of his exposing
himself to the night air during the celebration of the first Spanish victories
in Lombardy. With them the war was by no means over, for Francis I returned to the attack, without, however, scoring any notable success. In the
autumn of 1524 he made a supreme effort and conducted a large and magnificently equipped army across the Alps into the Lombard plain. The Imperialists, outnumbered, gave way before him except for a small force of four
thousand men who continued to hold Pavia. To this city King Francis laid
siege, but it resisted him so stubbornly that the Imperialists were enabled to
gather a relief army of Spanish and German troops. As it was contrary to
King Francis' chivalrous code of conduct to retreat on vulgar considerations
of safety, his forces were, on February 24, 1525, caught between the new Imperialist army and the garrison of Pavia and virtually annihilated. Francis
himself was captured and carried a prisoner to Spain. The war came to an
abrupt end with the Imperialists in unchallenged control throughout the
peninsula.

The blow of Pavia fell almost as heavily on the pope as on France and its
sovereign. During the preceding years Clement had been almost bled white
by the continual and unrelenting demands of the Imperialists for subsidies.
Sorely put out with them, he submitted to their exactions in the secret hope
that the French would presently re-establish a balance of power, enabling him
to reassert his independence. That hope was so completely blasted by Pavia
that in his disillusioned eyes he was now himself no better than a Spanish
prisoner. He made up his mind that his only possible escape was a national
league of all the remaining Italian states backed by the power of France. That
a nation so proud as the French would not accept the verdict of Pavia as final
was accepted by Clement as certain. To be sure, little or nothing was to be
expected from France while the king languished in captivity. Therefore it was
welcome news to the pope when, a year after his capture, Francis came to
terms with his jailer. By the treaty of Madrid (March 18, 1526) he gained his
freedom in return for the surrender to Charles of all his Italian claims together
with the duchy of Burgundy, a province of eastern France. Charles V was still
young and inexperienced or he would not have believed for a moment that his
rival would abide by terms of such crushing severity. It was no more than
what the rest of the world expected when Francis, hardly back on French
soil, entered into relations with the pope and the other Italian states with a
view to renewing the war with Spain at the earliest possible moment.

Pope Clement met the urgent overtures of the French monarch with the
greatest eagerness, although in the manner of the weak and timid he did his
best to conceal from the emperor that he was about to desert him. As Clement
controlled both the papacy and Florence, his act tied both states to the French

cause. Venice, too, was won over to the new league, and with this important addition the list of Italian allies was closed. It was still remembered
in the peninsula that the mighty Julius II had attempted to organize a national
movement for the expulsion of the invaders; but it was also remembered that
he had failed because, apart from an occasional enlightened individual, there
was no national sentiment to be found among the Italians. In plain truth the
anti-Imperialist league of 1526 was never anything more than a frail, hurriedly
patched-up improvisation. The French had gone ahead diplomatically before
they were militarily ready, and as a result, in spite of the lavish promises of
Paris, no French army appeared on Italian soil. The pope and Venice, aided
by the money of Florence, duly collected soldiers up to their limited capacity;
but owing to the inveterate suspicions dividing them, they could not be
brought to act on a common plan. Luckily the Imperialists were during the
year 1526 in almost equally evil case. It was characteristic of them throughout
this period that they lacked adequate funds, and that consequently, as soon
as a campaign was over, they would be obliged, in order to lighten their financial burden, to disband their troops. Charles could not therefore act promptly
in the face of the new danger. An advantage, however, that was bound to
tell in the long run was that he had a better political head than his rival,
Francis, and was served in the field by better commanders. During the winter
of 1526–27 he succeeded in again assembling German and Spanish troops in
northern Italy. In his opinion he would have only to possses himself of the
person of the pope for the whole conspiracy against his domination of Italy
to be completely disrupted.

It will not be possible to do more than indicate the strange vicissitudes of
the campaign of 1527. All the action that took place was supplied by a body of
German Landsknechts under their leader, Frundsberg, and an army of Spaniards under the duke of Bourbon, a French nobleman who had deserted his
king to join the enemy. Both armies were in a rebellious frame of mind owing
to arrears of pay and an incurable lack of provisions. To have stopped them
as they moved southward, plundering as they went, would not have been
difficult if the armies of the anti-Spanish league had been able to come to an
agreement. Instead of action, there was on the part of both generals and
governments nothing but bickering, bad faith, ineptitude, and cowardice. It
was the confession to the world of the complete political and military bankruptcy of Italy. Without being obliged to strike a single blow the Spaniards
and Germans, having united their forces, on May 4 reached the meadows outside the Vatican quarter. Two days later they had breached the wall and,
streaming over the bridges of the Tiber, held Rome at their mercy. The pope
and the cardinals were just able to save their lives by taking refuge in the
Castle of Sant' Angelo. Around them raged unchecked such a sack as the
Eternal City had not experienced even in the far days of the migrations.
Many of the German Landsknechts, as followers of Martin Luther, delighted
in venting their spite on the rich furnishings of the altars and on the persons
of great prelates, whom they held to extravagant ransom, while the Spaniards
in their house-to-house visits seized the gold, silver, jewels, and portable wealth
of every kind which the past generations had accumulated in the capital of

Christianity. The wild orgy ceased only when the pope accepted the terms dictated by the victors and in pledge of their fulfilment agreed to remain a prisoner in the Castle of Sant' Angelo at the discretion of the emperor.

The news of the capture of Rome reached Florence on May 11 and immediately produced a popular commotion. Ever since 1512 the city had made the best of the turn of chance that had converted it, through its renewed subjection to the Medici, into an annex of the papacy. Under Leo X the connection, distasteful though it was to the strong republican sentiment, had carried with it numerous compensatory advantages. These had continued for a time under Clement VII. They entirely disappeared, however, when the new pope's vacillating policy drew the plundering Imperialist hordes into central Italy and precipitated the awful Roman catastrophe. Immediately the old republican memories slumbering just below the surface of consciousness asserted themselves with elemental vehemence. There was nothing more to be expected from these latter-day Medici; besides, the only member of the family the citizens had reason to fear cowered, a broken man, behind the stout walls of his Roman prison. Cardinal Passerini, the unpopular personal representative of Clement in the city, was soon convinced that his position was hopeless. There was no violence to speak of, just a rising tide of irresistible opinion. Prudently yielding to its pressure, the cardinal on May 17 left the city accompanied by his two young Medicean charges.

Songs of thanksgiving sounded through the streets, as once again the yoke of tyranny was broken and the city enthusiastically assumed its republican vestments. Besmirched though they had been by the confirmed dishonest practices of knavish politicians, against every probability in this, the last phase of the free state, they took on once more the luster of their prime.

XXIX. Heroic End of the Republic (1527–30)

WITH a swiftness and spontaneity that testify to the abiding affection of the Florentines for the republican regime, the political arrangements imposed during the recent Medicean ascendancy were swept aside and replaced by the constitution elaborated after the expulsion in 1494 of young Piero de' Medici and sanctified for a large section of the population by the memory of Brother Girolamo Savonarola. The outstanding feature of this constitution was the Grand Council, to which over three thousand citizens were eligible and which was charged with the duty of electing the magistrates and validating the laws proposed by the signory. There were also set up again the smaller council of eighty members, the *Ottanta,* the *Dieci* or Ten charged with the conduct of war, and the signory of eight priors presided over by a gonfalonier of Justice. Instead, however, of conceding the gonfalonier a life-appointment, it was agreed that he should serve for one year only, but that at the expiration of his term he might be eligible for re-election.

When, on the last day of May, 1527, the Grand Council proceeded to vote on the new head of the state, its choice fell on Niccolò Capponi. Niccolò was the son of that Piero Capponi who, on the occasion of Charles VIII's occupation of the city, had spoken a word which had taken the hearts of the Florentines by storm. On the royal puppet's threatening to sound the trumpets summoning his soldiers to assault the town, Piero had cowed him with the bold reply: "And we shall ring our bells!" Other forebears of Niccolò had in their day played an equally important part in Florentine affairs so that the Capponi took rank among the greatest families of the city. Until recently Niccolò had figured as a partisan of the Medici; and although he had broken with them and been a prime mover in their most recent expulsion, he was so far from being their irreconcilable enemy that he openly favored sparing their partisans within the city the usual reprisals and planned, besides, to do his utmost to reach an accommodation with Pope Clement himself. In short, the gonfalonier was a moderate; and that a moderate was elected to the highest office of the state is conclusive proof that, at least in the first stage of the revolution, a considerable majority of the citizens were animated by peaceful sentiments and wished to come to terms with their former ruler, who, though momentarily a prisoner and not to be feared, nevertheless still was the pope and capable in the long run of rallying enormous resources to himself.

Undeniably, however, Florentine opinion, like opinion everywhere and always, was in a state of flux and might under changed conditions exhibit an entirely different complexion. Again let us note, there were in the town no political parties in our sense with an organization, officials, and a platform. There were merely voluntary groupings in the councils and magistracies determined in part by political principles, in larger part still by nothing more calculable than momentary emotional discharges. With this in mind we may speak of Capponi enjoying in the first place the support of the *Frateschi* or *Piagnoni,* composed in the main of the small shopkeepers who had constituted the solid kernel of Savonarola's following. That the gonfalonier was a man of sincere, if somewhat ostentatious, virtue grappled these people to him with bonds of steel. The Mediceans or *Palleschi,* still numerous in the city though now singing small, also gave their suffrages to a gonfalonier, whose main conviction was that the city must at all costs be pacified. A numerically feeble body of Optimates (*Ottimati*) were sworn enemies of the re-established democratic regime. While, owing to their insignificant representation in the Grand Council, they did not count for much, still they, too, were quick to sense that they were better off with Niccolò Capponi, socially if not politically of their own persuasion, than with any other available chief executive and lent him their somewhat equivocal support. Active, systematic opposition to the gonfalonier was reserved to the extreme democrats, whose animating principle was uncompromising hostility to the Medici. They went so far in their fear and hatred of the former ruling house that they received the name of mad men or *Arrabbiati.* Although the Arrabbiati, not to be confused with the Arrabbiati of the Savonarola period, commanded no great following, they embraced the most daring and vigorous youths of the city and furnish a good illustration of the disproportionate influence a coherent and spirited minority may attain in a society, the majority of whose members are as unwilling as they are unfit to accept responsibility. The capable head of this group was Baldasarre Carducci. Although himself an old man of grave bearing, he was as violent in his denunciations of the Medici as the young Hotspurs who frequented the piazza and the palace and was vociferously acclaimed by them as their leader.

While in view of the desperate Italian situation we may argue with a fair degree of assurance that the renewed republic was doomed, the fact remains and is forever memorable that, although it did perish after only three years, on the occasion of the second demise it went down gallantly with flying banners. Undeniably, too, the heroic exit of the later and, as the result proved, the last republic resulted as certainly from the fiery quality of its democratic temper, as this temper in its flaccid aspect had been the cause of the earlier disgraceful collapse. The strength of a democracy is an aroused popular emotion directed by competent leadership toward an inalterable goal. This strength the Florentine democracy of 1527 exhibited, bringing a glory to its last stand which nothing can ever dim. However, when, instead of acting bravely on impulse, the democracy was obliged to make important practical decisions in the business routine of each day, it developed violently opposed opinions and, after irritating debate, usually adopted the wrong course. Here lies, in part at least, the explanation of its failure; and a fateful decision taken in June, 1527, in the second month of its existence, will serve strikingly to illustrate how the lack of reflective discipline operated to nullify the emotional resolution of the embattled citizens.

For the new Florentine government looking out over the Italian world, the salient fact was that it would have to reckon with an attack by Pope Clement VII, even though that attack was not imminent since Clement was living in the Castle of Sant' Angelo as a Spanish prisoner. Filled to overflowing with passionate resentment against the emperor, Clement would hesitate to come to terms with that ruler, even though the orthodox Charles, in sympathetic response to his profoundly orthodox subjects, might be disposed to smooth the path for a reconciliation by offering notable concessions. However, concessions no matter how liberal would not be able to conceal the pope's virtual subjection to the emperor; and before Clement would submit to this humiliation, he would have to be assured that there was no longer the slightest prospect of his rescue from Spanish clutches by the intervention of France. For France was his sole hope; only France, as matters stood, possessed even the potential power to challenge the emperor's ascendancy in Italy, spectacularly declared to the world by the recent terrible sack of Rome. While it was therefore inevitable that the pope should look to France, the fact stood out that he had thus far been ill served by that power. For, having been persuaded by King Francis I to join the league of Cognac of 1526, Clement had been left without support when the army of the duke of Bourbon singled him out for attack. Hardly less angry with the king, because of his broken promises, than with the emperor, Clement still clung to Paris in the hope of escaping the dictation of Charles. Following the monstrous insult offered the head of Christendom by his brutal imprisonment, a wave of indignation had swept through the whole Catholic world. Himself carried along by it, King Francis hastened to express his devotion to the papacy, coupling it with the assurance that an army about to be dispatched across the Alps was evidence that he was at last done with delay. In sum, dissuading the pope from coming to terms with the emperor, Francis offered the alternative of a vigorous renewal of the war to the end of bursting open the papal prison by force. Thus hotly importuned by representatives of both France and Spain, Clement acted as he had always done. His many calamities had not changed his character by an iota. He refused to commit himself to either side, and with the indecision and ambiguity that had become his second nature awaited developments.

As soon as a new campaign loomed between France and Spain the Florentine signory, exactly like the pope, was exposed to the solicitations of both combatants. The struggle between the two powers over the control of Italy had now been going on for over thirty years and there was no telling how much longer it would last. What was already plainly apparent, however, was that Italy had lost its independence and was being slowly ground to pieces between an upper and a nether millstone. Its best hope under the circumstances was the early cessation of the terrible grinding process by the decisive victory of one power or the other. It did not much matter which, since in either case the peninsula would fall under foreign direction. As no Italian state, and certainly not Florence, possessed enough strength to count in the result, from a strictly peninsular point of view it was immaterial with which power Florence would elect to stand. From the point of view of the preservation of the republican form of government, on the other hand, the choice was of capital importance. For, if Florence should have the good fortune to align itself with the victor, it might with some measure of assurance count on its government being left undisturbed, whereas, in case it fought on the losing side, it would unescapably have to submit to such constitutional changes as the victor might see fit to impose.

Examined in this light, the foreign issue before Florence in the late spring of 1527 hinged on the question of which side would win, France or Spain. Conceding that it was impossible to forecast the outcome with certainty, we may nevertheless aver that ever since the campaign of Don Gonsalvo of Cordova there had been a firmness in Spanish policy and a vigor in Spanish arms which indicated that the ultimate victory would go to Spain. The Gonfalonier Capponi himself inclined to this view and a number of hard-headed friends lent him their support. They therefore advocated the alliance with Spain, especially as in their opinion, if Clement ever submitted to the emperor, he would stipulate as his very first condition that Florence should again be subjected to the Medici. According to the gonfalonier the best measure with which to parry that prospective blow would be for Florence to anticipate the pope by concluding an alliance with the emperor without delay. This cool calculation roused the Francophiles to fury. They pointed to the long tradition of friendship between the kings of the line of Capet and the Arno commonwealth, receiving their strongest support in the altered circumstances of the town no longer from the great merchants, as had once been the case, but from the honorable trade folk who, in spite of the thirty years that had passed since Savonarola had been reduced to ashes by a tragic miscarriage of justice, still tenderly cherished his memory and his words. A central point of the dead prophet's preachment, it will be recalled, had been that the reforms he advocated would be effected under the French aegis. By continuing to ascribe this protective role to France the large Savonarolist element of the population permitted itself to be swayed by a misguided and unreasoning sentiment. Unfortunately it was strong enough to turn the scales. The Spanish party, headed by the gonfalonier himself, was overwhelmed by the French party dominated by Frateschi sentiments, and on June 22, 1527, Florence recommitted itself to the French league of Cognac by agreeing to contribute an army of four thousand foot and four hundred horse to the common cause.

The decision was not immediately disastrous. Stung by the papal reproaches, King Francis in the late summer of 1527 sent a large army into Italy under the command of the very competent Lautrec. In the course of a few months this enterprising general succeeded in gaining a dominant position throughout northern Italy. As had frequently happened before, the Imperialists, whose chronically depleted funds regularly compelled them to dismiss most of their troops as soon as a campaign was over and to leave the remainder unpaid, were not prepared for the French thrust and gave way at every point. Pushing his advantage, Lautrec in the spring of 1528 drove southward into the kingdom of Naples and was, to all appearances, on the verge of capturing this chief Spanish stronghold when an incalculable event occurred. The contemporary historians, who have recounted the tenacious duel between France and

Spain over the possession of Italy, convey a puzzled impression that fate or the gods, indistinguishable from fate, fought all along on the side of Spain. In view of what happened in 1528 to Lautrec with victory almost in his grasp the modern historian is tempted to agree. While the French were laying siege to the city of Naples, a pestilence visited their camp which swung its scythe among them till the stricken handful of soldiers that was left beat a panicky retreat. Surrounded by the enemy among the mountains, this remnant was obliged to lay down its arms (August) and the campaign was over.

Although King Francis had tried to revive the faith of his Italian adherents by means of Lautrec's expedition and although the Florentines had yielded to his persuasions, the pope had obstinately remained deaf to the French pleas. We left Clement a prisoner in the Castle of Sant' Angelo at the mercy of the emperor. So great throughout the Catholic world was the scandal of this confinement that, after some six months, Charles agreed (December, 1527) to release the Holy Father on the strength of a few shadowy, unfulfillable promises. Thereupon Clement had made his escape to Orvieto, where he was comparatively free from imperial supervision. By this time the new French action in his behalf was well under way and, although Clement accompanied it with his secret prayers, he had too recently been personally terrorized by the Spaniards to risk any other official stand save that of neutrality. For once luck was with him, for, when in the summer of 1528 the French invasion of Naples ended, as we have seen, with the total destruction of the French army, Clement did not again, as in 1527, draw down on his head the imperial avalanche. Sadly no doubt but wisely he concluded that no further help was to be expected from France and that the time was at hand to make the best bargain in his power with the triumphant emperor. Charles was far away in Spain and the negotiations were greatly hampered by this circumstance; also the imperial and papal positions were at first separated by a wide gap, which it required much patient correspondence to close. Nonetheless already by the autumn of 1528 it was clear to every intelligent observer that pope and emperor had taken the preliminary steps toward a settlement, the aim and substance of which, so far as the Emperor Charles was concerned, would be the pacification of Italy under his hegemony.

With the give-and-take inevitable when two parties draw up a contract, it was patent that the pope would insist on being paid for his acceptance of Spanish preponderance in Italy with important benefits. In the forefront of these, according to everyone who had any knowledge of Clement's character, would be the restoration of the Medici to their native city. So thoroughly was this understood on the Arno that, no sooner had the rumor of negotiations between Rome and Madrid gone abroad, than the Florentines became convinced that the crisis hitherto latent between Clement and themselves was about to burst into the open. The period of domestic quiet was therefore over. Of course it had never been more than a relative quiet and, such as it was, may be ascribed to Gonfalonier Capponi's resolve to hold to a middle course. Never from the first day of the restored republic had the clash of opinion among the citizens ceased. Many acts of violence, which Capponi was helpless to repress, had occurred in consequence of the periodic overflowing of the animosity of the anti-Medicean Arrabbiati. A much more effective curb of their insolence, at least for the time being, than the soft-treading gonfalonier was the pestilence which had swept Florence and Italy in the years 1527 and 1528. We have already noted how in the summer of the latter year it wiped out the French army which had invaded Naples. It visited Florence in both years, although it was more virulent in 1527 than on its return. The number of deaths in the city and suburbs from both visitations is given, let us hope with the usual exaggeration in these matters, at 30,000, approximately one-third of the population! The famous Black Death which had raged at Florence almost two hundred years before had not been much more destructive. It comes to us with something of a shock to learn that at the height of the Renaissance, when the Italians had been engaged for some generations in revising their medieval outlook, they had done nothing whatever to improve the monstrous hygienic conditions of their towns. We are obliged to conclude that abstract intellectual activity is one thing and social reform directed by scientific inquiry quite another thing. In any case the recovery of classical antiquity, the main aim of Renaissance humanism, does not seem either to have stimulated medical knowledge or to have promoted the cause of public health.

An incident which occurred during the harrowing Florentine pestilence is commemorated by an intriguing inscription still to be read over the entrance to the Palazzo Pubblico. This inscription solemnly declares that the Florentine people recognize no other king than Jesus Christ. Already in Savonarola's time this curious sentiment had received official sanction and its revival during Capponi's gonfalonierat proves how living the memory of the great Dominican still was. The pious Capponi himself was so strongly under its ban that on February 9, 1528, apparently on the spur of the moment he made a speech to the Grand Council on the need of the citizens in their present affliction to put their trust in God. He imitated the hortatory manner of Savonarola even to repeating the prophet's actual words, and at the climax of his appeal threw himself on his knees calling on Heaven to have mercy. Immediately the whole assembly did the same, and before the rapture subsided the motion to make Christ perpetual king had been offered and carried.[1]

The upshot of the republic's first year was so favorable to the moderate policy of the gonfalonier that on the expiration of his term he was re-elected to office (July 1, 1528). Immediately after this event the pestilence destroyed the French army under Lautrec, the pope and the emperor began the maneuvering which foreshadowed their reconciliation, and a justified alarm stole its way into the hearts of the Florentines. From the moment of their return to the republic they had recognized the necessity of providing for their defense by re-establishing the militia, which, Machiavelli's proudest achievement, had been

[1] A recent thoroughgoing study of the years treated in this chapter is by C. Roth, *The Last Florentine Republic.* London, 1925. The bibliography on pp. xi-xii lists the leading printed and documentary authorities. The contemporary historians, Guicciardini, Segni, Nardi, Nerli, and Pitti, by treating this period each from his particular angle, build up an effective composite picture. The crown in this group, however, undoubtedly goes to Varchi, whose presentation is at the same time comprehensive and penetrating. Among the printed sources the most important are the reports of the Venetian ambassador, Carlo Capello. They have been published by E. Albèri, *L'Italia nel Secolo Decimosesto.* Florence, 1858.

abolished on the restoration of the Medici. It would have been a deserved recognition of merit to have again put Machiavelli in charge as secretary of the governing committee, but he had forfeited that honor by his recent acceptance of service under Pope Clement. As suspect to the republicans of 1527 as he had been to the Medici in 1512, he once again experienced the bitterness of finding himself tossed aside as a useless tool. He did not have to grieve long at this new misfortune, for, after a brief illness, on June 22, 1527, he came to the end of his many tribulations. With his successors lacking his tireless initiative the reorganization of the militia proceeded at such a leisurely pace that very little had yet been done when the crisis of 1528 descended upon the town. For reasons already explained the original militia law applied only to the country residents, the peasantry. Excited by the threat of war, the young enthusiasts of liberty within the walls clamored to be armed in their turn; and under pressure from them in November, 1528, the momentous forward step was taken of putting arms once more into the hands of the citizens. Ranged in the traditional sixteen companies (*gonfaloni*), they reached a total of four thousand men, who took upon themselves the unfamiliar obligation to march and drill with a zeal which put heart in all that beheld them. As the peasants, already enrolled, could be brought at need to about ten thousand foot, the two militias together constituted a far from negligible force, always provided they could be filled with the stubborn spirit of combat. Nobody doubted, however, that for a successful defense hired professional troops could not be dispensed with, and hesitatingly, for action under Gonfalonier Capponi proceeded with the greatest deliberation, the hiring of mercenaries and the providing of funds for their pay were taken under consideration.

Among the numerous measures made necessary by the coming struggle the most pressing of all was the strengthening of the city walls and the addition of such improvements as were imposed by recent changes in the art of war and the more general use of artillery. Pope Clement himself, before his overthrow, had set up a commission to consider the problem presented by the walls in the light of these innovations. The most conspicuous member of the commission was none other than our old friend Machiavelli. On being thus again absorbed into the service of the state, the former chancellor had elaborated a plan for a thorough overhauling of the Florentine fortifications. To be sure, not very much had been done by the time the revolution of 1527 terminated Clement's rule and Machiavelli's commission. Nor did the situation experience any immediate improvement under the republic. It required the slowly developing crisis of 1528 to make the fortifications the order of the day, while tangible results did not put in an appearance till the election in January, 1529, to the board of works, called the Nine, of Michelangelo Buonarotti. Like many other artists of the age, Michelangelo was also an engineer and was appointed to the Nine not to honor a famous fellow-citizen but for strictly professional reasons. A few months later, in April, he was given sweeping authority as governor of the fortifications and as such, elaborated a scheme of defense, the main feature of which has survived to our day. He took the position that the most vulnerable section of the vast urban girdle of brick and stone lay on the left bank of the river and that indispensable to a successful resistance was the inclusion of the hill of San Miniato within the system of defense. Accordingly, the work of fortifying San Miniato was begun and had well advanced when the general of fortifications suddenly ran away. In this strange evasion we are confronted with an episode in the personal history of the great artist which, in spite of the ready apologies of his biographers, will always be a blot upon his record. Apparently the constitutionally timorous Michelangelo was swept off his feet and stampeded into flight by rumors of treason among his associates. After an absence of some weeks he happily recovered his mental balance and was permitted to return under a pardon from the government. His removal from his post did not cause any alteration in the program he had worked out. In point of fact work on the fortifications was greatly accelerated following the artist's flight and was conducted with such thoroughness and industry that, when in due time the siege befell, Florence proved impregnable to direct assault.

While much of the hesitation and delay connected with the measures of military preparation may be ascribed to the paralyzing cross-currents of opinion inevitable in a democratic society, the most important individual cause of the unsteady course pursued was the head of the state, the Gonfalonier Capponi. It was explicable and pardonable that he should wish to spare Florence the harrowing experience of a siege, and it was at least intelligible that as a middle-of-the-road politician he should attempt to come to a peaceful understanding with Pope Clement. Unquestionably it would have to be a very secret understanding, for the violent anti-Mediceans of the Grand Council, to whom he was under constant suspicion on account of his moderation, had passed a motion expressly forbidding him to conduct negotiations on his own account with Rome. When he did so just the same, and when in April, 1529, an accident disclosed his disobedience, a tremendous storm was precipitated which swept him out of office. His followers were just strong enough to cause his life to be spared. A successor was at once elected and inevitably, under the circumstances, it was the leader of the Arrabbiati opposition, Francesco Carducci. Francesco was the younger brother of Baldassare Carducci, the original Arrabbiati head; and when late in 1528 Baldassare was sent as the republic's ambassador to France, Francesco had inherited his brother's position. The new gonfalonier must have proved a disappointment to his more extreme adherents, for, while conducting his office with an admirable firmness, he was so far from submitting to the violent spirit of party that he proved an excellent head of the state.

Not till June 29, 1529, were the long-drawn-out negotiations between the pope and the emperor brought to a conclusion by a peace and alliance signed at Barcelona. It bristled with concessions to Clement having as their object the return to his control of the State of the Church and the republic of Florence. A notable article revealed Clement's determination to establish the bastard Alessandro in the city as the representative of his house; and Charles's support of the plan was guaranteed by his promise to give to Alessandro his illegitimate daughter, Margherita, to wife. A month later (August 5) the emperor crowned his program of Italian and European pacification with the peace of Cambray. This is the famous Ladies' peace, so called from the circumstance that it was negotiated by the mother of Francis I and the aunt of Charles V acting for their respective relatives. The only feature of the Cambray document that immediately concerns us is that Francis gave up his Italian claims, thereby accepting the Spanish control of the peninsula. He made his surrender, unquestionably with the usual mental reservations, because his repeated defeats in the field had stripped him of his power of resistance. Granting that at the moment no other course was open to him, we have nonetheless no difficulty in understanding the indignation of the Florentines, whom he duped with promises of help to the very day the negotiations were completed and whom, even after the peace was signed, he privately encouraged to resist the Spanish hegemony with promises of help. With this monstrous deception of the trusting republic by Francis I the age-old intimacy of the two states so long united by a common interest and a common emblem came to a disastrous conclusion.

The treaties negotiated by the emperor with King Francis and Pope Clement respectively having cleared the way for the pacification of Italy under his control, in the late summer of 1529 Charles came by sea to Genoa attended by a formidable army and acclaimed by an expectant population. From Genoa he proceeded by slow stages to Bologna, where he set up his court for many months, during which he patiently negotiated a settlement of the many issues still awaiting adjustment between himself and the various Italian governments and among the contentious governments themselves. As a large part in the settlement had been assigned to the pope, Clement, too, came to Bologna, where he abode in close and friendly communication with his late enemy. To mark the triumphant conclusion of Charles's intervention, he was, by the terms of his recent treaty with the pope, to receive the imperial crown at the hands of Clement. This culminating event took place on February 24, 1530, amidst scenes of unrivaled magnificence. Thus during the winter of 1529-30 pope and emperor were the ·cynosure of all eyes and Bologna to all intents the capital of Europe. We must keep constantly before our eyes the congress of potentates and princes conducted just across the Apennines from Florence, if we would appreciate the isolation and also the heroism of the republic stubbornly bent on independence. For, with Pope Clement and King Francis reconciled with Charles, the many small states of the peninsula had no choice but to make the best terms possible with the emperor and accept him as the arbiter of the Italian destinies. The last state to come to heel was Venice. The republic of St. Mark was the final hope of the republic of the Baptist for support in its dire necessity. Turning a deaf ear to the frantic appeals of its Italian sister, in December, 1529, Venice reached a satisfactory, if selfish, settlement with Charles. The abandonment of Florence was complete.

To avoid a war, regarding the outcome of which there could be no reasonable doubt, the republic sent not one but several embassies to Charles to plead for an amicable settlement. Faithful to the obligations of his treaty with the pope, the emperor consistently referred the negotiators to Clement, and with the utmost reluctance they consented at last to treat directly with their adversary. It was a concession as futile as it was humiliating. The pope insisted on the restoration of his house to its traditional position, and as the Florentine

government and people stood unbendingly by the restored republic the ex-
changes came to nothing. Reluctantly but unescapably the issue was referred
to a decision in the field, for which pope and emperor had been prepared
from the beginning. In the view of the two allies the war was the pope's war
to be conducted at the pope's expense with forces put at his disposal by the
emperor.

Owing to these hesitations and delays the papal war against Florence was
slow in getting under way, and when it started in the autumn of 1529 reduced
itself, in the main, to a single action, the siege of the city. A memorable feature
of the siege, essentially the only feature worth remembering, are the resolution and valor displayed by the beleaguered citizens. While intrusting their
defense, according to custom, to hired troops under the Perugian condottiere,
Malatesta Baglioni, they supported the action of the professional soldiers by
devoted service in the newly established militia. The commander of the besieg-
ing Imperialist host was the Prince of Orange. After a few preliminary maneu-
vers he paid tribute to the stalwart character of the defense which he encountered by recognizing his inability to take the city by storm. Thereupon he settled
down to reduce it to surrender by starvation. As the emperor's captain-general
had at his disposal a mobile field force two or three times as large as that of
the republic, he had met with no resistance on his pouring into Tuscany by
the upper Arno Valley and had been able to lead his army right up to the city
walls. The strategy adopted by the Florentines was to let the enemy exhaust
his strength in attacking the fortifications. A necessary corollary of this strategy,
however, was that the defenders would have to bend every effort to retain
command of the lower Arno Valley as far as Pisa to serve as a source of bread,
meat, and the other necessities of life.

Under these circumstances it became clear to the Prince of Orange that he
could not hope to force the city to its knees until he had cut it off from its
markets. Relatively large as his army was, he did not have enough troops
completely to encircle so considerable a town. He had therefore been obliged
to content himself with investing that part of Florence which lay on the left
bank of the Arno and to utilize such forces as he could spare to patrol the
highways of the right bank in order to intercept the food caravans directed to
the city. At the same time no opportunity was to be permitted to escape for
seizing the fortresses in the lower Arno basin which served the Florentines
as points of concentration and support. In this manner it came about that while
the campaign, as already said, reduced itself to a siege, the successful resistance
of the beleagured citizens depended on their keeping command of the fertile
country extending westward to the sea. All the really crucial actions of the
winter of 1529-30 turned about the effort of the Florentines to keep their grip
on this area. While in the face of the large Imperialist re-enforcements continually pouring into Tuscany from the north the defenders slowly but steadily lost ground, they offered a stout resistance, all the high moments of which
were due to a Florentine citizen, who in the daily skirmishes for control of the
highways rose to amazing heights of gallantry. This surprising and un-
heralded hero was Francesco Ferrucci. If the republic went down in a blaze
of glory, more than to the actual siege it owed this distinction to the

struggle for the possession of the open country carried on by this resourceful, vigorous partisan.[2]

It is a curious circumstance that Florence, from whose fertile womb there had, in the course of the ages, issued so many sons of the rarest worth in every conceivable field of human striving, had never given birth to a soldier, who by his deeds in her behalf had shed a special luster on her long and troubled military annals. In her very last phase she made amends for this lapse with Francesco Ferrucci. Son of an impoverished father of good family, Francesco was, like the average middle-class lad of the city, apprenticed at an early age to a commercial firm but developed such aversion for the work in office and warehouse that he broke away from it in uncontrollable revolt. His mind was set on adventure, and after many hazards he was, although not till after the death of Giovanni de' Medici, absorbed into the latter's famous *Bande Nere*. Giovanni, a captain of great renown in his day, was, as his name suffices to declare, of Florentine birth; but never in his condottiere career, cut short by an early death, did he have the good fortune to fight under the lily banner. Such soldier glory as was his is therefore of a strictly personal nature. At best only in a roundabout way may he be considered to figure in Florentine military history through the circumstance that from his Black Bands a fellow countryman, Francesco Ferrucci, learned the art of war, which with a devotion beyond praise he put at the service of his city.

When the investment of Florence began, the war committee of the Dieci resolved to make use of Francesco's talents by employing him in the open country and gave him the command of Empoli. This small fortified town on the Arno midway between Florence and Pisa and commanding the entrance to the Elsa Valley was absolutely pivotal in the system of defensive warfare devised by the Ten. Not only did Ferrucci hold Empoli against attack but he tirelessly scoured the countryside for enemy raiders and kept an uninterrupted stream of supplies flowing to the beleaguered city. As the winter wore on his task became more and more difficult. The ever-increasing forces of the Prince of Orange took town after town in the disputed western area till the noose around the Florentine throat became steadily more galling. When still another body of Imperialists began to move in from the south, from the direction of Siena, with the plan of occupying the Elsa Valley, Ferrucci resolved to show them his teeth. The most audacious single action of his whole career was his recapture in April, 1530, of the hill town of Volterra. Although he fought like a lion to hold Volterra against repeated assaults, his long-drawn-out operations at a peripheral point of the scene of action proved a misfortune, for, taking advantage of his absence, an Imperialist troop surrounded and stormed the centrally located Empoli. The event occurred in June and was nothing short of decisive. The supplies which had been gradually failing during the preceding months now ceased entirely, and Florence was faced with that cruelest of alternatives, surrender or starvation. Not yet ready for surrender, the Dieci elaborated a last desperate plan of rescue, in which the liberator role was as-

---

[2] On the occasion of an anniversary celebration for Francesco Ferrucci a valuable collection of sources dealing with his career was published under the title: *Francesco Ferruccio e la Guerra di Firenze del 1529-30*. Florence, 1889.

signed to the native son whose brilliant defense of the open country had
aroused an unbounded enthusiasm in every Florentine bosom.

The plan of the Ten was for Ferrucci to attempt with the forces at his command to come to the relief of Florence, which, now completely surrounded,
was drawing a more anguished breath with every revolving hour. Although
to his fine military intelligence the proposal must have appeared wildly uto-
pian, he accepted it with the born soldier's invariable preference for action in
every paralyzing crisis. Moving first from Volterra to Pisa, he swung thence
northeastward in a wide circle along the foothills of the Apennines toward
Pistoia in the hope of sifting unobserved through the enemy lines and reaching the city. Informed of the enterprise by intercepted letters, the Prince of
Orange made all the arrangements necessary to smother his adversary before
he should arrive at his goal. Accordingly, when, on August 3, Ferrucci with
three thousand foot and three hundred horse tried to pass through the village
of Gavinana in the mountains above Pistoia, he was met by several converging
columns of Imperialists. One of the first victims of the ensuing ferocious
struggle was the Prince of Orange himself. Several times was Gavinana taken
and lost by the Florentines, but in the end the immense numerical superiority
of the Imperialists decided the issue and the few surviving members of Ferrucci's expeditionary force were surrounded and captured. Among them was
the wounded and exhausted leader of the troop. On being brought before a
Neapolitan captain in the imperial employ he was set upon and murdered
by this tiger in human form, in whom war had destroyed every sentiment of
kindliness and mercy.

When the news of Gavinana reached Florence, the whole citizen body with
the exception of a small band of frenzied young republicans knew that there
was now no escape from surrender. The Florentine captain-general, Malatesta
Baglioni, had been coming to this same opinion for some time past. He was
a professional soldier as well as a foreigner and had never viewed the situation
with the unbalanced enthusiasm of a hot, patriotic partisan. On first taking it
on himself during the mounting difficulties of the spring of 1530 cautiously to
advise the government to open negotiations with the Prince of Orange he had
found some support among the leaders. It was hurriedly withdrawn as soon as
the fiery young Jacobins of the piazza learned what was in the wind and staged
a demonstration against the traitor element in the signory. The result was that
Malatesta took the bit between his teeth and some time in either June or July
entered into relations with the Prince of Orange on his own account. In any
case he was in secret touch with his opponent before Francesco Ferrucci's
great stroke was carried out; and it is not unlikely, although unproved, that
the general of the Florentines contributed to the extinction of the Red Lily's
last hope of rescue by stipulating not to attack the Imperialist camp while
Orange was engaged in the man-hunt that ended with his own death at Gavinana, but also with that of his heroic opponent. By his independent negotiations
the Perugian condottiere became a traitor, and no argument can free him from
that blot, not even the argument that in his soldier's judgment Florence had
arrived at the end of its tether and that, taken, as the next step, by the enemy
at the point of the sword, it would be subjected to the nameless horrors of a

sack. Following the blow of Gavinana, Malatesta pressed his negotiations with the successor of Orange more urgently than ever and gradually forced the distraught Florentine government to submit to his authority. The leading official of the city was no longer the radical Francesco Carducci. On January 1, 1530, he had been succeeded as gonfalonier of Justice by Raffaelo Girolami, who owed his election to the strong moderate opinion reasserting itself in the Grand Council. The gonfalonier as well as the other leading officials, such as the priors and the Ten, continued to make a public display of reluctance, but in their hearts they were far more willing to negotiate than they were prepared to admit in the face of the loudly declared determination of a handful of overwrought youths rather than surrender to let Florence be destroyed and its people be buried under the ruins. However, with negotiations once under way the sentiment in favor of peace quickly swelled to such irresistible proportions that the opposition was silenced and a treaty signed which brought the siege to a close.

The peace, signed on August 12, was not an abject surrender. It carried a number of palliative, face-saving articles, as, for instance, that the city submitted not to the pope but to the emperor, who within a stipulated number of months, on the understanding that its liberty should be preserved, was to determine the future form of its government. The truly determinative articles, however, declared that the imprisoned Medicean partisans should be set free and that the numerous exiled followers of the former ruling family should be permitted to return. If any Florentine was so blind to the realities of politics as not to know what these concessions signified he was destined to be promptly disillusioned. Only a week after the fateful peace the citizens, still dazed by the recent disaster, were summoned to a parlamentum—the old, old trick!— and under the usual duress granted supreme power (balìa) to twelve fellow-townsmen, all of them proved and tested Mediceans. Thereafter no Florentine with even the rudiments of an intelligence could doubt that on August 12 the republic had perished to be succeeded by the re-established regime of the Medici.

When in the years following the return of the Medici the disappointed and embittered citizens, who, whether strict republicans or not, stood together as enemies of tyranny, reviewed the tremendous crisis of the siege, they inclined with steadily increasing assurance to ascribe the disastrous conclusion to the treason of Malatesta Baglioni. With the patriotic bias unescapable in times of war they finally went so far as to persuade themselves they would have triumphed save for their false leader, and with mounting animosity they charged him with having diabolically plotted against the city he was supposed to serve from the very day he accepted his command. With all but complete unanimity the native-born historians of Florence of all periods have incorporated this viewpoint in their books. But it will not stand up under investigation. The judicial present-day writer will not even be prepared to concede that the late, eleventh-hour treason of Malastesta, which he accepts as proved, did more than slightly to accelerate the surrender which had become a military necessity. Florence fell not on account of Malatesta's betrayal, or Ferrucci's death, or of any other single incident of the siege, but because the completely isolated republic could not sustain itself in the long run against the overwhelm-ing strength of the two allied world-powers, the pope and the emperor.

While this is the cold verdict of historical logic, we cannot thus impersonally conclude our story of the agony of Florence. With our generation still as with our earliest ancestors the heart is enthroned above the calculating intelligence; and if we still peruse with eagerness the records of the past, it is, in spite of the sage counsel of the philosophers, not so much to discover the safest course to be followed among the mazes of life as to lift up our spirit with examples of devotion to a great cause and with instances of a courage that does not flinch before sacrifice and death. Florence defended its independence against over-whelming odds because it believed that independence was a jewel beyond price. It is a relatively unimportant matter that for independence there were substi-tuted in the minds of many the more elastic and ambiguous concepts of liberty and democracy. Undoubtedly these, too, elicited a genuine enthusiasm; but what leaped as a spark from heart to heart until a whole people was kindled to a self-forgetful blaze was independence. It was to retain the dignity of free political agents that the Florentines fought their hazardous fight; and while such a fight has always been accounted good in itself, what matters much more than its universally conceded goodness is how those who undertake it meet the challenge they invite. We have learned in these pages that the Florentines stood their ground undauntedly on the walls and in the field; that they cheerfully yielded up their money and possessions; that they un-complainingly supported intolerable privations of body and of soul. In the light of such heroism their defeat loses its temporal sting, and we, its awed spectators, experience that elevation of spirit which permits us to see the siege of 1530 as the fitting end of a community, which had always lived adventurously and which owed its amazing achievements to its resolute pur-suit during five centuries of an obstinate dream of self-realization.

XXX. The Cinquecento: Climax and Disintegration of Florentine Culture

B Y THE beginning of the sixteenth century the cultural autonomy of Florence was drawing to a close. Not even in the fourteenth and fifteenth centuries, when its heart-beat was most vigorous, had Florentine culture been other than an offshoot of the ruling culture of the occident, within which it was embraced and with which it was in substantial accord. Like the culture of Venice, Padua, Siena, Ferrara, and like the similar cultures of the towns of the other European countries, it owed its existence to the social order of the Middle Ages with its innumerable independent political units. When these tiny polities began to be assembled into the large national wholes characteristic of the new, the modern social order, an inevitable consequence was that broad national cultures superseded the many provincial varieties that had germinated within the range of the European occident. To be sure, the political unification of Italy lagged considerably and, as we have seen, with tragic consequences behind that of France and Spain; but Italian cultural unification was another matter and by the sixteenth century had acquired a measure of coherence approximately equal to that of its politically more fortunate rivals. With the unconsciousness as well as with the irresistibleness of movements in the mental realm the separate cultures of the Italian towns were in the course of the cinquecento molded into a general Italian form. The cinquecento is therefore the last phase of a specifically Florentine culture. And like every final transformation it is both a culmination and a decline, that is to say, while marking the coming to a peak of forces which had been locally operative for many generations past, it also signifies their enfeeblement and disappearance. This double character of the cinquecento culture of our city is so important that it is indispensable to call attention to it at the outset. And since by about the year 1530, when the republic expired, the process by which the municipal culture was absorbed into the national culture was approaching completion, a second preliminary consideration may not be overlooked. It is that, culturally considered, the Florentine cinquecento embraces not the full century but only the first three decades, and that even its extreme manifestations hardly extend beyond the mid-century.

Vigorously as Florentine cultural expression had set in from about the middle of the dugento, it showed steady and cumulative development only in the Fine Arts, whereas in literature and thought the record was broken and uneven. Although we have already considered this phenomenon, it is

497

proper that in this concluding review we should bring it once more into focus. Sprung from an indefinable inner urge, architecture, sculpture, and painting were subjected to extraneous influences in the course of their development which they managed to assimilate without impairment of the creative energy of their practitioners, while literature and thought, on the contrary, were overwhelmed from without until they were repeatedly threatened with extinction. Let us begin with literature and again take note that its first great figure was Dante. With its very first manifestation therefore literature reached its apex and from Dante's time may be considered to have been in uninterrupted decline. True, the decline was gradual since Dante was followed by Petrarch and Boccaccio and these two poets and writers boasted an original talent enabling them to strike out on important literary paths of their own. With Boccaccio's death at the end of the third quarter of the trecento Florentine literary creativeness came to a temporary close. Of course writing as such did not cease, especially of *novelle* or short stories, but with the single exception of Sachetti, a story-teller of an admirable raciness of speech and matter, the literature of the imagination remained negligible for a hundred years. Then in the age of the magnificent Lorenzo there was a revival championed by Lorenzo himself; but it would be a manifest exaggeration to attribute either to Lorenzo's work or to that of Poliziano much more than the fluency and elegance of a high cultivation. To bring the work of the latter group into comparison with that of the three giants of the trecento is to see it at once as the artificial production which, in the main, it was.

After Lorenzo, in the cinquecento, to which this chapter is devoted, there was only very sporadic achievement. Fortunately, imaginative literature attained a fresh and memorable utterance in other Italian centers, such as Ferrara and Naples, and therefore went marching on as a manifestation of national life, but the specifically Florentine contribution of this period may be set down as unimportant. The appearance of a few comedies by Machiavelli, among them the pungent *Mandragola,* does not alter this judgment. Refusing to adorn the *Mandragola* with the stolen finery of Plautus and Terence, Machiavelli developed his theme from its own inner necessities and sustained it with a dialogue which is the very echo of life. No less true is the statement that the play, an appalling parade of obscenities, reveals local manners so corrupt that we experience a sudden rush of sympathy with Savonarola's reforming zeal. Its considerable merits notwithstanding, the *Mandragola* proved an erratic flare, a mere will-o'-the-wisp, and founded a theater neither in Florence nor in Italy.[1]

An explanation of this aridity has already been attempted by referring it

---

[1] It see.ms impossible to pass over without mention a work which, although written in the third quarter of the sixteenth century, by virtue of its content and its spirit is inseparable from the age treated in this chapter. I am referring to the *Autobiography* of the artist, Benvenuto Cellini (1500-1571). It unfolds a picture of the writer's period which for directness of speech, spiciness of detail, and general animation is without example. Although in the universalized quality of his art as well as in the innumerable dislocations of his life Cellini definitely marks the replacement of a specifically Florentine by a general Italian culture, he is in his writing a Florentine of Florentines, who, owing to his having been born a man of the people, had the good fortune to escape the cramping effects of a humanistic education. The *Autobiography* is one of the most fascinating works of its kind within the whole range of European literature.

to the revival of classical antiquity with its imposed imitation of famous models and its exaltation of a dead over the living language of the people. That may not, however, be the whole story. If we cast a glance at other culture groups of the European occident, we encounter instances in which the creative impulse spent itself in a single meteoric flash, and other and even more numerous instances in which it exhibited a specializing tendency in favor of a particular form of expression. We are herewith broaching the mystery presented by the diversity and sporadic nature of regional and national traits. In spite of the impressive display made by Dante, Petrarch, and Boccaccio, it may well be that the Florentines were chiefly gifted in the direction of the Fine Arts; and it may also be that, originally gifted in literature, they quickly exhausted this strain. With the mere mention of this puzzling matter we are content to let it fall. It brings us to a *terra incognita,* for the critical penetration of which neither biology nor psychology have as yet succeeded in providing us with a reliable road map.

Since, regardless of the emotional origin of great literature, it cannot live without thought, we have already in earlier chapters gone into the intellectual history of Florence. With Petrarch there came the great change which we have called humanism and which unfortunately was narrowed by its literary champions to the single purpose of reviving classical antiquity. Its most valuable outcome was scholarship, which, aiming at improved texts and accurate knowledge, developed norms of criticism basic to the whole subsequent structure of human knowledge. Engaged in uncovering buried antiquity, the humanists came also upon the treasure of classical philosophy. From this discovery sprang the Platonic academy, which, although native to Florence, developed sufficient force to spread its influence throughout the dominion of Italian speech. However, the academy died with its promoters of the Laurentian age, and the brief reign of philosophy on the Arno came to an end. Philosophy itself, it need hardly be said, did not die; but it was left to other centers than Florence to free it from both its medieval and its classical leading-strings and by a fresh examination of the facts of experience to establish it on definitely modern ground.

There remains a field of literary expression embraced within the dominion of *belles lettres,* in which the Florentine cinquecento attained a high originality and distinction. It is the field of history, of which something has already been said in the Introduction. Its leading figures are Machiavelli and Guicciardini, but around these central luminaries there circles a stately body of satellites, each of which boasts an individual energy imposing consideration and respect. These lesser but still important historians are Nerli, Vettori, Segni, Nardi, Giannotti, and Varchi. The fragmentary history of the last phase of the Florentine democracy left by Jacopo Pitti is hardly of sufficient merit to win him a place among this group, although, as the warm champion of a lost cause, he will always command a partisan following. Regard for the proportions of this book makes it impossible to consider these minor authors individually. We must content ourselves with the sweeping statement that, while each in writing the history of his native city maintained a point of view imposed by his personal circumstances and experience, they one and all lifted themselves to the level of critical historians by subjecting their material to an independent examination. Considered as a group, together of course with Machiavelli and Guicciardini, they signify the arrival of a new, a modern variety of historiography.[2]

Bracketed as Niccolò Machiavelli (1469–1527) and Francesco Guicciardini (1482–1540) usually are, they represent such diametrically opposed approaches to history that an examination of their method tempts us almost to lose sight of their resemblances. Resemblances, however, there are, of which the most important derive from the circumstance that, Florentine contemporaries and functionaries, they went through an identical political experience. Their striking differences spring from the possession by each of an independent personality which moved him to react to his experience in a very particular way. Wounded and heart-sore over the sorrows of Italy, Machiavelli diligently searched the pages of the past for a remedy of her ills. The record was far from clear, but pondering it through long years, he finally concluded that if he should succeed in reducing the confusing multiplicity of events to compact generalizations, he might arrive at a cure and prove the physician and savior of his country. This search for general rules or principles makes the Florentine secretary not so much a historian as a political scientist. While at the command of the Cardinal de' Medici (the later Pope Clement VII) he wrote a history, the *Istorie Fiorentine,* if the truth be told it is, in spite of a certain spice of comment inseparable from a mind so vigorous as Machiavelli's, a rather stiff and lifeless affair. For convincing evidence of Machiavelli's genius we must go not to his narrative but to his reflective works, *The Discourses* (*Discorsi sopra la Prima Deca di Tito Livio*), *The Art of War,* and *The Prince.* They constitute in their sum the first fruits of a political science of a distinctly modern inspiration. Guicciardini, on the other hand, distrusted generalizations and frankly expressed his skepticism in regard to those set forth by his friend Niccolò. What chiefly struck Guicciardini about life and history was a variety and mutability so overwhelming that it was a hopeless undertaking to reduce the chaos to an ordered system. Frankly rejecting therefore Machiavelli's procedure of assembling the mass of instances into classes, he was content, like his classical predecessors whom he admired but did not copy, to be a narrative historian, albeit one equipped with sharp critical powers developed by wide reading and, immeasurably more valuable, by a practical, first-hand knowledge of the motivating forces of states and politicians.

We learned in an earlier chapter that it was only on being excluded from the public service that Machiavelli took up as a solace and a pastime the speculative considerations of government on which his fame mainly rests. However, at bottom much more of a practical than of a speculative turn of mind, he was less interested in government in general than in finding an answer to the specific question imposed on him by his own troubled experi-

[2] For an estimate of the significance of these men within the whole movement of European historiography see E. Fueter, *Geschichte der neueren Historiographie.* Munich, 1911. A French translation of Fueter appeared in 1914. See also J. A. Symonds, *Renaissance in Italy* ("Age of the Despots," chaps. V and VI; "Italian Literature," Vol. II, chap. XVI); M. Lupo Gentile, *Studi sulla Storiografia Fiorentina alla Corte di Cosimo I de' Medici.* Pisa, 1905.

ence: what kind of a government will end the ills of Florence and of Italy? This should always be kept in mind, as it constitutes his defense against the accusing voices which have never ceased to be raised against him. Without any doubt whatever the indignation which he has aroused is to a large measure due to a misunderstanding. Aligning Machiavelli with such earlier speculative thinkers on the state as Aristotle and St. Thomas Aquinas, his critics have represented the Florentine as engaged in formulating general rules applicable to human societies throughout the ages, whereas his sole concern was Florence and Italy at the particular moment of time when he, Machiavelli, was alive. While he desired to impress his readers with his wide knowledge and sound scholarship, he never for a moment disguised the fact that he was following an intensely practical quest. On this account he did not feel any obligation to preface his reflections with an exposition of the theories of his predecessors in the governmental field. Indeed he did not so much as mention either Aristotle or Aquinas, possibly for the reason that he had not read them, more probably because in his view they had no relevance for his investigation. This was particularly true of St. Thomas. Machiavelli belonged to the group of humanistic pagans who had made a clean escape from the world of Christian ideology. The Thomist view that state and church were divinely authorized institutions collaborating in the great task of helping the individual to attain salvation was to his mind too contemptible even to debate. The only guidance he accepted for his problem, save his own experience, was the practice of that great state of antiquity, Rome, for which, as he rejoicingly took note, religion was nothing more than an instrument of popular control, and which completely subordinated the whole citizen body to the solely conceivable purpose of a state, which is authority and power.

In *The Discourses* Machiavelli's plan reduces itself to an analysis of Roman policy to the end of determining the laws of the republic's successful rise to world-mastery; and in *The Art of War,* wherein he compares ancient Roman with recent Italian practice, he arrives at the conclusion that states cannot be maintained in power and honor except by the citizens themselves transformed into soldiers, that is, by what we would now call universal military service. With these two works *The Prince* forms a single unit of speculative thought, springing from the same preconceptions and unfolding according to the same method. However, while *The Discourses* and *The Art of War* have been accepted as excellent examples of a novel manner of interrogating history and have given no offense, *The Prince,* as already said, created a moral scandal which is as lively in the world today as it was when the work first appeared.

For the Italy of Machiavelli's time there was no escape from enslavement to foreign conquerors except through national unity, and there was no way of attaining national unity except through a prince or tyrant. This is the central doctrine underlying *The Prince,* and it is so unanswerable that it has not been and cannot be successfully disputed. Consequently this has not been the feature on which the critics have sharpened their indignation. They sharpened it in his time and have continued to sharpen it to our own day on Machiavelli's further position that the hoped-for super-tyrant, who will crush the many

small existing tyrants in order to fuse their states into a united Italy, is justified to resort to force, violence, and fraud to attain his end. In the writer's
eyes the nation-state was the political form to which western Europe was at
that precise moment manifestly tending. This being true, it was imperative
for Italy to follow the path which France, Spain, and England had already
taken; and in the winning for Italy of its sovereignty, than which there was
nothing greater in heaven above or on the earth below, the desiderated tyrant
was invited to balk at no measure calculated to help him reach his goal.

Since this is obviously not the place to discuss the truth and falseness, the
strength and weakness of Machiavelli's powerfully argued political tenets,
we shall content ourselves with making three statements which may serve
to explain why *The Prince* has remained a living document down to the
present generation. In the first place the treatise is the boldest and rudest
challenge of the specific ideology of Christianity which has ever been issued.
Seeing that Machiavelli did not even honor this ideology with a rebuttal, he
may have thought in his pagan self-assurance that it was dead. Should we
concede that he may have had some ground for this assumption so far as
Renaissance Italy was concerned, we should still have to insist that he was
most egregiously in error in regard to the rest of Europe. To prove the point
it will suffice to recall that at the very time that Machiavelli propounded his
doctrine of the state as power, Erasmus set forth a diametrically opposed and
strictly pacifist view in his *Plea of Peace* and his *Education of a Christian Prince*
and Sir Thomas More projected in his *Utopia* an ideal society patterned on
apostolic Christianity. Far more alive in his own time than our pagan Florentine was ready to admit, Christian ideology has maintained a vigorous existence through the centuries and has carried on a relentless war against him.
The second statement deals with the demonstrable realities underlying the
sovereign state, which was emerging in Machiavelli's day and which has held
the European stage ever since. This sovereign state is and has been a law to
itself: it dwells in a moral void. Its aim is power and it acts, on the whole,
exactly as Machiavelli affirms, with sole regard to its own welfare. Every
scientifically inspired study of the behavior pattern of the great powers during the four centuries that have passed since Machiavelli wrote must agree
that his description is astonishingly close to the facts. The third and last statement has to do not with Machiavelli's thought but with his person. While
maintaining outwardly the cold manner of a chemist engaged in laboratory
operations, he is sustained throughout his studies by a suppressed patriotic
emotion. At the close of *The Prince* it exceptionally bursts forth with the
vehemence of a volcano. Even today, four centuries after it was written, no
one can read this flaming peroration without a quickened pulse beat. To
modern Italians, therefore, not only is the Florentine secretary the man who
nursed the sacred concept *patria* at the moment when the very word became
taboo and the *patria* itself was locked in a Spanish prison, but he is also the
prophet of a national delivery, which after three hundred years of waiting
leveled the prison walls with the ground and enabled Italy once more to take
her place among the nations.

Guicciardini's reputation, which for many generations burned as brightly as that of his friend and fellow-citizen, has since the beginning of the nine-teenth century suffered a considerable eclipse, owing chiefly to the improved technique and enlarged scope of history in our day. As his youthful *Storia Fiorentina,* a lively presentation of penetrating judgment, was not published till 1859, Guicciardini owed his fame to a single work, the *Storia d'Italia,* which was the ripe product of his experience and which, following its first appearance shortly after his death, went through many editions. In this history he treats of Italy between 1492 and 1534, which is to say, during the period of enslavement prepared for it by France and Spain. With the same unwavering hand as Machiavelli's he brushed aside the hollow public pre-tensions of statesmen to disclose the hidden kernel of their thought. Stripped finally of every illusion and no longer believing in the reality of anything but self-interest, he was left without so much as a trace of what even to the critics of Machiavelli constitutes the latter's saving grace: his patriotic ardor and romantic hope. Not only is the *Storia d'Italia* the first thoroughly realistic history of modern times, but it has the further merit of being the first clear exposition of the European political system as it emerged in Guicciardini's time and has continued without a break to the present day.

At the exact middle of the sixteenth century there appeared a history which testifies to that ever-widening genetic curiosity destined to become the per-haps leading trait of the modern mind. I am referring to the *Vite (Lives) de' piu eccellenti Pittori, Scultori, ed Architetti* by Giorgio Vasari (1511–71). It may be taken as a sign that the creative urge had passed its peak that Vasari, a fine critical historian but a less than mediocre painter, felt moved to assemble the record of a magnificent burst of expression while the evidence was still relatively fresh and crowded on his attention wherever he went in Italy. Although the minute criticism of the last one hundred years has corrected in-numerable small errors of fact of which the author was guilty, it has not suc-ceeded in pushing him from his pedestal. Vasari is still the one indispensable guide to the unfolding of the Fine Arts in Italy between Cimabue and Michel-angelo. His *Lives* are a classic in the same sense in which Machiavelli's *Prince* and Cellini's *Autobiography* are classics and very few other literary works, which are not poetry. If the *Lives* have achieved this permanence, they owe it to their author's zealous scholarship, sympathetic understanding, and literary artistry, a rarely occurring combination of gifts but regularly present when a work qualifying as the history of any human movement or interest achieves a measure of immortality.

In turning to the Fine Arts we shall not follow, as we have done for the earlier periods, the separate development of architecture, sculpture, and paint-ing. For a general sketch like this the procedure becomes unprofitable in view of the fact that the energy giving all three of these arts their cinquecento character issued in so overwhelming a measure from two men that an ex-amination of their contribution is the best conceivable introduction to the new phase of expression. The two men, who carried Florentine art to its apogee, and just as certainly initiated its decline, were Leonardo da Vinci (1452–1519) and Michelangelo Buonarroti (1475–1564). Of course they did not appear in the stark isolation that this setting forth of their names would suggest. The practitioners of the arts were probably numerically as strong in the cinquecento as in any earlier period, but, overborne by the two geniuses in their midst, they were drawn from their individual orbits into the dependence of declared satellites. Not improbably a decline, if not in the number, at least in the quality of the individuals electing to follow the arts, had already set in by the turn of the century. How else account for the fact that, except in that most Florentine of arts, in painting, there was a decided dearth of men for whom we may claim a genuinely original gift? Where are the architects of the period? Where is the sculptor whom it is not absurd as much as to mention in the same breath with Michelangelo? In painting, on the other hand, we undeniably meet with a number of artists, who, regardless of the influence over them of the two titans, managed to maintain a fairly independent status. Outstanding among such would be Fra Bartolommeo (1475-1517), Andrea del Sarto (1486-1531), Pontormo (1494-1556), and Bronzino (1502-72). Let us salute them respectfully as we pass them by, intent upon our plan of making acquaintance with the age through the work of its two key-men.

While Leonardo interested himself in all the arts, including music, his influence on his contemporaries made itself felt chiefly in the realm of painting. The reason is simple: he *was* a painter. True as this statement is in the realm of objective fact, it tells us nothing of the spiritual significance of Leonardo, the real clue to his wide sway. His puzzling personality must already have begun to disclose itself when, at the age of thirteen, he entered on his apprenticeship in the *bottega* of Verrocchio. Under this excellent master he absorbed the aims and traditions of the Florentine school of painting and prepared himself to make that magnificent contribution to the art which we shall presently examine. However, presented as a free gift from the gods with a restless, inquiring spirit, he found it impossible to restrict himself to the role of an obedient apprentice. Not only was he compelled to subject the teaching of Verrocchio to a critical examination but he found himself driven by an instinctive and irresistible force to go behind every finished work of his master to the infinite forms of life from which Verrocchio and all his contemporaries as well, according to their own statement, derived their inspiration.

Whether Leonardo experimented with painting, or, as was traditional with every ambitious Florentine craftsman, with one or all of the other arts, he regularly found himself in the end brought face to face with nature. He was still a young man when the infinite variety of natural phenomena took possession of his mind. As through the advancing years he saturated himself with this bewildering multiplicity, he became convinced that it represented nothing more than the surface play of hidden principles, by the discovery of which the whole apparently chaotic universe would fall into an ordered system. Starting his observations with the art with which he had embarked on life and gradually extending them to all the cognate arts, he found himself in the end drawn into the realm of science and broadened his studies till they embraced anatomy, physiology, mathematics, astronomy, physics, botany, zoölogy, and mechanical invention. To keep this crowding wealth of material from getting out of hand he adopted the practice of recording it in the form of notes in private diaries, which, scattered at his death but partially recovered in our day, furnish us with the indispensable means of becoming acquainted with the incomparable energy of his inquiring spirit. It goes to show that, after all, it was painting that served as the point of departure for his studies, that only in this field did he sufficiently systematize his observations to enable a later editor to produce a continuous document, the admirable *Treatise on Painting*. In this work Leonardo frequently packs the central purpose animating him into pithy aphorisms. Such are: "Practice must always be founded on sound theory"; and again, "My works are the issue of pure and simple experience, which is the only true mistress." [3]

These statements, which are borne to us down the ages with the very quality of the master's voice, deserve the most careful consideration. While formulated in regard to painting, they affirm guiding principles laid down by Leonardo for his procedure in all his studies. And they tell us in no uncertain manner that, after having begun life as an artist rejoicing in his senses and trusting to a blind inner urge, he passed into the world of experimentation and reflection and became engrossed with the task of reducing experience, his only mistress, to the laws by which it might be comprehended and controlled. Before he had reached middle age his interest in the arts had dwindled till they had become no more than a function of his all-embracing thought. He became in essence a scientist, one of the greatest the world has ever seen, although less by reason of his measurable achievements than by his formulation of an effective scientific method and by his prophetic hints of discoveries, such as the geologic ages of the earth, and of mechanical inventions, such as the submarine and the airplane. In the eyes of the living generation, the mind of which has received its special imprint from the vast scientific development since the cinquecento, Leonardo looms as a pathfinder and forerunner. While no one will begrudge him his belated fame, the historian of the arts may be permitted to point out that he did not achieve his scientific eminence without a severe loss. Concerned more and more with theory and abstractions, he inevitably gave himself less and less to practice. The time came when he dawdled painfully over the few paintings that he was still willing to undertake and which in the end he usually abandoned in a half-finished state. In the last ten years of his life he did nothing at all but think and dream. The paralysis of the will, as most of his biographers have called this curious lethargy, has been treated by them as the "problem" of the master's later years, but it is hardly so inexplicable as they would have us believe. Leonardo's glory as an artist lies without any question in the adjustment which he effected of an amazing natural endowment, essentially irrational, to the demands of a supreme intelligence. He marks a sum-

---

[3] Quoted from pages 15 and 18 of the *Literary Works of Leonardo da Vinci Compiled and Edited from Original Documents* by J. P. Richter. 2 vols. London, 1883. These writings, together of course with Leonardo's paintings examined directly or in reproduction, constitute the best approach to the master. Among the innumerable literary guides the reader is referred to Vasari and to the moderns already mentioned, such as Berenson and Mather. No one can afford to miss the appreciation of the master by Walter Pater in his volume *The Renaissance*. Leonardo's drawings have received an incomparable analysis and are in part magnificently reproduced by Berenson in his *Drawings of the Florentine Painters*. 2 folio vols. London, 1903.

mit in the arts because he achieved a balance such as has been only rarely brought about between the rational and irrational elements present in all great and sustained expression. Then slowly, as his reason mastered his instincts, the balance was disturbed and the fire at the core of his being was banked and subdued. There is no evidence that he ever analyzed his case or regretted the multiplying inhibitions that palsied his hand. He went, like all of us, his fated way, in the course of which the scientist in him, become too strong, devoured the artist.

Having dealt with the total man, we now turn to his particular achievement in the art of painting. Its indubitable magnitude is enhanced by the relatively small number of his extant works. Many a respectable modern painter, Renoir for instance, probably turned out more pictures in an average year than stand to Leonardo's total credit. The earliest evidence of his hand is the angel at the left of Verrocchio's picture of the Baptism of Christ in the Uffizi gallery. In the same gallery is an Annunciation, in which, designed in the main by Verrocchio, he had a much larger share than in the earlier work by supplying the gracious Gabriel and the characteristic Tuscan landscape. Finally, the Uffizi has also the large unfinished Adoration of the Magi, by which Leonardo disclosed (1481) for the first time his new principles of composition. His other leading works are the Last Supper at Milan; the Virgin of the Rocks, the Virgin with St. Anne and the Infant Jesus, the Mona Lisa— these three at Paris.

Beginning with the very first work of the young apprentice, the angel of Verrocchio's Baptism, we catch the challenge of his genius. It flashes more effectively still from the Annunciation and, excitedly increasing in the Adoration of the Magi, reaches its peak in the works at Milan and at Paris. Let us consider what these creations in their totality bring us that is new, and let our attention turn first to the matter of technique. Leonardo has caught and improved on Masaccio's chiaroscuro, the infinitely subtle transitions from light to dark. A logical consequence of this addiction to tonal finesse was that he sacrificed the frank color planes of the Florentine tradition and threw his influence on the side of the new oil technique recently imported from northern Europe, since only oil was able to render the *sfumature,* the imperceptible gradations of light and shade at which he aimed. His second novelty is that he turned away from the simple-hearted realism of the quattrocento which had made the pictures of the period an enchanting mirror of the throbbing life of town and country. The reflective bent of Leonardo, which prompted him to look for uniformity behind the endless individualizations of nature, sent him on the quest for the ideal man and woman never actually to be met with but definitely implied in all existing human forms. The search for the type, a passionate and characteristic pursuit of classical art, has always involved the attempt to create as a counterpart to our fleeting mundane existence a super-realm of permanence, serenity, and beauty. While Leonardo never wholly abandoned the traditional native realism, of which there is still abundant evidence in the rich characterization of the apostles in so relatively late a work as the Last Supper, we already get a glimpse of the artist's sublimated vision in that very first angel of his in Verrocchio's Baptism. That delicate celestial

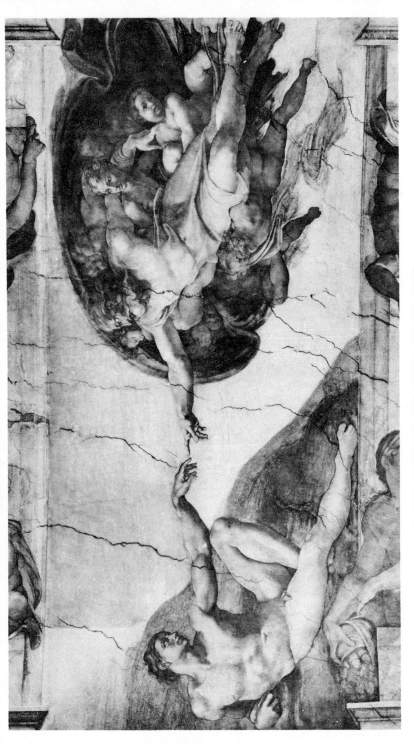

MICHELANGELO. CREATION OF ADAM. FRESCO IN THE SISTINE CHAPEL, ROME

Left: MICHELANGELO. JEREMIAH. SISTINE CHAPEL. ROME. *Right:* MICHEL-
ANGELO. DELPHIC SIBYL. SISTINE CHAPEL. ROME

MICHELANGELO. THE MEDICI CHAPEL OR NEW SACRISTY, SHOWING THE MONU-
MENT TO LORENZO DE' MEDICI

MICHELANGELO. MONUMENT TO GIULIANO DE'
MEDICI. MEDICI CHAPEL

visitor, completely out of tune with the harsh literalness of the rest of the composition, carries the unmistakable Leonardesque note. Struck in every subsequent creation with increasing clearness, it achieved its perfection in the unmatched loveliness of the women and children of the Paris altar pieces.

The third important contribution of the master is a new style of composition. In his view the quattrocentists, his immediate predecessors, had been guilty of cluttering their pictures with too much distracting detail. However, the greater compactness at which he aimed was not to be won by a simple process of elimination. Master of mathematics that he had become, he recognized that every good picture that has ever been painted possessed a geometrical substructure, whether consciously or unconsciously introduced by the artist. As a reflective, highly analytical painter Leonardo isolated this tectonic core as part of that theory which, according to his already quoted dictum, was a prerequisite of effective practice. The result was the triangle which, subtly broken and varied with straight and curved lines, constitutes his fundamental pictorial pattern. If his contemporaries detected a monumentality in Leonardo's works which even Masaccio had not attained and which swept them off their feet, it derived from the firm tectonic configuration of his designs.

Simple courtesy demands that we do not pass the Mona Lisa by without paying brief homage to her impassioned reticence. She is Leonardo's one indubitable work of portraiture. In view of the fact that the task which in this case he assigned himself was the likeness of a particular woman, he was obliged somewhat to disguise his preference for the type. The lady was the wife of a Florentine citizen, Francesco del Giocondo, who would not have been the successful business man he was if he had been satisfied with a feminine abstraction. Nevertheless Leonardo's philosophic passion for the universal over the particular showed itself clearly in his representing his sitter withdrawn into the world of dreams, where she is no longer reached by the earth and its affairs. Her fleeting, inscrutable smile reveals a soul which, having done with doubt and fear, is rapturously at peace with God. Only mystics will respond pleasurably to this pictured transfiguration; but all lovers alike of good painting will linger over and be thrilled by the artist's consummate chiaroscuro, which in this instance at least, far from being just another technical conquest, serves as the vehicle of a wholly novel kind of psychological portraiture.

As fascinating and unfathomable in his character of genius as Leonardo, Michelangelo Buonarroti does not present the same personal problem by reason of an attempted conquest of experience by an advance along too many and often contradictory lines. At no time of his long life did he desire to be anything other than an artist; and if, in addition to sculpture, which he preferred, he also practiced painting and architecture, he did no more in this than follow an honored Florentine tradition and, what is still more important, regardless of his medium of expression, he unfailingly brought to bear upon it the same compact and unified personality. Articled as a lad to the painter, Domenico Ghirlandaio, he broke away from his master after a few years to take up the study of sculpture among the collection of ancient and modern masterpieces assembled by Lorenzo the Magnificent in his garden hard by the monastery of San Marco. Lorenzo himself encouraged the lad to follow his natural bent by providing him with bed and board in the Medici palace. Under no other guidance than his own unerring instinct he absorbed the Florentine tradition as manifested in its most rugged representatives, Giotto, Masaccio, Donatello, Pollaiuolo, and Signorelli. Their continuous problem had been the mastery of the human form at rest or in the endlessly varied movements of which it is capable. Beginning with Masaccio, they had come to closer grips with the body by stripping it of its vestments and studying it in the state of nature. Michelangelo, the latecomer, enjoyed the advantage of starting where his predecessors had left off. With a masterful will that leveled every barrier he concentrated on the naked human form till by tireless drawing from models and with the aid of anatomical studies conducted with the eagerness of a surgical apprentice, he acquired a mastery of this instrument such as we can unhesitatingly pronounce unique in the history of the arts. The nude and nothing but the nude became for Michelangelo the medium of artistic expression.[4]

His draughtmanship and plastic modeling directed exclusively at the human body constitute the technical basis of Michelangelo's art. The art itself sprang from the mighty spirit which surged within his small, ill-favored body and clamored for expression. Conceding that this spirit was his very own marked with the uniqueness of every great soul from the dawn of history, still we cannot but be struck with the character stamped upon it by his age, by the Renaissance. This period which in his youth was approaching its meridian had steeped a succession of Italian generations in thoughts and plans of subjugation of the earth. It had stimulated the human will to a veritable riot of competition in all the fields of action, and it had glorified the essentially anti-Christian emotions, without the support of which the fierce mundane struggle could not have been sustained. Chanting the praises of *virtù,* the quality of undaunted manliness, the leading spokesmen of the age had summed up the medieval ideal of conduct as *bontà* (goodness) and had dismissed it contemptuously from consideration. It was the thoughts and ideas of his age which constituted the inner life of Michelangelo and which to have brought to their fullest and most concentrated expression is the explanation of his fame. In his view the human body, that most flexible of instruments, was the supreme medium for manifesting power in its material and, above all, in its innumerable and far more important spiritual aspects. It is an arresting circumstance that Buonarroti was personally a rather timorous man, whose consistent prescription for meeting a physical hazard was to run away from it. It is also true that he never even in play assumed the pagan religious attitude of so many of his cultivated contemporaries but remained throughout his life a true Christian believer and an earnest communicant of the Catholic church. There is a contradiction here between the man and the artist, which is not unex-

[4] In addition to such guides as Vasari, Berenson, Mather, the reader will find it advantageous to consult on Michelangelo one or another of the many biographies. Such are J. A. Symonds, *Michelangelo Buonarroti.* 2 vols. New York, 1893; C. Holroyd, *Michelangelo Buonarroti.* London, 1903. The Holroyd volume contains in translation the valuable contemporary life by Condivi, for which Michelangelo himself provided the material.

ampled and which it is not our business to resolve. It suffices for us, concerned exclusively with the Florentine's significance as an artist, that he used his marvelous technical mastery over the human body to render and exalt the resolution, the courage, the dignity, and the majesty of man under the ruling secular dispensation of the Renaissance.

Although his earliest works already have the touch of genius, we would not expect and do not get his full message at the start. He is engaged in finding himself in a group of works which we may assemble under the rubric of the Young Michelangelo. Among these are the Drunken Bacchus in the Museo Nazionale of Florence, the Bruges Madonna, and the Pietà at Rome. While exhibiting an excellent command of form, they indicate a lingering enslavement to the past and to the model. Already, however, it is apparent that the young sculptor desired to break away from the naturalist Florentine tradition and arrive at a more generalized version of the human body which would eliminate the distractions produced by a parade of individual idiosyncrasies. Since in the David (1504) he made in this respect a great forward stride, we may accept it as marking the transition from his first to his second phase. The David is a colossal figure representing the young shepherd at the moment of suspense preceding the discharge of the stone with which he will slay Goliath. He fixes his opponent with a level gaze; his whole body is taut with a stored power at the point of explosive release. While the David is a finely modeled body dramatically aglow with the idea that dominates it, it does not yet give us the entirely liberated Michelangelo. The head, hands, and feet are too large for the trunk and proclaim a carefully particularized and almost repulsively gawky adolescent, probably imposed on the sculptor by the actual youth who served him as a model.

It was not till the year 1508, when the artist undertook the frescos of the ceiling of the Sistine chapel at Rome that he achieved his rounded and matured style. Overruling Michelangelo's plea that painting was not his trade, Julius II, as lordly and, in his way, as typical a Renaissance figure as the artist, commanded that he slough his sculptor's skin to serve the pleasure of a pope. Amazing as is the fact that Buonarroti could thus transform himself, we accept his versatility without astonishment before the breath-taking miracle of this work. Besides, as, searching the slightly arched chapel vault, we become more familiar with the plan and its details, we have no difficulty in persuading ourselves that, although here is fresco painting even on the technical side of rarest excellence, it is the handiwork of one who has taught himself to think exclusively in plastic terms and who rigorously eschews pictorial effect. Not by a hair's breadth did Michelangelo in accepting an uncongenial medium depart from the sculptural quality imposed upon him by his genius. So complicated and elaborate is the design of this ceiling that it defies compact description. We shall have to content ourselves with few and distressingly futile words. The main, the central section consists of a series of nine scenes picturing the successive acts of Creation, the Fall of Adam, and the Flood. Around them runs a frame of twelve Prophets and Sibyls, who in the leaden days after the Fall nursed the faith of a Messiah destined to redeem mankind. The majesty of the Creator in his successive evocations of the world and its inhabitants, the relaxed supple vigor of Adam extending his hand to receive the divine spark, the massive dignity of the twelve heralds of redemption overcame and bewildered the spectators when the ceiling was uncovered. A new word, *terribilità,* was coined to express the awe which invaded the beholder before this unrivaled grandeur. Nor did the scenes from Genesis in their figured frame complete the undertaking. Beyond the inner there was a sweeping outer frame of lesser prophets and human ancestors of Christ reaching down to the arched window heads. Each single form of the vast composition was individually conceived and masterfully interwoven with the central panels into a varied and harmonious pattern. A census has revealed the presence in this vast picture book of three hundred and forty-three figures in every conceivable posture, each figure animated with that magic vigor by which art affirms itself to be not the imitator but the lord and the enhancer of life.

The only other work of Michelangelo's comparable to this masterpiece is the New Sacristy of San Lorenzo at Florence with the Medici monuments. This work, too, was evoked at the behest of a pope, the unhappy Clement VII, to whose honor it should always be remembered that, a man of unfixed and wavering purpose, he never wavered in his attachment to his great countryman's genius. Michelangelo's assignment was to construct the New Sacristy as a mausoleum or chapel to be filled with sculptured memorials of the more recent Medici dead. The building had been completed and the sculptural monuments were under way when the expulsion of the Medici in 1527 put an end to a labor, which was afterward never more than half-heartedly resumed. While what we now have is only a part of the original project, still it is for the lovers of Michelangelo the greatest shrine of art within the compass of his native city.

The chapel itself is a structure which shows that Buonarroti, working as an architect, reduced the classical principles revived by Brunelleschi to a greater precision and applied them with a greater freedom. By these innovations, according to Vasari, he prepared the way for the last or High Renaissance phase of this art, of which the cupola of St. Peter's at Rome, the work of Michelangelo's old age, is the finest single example. The New Sacristy is a medium-sized, rectangular structure crowned by a dome. Its inner walls constitute a handsome Renaissance decoration indented with numerous niches of a classical design. Had all these niches been filled with statues, as was originally planned, a most painful overcrowding would have been the result. It was probably not unfortunate that Michelangelo did not carry the work beyond the figures which commemorate the two princes, the duke of Nemours (Giuliano de' Medici) and the duke of Urbino (Lorenzo de' Medici). The two statues occupy opposite, elevated niches behind their respective sarcophagi, which rest upon the floor. On each sarcophagus repose two allegorical figures, one male the other female. They are known traditionally as Dawn and Twilight and Day and Night, and the most suggestive hint as to their significance was dropped by Michelangelo himself. Considered together, he is reported to have said, they represent "Time who consumes all things." Each prince with the tomb and its recumbent figures at his feet constitutes a composition employing the plastic idiom so magnificently realized for the first time in the Sistine chapel. Unalterably sure now of his purpose, the artist flatly refused to undertake portrait statues of the two dukes. With very little truth to fact he represented these rather insignificant Medici as warriors, and then, elaborating this concept, differentiated them respectively as the active and the thinking type of soldier. It is Giuliano who is the man of action, for his left leg, drawn back, shows that he is on the point of rising to issue a command, while Lorenzo, his chin dropped into his left hand and his face shadowed by his helmet, is brooding over problems which, vaster than war, plumb the depths of life itself. Every even fleeting consideration reveals the two princes as allegories, exactly like the male and female figures reclining on the tombs. So potent is this generalizing art and so unfathomable, let us add, is its secret that the two monumental compositions completely blot out for the beholder this multifold and confusing world to transport him on the wings of the imagination to a realm of beauty and permanence, which for Michelangelo, as for all thinkers of his mystic temper, is both the cradle and the goal of man.

It remains to justify an earlier remark to the effect that if Florentine art came to its efflorescence in Leonardo and Michelangelo, they too prepared the way for its decline. In this connection what we must never lose from mind is the subjugation these two titans effected of the contemporary practitioners of the arts. So complete a conquest as they made imposes the thought that the artistic vitality of the population was no longer what it had been. The followers of all the arts alike fell under the spell of the two magicians and, gathering around their works, searched them for the secret of the power with which they seemed to strike dumb whoever beheld them. To such an investigation by overawed admirers certain elements of a purely technical nature would not be slow to disclose themselves. It would, for example, be clear that Leonardo's chiaroscuro made for an intriguing mystery, and that his compositions owed their compactness to their tectonic, their triangular pattern. In the case of Michelangelo the *terribilità*, which prostrated the overwhelmed spectator, plainly emanated from his nudes monumentally conceived and violently agitated.[5]

The enumerated features lent themselves, one and all, to imitation. Industriously applied by sculptors and painters, they would give birth to a period of expression completely dominated by the recognizable outward characteristics of the two masters. It need hardly be expressly said, however, that a work composed on this copy-book recipe is bound to lack the vital spark. We recognize it at once as a piece of pretentious exhibitionism and turn away from it in disgust. Michelangelo in particular proved direct poison for the succeeding generation, which aped his lofty style and transformed it into a vulgar mannerism. The nudes of his followers tended to become bigger and bigger, their muscles more bulging, their movement more vehement till what emerged on canvas or in marble was a travesty utterly bare of meaning. Vasari, the excellent historian but execrable artist, is a fair illustration of the general degradation. He was the favorite painter of the new Medici lord of Florence, the grand duke Cosimo I, and not content to cover the walls of the great council chamber

[5] For an excellent analysis of the formal elements in the art of the two masters, so skimpily treated in this summary, see H. Woelfflin, *The Art of the Italian Renaissance*. New York, 1903.

of the Palazzo Pubblico with a series of hollow rhetorical compositions, he spilled a second series in even madder welter over the inner surface of Brunelleschi's cupola. In Vasari's own eyes he was with these empty declamations obediently following in the footsteps of Michelangelo, whom he idolized. Flying the flag of either Michelangelo or Leonardo or of both, the Florentine artists of the second half of the cinquecento plunged violently to destruction; but only by a prejudiced and too narrowly technical attack of the problem will the two leaders be made responsible for the disaster. Certainly the historically informed critic is bound to take another and a larger view. For him the problem of art is part of the general problem of the rise and fall of peoples, and in attempting to understand this tidal or, perhaps more truly, cyclic movement, he refuses to study it in isolation from the social, economic, and political situation. He must therefore insist on taking account of the sum of the influences operating in the Florentine area, and in order fully to understand Florence he must not fail to embrace all Italy in his consideration. Now the decline so manifest throughout Italy in the Fine Arts in the second half of the sixteenth century was at that same time overtaking every department of human activity. An ever-thickening fog was descending on the Italian cultural scene and blotting it from view; but as this disaster is a general and, in the main, a political event, which considerably transcends the history of Florentine art, we shall reserve consideration of it to our concluding pages.

Epilogue: The Great Lethargy

WHEN after the ever-memorable affirmation of their will to remain the masters of their destiny, the resolution of the Florentines was broken by the irresistible might of the two greatest lords of Europe, the pope and the emperor, it was clear that the city would become the prize of Clement VII in accordance with the terms of his alliance with his great secular rival. By making formal submission on August 12, 1530, to the emperor the city hoped to escape the noose that had been prepared for it, but the hope was one of those vain illusions to which the defeated have ever been prone to cling. A few days after the capitulation, on August 20, a parliament, held under the eyes of the victorious troops, conceded extraordinary power to a committee of Medicean partisans to reform the state. On that day and by that act was inaugurated the absentee rule of Clement VII; and its first measure was the extortion from his local enemies of the money promised by the treaty to the victorious troops and necessary to bring about their departure from the territory their savage forays had reduced to the extreme of misery. Fast on this measure there followed a long succession of similarly vengeful acts. In consequence the safeguards accorded in the treaty were canceled, the leading figures in the late uprising punished by exile, imprisonment, or death, and the terrorized citizens reduced to the abject docility which would enable the pope to lay such a yoke upon them as they should never again be strong enough to shake off.

After the unprecedented humiliations to which, since his mounting the chair of St. Peter, Clement had been subjected both at Rome and at Florence, he was prepared to proceed with a certain caution and to take one step at a time in order not unduly to imperil his renewed possession of his native town. Above all, for the present at least he was resolved to do nothing calculated to disturb his harmonious relations with Charles V, without whose co-operation he would not again have laid his hands upon Florence. As his representative on the Arno and as future lord of the Florentine dominion, he had fixed upon the youthful Alessandro; and on his first plotting with Charles in the treaty of Barcelona (1529) to reduce Florence to submission, he had already revealed his intention by having the emperor formally pledge to Alessandro as his bride Charles's illegitimate daughter, Margaret, although she was not yet of marriageable age. It will not be necessary to indicate all the steps by which the way was smoothed for Alessandro's assumption of power. Not till the summer of 1531, on July 5 to be precise, did the young man enter the city, dispatched thither with the blessings of his prospective father-in-law and fortified by the charter, whereby the imperial overlord, in accordance with the power granted him by the articles of capitulation, regulated the government of Florence. The document declared Alessandro and his heirs after him to be the lawful heads of the state; however, by permitting the traditional constitution to remain in operation it conspicuously failed to provide against a repetition of the two previous risings against Medicean rule. In the eyes of Clement this was an intolerable concession to his opponents. He was in poor health and, in expectation of his early death, focused with fanatical intensity on achieving through the exercise of the vast power of the papacy, if nothing else within the wide range of his mental vision, at least the establishment in perpetuity of his family in Florence. Accordingly he resolved to sweep the old constitution, which after the frequent tinkering it had experienced was, if the truth be told, a rubbishy assortment of ruins, onto the ash-heap and to make an entirely new start. In conformity with orders sent by him from Rome, on April 27, 1532, the old constitution with its familiar and cherished executive of priors and gonfalonier was declared abolished and the state entrusted to Alessandro as hereditary duke exercising his power in connection with three bodies, to wit, a council of Two Hundred, a senate of Forty-eight, and an inner administrative committee of Four. In strict fact these bodies were, one and all, no more than window-dressing intended to conceal from a people still clinging to its dream of freedom that they had at last succumbed to that long threatening specter, *il governo d'un solo*. The republic had been definitely and, as it turned out, finally superseded by a monarchy, and young Alessandro was master and duke of Florence.

In spite of his illegitimate birth and his repulsive negroid appearance, the young duke at first won a certain amount of favor by seriously devoting himself to his duties. So rapidly did he consolidate his position that even the death in 1534 of his exalted sponsor, Clement VII, did not impair his hold on the state. Before long, however, his head was turned by his new eminence and he became the object of a very general aversion by engaging in indecent orgies and indulging an unbridled lust. Consequently, when on the night of January 5, 1537, he was murdered in his bed by his relative, Lorenzino de' Medici, not a single Florentine experienced even a passing regret. As he was the last male member of the older Medicean line, the succession to the duchy now passed automatically to the younger line, which descended from Lorenzo, the younger son of old Giovanni di Bicci.[1] In point of fact the murderer of Alessandro, young Lorenzino, was Alessandro's next of kin; but as he had made himself impossible by his deed and, furthermore, had sought safety in precipitate flight, the succession was claimed by Cosimo, the most immediately available male of the younger line. Cosimo was the son of the famous soldier, Giovanni delle Bande Nere, whose career had been cut short by death in battle at the early age of twenty-eight. Had there been an effective republican sentiment still to be found in Florence, the occasion of Alessandro's sudden removal

---

[1] See genealogical tree at end of this chapter.

might have been utilized to put an end to the young and as yet precarious regime of tyranny. As not so much as a single voice made itself heard in protest against Cosimo's assumption of power, the son of the condottiere encountered no difficulty in mounting the throne that had been vacated by Alessandro's murder.

The new duke was not yet eighteen years of age. He was a tall, vigorous youth, expert in every form of athletic exercise, handsome to look upon, of a penetrating intelligence, and prepared to give his energies ungrudgingly to the obligations of his office. In short, he was the kind of man whom Florence, become a tyranny, required if the tyranny was to be transformed into an established monarchical form of government. Cosimo reigned from 1537 to 1574 and in that period so thoroughly reorganized the state that at his death it presented itself to view in the character which it substantially retained for two centuries, retained in fact till the great changes precipitated throughout Europe by the French Revolution. He, the second duke, and not Alessandro, the first duke, is the true founder of the dynasty. If we agree, as agree we must, that the atmosphere in which republics thrive was no longer to be encountered in the cinquecento, and that not only in Italy but everywhere in Europe the stage was set for the advent of the absolute monarchy, we cannot deny that Cosimo is a notable political figure. The numerous Florentine exiles, victims of the catastrophe of 1530 and therefore champions of the republican idea, regarded him with an understandable detestation. They assiduously spread slanderous stories about him by which they so successfully blackened his character in the court of public opinion that he is still very generally held to have been one of the most sinister figures of his age. Let it be conceded at once that, engaged during a long reign in establishing his rule upon unshakable foundations, he committed many a hideous excess against his enemies. Similar excesses can be brought home to every sovereign of the period intent on the same kind of work, the statement being as true of the kings of such great states as Spain, France, and England as it is true of the smaller lords of the Lilliputian subdivisions of Germany and Italy. Within narrow Tuscan limits Cosimo is the "Prince," whom Machiavelli in his day attempted to wrest by prayer from the reluctant gods. If Cosimo was not able to operate on a national scale, as Machiavelli would have had his "Prince" do, that was not Cosimo's fault but the result of peninsular conditions reaching far back into the past. It is not likely that a student of the Renaissance acquainted with the forces operating in the field of political history will fail to accept him as an effective example of the tyrant type current in his age. To a striking degree, moreover, he exhibited the most characteristic traits of the outstanding rulers of his day. He relied chiefly on himself for counsel, was taciturn and sphinx-like; and while reasonably accessible to his subjects, especially of the lower orders, he practiced a cold aristocratic aloofness and made no effort to found his rule on a specious popularity. Conceding that Cosimo neither in his individual capacity nor as the representative of a new type of absolute sovereign is capable of eliciting a warm enthusiasm, we may yet attribute to him such a combination of qualities of will and mind that we cannot withhold from him a measure of sincere, if cold, respect.[2]

To put Duke Cosimo's achievement in a nut-shell he consolidated his state to a notable degree both within and without. The republic of Florence had never been anything other than a victorious town, powerful by reason of its population, wealth, and unrivaled energy, lording it over lesser towns, castles, and villages which by gradual stages had been reduced to obedience. By Cosimo's legislation Florentine citizenship was extended to the whole state; the ancient distinction between major and minor gilds was suppressed, as was indeed the far more fundamental distinction between gildsmen who enjoyed political rights and non-gildsmen who did not enjoy them; in short, the whole population was systematically reduced to an indistinguishable mass of subjects under a single master. This summary statement should serve to make clear that Cosimo envisaged not Florence but Tuscany as his inheritance. This same Tuscan outlook is also the key to his foreign policy. So long as the republic of Siena maintained a separate existence in southern Tuscany, his own state was, in Cosimo's eyes, no better than a torso. Firmly resolved to round off his dominion by the acquisition of Siena he adopted the only policy calculated to bring him success. This was to attach himself closely and unswervingly to that power, Spain, whose Italian hegemony had become the determining factor in the general peninsular situation. With the patience of a hunter stalking a deer, he bided his time, and on the occasion of a new war, in which France once again challenged the Spanish ascendancy and in which Siena, ever given to ill-considered, headstrong action, sided with France, the duke's help was welcomed by Emperor Charles V with open arms. As a result, when in the year 1555 Siena was captured after a ferocious and memorable siege, Cosimo could put forth an excellent claim to it as his share of the common spoils. On his taking over the Sienese state the duke, whose reputation as a competent autocrat had steadily mounted ever since his accession, was widely looked upon as the leading prince of Italy. He was therefore not succumbing to an inordinate ambition when he determined to mark his increased dignity and power by adopting a new title. In the year 1569 he proclaimed himself grand duke of Tuscany. By that act he swept from the public stage the last few properties recalling the old Florentine republic, which, having long lost the power to rouse men to action, now definitely took its place in the mausoleum dedicated to the memories of the past.

In earlier times than ours, when life moved at a more deliberate pace and boasted a greater dignity, it was customary for historians to mark the passing of the state which has engaged their attention with a solemn funeral oration, wherein they attempted to gather into a final estimate the manifold achievements of the polity which they had followed through its appointed cycle. Quite apart from the changed manners of our day which would make such a performance ludicrous, a review of the achievements of Florence coupled with an effort to define its place in the movements of European thought and life would

---

[2] The many contemporary historians, Varchi, Segni, Nardi, and Nerli deserve to be heard on the subject of Cosimo. The best modern presentation of Cosimo and the state he founded is by A. Reumont, *Geschichte Toscanas*. 2 vols. Gotha, 1876-77. A recent biography is by C. Booth, *Cosimo I Duke of Florence*. Cambridge, 1921.

be to squeeze into a dry summary the animated story, to which the many hundred pages of this book have not sufficed to do justice. We shall content ourselves therefore with a few words concerned with the significance for Tuscan and Italian history in general of the disappearance of the Florentine republic. The writer has not concealed his recognition of the considerable accomplishment of Duke Cosimo in reshaping the broken administrative mechanism that had come into his hands into a monarchical unit which succeeded in fitting itself into the ruling European system of his day. But he is sharply indisposed to leave his readers with the impression that he regards the grand duchy of Tuscany as marking in any other than a purely formal sense a continuation of the republic to which it succeeded. In his view the republic expired with the heroic spasm culminating in the siege of 1530; and if it did not again revive, that was because the exceptional energies that had sustained the citizens for a span of four amazing centuries had during recent generations gradually diminished until with the famous siege they were finally and tragically dispersed. The magnificent Florentine will-to-power, around which the history of the Red Lily revolves as around its axis, can with arguments of an undeniable plausibility be ascribed to the pressure of external conditions calculable as "forces," such as the geographical situation of the town in respect of the communal revolution and the consequent economic stimulations which pricked the citizens to an unwonted daring. But that would very decisively not be the whole story. In the record of the Florentines there clearly is something akin to what, vaguely enough, we call genius when manifested by an individual. Genius falls where it chooses to fall; it is given and taken away. Nobody earnestly contemplating the demise of the republic can come to any other conclusion than that its peculiar genius or, if a less symbolical term is preferred, the historical energies of the citizens were by that catastrophe extinguished. Of course the extinction did not occur with anything like the dramatic suddenness suggested by our statement. It was a gradual process which had unquestionably set in some generations before 1530 and which even with the establishment of the duchy was not complete, as the single name of Galileo, mathematician, physicist, and astronomer, will suffice to prove. Substantially, however, the statement is true that in the year 1530 the spirit or genius or soul of Florence— call it what you will—took its departure. The unfathomed event is reflected in the uncertain terms employed to describe it. Physically the town survived, has indeed survived to this day, but as a cultural manifestation it had reached the end of the trail.

And yet, after admitting the presence of an incalculable factor in the fall of this state, its historian, prompted to defend the rational and systematic character of his studies, cannot but insist on submitting the issue to an analysis. The insistence becomes unescapable in the present instance, since the growth and expansion of Florence has through many chapters and with abundant detail been referred to a complex of forces, political, economic, social, religious, and intellectual, which have been carefully identified and which never for a moment ceased to operate. The judgment may be ventured that the incidence of these various forces was most favorable to Florence in the fourteenth and early fifteenth centuries, and that consequently this period marks the culmination, the indisputable heyday of the Arno community. A scrutiny of these same determinative agencies will disclose, beginning approximately with the rise of the Medici, a gradual shift in their volume and direction, with the result that Florence was progressively deprived of the advantages hitherto enjoyed and subjected to disadvantages of a cumulative vigor. Although scattered reference has already been had to these increasing handicaps, it is proper that the many circumstances revealing how Florence, originally so greatly favored and exalted by fortune, sank to the level of fortune's step-child, should be assembled into a co-ordinated picture.

The material prosperity of Florence, which rested mainly on the two pillars of its banking facilities and the trade in woolen cloth financed by its bankers, probably reached its highest level in the first half of the fourteenth century. The ability of the Florentines to sell their cloth profitably in all the markets of the world and particularly in France, Flanders, and England resulted from the cheapening of costs through the adoption of a capitalistic form of production and from an improved product due to the special skills developed by the local artisans. Inevitably these advantages disappeared in measure as competitors imitated the industrial organization of the Arno merchants and copied and in some cases even improved on the original Florentine techniques. By the fifteenth century the home production of the northern countries had already taken such a development that, had not the sons of the Baptist made a quick adjustment to the altered situation, they would with very little delay have seen the end of their material power. Still splendidly elastic at that time, they found a substitute for the vanishing woolen markets of the north by gaining admission for their goods to the markets of the Levant, while at the same time they tapped a fresh source of prosperity by calling into life a new industry, the manufacture of silk. However, in the course of the sixteenth century they were once again checkmated. On the one hand, France, from of old a leading economic dependency of the Arno city, developed an infant silk industry of its own; on the other hand, the woolen industries of Flanders, France, and England, already long escaped from their swaddling clothes, pushed their emancipation from Florentine production still further by the adoption of a high tariff policy. Unscalable tariff walls completed the rout which the successful imitation of Florentine business methods had begun.

If we now add to these blows the economic revolution precipitated by the Portuguese discovery of a sea-route to Asia and by the Spanish discovery of the western hemisphere, the main factors in the economic decline of Florence are before us. The situation is so entirely familiar to everyone that it would be tiresome to rehearse it in detail. With Asia and the Americas opened to exploitation western civilization was launched on a new era of an all but unbounded horizon. It followed that Europe, which for many centuries had contentedly spent its energies upon the Mediterranean, swung about, and turning its back on this ancient sea, faced toward the Atlantic. At the same time, as chance would have it, the Atlantic powers, Spain, France, and England, succeeded in reorganizing themselves into compact monarchies and, thus fortified, they prepared to appropriate the trade and all the many other advantages which the voyages of discovery had made accessible. The conversion of the republic of Florence into a grand duchy of Tuscany may not improperly be interpreted as an attempt to keep abreast of the contemporary and compelling movement of political consolidation. But that so feeble a state as the grand duchy could operate with effectiveness on the enlarged stage of the world and enter into rivalry with the Atlantic powers for the great Atlantic prizes was not to be thought of.

Since men do not live by bread alone there are other than geographico-economic reasons for the cinquecento Florentine and, let us add, the concomitant Italian decline. Humanism, still so extravagantly celebrated in many quarters in our day, had proved to be a very doubtful benefit to the self-styled heirs of Rome ever since Petrarch and his collaborators had given the movement the narrowly circumscribed character of a revival of antiquity. In its final sixteenth-century metamorphosis this Petrarchan humanism took the form of a command to its followers to imitate as slavishly as possible the letters and arts of the ancients. What this signified in the way of systematically cultivating a sterility which a laughably pretentious façade served to disclose rather than to conceal has been briefly expounded in the preceding chapter. We are asserting what cannot be successfully challenged when we declare that it was the arid imitative classicism of the cinquecento which first laid a disturbing palsy on the Italian spirit. But that the classical inhibition became an enduring paralysis followed from the impact of a movement of an entirely different nature. I am referring to the Counter Reformation. It is well known that the Counter Reformation first gathered strength in Spain and that its gradual subjugation of Italy was a consequence of the Spanish political hegemony, with the main stages of which we have become familiar. Developing into a movement fiercely repressive of the free exercise of the human mind, the Counter Reformation fashioned to its use in such institutions as the Inquisition and the Order of the Jesuits a set of instruments with which it was able, first, to check and, finally, to stifle the fiery initiative of the Italian spirit. With the second half of the sixteenth century the breath of that spirit became steadily more feeble until the whole nation quietly subsided into a kind of winter sleep. While there continued to take place here and there splendid individual manifestations of that creativeness with which this so highly endowed people had projected itself into the story of western civilization, taken as a whole the nation exhibited multiplying symptoms of a steadily advancing mortal lethargy. We may sum up the arresting event in the words with which the Italians themselves have long since formulated their national tragedy: Italy entered the prison of Spain and the Counter Reformation and had the key turned on its spirit for over two hundred years.

A history of Florence cannot fittingly close on a note of lethargy and death. To be sure, the republic, the concern of this book, died, as we have seen, and has had its end duly recorded. But from the physical corruption of the Florentine state the great achievements of that state, products of the not equally corruptible mind, have been largely immune. These mental achievements belong to every field of human endeavor, to government, justice, trade, industry, finance and, notably, far more notably, to those highest ranges of the spirit where literature and art bring forth their golden fruit. In the great works of the imagination handed down to us from the past of the human race we of to-day still recognize, as have all the generations who have gone before, spiritual manifestations which serve as a fountain of youth for our perpetual renewal. Surely the best of what the Florentine artists, writers, and thinkers have left behind is such a refreshing fount. Partaking of its vitalizing waters, we slough off the fetters of the flesh and rise to a realm of serenity and understanding than which our mortal state holds no higher reward.

THE HOUSE OF MEDICI

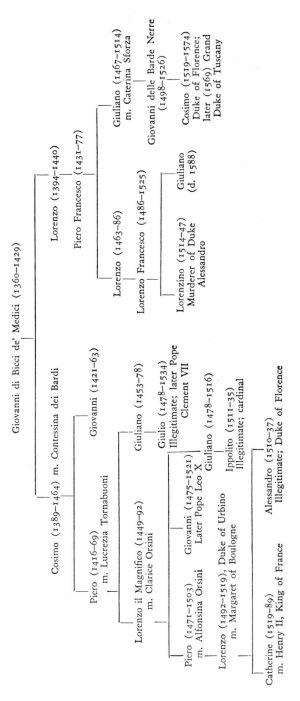

Giovanni di Bicci de' Medici (1360–1429)

Lorenzo (1394–1440)

Piero Francesco (1431–77)

Giuliano (1467–1514)
m. Caterina Sforza

Giovanni delle Barde Nerre
(1498–1526)

Cosimo (1519–1574)
Duke of Florence;
later (1569) Grand
Duke of Tuscany

Lorenzo (1463–86)

Lorenzo Francesco (1486–1525)

Giuliano
(d. 1588)

Lorenzino (1514–47)
Murderer of Duke
Alessandro

Cosimo (1389–1464) m. Contessina dei Bardi

Giovanni (1421–63)

Giuliano (1453–78)

Giulio (1478–1534)
Illegitimate; later Pope
Clement VII

Giuliano (1478–1516)

Ippolito (1511–35)
Illegitimate; cardinal

Alessandro (1510–37)
Illegitimate; Duke of Florence

Piero (1416–69)
m. Lucrezia Tornabuoni

Lorenzo il Magnifico (1449–92)
m. Clarice Orsini

Giovanni (1475–1521)
Later Pope Leo X

Piero (1471–1503)
m. Alfonsina Orsini

Lorenzo (1492–1519), Duke of Urbino
m. Margaret of Boulogne

Catherine (1519–89)
m. Henry II, King of France

INDEX TO BOTH VOLUMES

Niccolò Niccoli, 323

Nogaret, Guillaume de, impresario of the Anagni outrage, 177

Odoacer, 13

Oligarchy, rules at Florence, 210, 259, 306, 308; challenged on account of its failure, 259-260; renewed ascendancy, 282-283, 337; its governing system; 338-342; and the Catasto of 1427, 345; as operated under Cosimo, 354-357. See *Popolami grassi;* Gilds of merchants

Opera, meaning of term, 242

Operaio, defined, 242

Or San Michele, a Lombard foundation, 31; history of, 252; Orcagna fashions tabernacle for, 252, 329-330

Or San Michele, piazza of, grain-market, 236, 237, 252; discontinued as grain-market, 252

Orange, Prince of, imperial general, 432, 494

Orcagna, fashions tabernacle of Or San Michele, 252, 329-330; not the architect of the Loggia dei Lanzi, 254; as painter, 334

Ordeal by Fire (1498), 451-452

Ordinances of Justice, described, 158-159; modified (1295), 164; as constitution of the priors, 200; abolished, 222; reenacted, 223; manipulated for party purposes, 340, 367

Orsini, Alfonsina, wife of Piero de' Medici, 404

Orsini, Clarice, wife of the Magnificent, 377, 405

Orsini, Roman family, 148, 168, 376, 404

Ostrogoths, invade Italy, 14; establish a state, 14-15

Otranto, captured by the Turks, 389

Ottanta, the small council, 442, 483

Otto I, crowned emperor, 24; character of Italian rule, 35-36

Otto IV, emperor, 93, 94, 108

Otto di Guardia, their function, 342, 397; increased power of, 367

Otto di Pratica, instituted by Lorenzo, 396-397; reestablished (1512), 475

Otto Santi, war of the, 275-276, 304

Ottokar (historian), 156

Paganism, spread of, 324-325, 411-412, 440

Painting, and antiquity, 418-419

Palace of the Priors. See Palazzo Vecchio

Palazzo Vecchio (Palace of the Priors), 210; erection of, 247-248

Palleschi, partisans of the Medici, 484

Panni franceschi, 297

Paoli, C., Florentine scholar, xxxii

Papacy, degradation of, 49; financial operations of, 135-136; falls into dependence on Charles I, 146; strengthened territorially by Nicholas III, 149; subjected to France, 178; return of to Rome, 272, 275; and the bankers, 295-296. See State of the Church

Parlamentum, 67, 91-92; becomes a mockery, 338, 353, 365-366, 373; reestablished (1512), 471; tricky resort to (1530), 495

Passerini, Cardinal, 479, 482

Pater patriae, title accorded Cosimo, 370

Pavia, battle of (1525), 480

Pavia, Lombard capital, 30

Pazzi, Florentine magnate family, 383

Pazzi, Francesco, his share in plot against the Medici, 383-386

Pazzi, Jacopo, his share in the Pazzi plot (1478), 384-386

Pazzi Plot (The), 382-386

Pedites, described, 69; deficiencies of, 194-195

Perrens, P. T., historian of Florence, xxix

Peruzzi chapel (at Santa Croce), 332, 333

Peruzzi, trading company, 218-219; bankruptcy of, 224

Pestilence, a frequent consequence of famine, 237, 266; instance of 1340, 238-239; Black Death (1348), 224, 225, 239-240, 269; instance of 1527, 488

Peter Mezzabarba, bishop of Florence, 47-48

Peter (Petrus Igneus), sustains the ordeal of fire, 48, 452

Petrarch, son of ser Petracco, 174; champion of humanism, 314; life of, 315-316; champion of classical Latin, 316-317; as a book-collector, 323; climbs Mont Ventoux, 324

Philip IV, king of France, appealed to by Boniface VIII to send his brother to Italy, 169; struggle with and victory over Boniface VIII, 175-178

Piagnoni, 442, 450, 456, 484

Piccinino (condottiere), 359

Pico della Mirandola, 405, 412, 414-415

Pietrasanta, 394, 436, 443

Pippin, Frank king, 20

Pisa, struggle of against Saracens, 57, 61, 285, 287; charter of, 58-59, 85; early alliance with Florence, 90, 287-288; struggle with Florence, 91, 121, 157, 288; aids Conradin, 140; supports Henry VII, 188, 190, 191; seized by Uguccione, 197-199; captures Lucca, 217; war of 1362 with